CW01572711

From Fratricide to Forgiveness

Siphrut
Literature and Theology of the Hebrew Scriptures

Editorial Board

STEPHEN B. CHAPMAN   *Duke University*
TREMPER LONGMAN III   *Westmont College*
NATHAN MacDONALD   *Universität Göttingen*
and University of St. Andrews

From Fratricide to Forgiveness

The Language and Ethics of Anger in Genesis

Matthew Richard Schlimm

Winona Lake, Indiana
EISENBRAUNS
2011

© 2011 by Eisenbrauns Inc.
All rights reserved
Printed in the United States of America

www.eisenbrauns.com

Library of Congress Cataloging-in-Publication Data

Schlimm, Matthew Richard.
  From fratricide to forgiveness : the language and ethics of anger in Genesis /
  Matthew Richard Schlimm.
      p.   cm. — (Siphrut, literature and theology of the Hebrew Scriptures ; v. 7)
  Includes bibliographical references and index.
  ISBN 978-1-57506-224-2 (hardback : alk. paper)
  1. Anger in the Bible.   2. Bible. O.T. Genesis—Criticism, interpretation,
  etc.   I. Title.
    BS1199.A53S35   2011
    222′.110815247—dc23
                                                                    2011034551

The paper used in this publication meets the minimum requirements of the American National Standard for Information Sciences—Permanence of Paper for Printed Library Materials, ANSI Z39.48-1984. ⊗™

To

Isaiah Matthew Schlimm
(born August 22, 2004)

In Loving Memory of

Doris Jane Sieplinga
(born August 22, 1922,
died January 3, 2011)

Contents

Part 2
Daybreak after the Dim Glow of the Enlightenment:
Approaching the Ethics of Genesis

Part 3
In Search of A Brother's Keeper:
Anger and Its Antitheses in Genesis

List of Tables

List of Figures

Acknowledgments

Many people have helped form not only this manuscript but also me as a person.

Foremost, I thank my dissertation committee, under whose guidance this work originally took form. James Crenshaw chaired the committee, and he was joined by Ellen Davis, Anathea Portier-Young, Randy Maddox, and J. Robert Cox. These mentors are incredible scholars and wonderful people. They inspire me daily.

I also thank the University of Dubuque for its commitment to me and for giving me the time, resources, and means to finish this project.

I thank conversation partners who have given of their own precious time to help me with this project. These include Jacob Stromberg, Chadwick Eggleston, Amanda Benckhuysen, Bryan Dik, Becky Nicol, Rebekkah Shrimplin, James Drury, Monica Meissen, and Glenn Weaver. I also appreciate the staff at Eisenbrauns, including Beverly McCoy and Jim Eisenbraun.

Finally, I thank my family for their extraordinary support. My parents, Richard Schlimm and Sheila Bluhm, as well as my sister, Amanda Schlimm, have always found ways to make me smile.

Special mention goes to two family members who appear on the dedication page. One is my great-aunt Doris Sieplinga. She was a constant blessing, and much of the good in my life is due to her undying generosity and faith. I have her to thank for my love of studying the Bible. This book is inscribed in memory of her.

Aunt Dori shared her birthday with my son Isaiah, to whom I dedicate this book. Isaiah, may you find peace and goodness, even when options are limited and resources are thin. May you grow up and be blessed with grace, generosity, and laughter, even in this land outside Eden.

Abbreviations

General

Eth. nic.	*Ethica nichomachea* (*Nichomachean Ethics*) by Aristotle
Ira	*De ira* (*On Anger*) by Seneca
Leg.	*Leges* (*Laws*) by Plato
NRSV	New Revised Standard Version
Phaedr.	*Phaedrus* by Plato
Poet.	*Poetica* (*Poetics*) by Aristotle
Resp.	*Respublica* (*Republic*) by Plato

Reference Works

AB	Anchor Bible
ABD	*Anchor Bible Dictionary*. Edited by D. N. Freedman et al. New York: Doubleday, 1992
AEL	*Ancient Egyptian Literature*. M. Lichtheim. 3 volumes. Berkeley: University of California Press, 1973–80
ANEP	*The Ancient Near East in Pictures Relating to the Old Testament*. Edited by J. B. Pritchard. 2nd edition. Princeton: Princeton University Press, 1969
ANET	*Ancient Near Eastern Texts Relating to the Old Testament*. Edited by J. B. Pritchard. 3rd edition. Princeton: Princeton University Press, 1969
BA	*Biblical Archaeologist*
BAR	*Biblical Archaeology Review*
BDB	Francis Brown, S. R. Driver, and Charles A. Briggs. *Hebrew and English Lexicon: With an Appendix Containing the Biblical Aramaic*. Peabody, MA: Hendrickson, 2003
BibInt	*Biblical Interpretation*
BN	*Biblische Notizen*
BR	*Biblical Research*
BZ	*Biblische Zeitschrift*
CAD	*The Assyrian Dictionary of the Oriental Institute of the University of Chicago*. Chicago: Oriental Institute, 1956–2011
CBQ	*Catholic Biblical Quarterly*
ChrCent	*Christian Century*
COS	*The Context of Scripture*. Edited by W. W. Hallo. 3 volumes. Leiden: Brill, 1997–2003
CTJ	*Calvin Theological Journal*
DDD	*Dictionary of Deities and Demons in the Bible*. Edited by Karel van der Toorn et al. 2nd edition. Leiden: Brill, 1999
EgT	*Eglise et théologie*
ExAud	*Ex Auditu*

GKC   *Gesenius' Hebrew Grammar.* Edited by E. Kautzsch. Translated by A. E. Cowley. 2nd ed. Oxford: Oxford University Press, 1910

HALOT (study ed.)   *The Hebrew and Aramaic Lexicon of the Old Testament.* Ludwig Koehler, Walter Baumgartner, and Johann Jakob Stamm. Translated by M. E. J. Richardson. Study edition. 2 volumes. Leiden: Brill, 2001

HvTSt   *Hervormde teologiese studies*

IBC   Interpretation: A Bible Commentary for Teaching and Preaching

IBHS   *An Introduction to Biblical Hebrew Syntax.* B. K. Waltke and M. O'Connor. Winona Lake, IN: Eisenbrauns, 1990

IDB   *The Interpreter's Dictionary of the Bible.* Edited by G. A. Buttrick. New York: Abingdon, 1962

Int   *Interpretation*

ITC   International Theological Commentary

JAAR   *Journal of the American Academy of Religion*

JBL   *Journal of Biblical Literature*

JBQ   *Jewish Bible Quarterly*

JETS   *Journal of the Evangelical Theological Society*

JNES   *Journal of Near Eastern Studies*

JNSL   *Journal of Northwest Semitic Languages*

JQR   *Jewish Quarterly Review*

JR   *Journal of Religion*

JSOT   *Journal for the Study of the Old Testament*

JSOTSup   Journal for the Study of the Old Testament: Supplement Series

JSSSup   Journal of Semitic Studies Supplements

KAI   *Kanaanäische und aramäische Inschriften.* Edited by H. Donner and W. Röllig. Wiesbaden: Harrassowitz, 1962–64

LCL   Loeb Classical Library

LHBOTS   Library of Hebrew Bible/Old Testament Studies

NICOT   New International Commentary on the Old Testament

NIDOTTE   *New International Dictionary of Old Testament Theology and Exegesis.* Edited by W. A. VanGemeren. 5 volumes. Grand Rapids, MI: Zondervan, 1997

OBO   Orbis Biblicus et Orientalis

OBT   Overtures to Biblical Theology

OTL   Old Testament Library

RB   *Revue biblique*

RBL   *Review of Biblical Literature*

RelSRev   *Religious Studies Review*

SBLSymS   Society of Biblical Literature Symposium Series

TDOT   *Theological Dictionary of the Old Testament.* Edited by G. Johannes Botterweck, Helmer Ringgren, and Heinz-Josef Fabry. 15 volumes. Grand Rapids, MI: Eerdmans, 1974–2003

ThTo   *Theology Today*

TLOT   *Theological Lexicon of the Old Testament.* Edited by E. Jenni and C. Westermann. Translated by M. E. Biddle. 3 volumes. Peabody, MA: Hendrickson, 1997

VT   *Vetus Testamentum*

WBC   Word Biblical Commentary

WTJ	*Westminster Theological Journal*
WW	*Word and World*
ZAH	*Zeitschrift für Althebräistik*

Chapter 1

Introduction

1.1 The Value of Studying Emotion

In a recent article in the *Journal of the American Academy of Religion*, Robert Fuller writes, "There is no such thing as emotion-free religiosity."[1] He argues that emotions are integral elements of the human religious experience that should not be ignored, even if scholars of religion have sometimes neglected them.[2] In presenting his argument, Fuller joins a consensus growing across the humanities that, although the emotions were formerly overlooked (even in fields such as psychology), the feelings that individuals experience and the beliefs ascribed to them constitute a fascinating field of study.[3]

In biblical studies, analyses of human emotion were relatively scarce prior to the 1990s.[4] A decade ago, Paul Krüger observed, "The subject of emotions in the Hebrew Bible is a most neglected theme and deserves an extensive treatment."[5] Thanks in part to scholars such as Krüger, a shift has taken place.[6] A growing number of interpreters have undertaken intriguing projects leading to fruitful results. Prominent scholars such as Gary

---

1. Robert C. Fuller, "Spirituality in the Flesh: The Role of Discrete Emotions in Religious Life," *JAAR* 75 (2007) 25–51, esp. p. 45.

2. While this article begins by noting that emotions played a role in discussions of religion by previous thinkers such as Freud (guilt), Schleiermacher (absolute dependency), and Otto (the numinous), the conclusion stresses that "the study of religion has failed to keep abreast of recent scholarship in the natural and social sciences," leading to "a regrettable paucity of truly interdisciplinary understandings of religious thought and feeling" (ibid., 46).

3. Regarding the tendency for even psychologists to overlook emotions, Ronald L. Koteskey writes, "Strangely enough, emotion has been outside the mainstream of both psychology and Christianity" ("Toward the Development of a Christian Psychology: Emotion," *Journal of Psychology and Theology* 8 [1980] 303–13, esp. p. 303).

4. Zacharias Kotzé notes that the study of human emotion has been especially neglected ("Research on the Emotion of Anger in the Old Testament: Recent Trends," *HvTSt* 60 [2004] 843–63). While many have studied divine emotion, and although there are a variety of studies that examine Hebrew terms such as נפש 'life', רוח 'spirit', לבב 'heart', and בשׂר 'flesh', "few have attempted a detailed description of distinct emotions" (ibid., 856).

5. Paul A. Krüger, "A Cognitive Interpretation of the Emotion of Anger in the Hebrew Bible," *JNSL* 26 (2000) 181–93, esp. p. 181 n. 1. See also idem, "On Emotions and the Expression of Emotions," *BZ* 48 (2004) 213–28, esp. pp. 213–16.

6. Krüger has a variety of additional publications on this topic, including "'Nonverbal Communication' in the Hebrew Bible: A Few Comments," *JNSL* 24 (1998) 141–64; and

1

Anderson, Mark Smith, and Jacqueline Lapsley, as well as many others have investigated various aspects of emotion in the Hebrew Bible.[7] Furthermore, at the 2007 Annual Meeting of the Society of Biblical Literature, the Character Ethics and Biblical Interpretation Group held a session on "Whither the Bible and ethics? What directions should future engagement between the Bible and ethics take?" The three presenters, myself included, focused on the topic of human emotion in the Hebrew Bible.[8] While there is need for methodological refinement in this underexplored subfield, it is clear that analyses of emotion are becoming an important area of research among interpreters of the Hebrew Bible.

There are several reasons why emotions were overlooked for much of the 20th century.[9] First, as Lutz and White observe, literature on emotion is filled with theoretical tensions that affect the way that emotions are described, tensions between "materialism and idealism, positivism and interpretivism, universalism and relativism, individual and culture, and romanticism and rationalism."[10] In light of so many perplexing issues, the academic study of emotions seems fraught with difficulty from the outset. Second, a hallmark of Western assumptions about emotions is that they are irrational. As such, scholars have not seen them as a particularly

---

"A Cognitive Interpretation of the Emotion of Fear in the Hebrew Bible," *JNSL* 27 (2001) 77–89.

7. G. A. Anderson, *A Time to Mourn, a Time to Dance: The Expression of Grief and Joy in Israelite Religion* (University Park, PA: Pennsylvania State University Press, 1991); Mark S. Smith, "The Heart and Innards in Israelite Emotional Expressions: Notes from Anthropology and Psychobiology," *JBL* 117 (1998) 427–36; Jacqueline E. Lapsley, "A Feeling for God: Emotions and Moral Formation in Ezekiel 24:15–27," in *Character Ethics and the Old Testament: Moral Dimensions of Scripture* (ed. M. Daniel Carroll R. and Jacqueline E. Lapsley; Louisville: Westminster John Knox, 2007) 93–102. Regarding the New Testament, see Matthew A. Elliott, *Faithful Feelings: Rethinking Emotion in the New Testament* (Grand Rapids, MI: Kregel, 2006); and Karl Allen Kuhn, *The Heart of Biblical Narrative: Rediscovering Biblical Appeal to the Emotions* (Minneapolis: Fortress, 2009).

8. Stuart Lasine, "Breaking the 'Spell of Identification': Ethics and the Evaluation of Biblical Characters"; Matthew R. Schlimm, "From Fratricide to Forgiveness: The Ethics of Anger in Genesis"; Thomas Kazen, "Emotions, Biblical Interpretation and the Ethics of Ethnicity" (papers presented at the Annual Meeting of the Society of Biblical Literature, San Diego, CA, November 18, 2007). Kent Richards was the session respondent. Kazen also has a recent essay related to his presentation: "Dirt and Disgust: Body and Morality in Biblical Purity Laws," in *Perspectives on Purity and Purification in the Bible* (ed. Baruch J. Schwartz et al.; New York: T. & T. Clark, 2008) 43–64.

9. This neglect of the emotions is primarily a 20th-century problem. Although many Stoics preached the avoidance of at least certain types of emotions, they actually spent considerable time reflecting on the emotions (for example, Seneca, *Ira*). Similarly, while one can accuse Victorianism of being repressive, it actually dealt with emotions extensively and suggested that they should be experienced, with the exception of emotions that were considered unethical, such as lust (Peter N. Stearns, *American Cool: Constructing a Twentieth-Century Emotional Style* [New York: New York University Press, 1994] chaps. 2–3).

10. Catherine A. Lutz and Geoffrey M. White, "The Anthropology of Emotions," *Annual Review of Anthropology* 15 (1986) 405–36, esp. pp. 406–9.

important area of exploration. Individuals have set emotions in contrast to reason, seeing the former as private and subjective, with the potential for displaying characteristics that are primitive, immature, animalistic, and even pathological.[11] Third and consequently, as Niko Besnier remarks, academic style calls for muted emotions.[12] When the very medium by which academics express their thoughts tends to minimize the expression of emotions, it is hardly surprising that emotions have not been at the forefront of research. Fourth and closely related, traditional academic research has emphasized the importance of serving as a detached observer. Such an emphasis has led to ignoring and even "tidying up" the emotions.[13] Fifth, modern Western societies place great emphasis on efficiency of labor and advances in technology. Within these cultures, emotions are often seen as an impediment to achievement.[14] They thus do not receive priority in many research agendas. Finally, scholars have traditionally tended to ignore or at least disregard the body in fields outside of science. The lack of attention to the emotions in academic study can be seen as part of this broader trend of giving insufficient attention to issues of the body and embodiment.[15]

The times have changed, due to several factors. First, several scientists and scholars working in the fields of neuroscience, psychology, and philosophy have questioned the traditional notion that emotions are irrational.[16] Those studying emotions have begun to see conventional ideas about the irrationality of the emotions as simplistic and problematic. Second, the emphasis on serving as a detached observer has given way to alternate models. In many fields, for example, publications call for researchers to strive for empathy rather than cool detachment.[17] Finally, many disciplines now

---

11. Krüger, "On Emotions and the Expression of Emotions," 214; Catherine A. Lutz, *Unnatural Emotions: Everyday Sentiments on a Micronesian Atoll and Their Challenge to Western Theory* (Chicago: University of Chicago Press, 1998) 40–47, esp. pp. 40–42.

12. Niko Besnier, "Language and Affect," *Annual Review of Anthropology* 19 (1990) 419–51, esp. pp. 431, 434–36.

13. Lutz, *Unnatural Emotions*, 43.

14. Stearns, *American Cool*, passim; Lutz, *Unnatural Emotions*, 41; Arlie Russell Hochschild, *The Managed Heart: Commercialization of Human Feeling* (Berkeley: University of California Press, 1983).

15. For related matters, see Susan Koch, "Review of *Metaphors We Live By*," *Quarterly Journal of Speech* 67 (1981) 446–47; Fuller, "Spirituality in the Flesh," 26–31; Paula M. Niedenthal et al., "Embodiment in Attitudes, Social Perception, and Emotion," *Personality and Social Psychology Review* 9 (2005) 184–211, esp. pp. 185–86.

16. See esp. §3.2 below for a detailed discussion of this topic.

17. To name some examples: Mauro Adenzato and Francesca Garbarini, "The *As If* in Cognitive Science, Neuroscience and Anthropology: A Journey among Robots, Blacksmiths and Neurons," *Theory Psychology* 16 (2006) 747–59; Celeste M. Condit, "The Critic as Empath: Moving Away from Totalizing Theory," *Western Journal of Communication* 57 (1993) 178–90; Lutz, *Unnatural Emotions*, 43; Jacqueline E. Lapsley, *Whispering the Word: Hearing Women's Stories in the Old Testament* (Louisville: Westminster John Knox, 2005) 11–12.

recognize embodiment as integral to critical study.[18] One implication of the body's critical importance is that scholars cannot ignore the emotions, which lie at the intersection of body and mind. In biblical studies and beyond, these shifts have allowed many to see the value of studying emotion.

1.2 Genesis and Anger

To find fertile ground for continuing the study of emotion in the Bible, one needs to look no further than the Bible's first book. Few themes in Genesis are more significant and more understudied than human anger. Genesis has two bookends, which expose readers to the opposite extremes of what can happen as a result of anger. In Gen 4:1–16, readers receive their first glimpse of life outside Eden. There, anger takes center stage as Cain becomes enraged when God ignores his offering but regards his brother's offering. God intervenes and speaks to Cain about his anger, which is quite remarkable given that the divine word in Genesis is reserved for the most significant of developments, including the creation and salvation of the world. In sharp contrast to divine words elsewhere, God's speech in chap. 4 falls flat. Cain refuses to heed God's warning. He kills his brother although Abel has done nothing wrong. Fratricide represents one extreme on the spectrum of what can happen as a result of anger.

In the final chapter of the book, readers encounter the opposite extreme, forgiveness. There, Joseph and his brothers forgive one another after a long history of jealousy, anger, deception, and abuse. Jacob is at death's door, and Joseph's brothers fear that Joseph is harboring anger against them and plotting to kill them after their father's death, much as Esau planned to do with Jacob (50:15; see 27:41). So Joseph's brothers claim that their father has ordered Joseph to forgive them (50:16–17). When Joseph hears their words, he weeps. The brothers offer themselves as Joseph's servants (50:18; see also 32:19[18], 21[20]), but Joseph instead speaks graciously to them and reassures them that he will provide for both them and their children. It is a moment of reconciliation offered just before the book closes, allowing readers to see Joseph as an anti-Cain—a brother who has all the power and all the reasons to harm his brothers but instead turns away from anger and, despite the inherent difficulties, offers forgiveness. Whereas Cain suggested that he never was and never should have been his brother's keeper, Joseph shows himself to be in precisely this role, providing protection and provisions for his brothers in a foreign land.

While Genesis frames its post-Edenic narratives with two contrasting outcomes of anger, fratricide and forgiveness, it avoids simplistic moral rea-

---

18. William R. LaFleur, "Body," in *Critical Terms for Religious Studies* (ed. Mark C. Taylor; Chicago: University of Chicago Press, 1998) 36–54, esp. p. 36. See also Tamar Kamionkowski and Wonil Kim, eds., *Bodies, Embodiment and Theology of the Hebrew Bible* (LHBOTS; New York: T. & T. Clark, 2010).

soning that demands from its readers that they respond to being angry with someone by forgiving the person. Rather, between these two bookends, it offers a variety of other episodes that give readers resources for dealing with this emotion. Many of Genesis' most significant plots revolve around anger that is either explicitly named or implicitly present in the text:

1. In Gen 4:5–8, Cain's anger (וַיִּחַר לְקַיִן מְאֹד) leads to the Bible's first death and the first explicit mention of sin.
2. In Gen 13:5–12, the anger between the herders of Abram and Lot (implicit with ריב 'strife' and מריבה 'quarreling') leads to their separation, on which several subsequent events depend.[19]
3. In Genesis 16 and 21, Sarai/h's anger, implied by her actions, leads to the expulsion of Hagar from the household.[20]
4. In Gen 26:12–22, one of the few narratives featuring Isaac as an adult, anger (implied with ריב 'strife') and jealousy (קנא) on the part of the herders of Gerar lead to the forced migrations of this patriarch.[21]
5. In Genesis 27, Jacob deceives his father and steals his brother's birthright, which enrages Esau (אף; חמה; שטם) and causes Jacob's flight and subsequent residence with Laban (esp. 27:41–45).
6. In Gen 30:1–4, a barren Rachel is jealous (קנא) of Leah's fertility, and the text says specifically that Jacob becomes angry (וַיִּחַר־אַף יַעֲקֹב) with Rachel after she demands children.
7. In Gen 31:35–32:1[31:35–55], an enraged (חרה) Jacob and Laban contend fiercely (ריב) with one another, eventually agreeing to a legal separation.
8. In Genesis 33, a tense interchange transpires between Jacob and Esau in which the anger of 27:41–45 is not far in the background.
9. In Genesis 34 (see also 49:5–7), Dinah's brothers become furious (עברה; אף; וַיִּחַר לָהֶם מְאֹד) with Shechem and consequently slaughter both him and the inhabitants of his city (esp. 34:7, 49:6–7).
10. In Gen 39:17–20, an angry Potiphar (וַיִּחַר אַפּוֹ) imprisons Joseph after he hears his wife's allegations.
11. In Gen 40:1–3 (see also 41:10), Pharaoh's anger (קצף) leads to the imprisonment of two of his servants.

---

19. As explained in §5.6 below, words from the root ריב are closely related to anger.

20. As explained in §4.3.3 below, the Hebrew Bible refrains from explicitly calling women angry. Nevertheless, in §4.3.3 below, the interactions between Sarai/h and Hagar closely match the portrayal of angry actions throughout the Hebrew Bible, suggesting that at least on implicit levels there was some degree of anger between them.

21. As explained in §5.1 below, there are strong associations between jealousy and anger throughout the Hebrew Bible. Jealousy may even constitute a particular type of anger. Thus, it is appropriate to include instances of jealousy in this study. These cases include the jealousy that the Philistines have toward Isaac and his wealth (26:14); Rachel's jealousy of her sister and her fertility (30:1); and Joseph's brothers' jealousy of him, his dreams, and his preferential treatment (37:11).

12. In Genesis 37, 44, 45, and 50, various interactions occur between Joseph and his brothers in which jealousy and anger (קנא ;אָף ;חרה; רגז ;שׂטם) play important roles (esp. 37:11; 44:18; 45:5, 24; 50:15).

The recurrence of significant episodes involving anger suggests that it is an important motif, meriting close attention.

However, critical interpreters of Genesis have tended to ignore this emotion. Much has been written about topics in Genesis that are closely related to anger, such as sibling rivalry, family conflict, election, inclusion and exclusion, and deception.[22] However, these studies typically give anger the briefest treatment, if any at all. To name a prominent example, David Petersen's 2004 presidential address to the Society of Biblical Literature focuses on family conflict in Genesis, examining the strife between the herders of Abram and Lot (Genesis 13), Jacob and Laban (Genesis 31), and Jacob and Esau (Genesis 27, 33). When one examines what the text says about characters in the midst of these conflicts, it is clear that they are angry. There is ריב ('strife') between the herders of Abram and Lot, which as shown in §5.6 below, has close associations with anger. Meanwhile, the terminology for anger is used explicitly to describe the conflicts that Jacob has with both Esau and Laban (Gen 27:41–45 and chap. 33 for Esau; Gen 31:35–36 for Laban). Although anger is key to understanding what the protagonists in these stories actually experience, and although this emotion is portrayed in all three cases as the potential cause of violence and great physical harm (which Petersen focuses on), anger is never explicitly mentioned in Petersen's study.[23] Given the critical importance of emotion to religious experience, and given the way anger resurfaces throughout Genesis, this motif merits a thorough study.

1.3 The Primary Aims of This Project

This work aims, first and foremost, at understanding what the book of Genesis conveys to its readers about anger. Why does Genesis return to the emotion of anger so many times on so many occasions? What impact

---

22. To name only a few examples: Mark G. Brett, *Genesis: Procreation and the Politics of Identity* (Old Testament Readings; London: Routledge, 2000); R. Christopher Heard, *Dynamics of Diselection: Ambiguity in Genesis 12–36 and Ethnic Boundaries in Post-Exilic Judah* (Atlanta: Society of Biblical Literature, 2001); Roger Syrén, *The Forsaken First-born: A Study of a Recurrent Motif in the Patriarchal Narratives* (JSOTSup 133; Sheffield: JSOT Press, 1993); Naomi A. Steinberg, *Kinship and Marriage in Genesis: A Household Economics Perspective* (Minneapolis: Fortress, 1993); Michael James Williams, *Deception in Genesis: An Investigation into the Morality of a Unique Biblical Phenomenon* (Studies in Biblical Literature 32; New York: Peter Lang, 2001).

23. David L. Petersen, "Genesis and Family Values," *JBL* 124 (2005) 5–23, esp. pp. 18–20. Similarly, Devora Steinmetz gives exceedingly little attention to anger when reflecting on family conflict in Genesis (*From Father to Son: Kinship, Conflict, and Continuity in Genesis* [Literary Currents in Biblical Interpretation; Louisville: Westminster John Knox, 1991] 28–29).

does this emotion have on the moral life? What dangers does it present? Is it possible to avoid anger? What resources does Genesis give readers for engaging this emotion in others and in themselves? Above all, how does Genesis function as Torah ('instruction, direction, law'), offering moral guidance about anger for its readers?

To answer these questions, I will provide a methodological model that is useful both for exegetes studying biblical emotion and for interpreters interested in biblical ethics. The foremost goal of this sort of model is to understand the text on its own terms.[24] Although exegetes have sought to understand the text in this way since its inception, both emotions and ethics constitute complex subjects of investigation that require special interpretive moves to avoid a host of errors. As will be shown below, many modern interpreters have approached the text with preconceived ideas of emotion and ethics that are incongruent with the text itself. In this book, I seek to correct errors in past studies, provide methodological resources for future studies, and explain Genesis' understanding of anger and ethics in contradistinction to modern preconceptions.

The driving thesis of this book is that the emotion of anger appears in Genesis not merely to embellish story lines or add color to characters but to express a multifaceted message about the ethical significance of anger. The text does not give readers simplistic instructions about what to do with anger but instead is quite realistic about the limitations that individuals face and the paradoxes presented by this emotion. Genesis presents anger as an emotion that arises from one's moral sensitivities in response to the perception of wrongdoing. At the same time, the text presents anger as a great threat to the moral life. Genesis warns readers about the dangers of anger, but it never suggests that one can lead a life free from anger. Instead, it portrays every patriarch and many of the matriarchs as having significant encounters with this emotion, presenting them with dilemmas that defy easy resolution. It depicts anger as an inevitable part of a world marked by profound limitations. It also invites readers to imagine ways of alleviating anger. It suggests that humility and generosity may ameliorate the worst outcomes of anger, and it illustrates the possibility of reconciliation after anger has caused harm. At the same time, it is painfully realistic about how difficult, threatening, and short-lived human attempts at ending anger may be.

---

24. This language of "understand[ing] the text on its own terms" is not meant to suggest that a given text has a singular meaning. Every reader plays a role in the creation of a text's meaning, and there are as many meanings of a text as there are readers. Nevertheless, there are readings and interpretations that are not supported by the text itself. A key goal of honest, critical interpretation is minimizing misunderstandings of what is posited in the text. If a field of meaning is opened by the text, then responsible scholarship will hopefully point toward interpretations that fall within this field.

1.4 Methodological Overview

Academics have tended to neglect not only biblical emotions but also Old Testament ethics until relatively recently. Although newer works have been written on these topics, these subfields are still in their infancy. Existing literature on both biblical emotions and biblical ethics stand in need of modification. On the one hand, many misunderstandings exist and have gone unchecked. On the other, several proposals that work well with some pieces of biblical evidence are less applicable to the study of anger in Genesis. Therefore, it is necessary to spend considerable time clarifying the best ways to approach these topics before diving into Genesis' narratives involving anger. When scholars examine other literary motifs in other biblical books, this sort of spadework may be unnecessary. Here, however, it is important to correct previous misunderstandings and lay the framework for future examinations of emotion and ethics in a text such as Genesis.

Thus, this book has three parts. The first examines the language and concept of anger in the Hebrew Bible; the second examines Old Testament ethics; and the last turns specifically to the ethics of anger in Genesis. Part 1 begins by bringing together insights from translation theory, anthropology, and cross-cultural psychology to answer the question, How can one best study an emotion described in another language by another culture (chap. 2)? The answers to this question are then brought into conversation with the ways that biblical anger has been characterized in the past, giving particular attention to whether this emotion is appropriately characterized as irrational (chap. 3). Next, the findings of cognitive linguistics, particularly prototype theory, are brought to bear on how the Hebrew Bible presents anger and the events surrounding it (chap. 4). Attention is also given to the concepts most frequently associated with anger in the Hebrew Bible (chap. 5). Part 1 concludes with a chapter that examines the conceptual metaphors for anger at work in the Hebrew Bible (chap. 6).[25]

In part 2, attention shifts to the field of biblical ethics. I examine the advances that have taken place in this field in recent decades, evaluating their usefulness for studying anger in the narratives of Genesis (chap. 7). Supplementing these works in biblical studies with theoretical insights from Mikhail Bakhtin, Paul Ricoeur, Jean-François Lyotard, Martha Nussbaum, Wayne Booth, and Kenneth Burke, I outline in the following chapter an understanding of ethics and narrative that aligns with the contours of Genesis (chap. 8).

Part 3 employs a rhetorical-literary approach to analyze the texts of Genesis dealing with anger. Attention is given first to the foundational narrative

---

25. Rather than defining *anger* in this introductory chapter, I will provide brief definitions of the individual Hebrew terms in chap. 6 (esp. §6.5) as well as detailed explanations in appendix B (pp. 193–201). The broader concept of anger in the Hebrew Bible is also explicated in chaps. 4 and 5 (esp. §4.3–§5).

of Cain and Abel (chap. 9) and second to a series of narratives involving anger among shepherds (chap. 10). Next, this book focuses on Genesis' accounts of anger involving those who are marginalized, particularly women and slaves (chap. 11). Finally, close readings are conducted of the attempts at reconciliation made first between Jacob and Esau and then between Joseph and his brothers (chap. 12). As a whole, part 3 examines how these texts provide a conversation with one another about anger and its moral perplexities. Various themes from this study are collected and summarized in the concluding chapter (chap. 13).

Last, two appendixes have been provided. Appendix A explains how the statistics mentioned in chap. 3 were attained. Appendix B provides additional details about the terminology for anger used in Biblical Hebrew.

1.5 Literary Approaches and Historical Criticism

Literary approaches and historical criticism constitute two of the broadest and most popular methods in biblical studies. As such, they merit an extra word at the outset of this study. As is well known, the field of biblical studies focused primarily on source and form criticism throughout much of the 20th century. By the late 1960s, however, the methodological limitations of these enterprises were becoming increasingly apparent.[26] In particular, the focus on getting behind the text (that is, unearthing the sources and settings that gave rise to passages) led to a neglect of the content of the biblical text and the means by which this content is conveyed. To remedy this problem, literary and rhetorical approaches entered the scene, appearing in full force in the 1980s and beyond. A favored method of these approaches is closely reading biblical pericopes, seeking to understand the final form of the text on its own terms.[27] This method has proved enormously useful for the fields of biblical theology and biblical ethics, and it will be used to approach the text of Genesis in this book.[28]

Early on, many writers who used literary approaches were quite adverse to historical criticism, calling it idolatrous, stubborn, "senseless," "futile," and "incongruent with the text itself."[29] However, several scholars in more

---

26. See, for example, James Muilenburg, "Form Criticism and Beyond," *JBL* 88 (1969) 1–18, esp. pp. 4–7.

27. The term *close reading* is here used in a broad sense rather than in the sometimes technical way it has been employed, for example, by practitioners of the so-called New Criticism.

28. On its usefulness, see, for example, James L. Crenshaw, *Defending God: Biblical Responses to the Problem of Evil* (New York: Oxford University Press, 2005) esp. pp. 12–14.

29. These quotations are taken from J. P. Fokkelman, *Narrative Art in Genesis: Specimens of Stylistic and Structural Analysis* (2nd ed.; Biblical Seminar 12; Sheffield: JSOT Press, 1991) vii–viii; Meir Sternberg, *The Poetics of Biblical Narrative: Ideological Literature and the Drama of Reading* (Indiana Studies in Biblical Literature; Bloomington: Indiana University Press, 1985) 13; and Walter Brueggemann, *Theology of the Old Testament: Testimony, Dispute, Advocacy* (Minneapolis: Fortress, 1997) 103–5, 726–29, esp. p. 104.

recent times have stressed the importance of combining a literary approach with historical, sociological, and ideological methods.[30] These more integrated approaches raise the question of how to relate the literary approach taken in this book with these other methods.

It is useful to begin by noting that even literary works opposed to historical-critical methodologies have tended to make room for comparative studies of ancient Near Eastern literature as a way of illuminating the biblical text.[31] While parallels to Genesis' creation and flood narratives are well known (for example, *Atrahasis*, *Gilgamesh*, and *Enuma Elish*), there are also several texts that provide useful points of comparison with Genesis' texts dealing with anger. A number of narratives, for example, deal with anger and strife among brothers, akin to what one finds in Genesis.[32] Material of this sort provides interpreters with the types of cultural ideas and narrative forms in existence prior to and concomitant with the formation of Genesis, allowing readers to gain a better grasp of the conventions in the biblical text.[33]

Although scholars have access to texts from the ancient Near East that may have influenced the formation of Genesis in one way or another, none of Genesis' composite sources has survived. While few dispute that the book has emerged from a lengthy process of composition involving multiple authors and redactors, there is great disagreement about who these writers were, how they interacted with one another, and which texts stem from which sources. What consensus existed in source criticism a generation ago has given rise to (in the words of individuals working in this field) "uproar" and "confusion."[34] While many valiant scholars have sought to

---

30. See, for example, Heard, *Dynamics of Diselection*; J. David Pleins, *The Social Visions of the Hebrew Bible: A Theological Introduction* (Louisville: Westminster John Knox, 2000); David McLain Carr, *Reading the Fractures of Genesis: Historical and Literary Approaches* (1st ed.; Louisville: Westminster John Knox, 1996) vii.

31. See, for example, Sternberg, *The Poetics of Biblical Narrative*, 12–13.

32. These texts include (1) the Sumerian Narrative "Emesh and Enten: Enlil Chooses the Farmer-God" (S. N. Kramer, *Sumerian Mythology: A Study of Spiritual and Literary Achievement in the Third Millennium b.c.* [Memoirs of the American Philosophical Society; Philadelphia: American Philosophical Society, 1944] 49–51); (2) the Hittite Myth "Appu and His Two Sons" (*COS* 1.58:153–55); (3) the Ugaritic "Kirta Epic" (*COS* 1.102.333–43); (4) the Assyrian "Prism of Esarhaddon" (*ANET*, 289–90); (5) "The Story of Idrimi, King of Alalakh" (*ANET*, 557–58); and (6) various Egyptian sources, including *The Instruction of Amenemope* (*COS* 1.47.115–22), "The Memphite Theology" (*AEL* 1:51–57), "The Two Brothers" (*AEL* 2:203–11), and "Horus and Seth" (*AEL* 2:214–23).

33. A similar point is made by Simon B. Parker, *Stories in Scripture and Inscriptions: Comparative Studies on Narratives in Northwest Semitic Inscriptions and the Hebrew Bible* (New York: Oxford University Press, 1997) 5.

34. The term "uproar" is used in Pleins, *The Social Visions of the Hebrew Bible*, 24. David McLain Carr uses the term "confusion" in "Controversy and Convergence in Recent Studies of the Formation of the Pentateuch," *RelSRev* 23 (1997) 22–31, esp. p. 22.

create order out of this תֹהוּ וָבֹהוּ [35] surrounding Genesis' textual origins, there is admittedly a conjectural nature to these analyses. [36] Given these limitations, one can see the value of closely reading biblical texts to determine what messages they elicit without tying the messages to hypothetical reconstructions of what the texts might have looked like in previous forms. Thus, to keep this project manageable, source-critical discussions will not factor into this book.

Though scholars have become increasingly divided about many pillars of source criticism, they increasingly agree that, whatever Genesis' compositional history, it probably reached a final form in an exilic or postexilic setting. [37] A fruitful area of examination is how this book's message about anger interacted with historical, sociological, and ideological forces in this period. One suspects that anger was not uncommon during this period, when Jewish populations wrestled with competing ideas about a variety of topics including self-identity, land ownership, cultural assimilation, and religious practices. As Paul Hanson puts it, "We are dealing with a period of deep divisions and unprecedented crises within the Jewish community, as an independent-minded people suddenly finds itself both subjugated by a pagan power (Persia) and splintered internally by contending parties." [38] It would be quite interesting to examine how Genesis' message about anger interacted with the vexing dynamics of this period. Unfortunately, two factors cause this area of research to be exceedingly complex and beyond what can be treated in this book. The first pertains to evidence. There is not as much evidence from this time period as one would like, and the evidence

---

35. These are the Hebrew words in Gen 1:2 that are traditionally translated 'formless and void'.

36. Granted, literary-rhetorical criticism has a conjectural nature as well. For example, it is not always clear whether an alleged wordplay is truly significant or merely coincidental. Thus, one need not go as far as scholars who claim that literary-rhetorical methods are vastly superior to historical-critical methods. A level of humility is required among the practitioners of all critical methodologies.

37. Steinberg's *Kinship and Marriage in Genesis* was one of the earlier works (published in 1993) to argue that Genesis achieved its formation in the exilic or postexilic period. Others have followed Steinberg's lead. Rainer Albertz concisely surveys important works of scholarship while making the case that two key redactions of Genesis 12–50 took place during the exilic period (*Israel in Exile: The History and Literature of the Sixth Century B.C.E.* [trans. David Green; SBLSBL; Atlanta: Society of Biblical Literature, 2003] 246–71). See also the Persian Authorization Thesis, which asserts that the Pentateuch took form under a federal arrangement between the Persian imperial administration and local communities, an agreement that granted some autonomy to local peoples while ultimately reinforcing Persian rule (for a summary in English, see Peter Frei, "Persian Imperial Authorization: A Summary," in *Persia and Torah: The Theory of Imperial Authorization of the Pentateuch* [ed. James W. Watts; SBLSymS 17; Atlanta: Society of Biblical Literature, 2001] 5–40). Other works connecting Genesis with this time period include Carr, *Reading the Fractures of Genesis*; Brett, *Genesis*; and Heard, *Dynamics of Diselection*.

38. Paul D. Hanson, *Old Testament Apocalyptic* (Nashville: Abingdon, 1987) 91.

that is available is frequently the subject of great debate.[39] Second, study of this time period is fraught with political and ideological implications, and thus even the term *exile* is fiercely contested.[40] These two factors lead to a wide variety of opinions about not only what Jewish populations experienced in the sixth and fifth centuries but also whether one can even be certain of any conclusions made about this time period. These complicated issues cannot be treated within the scope of this book, but they do constitute a promising avenue for future research.

1.6 Limitations of This Study

To keep this project well defined, I limited its scope in other ways. First, this study focuses on human anger rather than divine anger. It does so primarily because Genesis is not concerned with divine anger. While God is portrayed angrily in many books of the Bible, the book of Genesis contains no explicit, actualized references to divine anger. Although some parts of Genesis may imply that God is angry (for example, chaps. 3, 4, 6, 11, 18–19), none of them explicitly refers to the divine being in this way. The only time Hebrew terminology for anger is used of God in Genesis is in 18:30 and 32, where Abraham, while requesting that innocent people be spared from impending destruction, asks that the deity not become angry with him for making this request. The text suggests that God obliges Abraham and does not become angry.[41] All of the other explicit references to anger in Genesis pertain to humans. Genesis focuses on human anger, as I will.

Furthermore, it is not clear that studying the implicit or nonactualized references to divine anger in Genesis would shed considerable light on how this book characterizes human anger. Abraham Heschel argues that there is

---

39. Regarding extrabiblical texts, see the contrasting interpretations of the Murashu Texts from Nippur by Rainer Albertz, *A History of Israelite Religion in the Old Testament Period* (trans. John Bowden; 2 vols.; Louisville: Westminster John Knox, 1994) 2.373–74; and Daniel L. Smith-Christopher, *A Biblical Theology of Exile* (OBT; Minneapolis: Fortress, 2002) 69. Regarding field archaeology, see the nearly contradictory accounts in Hans M. Barstad, *The Myth of the Empty Land: A Study in the History and Archaeology of Judah during the "Exilic" Period* (Oslo: Scandinavian University Press, 1996) esp. p. 42; and Ephraim Stern, "The Babylonian Gap: The Archaeological Reality," *JSOT* 28 (2004) 273–77, esp. p. 273. Regarding the biblical evidence, see the contrast between James D. Purvis and Eric M. Meyers, "Exile and Return: From the Babylonian Destruction to the Reconstruction of the Jewish State," in *Ancient Israel: From Abraham to the Roman Destruction of the Temple* (ed. Hershel Shanks; Washington, DC: Biblical Archaeology Society, 1999) 201–29, esp. p. 205; and Peter R. Ackroyd, *Exile and Restoration: A Study of Hebrew Thought of the Sixth Century b.c.* (OTL; Philadelphia: Westminster, 1968) 32.

40. Barstad, *The Myth of the Empty Land*; Lester L. Grabbe, ed., *Leading Captivity Captive: 'The Exile' as History and Ideology* (Sheffield: Sheffield Academic Press, 1988).

41. Like Genesis, Numbers appears in the Pentateuch containing significant portions of narrative material, a fair amount of which is concerned with anger. However, the majority of these texts speak of divine anger. Genesis, by contrast, focuses on human anger much more than divine wrath.

a fundamental distinction between divine and human emotion: "What Isaiah (55:8f.) said concerning the thoughts of God may equally apply to His pathos: For My pathos is not your pathos, neither are your ways My ways, says the Lord. For as the heavens are higher than the earth, so are My ways higher than your ways, and My pathos than your pathos."[42] While Heschel may here engage in hyperbolic language, it is clear that one should not conflate human and divine anger. For example, human anger very frequently receives censure in biblical texts, but this is not the case with divine anger. Similarly, humans at times become angry with the wrong people for the wrong reasons (for example, Potiphar's anger toward the innocent Joseph in Gen 39:19), but the biblical text does not typically portray divine anger in these terms. Moreover, it is human anger, far more than divine anger, that has been ignored by many scholars. It merits careful study.[43]

A second limitation is that this book focuses primarily on Genesis rather than on other texts of the Hebrew Bible. As illustrated above (§1.2), anger is a prominent motif in Genesis that merits careful study in its own right. Although Proverbs, for example, joins Genesis in describing human anger on a variety of occasions, anger in Proverbs does not constitute a carefully arranged literary motif akin to what one finds in Genesis.[44] Nevertheless, while the focus here is on Genesis, other books of the Hebrew Bible are drawn on when they shed light on the text of Genesis. The Hebrew Bible is by no means monolithic, and one should not automatically assume that what one text says is echoed in another text. At the same time, when one studies Genesis, the books elsewhere in the Hebrew Bible provide the closest linguistic, temporal, and geographical parallels in existence.[45] Thus, part 1 relies on the entire Hebrew canon (as well as related ancient Near Eastern sources) to understand better the cultural-linguistic concept of anger drawn upon by the writers of Genesis.

A third limitation of this study is that it does not use Western psychological theories to illumine biblical texts. Approaches of that sort have been undertaken by a variety of scholars.[46] For example, some see Esau as the

---

42. Abraham J. Heschel, *The Prophets* (2 vols.; Peabody, MA: Prince, 1962) 2.56.

43. For an excellent overview of sources studying divine anger, see Kotzé, "Research on the Emotion of Anger," 844–47. For one of the most recent and most comprehensive sources, see Bruce Edward Baloian, *Anger in the Old Testament* (American University Studies 7, Theology and Religion 99; New York: Peter Lang, 1992) esp. pp. 65–179, 192–210.

44. It lacks, for example, the type of inclusio structure found in Genesis, where anger is treated in both the first post-Edenic episode and the book's penultimate episode.

45. Shemaryahu Talmon, "The 'Comparative Method' in Biblical Interpretation: Principles and Problems," in *Congress Volume: Göttingen 1977* (VTSup 29; Leiden: Brill, 1978) 320–55.

46. For two useful anthologies, see J. Harold Ellens and Wayne G. Rollins, eds., *Psychology and the Bible: A New Way to Read the Scriptures* (2 vols.; Praeger Perspectives: Psychology, Religion, and Spirituality; Westport, CT: Praeger, 2004); and Wayne G. Rollins and D. Andrew Kille, eds., *Psychological Insight into the Bible* (Grand Rapids, MI: Eerdmans, 2007).

equivalent of Jacob's Jungian shadow.[47] Others claim to have found Freud's Oedipus complex present among the Patriarchs.[48] Additional examples could be given.[49] These studies presuppose not merely that Jung, Freud, or another psychologist was correct but also that the dynamics described by the psychologist are universal, not limited by cultural constraints.[50] Presumptions of this sort are questionable, to say the least.[51] As we shall see in chap. 2, it is not apparent that the Hebrew Bible's understanding of anger aligns with Western conceptions of this emotion. When interpreters assume that the Western model of anger is universal and is presupposed by the text itself, they limit their ability to understand the text on its own terms. If something as fundamental as anger can vary significantly from culture to culture, then interpreters should be wary about assuming that more complex and hypothetical psychological ideas, such as the Oedipus complex, reflect archetypal features of humanity. Therefore, the use of psychology in this study is limited to cross-cultural psychology and related fields. Cross-cultural analyses, outlined in chap. 2, point to principles and cautions that interpreters should be aware of when interpreting the emotions of another culture.

1.7 Conclusion

Nearly all of the great classical philosophers wrote extensively about anger, seeing it as an essential topic when considering the ethical life.[52] To cite a prominent example, in *Moral Essays*, Seneca writes that anger is the most harmful force known to humanity. He asserts that anger, "the most hideous and frenzied of all the emotions," has done more to threaten the

---

47. D. Andrew Kille, "Jacob—A Study in Individuation," in *Jung and the Interpretation of the Bible* (ed. David L. Miller; New York: Continuum, 1995) 40–54. See also Maria Kassel, *Biblische Urbilder: Tiefenpsychologische Auslegung nach C. G. Jung* (Munich: Pfeiffer, 1980) esp. pp. 258–79.

48. Steinmetz, *From Father to Son*, passim; Kassel, *Biblische Urbilder*, 247; Marie Balmary, *Abel ou la traversée de l'Éden* (Paris: Bernard Grasset, 1999) 141–44. See also André LaCocque, *Onslaught against Innocence: Cain, Abel, and the Yahwist* (Eugene, OR: Cascade, 2008) 38, 47–51, 56–57, 89, 108–11.

49. See the essays by Huth, Meves, and Hirschberg in *Brudermord: Zum Mythos von Kain und Abel* (ed. Joachim Illies; München: Kösen-Verlag, 1975) 37–67, 123–55; Richard A. Hughes, *Theology and the Cain Complex* (Washington, DC: University Press of America, 1982); idem, "*Schicksalsanalyse* and Religious Studies," *JR* 87 (2007) 59–78, esp. pp. 64, 68–71, 75–76.

50. Steinmetz attempts to address this issue by considering whether the Oedipus complex is universal (*From Father to Son*, 11–34). However, there are problems with this analysis. It is based primarily on the Trobriand Islanders, rather than a more global study.

51. Bryan J. Dik, Department of Psychology, Colorado State University, private communication, Oct. 15, 2008.

52. David E. Aune, "Review of: William Harris, *Restraining Rage: The Ideology of Anger Control in Classical Antiquity*," *JR* 83 (2003) 678–80, esp. p. 678.

survival of humanity than even the deadliest plague (Seneca, *Ira* 1.1–2).[53] Although Genesis uses a different language and genre from Seneca, it likewise sees anger as a great threat to humanity—a permanent mark of the expulsion from Eden, the cause of the first recorded sin, and the force that brings death into the world. While Seneca's Stoic response to the harmful nature of anger is well known, Genesis' account of this emotion is not. The time has come to consider the language and ethics surrounding anger in the Bible's first book. This subject has been overlooked long enough.

---

53. *Seneca: Moral Essays* (trans. John W. Basore; LCL; Cambridge: Harvard University Press, 1928).

Part 1
The Language of Anger

Chapter 2

Traversing Foreign Terrain: The Troubles of Translating Emotion

Translation is the bedrock of interpretation. Unfortunately, biblical scholars sometimes give insufficient attention to this foundational enterprise and consequently make unsound interpretive moves. In this chapter, I examine the task of translation, first on a general level by drawing together insights from both accomplished translators and critical theorists. I then shift to particular areas that need attention when one is translating terms for emotion. In this discussion, I look beyond biblical studies to the fields of anthropology and linguistics, outlining an approach that does justice to the variety of issues that translators face. These findings are then brought into dialogue with broader issues of linguistic relativity, as well as the reigning assumptions in biblical studies. As a whole, this chapter points to the need for understanding anger in the Hebrew Bible as a foreign concept embodied in a set of terms that do not always align with modern Western concepts and language. Despite similarities, differences persist.

2.1 The Violence of Translation

Individuals who work extensively with foreign languages have stressed the violent nature of translation. They have described translation as both damaging the original work and warping the target language. They explain that the transference between languages is never perfect. There are always losses. Despite great precautions, casualties invariably take place. One of the most well-known individuals to speak of violence in translation is Saint Jerome. He compares the translator to a conqueror who invades the foreign, takes captive thoughts and meaning, and brings them back to Latin soil.[1] More than a thousand years after Jerome, Martin Luther, under heavy fire from his critics, describes himself as having only two choices, to demolish (*tun Abbruch*) the German language or to depart from (*weichen von*) the biblical word.[2] In passages of greatest significance, he asserts that he chose to commit violence against his native tongue rather than stray from the original text.

---

1. Saint Jerome, *To Pammachius: On the Best Method of Translating (St Jerome, Letter 57)* (trans. Louis G. Kelly; Ottawa: Ecole de Traducteurs et d'Interpretes, Universite d'Ottawa, 1976) 8, §6.
2. Martin Luther, "*Sendbrief vom Dolmetschen,*" in *An den christlichen Adel deutscher Nation; Von der Freiheit eines Christenmenschen; Sendbrief vom Dolmetschen* (ed. Ernst Kähler; 2nd ed.; Stuttgart: Reclam, 1970) 151–73, esp. p. 164.

19

In the modern era, Michel Foucault also portrays translation in violent terms. In his short essay "Les mots qui saignent," he evokes the image of a catapult, speaking of translations that "launch one language against another. . . . They take the original text for a projectile and treat the translating language as a target."[3] George Steiner goes further, understanding aggression and destruction to be integral elements of virtually all translations. He writes, "Unquestionably there is a dimension of loss, of breakage—hence . . . the fear of translation, the taboos on revelatory export which hedge sacred texts, ritual nominations, and formulas in many cultures."[4] Jacques Derrida also connects translation with violence, but with an interesting twist. In *Des tours de Babel*, he asserts that Yhwh has violently imposed translation on humanity while simultaneously forbidding it, making it both a human necessity and an impossibility.[5]

While many thinkers across the centuries have thus connected translation with violence, Antoine Berman offers one of the most systematic accounts of how this violence takes place.[6] He describes a variety of "deforming tendencies" that creep into translation, rendering the final product a distortion of the original. He explains that translators (perhaps unwittingly) embellish works, an occurrence that ironically leads to the loss of elements in the original. He observes the tendency to rationalize works in translation, rearranging elements to fit preconceived ideas of discursive order that stand at variance with the original. Abstraction, he notes, often accompanies rationalization, destroying the concreteness of the source text. Berman shows that original works are further effaced by the clarifications, explications, and illuminations that enter the translated work. The ambiguities, enigmas, and complexities of the original become buried. The limitations of language inhibit their full replication. Attempting to resemble the original, translators expand the source text, making it swollen and bloated. In the end, Berman observes, "The translating results in a text that is at once *poorer* and *longer*."[7]

---

3. The French uses the language of *choc*, which can refer to a collision or shock (Michel Foucault, "Les mots qui saignent," *L'express*, 29 Aug 1964, 21–22, esp. p. 21; translation mine).

4. George Steiner, *After Babel: Aspects of Language and Translation* (Oxford: Oxford University Press, 1975) 297–300, esp. p. 300.

5. Jacques Derrida, *"Des tours de Babel,"* in *Difference in Translation* (ed. Joseph F. Graham; Ithaca, NY: Cornell University Press, 1985) 214. For Derrida, "Yhwh" is a literary construct. Elsewhere in this book, I use "Yhwh" to signify the Hebrew name for God, יהוה, which English Bibles frequently translate as "the Lord."

6. Antoine Berman, "Translation and the Trials of the Foreign," in *The Translation Studies Reader* (ed. Lawrence Venuti; London: New York, 2000) 284–92. See also Wilhelm von Humboldt, "From the Introduction to His Translation of *Agamemnon*," in *Theories of Translation: An Anthology of Essays from Dryden to Derrida* (ed. Rainer Schulte and John Biguenet; Chicago: University of Chicago Press, 1992) 58–59.

7. Berman, "Translation and the Trials of the Foreign," 292, Berman's italics. See also Friedrich Schleiermacher, "On the Different Methods of Translating," in *Theories of Trans-*

Berman describes additional elements within the original work that cannot be perfectly replicated in the target language. These casualties of translation include the destruction of the original work's iconic richness, its precise rhythms, its underlying networks of signification, its linguistic patternings, its vernacular networks, and its expressions and idioms.[8] In the act of translation—and by implication, even in the act of interpreting foreign works—much is lost, far more than is typically realized. Every act of translation is an act of violence.

2.2 The Vulnerability of Terms Conveying Emotion

On the battlefield of translation, terms conveying emotion are particularly vulnerable to attack.[9] Several anthropologists have reached this conclusion after extensive studies of terms for emotion in other languages. Jean L. Briggs's *Never in Anger*, published in 1970, cleared the path for a great deal of subsequent scholarship by analyzing the appropriation of emotion by the Utku Eskimos in northern Canada. Briggs concludes that the "Utku do not classify emotions exactly as English speakers do; their words for various feelings cannot in every case be tidily subsumed under our words: affection, fear, hostility, and so on." She states that her use of English terms to describe Utku words for emotion, even when accompanied by extensive commentary, entails the "risk of doing violence to the Eskimo ways of conceptualizing feelings."[10] Briggs's basic point, that the categories represented by emotion terminology do not transfer well between languages, is true of not just Utku and English but virtually all languages. Not surprisingly, the difficulty of transference is greater when one compares the English language with languages outside the Indo-European family.

Studies after Briggs's have compared emotion terms across languages, ranging from the most abstract to the most specific. They have concluded that the categories for emotion differ from language to language, whether one examines basic-level emotion terms (such as *happiness*, *anger*, *fear*, and *sadness*), superordinate-level terms (such as *emotion*), or subordinate-level terms (such as *wrath*, *fury*, *revulsion*, *irritation*, and *hatred*, to name some of the terms subordinate to their hypernym *anger*).[11] With regard

---

lation: An Anthology of Essays from Dryden to Derrida (ed. Rainer Schulte and John Biguenet; trans. Waltraud Bartscht; Chicago: University of Chicago Press, 1992) 36–54, esp. p. 47.

8. Berman, "Translation and the Trials of the Foreign," 292–97. Much of the language above is used by Berman throughout this essay.

9. Catherine A. Lutz, *Unnatural Emotions: Everyday Sentiments on a Micronesian Atoll and Their Challenge to Western Theory* (Chicago: University of Chicago Press, 1998) 8; James A. Russell, "Culture and the Categorization of Emotions," *Psychological Bulletin* 110 (1991) 426–50, esp. p. 433.

10. Jean L. Briggs, *Never in Anger: Portrait of an Eskimo Family* (Cambridge: Harvard University Press, 1970) 311.

11. This type of hierarchical taxonomy is frequently used by cognitive linguists. For a concise introduction to the way these taxonomies work, see René Dirven and Marjolijn

to the superordinate term *emotion*, Anna Wierzbicka shows that this word does not align especially well with similar terms in other languages. Even among Indo-European languages, she demonstrates, there are significant differences between the English *emotion*, the German *Gefühl*, the Polish *uczucie*, the French *émotion*, the Italian *emozione*, and the Spanish *emoción*, especially when one considers the level of cognition presupposed by each word.[12] These words do not in every instance refer to the same thing, although there are obvious areas of semantic overlap. Incomplete lexical matches on the superordinate level raise questions not only about translation but also about the appropriateness of categorizing terminology from other languages with the term *emotion*, which may not correspond to any terms in the native language.[13]

Basic-level terms for emotions do not always align across languages either. Some of these terms, such as the equivalents of *sadness* and *fear*, are said to be missing altogether in other languages.[14] Furthermore, ethnographers have documented several languages that do not distinguish between the basic categories that English uses. Some African languages, for example, do not differentiate *anger* from *sadness*.[15] Meanwhile, for the Ilongot people in the northern Philippines, the term *liget* refers not only to what we would call *anger* but also to the passionate energy associated with difficult physical labor, as well as the youthful drive toward marrying and reproducing. It is even associated with headhunting.[16] To name another example, a prominent emotion word among the Ifaluk people of Micronesia is *song*, which has some connections with *anger* but is far more communal than individual. It is directly related to issues of social and interpersonal justice.[17] Linguists often speak of collocations, that is, the contextual associations and

---

Verspoor, eds., *Cognitive Exploration of Language and Linguistics* (Amsterdam: John Benjamins, 1998) 39–40.

12. Anna Wierzbicka, "Everyday Conceptions of Emotion: A Semantic Perspective," in *Everyday Conceptions of Emotion: An Introduction to the Psychology, Anthropology and Linguistics of Emotion* (ed. James A. Russell et al.; Dordrecht: Kluwer Academic, 1995) 17–47, esp. pp. 20–22.

13. Robert Alan LeVine, "Levy's *Tahitians*: A Model for Ethnopsychology," *Ethos* 33 (2005) 475. Other scholars such as Ellen van Wolde have been hesitant to use *emotion* to describe terms in the Hebrew Bible, preferring alternates such as *sentiment* ("Language of Sentiment," *SBL Forum* 5, 2007, http://sbl-site.org/Article.aspx?ArticleID=660 [accessed April 11, 2007]). One may question, however, whether alternatives of this sort are an improvement, because they likewise have their own connotations and meanings. The approach here is to use the term *emotion* but note ways that the biblical text reflects different conceptions.

14. Russell, "Culture and the Categorization of Emotions," 441, table 4.

15. Ibid., 430.

16. Michelle Z. Rosaldo, *Knowledge and Passion: Ilongot Notions of Self and Social Life* (Cambridge: Cambridge University Press, 1980) passim, with a concise introduction on pp. 20–30.

17. Lutz, *Unnatural Emotions*, 155–82.

restrictions that words carry with them. The collocations of *song* disallow its use in ways unrelated to matters of injustice, in contrast to the collocations of *anger* (for example, "I became angry when my computer crashed"). Whereas the Ifaluk see *song* as always being justified, the Utku Eskimos that Briggs describes are at the opposite end of the spectrum; they neither have words for "justified anger" nor conceptualize interpersonal anger as being justified.[18] As all of these examples illustrate, terms for emotions do not always align well with their closest counterparts in other languages.

While the above examples come from languages that are not Indo-European, there are also examples *within* this family of languages in which basic-level emotion terms do not transfer perfectly. Again, Anna Wierzbicka has provided useful insights. She discusses the Italian word *rabbia*. It refers to anger that is uncontrolled, intense, and explosive. In this sense, it corresponds with the English terms *fury* and *rage*. Italian expressions such as *la rabbia delle vento* can even be rendered literally in English as *the fury of the wind*. While there is thus a fairly close semantic match between the words *rabbia* and *fury*, there is also a key difference. The English word *fury* is understood as a departure from normal emotional states.[19] It is extraordinary, not something that most people experience on a fairly regular basis. The Italian *rabbia*, however, is a very popular word used in everyday conversation. In Italian, *rabbia* may be considered a basic-level emotion term—more so than *fury*, which in English is a subordinate-level term, a hyponym of *anger*.[20]

As this example illustrates, not only basic-level but also subordinate-level emotion terms do not always transfer easily from one sociolinguistic system to another. There are many lexical gaps on this level in both non-English and English languages. Anthropologists have documented a number of non-English languages that lack words for *depression*, *anxiety*, and *guilt*.[21] With regard to gaps in English, the Korean construction 쓸쓸한 느낌 refers to the specific type of sadness, emptiness, and loneliness that one experiences in autumn as life dies and days shorten.[22] Another lexical gap in English is the Japanese word 甘え, which indicates a pleasant feeling of

---

18. Briggs, *Never in Anger*, 328–37. Briggs argues that, for the Utku, anger is not justified in interactions with people over four years of age, although she does describe an occasion where the act of scolding (*huaq*), which has potential connections with anger, was seen as appropriate (p. 257).

19. See *Oxford English Dictionary Online*, s.v. "fury, *n*.," http://www.oed.com (accessed Oct. 11, 2007).

20. Wierzbicka, "Everyday Conceptions of Emotion," 31–33.

21. Russell, "Culture and the Categorization of Emotions," 431.

22. Dr. Sua Yoo, Duke University, private communication, June 20, 2007. American English may begin to articulate a similar concept in describing *seasonal affective disorder*, but there are obvious differences (for example, the English term suggests a medical condition more than a common sentiment in the general populace).

passive dependence on another (for example, an infant on her mother).[23] The literature on this topic contains many more examples of terms for emotion that lack adequate counterparts in other languages.[24]

English, by way of circumlocution, can convey some of the concepts behind these words in other languages, but these circumlocutions do not take place frequently. Individuals in different cultures tend to have different conceptions of emotion and, at least potentially, different emotional experiences. Even when words can be found with dictionary definitions that roughly align (for example, *rabbia* and *fury*), it is clear that most words carry with them an encyclopedic range of meaning and concepts, and these broader associations do not always match perfectly.[25] To use Max Black's terminology, a "system of associated commonplaces" develops around particular words that is far more complex than their basic definitions.[26]

2.3 Emotion and Culture

Emotion terms tend to carry complex associative networks with them that convey an array of cultural assumptions about how emotions can and should work.[27] Even if some emotional experiences are universal or nearly universal, societies differ greatly in the social norms that they construct around these emotions.[28] The norms of a given culture, which anthropologists collectively refer to as an "emotional style," include assumptions about the following:

- *Taxonomy*: what types of feelings people experience
- *Ecology*: which situations elicit which emotions

---

23. Russell, "Culture and the Categorization of Emotions," 432; Wierzbicka, "Everyday Conceptions of Emotion," 19–20.

24. An excellent source for these examples is Russell, "Culture and the Categorization of Emotions," 426–433.

25. See Ronald W. Langacker, "Context, Cognition, and Semantics: A Unified Dynamic Approach," in *Job 28: Cognition in Context* (ed. Ellen van Wolde; Leiden: Brill, 2003) 187–89; Ellen van Wolde, *Reframing Biblical Studies: When Language and Text Meet Culture, Cognition, and Context* (Winona Lake, IN: Eisenbrauns, 2009) 8, chap. 3.

26. Max Black, *Models and Metaphors: Studies in Language and Philosophy* (Ithaca, NY: Cornell University Press, 1962) 40–41. (Black may not agree with all of the implications drawn here from his work; see §2.4.) Langacker, "Context, Cognition, and Semantics," 187–92.

27. Lutz, *Unnatural Emotions*, 210–11.

28. There appears to be a growing consensus that, although universal human biology obviously plays a part in the physiology of emotion, culture determines a great deal of emotion meaning: what emotions are, their likely causes, their likely outcomes, their frequency, their accompanying behaviors, and their attachment to systems of value. See, for example, Russell, "Culture and the Categorization of Emotions," esp. p. 428; Wierzbicka, "Everyday Conceptions of Emotion," passim; Ralph B. Hupka et al., "Anger, Envy, Fear, and Jealousy as Felt in the Body: A Five-Nation Study," *Cross-Cultural Research* 30 (1996) 243–64; Lutz, *Unnatural Emotions*, passim.

- *Semantics*: what emotions imply (for example, action tendencies such as fear implies flight)
- *Communication*: how emotions can and should be expressed
- *Social regulation*: which emotions are appropriate and inappropriate in which situations
- *Management*: how to deal with emotions that cannot be expressed[29]

As this list illustrates, an emotional style entails a series of essential and normative judgments—that is, a variety of assessments about the nature of reality and how one should act within it. Over the course of time, these judgments have become attached to the corresponding language of emotion, imbuing particular words with positive and negative connotations.[30]

To come at the same point from a different angle, linguists have argued for decades that context is key to determining meaning.[31] This observation is true of not only textual context but also cultural context. As Leo Noordman explains, readers construct mental models of the content of a text.[32] This construction involves not only what the text explicitly conveys but also contextual information, cultural assumptions, and one's perceived knowledge of the world.[33] Therefore, to understand an ancient text on its own terms, interpreters must set aside their modern assumptions about emotions, removing the blinders that obstruct the associated commonplaces inherent in the text's original language and culture.[34] As much as possible, interpreters must draw attention to the various associations that particular terms carry with them in the source language.

---

29. These categories are adopted from R. A. Shweder's discussion of emotional functioning (*Thinking through Cultures: Expeditions in Cultural Psychology* [Cambridge: Harvard University Press, 1991] 242–52).

30. An obvious reflection of emotional style in ancient Near Eastern discourse is found in a memo written by Adad-shum-usur, a seventh-century Assyrian exorcist-priest, who urges his king to refrain from mourning because the king is the image of the sun god (Jeffrey H. Tigay, "The Image of God and the Flood: Some New Developments," in *Studies in Jewish Education and Judaica in Honor of Louis Newman* [New York: Ktav, 1984] 169–82, esp. p. 171). Here, one sees an obvious set of assumptions about the contexts and persons for whom mourning is and is not appropriate.

31. Ludwig Wittgenstein, *Philosophical Investigations* (trans. G. E. M. Anscombe; New York: Macmillan, 1953) 24, §49; G. Frege, *The Foundations of Arithmetic: A Logico-Mathematical Enquiry into the Concept of Number* (trans. J. L. Austin; New York: Philosophical Library, 1950, 1884) esp. x^c; V. N. Voloshinov, "'Language, Speech, and Utterance' and 'Verbal Interaction'," in *Bakhtinian Thought: An Introductory Reader* (ed. Simon Dentith; London: Routledge, 1995) 107–43, esp. p. 130.

32. Leo Noordman, "Some Reflections on the Relation between Cognitive Linguistics and Exegesis," in *Job 28: Cognition in Context* (ed. Ellen van Wolde; Leiden: Brill, 2003) 331–36, esp. p. 332. See also Lutz, *Unnatural Emotions*, 85.

33. For analogous concepts pertaining to metaphors, see Michael A. Osborn and Douglas Ehninger, "The Metaphor in Public Address," *Speech Monographs* 29 (1962) esp. pp. 228–30.

34. See Shweder, *Thinking through Cultures*, 66–69.

These associations can vary significantly from culture to culture.[35] In American English, for example, the word *fear* carries with it relatively few positive connotations. Individuals often try to conceal this emotion, as it frequently is a source of shame. In a number of languages of the South Pacific, however, the terms for fear have moral connotations, and the emotion is seen as something to be prized, even celebrated.[36] A common practice in these cultures is to tell stories of one's fear to others. Informing others of one's fear is seen as a way of communicating that one is harmless and therefore deserving of respect.[37] Words for fear in these languages carry with them a different set of associated commonplaces than fear-related words in English, which tend to be negative and point to weakness and inadequacy.[38]

To consider another example of different associations in different languages, on the Micronesian atoll of Ifaluk, the rough equivalent of the word *happiness* is *ker*. This Ifaluk word, however, does not have many positive associations. Rather, it is viewed as amoral, if not immoral. As a result, this word's associations differ greatly from those of the English word *happiness*, especially among individuals who believe that the pursuit of happiness is a fundamental goal that all of humanity has the right to seek.[39] As this brief example illustrates, words for emotion are linked to broader issues of ideology, morality, and world view.

Research across the humanities has come to understand in new ways the extent to which words can be ideologically charged. In the last few decades, rhetorical critics have recognized that individual words and phrases have the capacity to function as *ideographs*, that is, to convey entire ideologies that bespeak how the world works and how reality is governed.[40] Valentin Voloshinov (a colleague of Mikhail Bakhtin), in a move that foreshadowed some of the work on ideographs, stresses the relationships between language and cultural values, arguing, "Each and every word is ideological."[41] Lin-

---

35. For an overview of the relationship between culture and emotion, see Jerome Kagan, *What Is Emotion? History, Measures, and Meanings* (New Haven, CT: Yale University Press, 2007) 142–89.

36. Lutz, *Unnatural Emotions*, 184–85; Robert I. Levy, *Tahitians: Mind and Experience in the Society Islands* (Chicago: University of Chicago Press, 1973) 307–8.

37. Lutz, *Unnatural Emotions*, 184–85.

38. Incidentally, one wonders if יראת יהוה 'the fear of the Lord', which carries many positive connotations in the Hebrew Bible, is closer to these conceptions of fear in the South Pacific than the conceptions reflected in American English.

39. Lutz, *Unnatural Emotions*, 44. While the English word *pleasure* has some similarities with these features of *ker*, Lutz's text makes clear that there are also differences between *pleasure* and *ker*. Those who experience *ker*, for example, may cry if they are of a particular disposition (p. 115).

40. Michael Calvin McGee, "The 'Ideograph': A Link between Rhetoric and Ideology," *Quarterly Journal of Speech* 66 (1980) 1–16. See also Lutz, *Unnatural Emotions*, esp. p. 5.

41. Voloshinov, "'Language, Speech, and Utterance' and 'Verbal Interaction'," 138. The author may have been Mikhail Bakhtin, writing under Voloshinov's name. By "ideo-

guists and anthropologists have become increasingly aware of this point. A. L. Becker, for example, describes how messages trigger entire orientations: "Words [do not] represent *the* world; rather they specify *a* world."[42] In the case of emotion, the meaning of a particular word goes far beyond a denotative sense that indicates a perceived sentiment: the word encapsulates a series of connotations, collocations, and assumptions that reflect not only the emotional style of its culture, but also broader cultural values and ideologies.[43] This point has been stressed by many anthropologists studying emotions, such as Catherine Lutz, who argues:

> The pragmatic and associative networks of meaning in which each emotion word is embedded are extremely rich ones. The complex meaning of each emotion word is the result of the important role those words play in articulating the full range of a people's cultural values, social relations, and economic circumstances. Talk about emotions is simultaneously talk about society—about power and politics, about kinship and marriage, about normality and deviance—as several anthropologists have begun to document.[44]

As Lutz here intimates, terms for emotion are closely related to systems of value, and thus they are integral elements in a society's discourses. They are, as Foucault puts it, "tactical elements or blocks operating in the field of force relations."[45]

The preceding discussion has several key implications for a study of the biblical language for anger. Interpreters need to recognize that the categories of emotion in English do not necessarily align with the categories of emotion in the biblical text. Benjamin Lee Whorf, whose work is discussed in greater depth below (§2.4), makes the following point about language in general, which is applicable to emotion terminology:

> We dissect nature along lines laid down by our native languages. The categories and types that we isolate from the world of phenomena we do not find there because they stare every observer in the face; on the contrary, the world is presented in a kaleidoscopic flux of impressions which has

---

logical," the author means reflecting cultural values.

42. A. L. Becker, "A Short Essay on Languaging," in *Research and Reflexivity* (ed. Frederick Steier; London: Sage, 1991) 229–32. See also van Wolde, *Reframing Biblical Studies*, chap. 3, esp. pp. 58–59.

43. Niko Besnier, "Language and Affect," *Annual Review of Anthropology* 19 (1990) 419–51, esp. p. 433. Some argue to the contrary that the denotative meanings of emotion terms are more significant than the associative networks they carry with them. For a brief overview of this debate, see Zoltán Kövecses, "Introduction: Language and Emotion Concepts," in *Everyday Conceptions of Emotion: An Introduction to the Psychology, Anthropology and Linguistics of Emotion* (ed. James A. Russell et al.; Dordrecht: Kluwer Academic, 1995) 6–8.

44. Lutz, *Unnatural Emotions*, 5–8, 210–11, esp. pp. 5–6.

45. Michel Foucault, *The History of Sexuality: An Introduction* (trans. Robert Hurley; 3 vols.; New York: Vintage, 1990) 1.100–102.

to be organized by our minds—and this means largely by the linguistic systems in our minds.[46]

Whorf's point is essential for interpreters who are analyzing terms of emotion in the Bible. When English speakers fail to recognize the degree to which emotion terms can vary across cultures, they reify, as Wierzbicka puts it, "inherently fluid phenomena which could be conceptualized and categorized in many different ways."[47] English words such as *emotion, anger, fear,* and *happiness* do not necessarily align with universal brain functions. Rather, they are, in the words of James Russell, "hypotheses formulated by our linguistic ancestors."[48] By assuming that English terms are somehow universal or the best representations of reality, one can quickly enact violence when translating and interpreting foreign works because the networks of association presupposed by the source language are often missed. This type of interpretive practice subtly embodies neocolonialist discourse, wherein the Western model is assumed to be universal, and foreign conceptions are perceived as mere reflections of Western norms.[49] Such unself-conscious appropriation of Western emotion categories serves only to reinforce Western ideologies about the self, the individual, and the perceived dichotomy between reason and emotion.[50] Unfortunately, many analyses of anger in the Hebrew Bible make precisely this mistake.

2.4 Linguistic Relativity

Before turning to analyses of anger in the Hebrew Bible, we need to discuss linguistic relativity, an idea that has much in common with the preceding arguments. The discussion above stresses that terms for emotion within a particular language have the potential to carry with them vast associations of thought. This idea is not far removed from the concept of *linguistic relativity*, which asserts in its strong forms that language *determines* one's thinking. In its weaker forms, it suggests that language *influences* one's thinking. Many of the anthropologists and linguists mentioned above have expressed sympathy for the weaker forms of linguistic relativity. Observing the significant differences between emotion terms in languages, they have argued that language and cognition influence one another.[51]

---

46. Benjamin Lee Whorf, *Language, Thought, and Reality: Selected Writings of Benjamin Lee Whorf* (ed. John B. Carroll; New York: The Technology Press of Massachusetts Institute of Technology and John Wiley, 1956) 213.

47. Wierzbicka, "Everyday Conceptions of Emotion," 20–21. See also Besnier, "Language and Affect," 421.

48. Russell, "Culture and the Categorization of Emotions," 444.

49. I deal with neocolonial discourse more extensively in "The Necessity of Permanent Criticism: A Postcolonial Critique of Ridley Scott's *Kingdom of Heaven," Journal of Media and Religion* 9 (2010) 129–49.

50. Lutz, *Unnatural Emotions*, 218–25; Jane H. Hill and Bruce Mannheim, "Language and World View," *Annual Review of Anthropology* 21 (1992) 381–406, esp. p. 384.

51. Rosaldo, *Knowledge and Passion*, 20; Shweder, *Thinking through Cultures*, 155; Russell, "Culture and the Categorization of Emotions," 427.

The stronger forms of this theory date at least as far back as Wilhelm von Humboldt (1767–1835), who saw the language and the mental framework of a people as inextricably linked:

> The *mental individuality* of a people and the *shape of its language* are so intimately fused with one another that, if one were given, the other would have to be completely derivable from it. . . . Language is, as it were, the outer appearance of the spirit of a people; the language is their spirit and the spirit their language.[52]

This type of argument found new heights of popularity in the 1940s, when factors in the American intellectual climate led to a constellation of ideas formulated by Edward Sapir and Benjamin Lee Whorf (giving rise to the term "the Sapir-Whorf hypothesis").[53] Three quotations illustrate the types of claims they made. In a fairly concise statement, Sapir argues, "Human beings . . . are very much at the mercy of the particular language which has become the medium of expression for their society."[54] Whorf elaborates:

> the "linguistic relativity principle," . . . means, in informal terms, that users of markedly different [patterns of language] are pointed by [these patterns] toward different types of observations and different evaluations of externally similar acts of observation, and hence are not equivalent as observers but must arrive at somewhat different views of the world.[55]

When discussing the Hopi (a Native American people) model of the universe, Whorf makes similar claims, arguing, "Every language contains terms that have come to attain cosmic scope of reference, that crystallize in themselves the basic postulates of an unformulated philosophy, in which is couched the thought of a people, a culture, a civilization, even of an era."[56] Whorf and Sapir, like Humboldt, drew close lines of connection between language and cognition, even going so far as to argue that language determines one's orientation to reality.[57]

---

52. Wilhelm von Humboldt, *On Language: On the Diversity of Human Language Construction and Its Influence on the Mental Development of the Human Species* (trans. Peter Heath; Cambridge: Cambridge University Press, 1999) 46, Humboldt's italics.

53. For these factors, see the discussion in John J. Gumperz and Stephen C. Levinson, eds., *Rethinking Linguistic Relativity* (Cambridge: Cambridge University Press, 1996) 3–7.

54. Edward Sapir, *Selected Writings of Edward Sapir in Language, Culture, and Personality* (ed. David G. Mandelbaum; Berkeley: University of California Press, 1949) 162.

55. Whorf, *Language, Thought, and Reality*, 221. In the quotation above, I have substituted Whorf's word "grammar" with the words "patterns of language" because "grammar" is a technical term for Whorf referring to "automatic, involuntary patterns of language . . . —a term that includes much more than the grammar we learned in the textbooks of our school days" (ibid.).

56. Ibid., 61.

57. As William M. Schniedewind points out, Humboldt and Whorf do have some differences, particularly regarding how individualist their ideas were ("Prolegomena for the Sociolinguistics of Classical Hebrew," *Journal of Hebrew Scriptures* 5 [2005] esp. §2.3, http://www.arts.ualberta.ca/JHS/Articles/article_36.pdf [accessed Aug. 16, 2007]).

By the 1960s, two decades after the thinking of Sapir and Whorf reached its highpoint of popularity, the intellectual climate in Britain and America had changed. With the rise of cognitive sciences, attention focused on universal features of the human mind.[58] The work of Sapir and Whorf was called into question on the basis of empirical studies, at least with respect to perceptual terminology, such as words for colors.[59] Max Black, meanwhile, assailed the basic postulates of this theory, arguing, "Whorf commits the *linguist's fallacy* of imputing his own sophisticated attitudes to the speakers he is studying."[60] In this context of growing animosity toward notions of linguistic relativity, James Barr published *The Semantics of Biblical Language*, which launched a full, frontal attack on the ways that many biblical interpreters, especially within the biblical theology movement, simplistically and problematically made moves that aligned with the types of claims associated with Sapir and Whorf.[61]

Barr's work has been exceptionally influential, and it continues to provide the basis for many of the reigning assumptions in current linguistic work on the Bible.[62] It clearly opposes the strong forms of the linguistic relativity theory. Countering Kittel's *Theological Dictionary of the New Testament*, Barr maintains, "Theological thought of the type found in the NT has its characteristic linguistic expression not in the word individually but in the word-combination or sentence."[63] Barr argues that, unless the word at hand is a technical term, it does not contain within it vast conceptual networks. Assigning words large theological frameworks (as Barr contends that *TDNT* does) leads to terms' becoming "overloaded with interpretive suggestion."[64] Barr's argument raises important questions for studying emotion in a foreign language: Is it problematic to believe that cultural

---

58. For an excellent discussion, see Gumperz and Levinson, eds., *Rethinking Linguistic Relativity*, esp. pp. 2–7.

59. See for example Brent Berlin and Paul Kay, *Basic Color Terms: Their Universality and Evolution* (Berkeley: University of California Press, 1969); Eleanor Rosch, "Linguistic Relativity," in *Human Communication: Theoretical Explorations* (ed. A. Silverstein; New York: Halsted, 1974) 27–48. For criticism of this type of work, see C. Hoffman, I. Lau, and D. R. Johnson, "The Linguistic Relativity of Person Cognition: An English-Chinese Comparison," *Journal of Personality and Social Psychology* 51 (1986) esp. p. 1104; Shweder, *Thinking through Cultures*, esp. pp. 114–17; Zoltán Kövecses, *Language, Mind, and Culture* (Oxford: Oxford University Press, 2006) esp. pp. 34–35, 334–35; Russell, "Culture and the Categorization of Emotions," 427.

60. Max Black, "Linguistic Relativity: The Views of Benjamin Lee Whorf," *The Philosophical Review* 68 (1959) 228–38, esp. p. 230.

61. James Barr, *The Semantics of Biblical Language* (London: SCM, 1961).

62. A more recent work heavily indebted to Barr's earlier work is Moisés Silva, *Biblical Words and Their Meaning: An Introduction to Lexical Semantics* (rev. ed.; Grand Rapids, MI: Zondervan, 1994). On the influence of Barr's work shortly after its publication, see Brevard S. Childs, "Review of James Barr, *Semantics of Biblical Language*," *JBL* 80 (1961) 374–77.

63. Barr, *The Semantics of Biblical Language*, 233.

64. Ibid., 234.

assumptions about emotion are reflected in individual linguistic signs for emotion? Does one not risk overloading words for emotion with "interpretive suggestion"?

On the one hand, Barr is correct that interpreters must guard against what he calls the "illegitimate totality transfer"—that is, the error of taking the sum total of a word's potential associations and assuming that they can all be read into a particular appearance of the term.[65] On the other hand, it would be foolish not to study the full semantic range of key terms and the types of concepts that they frequently presuppose. It is necessary to understand the types of associations that words in the source language can have and compare them with associations in the target language. At one point, in a parenthetical remark, Barr essentially makes this point, conceding that individual words function semantically by carrying "emotional suggestion, reference to traditional patterns and ideas, references and values usually only in certain groups and speakers, and so on."[66] The types of references that Barr mentions here deserve careful attention.

When one looks beyond *The Semantics of Biblical Language*, one sees that Barr is not opposed to careful lexical analyses of particular words, as his review of the second volume of *TDOT* illustrates.[67] Thus, David Lambert correctly observes, "Barr pointed to the way in which linguistic data could be misused but never denied altogether the significance of philology for theology."[68] Moreover, Barr is aware that language at least dimly reflects the world view of its time and that interpreters must guard against imposing their modern presuppositions onto their definitions of biblical words. Thus, he faults Bauer's lexicon for being "too content to give semantic indications which presuppose, and are intelligible only in terms of, a more modern intellectual and cultural *Weltanschauung* than that of the NT."[69] Barr is more concerned with guarding against problematic linguistic moves than abandoning careful semantic analyses that examine the broader associative networks that particular words carry with them.

A key argument Barr makes is that the lexical gaps and lexical stock of a given language do not finally decide the types of thoughts one can form. Several individuals studying emotion and culture are quick to agree with him.[70] At the same time, a number of these scholars argue that lexical gaps and lexical stock can indicate levels of prominence and conceptualization

---

65. Ibid., 218.

66. Ibid., 245.

67. James Barr, "Review of G. Johannes Botterweck and Helmer Ringgren, eds., *Theological Dictionary of the Old Testament*, Vol. 2," *Int* 33 (1979) 90–91.

68. David Lambert, "Review of Michael Carasik, *Theologies of the Mind in Biblical Israel*," *RBL* (2007), http://www.bookreviews.org/pdf/6041_6434.pdf (accessed May 7, 2010).

69. Barr, *The Semantics of Biblical Language*, 254–55.

70. Russell, "Culture and the Categorization of Emotions," esp. p. 434; Silva, *Biblical Words and Their Meaning*, esp. p. 27.

that particular emotions achieve or fail to achieve in various languages.[71] As Robert Levy pointed out 30 years ago in a landmark study that continues to be a model for ethnopsychological research, when a language has many words to describe a type of emotion (in Levy's case, words for *anger* in Tahitian), the culture using this language tends to have considerable assumptions about that type of emotion. Levy calls these sorts of emotions *hypercognated*. In contrast, when a language has relatively few words for a type of emotion (in Levy's case, words for *sadness* in Tahitian), the corresponding culture tends to have far fewer discussions and assumptions about that type of emotion. It is *hypocognated*.[72]

While vocabulary grids are not the only factor to consider, they should not be ignored either. They are an indication, though not the final arbiter, of the degree of salience that particular concepts achieve in a given culture.[73] While they do not indicate what can *potentially* be conveyed in a given language, they can reflect what *habitually* is conveyed in this language.[74] Thus, Humboldt insightfully makes the following observation: "It is not too bold to contend that everything, from the most elevated to the most profound, from the most forceful to the most fragile, can be expressed in every language. . . . Nevertheless these undertones of language slumber, as do the sounds of an unplayed instrument, until a nation learns how to draw them out."[75] Implicit in this observation is the fundamental insight that every language has its limitations. While there are ways of counteracting these shortcomings (such as circumlocutions), they still exist. No language is ever perfect. J. L. Austin concurs, writing, "ordinary language is *not* the last word: in principle it can everywhere be supplemented and improved upon and superseded. Only remember, it *is* the *first* word."[76] Barr could have displayed greater sensitivity to these points.

On the whole, therefore, it appears wise to heed Barr's warnings (for example, with the illegitimate totality transfer), while taking a more balanced approach that recognizes that language forms an essential part of one's conceptual apparatus, serving as the building blocks of thought. An approach of this sort is similar to the course taken by many contemporary

---

71. Wierzbicka, "Everyday Conceptions of Emotion," esp. pp. 19, 25, 27; Lutz, *Unnatural Emotions*, esp. pp. 84–85; John A. Lucy, *Language Diversity and Thought: A Reformulation of the Linguistic Relativity Hypothesis* (Cambridge: Cambridge University Press, 1992) 136–37.

72. Levy, *Tahitians*, 284, 324; see also LeVine, "Levy's *Tahitians*," 477–78.

73. Wierzbicka, "Everyday Conceptions of Emotion," 19, 25–27.

74. For related ideas, see Lucy, *Language Diversity and Thought*, 7, 136–37.

75. Humboldt, "From the Introduction to His Translation of *Agamemnon*," 56–57.

76. J. L. Austin, *Philosophical Papers* (2nd ed.; Oxford: Clarendon, 1970) 185. Obviously, there are a number of philosophical issues at stake in the preceding discussion. For more on those issues, see Catherine A. Lutz and Geoffrey M. White, "The Anthropology of Emotions," *Annual Review of Anthropology* 15 (1986) 405–36; Shweder, *Thinking through Cultures*, 353–58.

linguists, who make modifications to the theories advanced by Sapir and Whorf while retaining significant continuity with them.[77] John Gumperz, for example, in his introduction to *Rethinking Linguistic Relativity*, observes that "the original idea of linguistic relativity is still alive, but functioning in a way that differs from how it was originally conceived." He shows that "there have been a whole range of recent intellectual shifts that make the ground more fertile for some of the original seeds [of this idea] to grow into new saplings."[78] These shifts have begun to make their presence known in biblical studies. For example, there is an increasing awareness of the interrelations between language and ideology.[79] Likewise, Mikhail Bakhtin has become a very fruitful dialogue partner for biblical scholars, and much of his work has similarities with notions of linguistic relativity.[80] One suspects that, in the future, increasing numbers of biblical interpreters will take balanced positions that are open to examining the interrelations between language, cognition, and cultural values.

2.5 Conclusion

While interpreters can obviously go too far and overload words with interpretive suggestion, there remains a valid place for careful analysis of

---

77. D. Slobin, "The Development from Child Speaker to Native Speaker," in *Cultural Psychology: Essays on Comparative Human Development* (ed. J. W. Stigler, R. A. Shweder, and G. Herdt; Cambridge: Cambridge University Press, 1990); Joel Sherzer, "A Discourse-Centered Approach to Language and Culture," *American Anthropologist* 89 (1987) 295–309; Lera Boroditsky, "Does Language Shape Thought?: Mandarin and English Speakers' Conceptions of Time," *Cognitive Psychology* 43 (2001) 1–22; Hill and Mannheim, "Language and World View," passim; Hoffman, Lau, and Johnson, "The Linguistic Relativity of Person Cognition," passim; Lucy, *Language Diversity and Thought*, passim.

78. Gumperz and Levinson, eds., *Rethinking Linguistic Relativity*, 1–11, quotes taken from 12, 17, respectively. One of these prominent intellectual shifts is an increasing recognition that language is not neutral but rather imbued with judgments and values. See for example Stanley Fish, *The Trouble with Principle* (Cambridge: Harvard University Press, 1999) 14; Kenneth Burke, *Permanence and Change: An Anatomy of Purpose* (3rd ed.; Berkeley: University of California Press, 1984) 176–77; idem, *Language as Symbolic Action: Essays on Life, Literature, and Method* (Berkeley: University of California Press, 1966) 44–62.

79. An obvious example would be studies that have shown how the term *exile* is related to broader ideological issues of who has rights to land. While these studies do not always make explicit appeals to linguistic relativity, they do show how the linguistic term *exile* brings with it a host of ideological assertions regarding material concerns, particularly land ownership. See for example Robert P. Carroll, "Exile! What Exile? Deportation and the Discourses of Diaspora," in *Leading Captivity Captive: 'The Exile' as History and Ideology* (ed. Lester L. Grabbe; Sheffield: Sheffield Academic Press, 1988) 62–79; Philip R. Davies, "Exile? What Exile? Whose Exile?" in *Leading Captivity Captive: 'The Exile' as History and Ideology* (ed. Lester L. Grabbe; Sheffield: Sheffield Academic Press, 1998) 128–38; Hans M. Barstad, *The Myth of the Empty Land: A Study in the History and Archaeology of Judah during the "Exilic" Period* (Oslo: Scandinavian University Press, 1996).

80. See Mikhail Bakhtin, *The Dialogic Imagination* (trans. C. Emerson and M. Holquist; Austin: University of Texas Press, 1981, 1935) 291–95; E. A. Schultz, *Dialogue at the Margins: Whorf, Bakhtin, and Linguistic Relativity* (Madison: University of Wisconsin Press, 1990).

particular concepts and terminology within the Hebrew Bible. That is to say, there is a danger in relying solely on the lexical meaning of terms found in dictionaries and lexicons. Attention needs to be given to the broader encyclopedic range of meanings, associations, and cultural values that surround terms and ideas. This is particularly true when one considers anger in the Hebrew Bible. As I will show in the next chapter, many inter-preters have conflated modern Western understandings of anger with the understandings present in the Hebrew Bible. While there are similarities between anger in past and present cultures, the broader encyclopedic range of ideas surrounding anger can differ, sometimes in significant ways. In the remainder of part 1, I will attend to this encyclopedic network of concepts surrounding anger in the Hebrew Bible.

Chapter 3

Imposing Western Assumptions on the Text: Irrationality as Senseless Violence

Past works that examine biblical anger have paid insufficient attention to the interrelations between language, cognition, and cultural values, instead imposing Western assumptions onto characterizations of biblical emotion. In particular, there has been a strong tendency to argue that the Hebrew Bible portrays human anger as irrational. This characterization merits extended treatment both because of its popularity and because it strikes at the heart of the Western conception of emotion. This chapter explains the close links that have been made between emotion and irrationality in Western discourse, shows how these links have been imposed on the biblical text by interpreters, and demonstrates the lack of textual evidence for these sorts of claims. In the end, this chapter illustrates how biblical interpreters can commit violence against the texts they translate and interpret.

3.1 Origins of a Folk Theory

In ancient times, Greek and Latin writers such as Plato, Aristotle, and Seneca associated the emotions, especially anger, with irrationality. Plato claimed that the soul pulls the individual in two opposing directions, one way by 'the rational' (λογιστικὸν) part of the soul and another direction by 'the irrational and appetitive' (ἀλόγιστικόν τε καὶ ἐπιθυμητικόν) part of the soul. This irrational direction Plato associated with 'affections and diseases' (παθημάτων τε καὶ νοσημάτων), thus linking irrationality with emotion.[1] Plato's student Aristotle argued that 'passion' (πάθεσιν), particularly 'anger' (θυμοὶ) and a few other emotions have the potential to 'cause madness' (μανίας

---

1. Both the Greek and its translation come from Plato, *Resp.* 4.14, §439C–D (*The Republic: Books 1–5* [trans. Paul Shorey; LCL; Cambridge: Harvard University Press, 1930]). See also Plato, *Leg.* 1, §644E–645A (*Laws: Books 1–6* [trans. R. G. Bury; LCL; Cambridge: Harvard University Press, 1926]); idem, *Phaedr.* 25–38, §246A–257B ("*Phaedrus,*" in *Euthyphro, Apology, Crito, Phaedo, Phaedrus* [ed. W. R. M. Lamb; LCL; Cambridge: Harvard University Press, 1914] 405–580); as well as Galen, *On the Doctrines of Hippocrates and Plato* (trans. Phillip de Lacy; 3 vols.; Berlin: Akademie, 1978) esp. 1.324–25, §V.5.34–35.

ποιοῦσιν).[2] Several centuries later, Seneca also associated emotion, including anger, with irrationality and insanity. Seneca maintained that anger
involves three stages: first an involuntary reaction to an injury, second the
judgment that the injury deserves retribution, and third the irrational, uncontrollable prompting to take vengeance. The third stage, Seneca says,
'has utterly vanquished reason' (*rationem evicit*).[3]

While there thus are many antecedents to seeing emotions as irrational, they took new forms amid developments in the 20th century. As Peter
Stearns has persuasively argued, between 1920 and 1950 a new emotional
style began to emerge in America that has continued to the present day, a
style marked above all else by dispassion, or to use the term popular since
the 1960s, by being "cool." With the growth of consumerism, corporate
management, and the service-sector, the American middle class adopted
an emotional style that places great stress on concealing emotional reac-
tions, especially in the workplace, where they could interfere with generating profits. Marked by an intolerance of emotions, this emotional style
deems individuals who display emotional intensity to be vulnerable, child-
ish, and irrational. This emphasis on dispassion has translated into other
spheres of life beyond the workplace. However, because emotions could
not be completely excised from the human experience, American leisure
was reshaped to allow for emotional expression through contrived means
such as sporting events, movies, television, rock music, and amusement
parks, all of which further contribute to generating profits in a consumer
society. Aside from these commercial avenues, however, people are largely
expected to act as though they are unaffected by emotions.[4] Ancient West-

---

2. Both the Greek and its translation are from Aristotle, *Eth. nic.* 7.3.7 (*The Nicomachean Ethics* [trans. H. Rackham; ed. Jeffrey Henderson; LCL; Cambridge: Harvard University Press, 1934]). It is also worth noting that for Aristotle (ibid., 10.7.8–9), our true self
is associated first and foremost with the intellect (νοῦς), although it has been argued that
Aristotle's point here is not his last word on the topic (Richard Sorabji, *Emotion and Peace
of Mind: From Stoic Agitation to Christian Temptation: The Gifford Lectures* [Oxford: Oxford
University Press, 2000] 190).

3. The Latin and its translation are quoted from Seneca, *Ira* 2.4.1 (*Moral Essays* [trans.
John W. Basore; LCL; Cambridge: Harvard University Press, 1928]). Seneca also joins Aristotle in associating anger with insanity and madness (ibid., 3.1.3–6). This tradition of
associating irrationality with emotion continued in the early modern period with René
Descartes, whose division of the mind and body played a key role in reinforcing the ascrip-
tion of irrationality to emotion, particularly with his emphasizing the mind, not the body,
as the true ground of being (*Cogito ergo sum*) (Antonio R. Damasio, *Descartes' Error: Emotion, Reason, and the Human Brain* [New York: Putnam's, 1994] esp. pp. 245–52). Though
Descartes admitted that emotions are often present in the mind and even have positive
qualities, he believed they were corrupted by their association with the body (R. Descartes,
The Passions of the Soule [London: A. C., 1650] 170 [Article 211]. Online: *Early English Books
Online EEBO*, http://eebo.chadwyck.com/ [accessed April 18, 2006]).

4. Peter N. Stearns, *American Cool: Constructing a Twentieth-Century Emotional Style*
(New York: New York University Press, 1994) passim. A key summary is found on pp. 300–
301, a discussion of the word "cool" on pp. 1–2, a discussion of dating on pp. 95–138, a

ern assumptions about the irrationality of emotion have thus become fused with discourses that serve vested interests in modern capitalist societies.

Catherine Lutz has also shown how characterizing emotions as irrational relates to broader issues of discourse and power in our society. She demonstrates that rationality, when viewed from a critical perspective, has less to do with operating in accordance with universal logic (if there is such a thing) and more with "the historically and culturally determined assessment of how a sensible, or fully mature, human ought to behave."[5] Within this rubric, rationality is closely related to dominant ideologies. Emotion, which is so frequently set in opposition to rationality, is used to label deviations from these ideologies. As Lutz puts it:

> When the emotional is defined as irrational, all those occasions and individuals in which emotion is identified can be dismissed. . . . In this society, those groups which have traditionally 'been conceived of as passional beings, incapable of sustained rationality' . . . include 'infants, children, adolescents, mental patients, primitive people, peasants, immigrants, Negroes, slumdwellers, urban masses, crowds, and most of all, women'. . . . Emotion becomes an important metaphor for perceived threats to established authority.[6]

In other words, the perceived connection between emotionality and irrationality serves to silence groups who are outraged and angered by the injustices committed by people with power. Even when the marginalized are not expressing such anger, the characterization of them as emotional (and therefore irrational) serves to reinforce their marginalized status. Thus, when discourses describe women as more emotional than men, they appeal to a broader set of assumptions within Western society that reinforces the culturally inferior status of women.

3.2 Beyond Faulty Characterizations

One may try to rebut the above arguments by claiming that there is scientific evidence for seeing emotions as irrational. These claims would be based on outdated assumptions and faulty scientific models. Ironically, the dichotomy between reason and emotion, so ingrained in Western consciousness, is fantasy, a mere invention that stands at odds with the

---

discussion of reasons for the emergence of this style (which are not completely limited to economic reasons) on pp. 193–228, and a discussion of recreation on pp. 264–84.

    5. Catherine A. Lutz, *Unnatural Emotions: Everyday Sentiments on a Micronesian Atoll & Their Challenge to Western Theory* (Chicago: University of Chicago Press, 1998) 62.

    6. Ibid., 58–80, esp. p. 62. Arlie Russell Hochschild makes a similar point with respect to the tendency to disregard female emotion by seeing it as irrational (*The Managed Heart: Commercialization of Human Feeling* [Berkeley: University of California Press, 1983] esp. pp. 172–73). Regarding the Hebrew Bible itself, see the discussion in Ellen van Wolde, *Reframing Biblical Studies: When Language and Text Meet Culture, Cognition, and Context* (Winona Lake, IN: Eisenbrauns., 2009) 70–72, esp. p. 72.

most recent scientific findings. Research demonstrates that "the substrates of complex emotion and cognition overlap considerably. It is simply not possible to identify regions of the brain devoted exclusively to affect or exclusively to cognition."[7] Antonio Damasio, an internationally recognized neurologist, has played a key role in demonstrating that the perceived dichotomy between reason and emotion is false. Feelings, he shows, are actually integral to rationality. Over the course of two decades, Damasio has studied several neurological patients who led normal lives until an accident, surgery, or tumor caused brain damage, typically lesions on the prefrontal cortex (PFC). In clinical tests, these patients score high on intelligence exams, but they have difficulty reasoning with everyday decisions, frequently displaying morally problematic behavior and an inability to maintain employment. Damasio finds that these patients also lack the ability to experience emotion. With the inability to experience emotion comes the inability for these patients to reason effectively, even though they remain extremely intelligent. Emotions play a key role in making everyday decisions.[8]

Another important study from the field of neuroscience is Joseph LeDoux's *Emotional Brain: The Mysterious Underpinnings of Emotional Life.* Although conventional Western assumptions link emotions with the heart and thinking with the brain, LeDoux demonstrates that "emotional feelings involve many more brain systems than thoughts."[9] While LeDoux does not want to equate emotion and cognition, he sees both of them as (1) operating on unconscious levels, (2) interacting with each other, and (3) being processed by the same mechanisms that make us consciously aware of them.[10] Viewing emotion and reason as two completely separate entities fails to do justice to the evidence.

Studies in the field of psychology have supported the findings of scholars such as Damasio and LeDoux. Keith Oatley, the former president of the International Society for Research on Emotions, has written an important essay entitled "Do Emotional States Produce Irrational Thinking?" Nuanced and articulate, this essay demonstrates that "there is no basis . . . for assuming that emotions are distinctively and inherently irrational, while non-emotional thinking is inherently rational. This is . . . a relic of

---

7. Richard J. Davidson, Klaus R. Scherer, and H. Hill Goldsmith, eds., *Handbook of Affective Sciences* (Series in Affective Science; Oxford: Oxford University Press, 2003) 5. Similar sentiments have been voiced by Caleb R. Schultz, M.D., Mayo Clinic, private communication, Sept. 21, 2007.

8. Damasio, *Descartes' Error*, esp. pp. 3–79, 245–52. See also Davidson, Scherer, and Goldsmith, eds., *Handbook of Affective Sciences*, 5–7, 66–92.

9. Joseph LeDoux, *The Emotional Brain: The Mysterious Underpinnings of Emotional Life* (New York: Simon & Schuster, 1996) 299.

10. Ibid., 19, 68–69.

a folk theory which in this case was false."[11] Oatley argues that irrationality is not a defining characteristic of emotion. While individuals who are "emotional" can display signs of irrationality, so can those who are not emotional. He concludes, "The appropriate way to see emotions is not as irrational elements in our lives, but as a clever biological solution to problems with which we are often confronted."[12]

Similar conclusions have also been reached in the field of philosophy.[13] Martha Nussbaum, one of the leading public intellectuals of our time, argues that emotions are not outcomes of irrational components in the human psyche but are judgments of value. Thus, she examines different emotions, showing that they stem not from a lack of common sense but from an assessment of events that matter greatly: "In fear, one sees oneself or what one loves as seriously threatened. In hope, one sees oneself or what one loves as in some uncertainty but with a good chance for a good outcome. In grief, one sees an important object or person as lost; in love, as invested with a special sort of radiance."[14] For Nussbaum, emotions are not the polar opposites of rationality but are part of the way that we judge the world around us.

3.3 Violent Distortions of the Biblical Text

The best ethnographic research reflects the findings of scholars such as Damasio, LeDoux, Oatley, and Nussbaum, recognizing that the opposition between thought and emotion is a Western construct that one should not presuppose is at work in non-Western cultures.[15] Unfortunately, many biblical interpreters appear insufficiently aware of the ways that emotions can

---

11. Keith Oatley, "Do Emotional States Produce Irrational Thinking?" in *Lines of Thinking: Reflections on the Psychology of Thought* (ed. K. J. Gilhooly et al.; 2 vols.; Chichester: John Wiley, 1990) 2.121–31, esp. p. 130.

12. Ibid., 130–31. In addition to the work done by Oatley, one thinks of the idea of "emotional intelligence," which has gained prominence in not only psychology but also education. Simply put, it contends that an essential skill in life is one's ability to recognize and manage one's emotions. It builds on the work of Damasio, LeDoux, and others, presenting interesting data on how regulating emotions can lead to success in one's career and the prevention of problematic behaviors. This idea has been popularized in part by Nancy Gibbs, "The EQ Factor," *Time*, Oct. 2, 1995, http://www.time.com/time/classroom/psych/unit5 _article1.html (accessed April 13, 2010). For a more scholarly discussion, see Reuven Bar-On and James D. A. Parker, eds., *The Handbook of Emotional Intelligence: Theory, Development, Assessment, and Application at Home, School, and in the Workplace* (San Francisco: Jossey-Bass, 2000).

13. Robert Solomon, *The Passions* (Garden City, NY: Anchor, 1976) xviii, 241–52; idem, *Not Passion's Slave: Emotions and Choice* (Oxford: Oxford University Press, 2003). See also Martha C. Nussbaum, *Upheavals of Thought: The Intelligence of Emotions* (Cambridge: Cambridge University Press, 2001) passim, esp. pp. 114–19.

14. Ibid., 28.

15. An excellent review article of this research is Niko Besnier, "Language and Affect," *Annual Review of Anthropology* 19 (1990) 419–51, esp. p. 420.

differ between cultures. A number of scholars have consistently emphasized the irrationality of emotion in the Hebrew Bible and thus imposed
modern, Western misunderstandings on a text that is neither modern nor
Western. One of the most prominent examples is Bruce Edward Baloian's
doctoral thesis on *The Aspect of Anger in the Old Testament.*[16]

On the whole, the published form of Baloian's dissertation has many
praiseworthy features. However, he goes further than most in imposing
Western assumptions about rationality onto the biblical text. Time and
again, Baloian finds it necessary to use the categories *rational* and *irrational* to characterize biblical anger.[17] He tends to characterize human anger
as irrational and divine anger as rational. While it may be that Baloian is
merely seeking to interpret biblical anger in terms that his Western audience would understand (that is, with reference to rationality and irrationality), there are several occasions where he goes further, nearly implying
that (ir)rationality is a category used by the Bible itself. For example, at
the conclusion of the book, when Baloian summarizes the Hebrew Bible's
portrayal of human anger, he writes, "The explicit demand of the Old Testament texts is to govern anger by the use of reason."[18]

Although Baloian's work is a prominent example of the tendency to characterize biblical anger along the Western categories of rationality and irrationality, he is not alone. With respect to divine anger, Heschel, Fretheim,
and Brueggemann discuss the extent to which God's anger should be seen
as rational.[19] With regard to human anger, Hans Walter Wolff characterizes
emotional acts ascribed to the (לב) לבב ('heart') as corresponding to 'the irrational levels of [humanity]' (*den irrationalen Schichten des Menschen*).[20] The
Theological Dictionary of the Old Testament, in treating the various words
for *anger* in the Hebrew Bible, concludes, "Anger characterizes the fool, *the
irrational*, and the evildoer."[21] Similarly, the *New International Dictionary of
Old Testament Theology and Exegesis* claims in its opening remarks about אַף
('anger') that this word, when used of humans, can "indicate an irrational,

---

16. Bruce Edward Baloian, *The Aspect of Anger in the Old Testament* (Ph.D. thesis, Claremont Graduate School, 1989). It was written under the direction of Rolf Knierim. The
published form is *Anger in the Old Testament* (American University Studies 7, Theology and
Religion 99; New York: Peter Lang, 1992).

17. Ibid., 23–26, 31, 33, 35, 37, 40–42, 46, 48, 151, 153, 157–58, 163.

18. Ibid., 151; see also pp. 35, 42.

19. See my "Different Perspectives on Divine Pathos: An Examination of Hermeneutics in Biblical Theology," *CBQ* 69 (2007) 673–94, esp. pp. 676–78, 681–84.

20. The English is quoted from Hans Walter Wolff, *Anthropology of the Old Testament*
(trans. Margaret Kohl; Philadelphia: Fortress, 1981) 44. Even when Wolff goes on to qualify this remark, it is problematic. He writes, "We must guard against the false impression
that biblical man is determined more by feeling than by reason" (p. 47). Later, he asserts
that the *lēb(āb)* "describes the seat and function of the reason" (p. 51). One wishes that,
in all of these instances, Wolff had abandoned the language of *reason* and *rationality* and
stressed that the Hebrew Bible does not perceive a dichotomy between *reason* and *emotion*.

21. J. Bergman and E. Johnson, "אָנַף; אַף," *TDOT* 1.348–60, esp. p. 356 (italics mine).

out-of-control anger."[22] In a comparable move, Ellen van Wolde describes verbs for anger in the Hebrew Bible by saying, "the irrational and destructive power of anger is all too apparent."[23]

One wonders what authors such as Baloian and van Wolde mean by *irrational*.[24] Biblical Hebrew has no words that easily align with the terms *rationality* or *irrationality*. It has no true equivalents of *reason* or *logic*.[25] It does focus on wisdom. However, חכמה ('wisdom') carries shades of meaning and associative networks that contrast sharply with *reason*. The Western term *reason* is concerned with logic, while biblical *wisdom* is concerned primarily with character formation.[26] In the Bible, wise decisions may or may not align with what Westerners call *logic*.[27] As the books of Job and Qoheleth illustrate, the pursuit of *wisdom* involves a fair amount of guesswork and in the end may lead to insufficient answers or escape humanity altogether.[28] If anything, the biblical concept of wisdom shares more in common with the Egyptian understanding of *maat* than Western notions of *rationality*.[29] The distance between Athens and Jerusalem should not be minimized.[30] Using the Western categories of rationality to characterize emotion in the Hebrew

---

22. Gale B. Struthers, "אַף, אָנַף," *NIDOTTE* 1.462–65, esp. p. 463.

23. Ellen van Wolde, "Language of Sentiment," *SBL Forum* 5 (2007), http://sbl-site.org/Article.aspx?ArticleID=660 (accessed April 11, 2007). Van Wolde does not emphasize the irrationality of biblical anger in a subsequent publication on the subject (*Reframing Biblical Studies*, 62–72, esp. pp. 70–72), though she continues to speak of similar concepts by describing biblical anger as both marked by a lack of control and having an immediate destructive result.

24. Baloian and van Wolde are mentioned because they, more than other sources, devote extensive portions of their writing to human anger.

25. Granted, Biblical Hebrew does not have terms for *theology* or *history* either. But the Hebrew Bible does focus clearly on both divinity and the events of the past. The Hebrew Bible does not focus on *reason* or *logic*.

26. Although biblical wisdom has connections with common sense (Prov 10:13, 21; 11:12) and even vocational skill (Exod 35:10, 25; 36:1–2, 4, 8), the Hebrew Bible as a whole associates it most closely with morality. As James L. Crenshaw puts it, "The goal of all wisdom was the formation of character" (*Old Testament Wisdom: An Introduction* [rev. ed.; Louisville: Westminster John Knox, 1998] 3).

27. For more on how wisdom differs strongly from modern Western modes of knowledge, reason, and power, see Ellen F. Davis, *Getting Involved with God: Rediscovering the Old Testament* (Cambridge, MA: Cowley, 2001) 91–103, esp. pp. 194–98.

28. Many verses in these books emphasize the elusiveness and insufficiency of wisdom for humanity, such as Job 5:13; 12:2; 28:20–21; 32:13; 38:36–37; Qoh 1:13, 16–18; 2:14–21; 6:8–9; 7:16, 23; 8:17; 9:11, 15–16.

29. On the Egyptian conception of *maat*, see Miriam Lichtheim, *Moral Values in Ancient Egypt* (OBO 155; Fribourg: University Press / Göttingen: Vandenhoeck & Ruprecht, 1997) 11–12, 43, 95.

30. There are some who argue in favor of Greek influences on wisdom literature, such as Joseph Blenkinsopp, "Ecclesiastes 3:1–15: Another Interpretation," *JSOT* 66 (1995) 55–64. However, even if there are some connections, they should not be pushed too far. See James L. Crenshaw, "Prolegomena," in *Studies in Ancient Israelite Wisdom* (ed. James L. Crenshaw; New York: Ktav, 1976) 8.

Bible is akin to using the word *democracy* as one's primary rubric for characterizing the political and religious rulers of ancient Israel. It corresponds to the problematic equation of נפש ('life') with *soul*. [31]

Whether one examines why people become angry or what they do when angry, biblical texts do not portray angry individuals as displaying flawed thinking or anything resembling *irrationality*. With regard to anger's various causes, the Hebrew Bible has few, if any, instances in which people become angry for no apparent reason (see §4.3.1), a point that both Baloian and van Wolde note. [32] Baloian suggests that, while anger usually arises for clear reasons, these reasons can be irrational, as is the case with "greed, irritation, pride, or the lust of war." [33] A chief example that he discusses is Uzziah in 2 Chronicles 26. As the text mentions (v. 16), Uzziah's 'heart grew proud' (גָּבַהּ לִבּוֹ). Three verses later, it says that he became angry (וּבְזַעְפּוֹ, וַיִּזְעַף) when priests challenged his authority to burn incense in the temple. Baloian seems to be suggesting that Uzziah made an irrational judgment in seeing himself as having the authority to burn incense. However, kings both in the Hebrew Bible and throughout the ancient Near East saw themselves as "responsible for the organization and administration of the cult including cultic reform." [34] If Uzziah believed that as king he had responsibility over the cult, then were his actions really irrational? Burning incense in the temple by a non-priest is portrayed on several occasions as violating the divine will (Lev 2:16, Num 4:16, 1 Sam 2:28). But is it useful to equate violations of God's will with irrationality? At least in the book of Isaiah, the divine will is not always portrayed as corresponding with human rationality or human ways of thinking (Isa 55:8–9). [35] One wonders if similar assumptions are at work here. At best, Baloian's separating emotion from reason detracts from what is at stake in the text itself. He could easily have associated this anger with the biblical category of *sin*. The use of the

---

31. The second example (soul) is more complex than the first (democracy). One could argue that pre-Platonic conceptions of *soul* have a fair amount in common with the biblical concept of נפש.

32. Baloian stresses that human anger has clear causes, such as frustration (*Anger in the Old Testament*, 29–37), pride (pp. 37–43), and a concern for justice (pp. 43–50). Likewise, van Wolde's work suggests that anger prototypically arises not in a vacuum but in response to having one's goals thwarted ("Sentiments as Culturally Constructed Emotions: *Anger* and *Love* in the Hebrew Bible," *BibInt* 16 [2008] 1–24, esp. p. 8). One of the rare places where readers are not told the cause of anger is in 2 Sam 24:1, where Yʜᴡʜ becomes angry with David, and no reason is given in the immediate context. Even in this case, however, Yʜᴡʜ's anger is not necessarily irrational. Readers do not know the reason for the anger, but this does not mean that there is none. The narrator's decision not to share elements of the story should not be confused with their nonexistence.

33. Baloian, *Anger in the Old Testament*, 42.

34. Keith W. Whitelam, "King and Kingship," *ABD* 4.40–48, esp. p. 46. As examples, Whitelam cites 1 Kgs 15:12–15; 2 Kgs 18:1–7, 22:3–23:23.

35. Consider also Job 42:7–8, where God rebukes Job's friends for their various thoughts that were not 'what is right' נְכוֹנָה.

Western category of *rationality*, on the other hand, is unmerited and leads only to confusion.

If *irrational* is not the best descriptor of biblical anger's *causes*, does it do justice to the *behavior* of angry individuals? Both Baloian and van Wolde suggest that biblical anger often leads to irrational actions. Following an ancient precedent (4 Macc 2:19), they both give the example of Gen 34:7, where Dinah's brothers become enraged at what has happened to her and subsequently slaughter the Shechemites. Baloian criticizes the brothers because they do not "cool down, so that the heat (חמה) of passion can cool and rational thinking can take hold."[36] Van Wolde, meanwhile, says that the brothers "lose all rational control and aim for but one thing: immediate revenge."[37]

Even with this example, where the action resulting from anger is extreme, one can question whether the description of this anger as being irrational really fits. The brother's revenge is certainly not immediate, as van Wolde contends. Rather, it is carefully calculated. Initially, the brothers deceive the Shechemites. They demand that they become circumcised, meaning that Shechem experiences pain on the same bodily organ with which he raped (or perhaps disgraced) Dinah. After a period of time, Simeon and Levi take the city while the men are still in pain and unable to defend themselves. Their vengeance is thoughtfully designed to inflict the maximum damage on the maximum number of people.[38]

Were the brothers irrational in becoming angry and judging that vengeance should take place? Though interpretations of this chapter differ greatly, there is a clear, logical reason for the brothers' anger.[39] Their sister has been severely mistreated, and the entire clan has been disgraced. Even the narrator explicitly condemns Shechem's treatment of Dinah (Gen 34:7), saying that Shechem 'committed an outrage in Israel by lying with Jacob's daughter, for such a thing ought not to be done' (NRSV; נְבָלָה עָשָׂה בְיִשְׂרָאֵל לִשְׁכַּב אֶת־בַּת־יַעֲקֹב וְכֵן לֹא יֵעָשֶׂה). This explicit condemnation is remarkable, given the rarity with which the narrator of Genesis offers explicit evaluations of events.[40] Unless one assumes a position of extreme Stoicism,

---

36. Baloian, *Anger in the Old Testament*, 39–40.

37. Van Wolde, "Sentiments as Culturally Constructed Emotions," 14.

38. Meir Sternberg, *The Poetics of Biblical Narrative: Ideological Literature and the Drama of Reading* (Bloomington: Indiana University Press, 1985) 466–67.

39. On the different interpretations, compare Sternberg (*The Poetics of Biblical Narrative*, esp. pp. 445–475) with Danna Nolan Fewell and David M. Gunn ("Tipping the Balance: Sternberg's Reader and the Rape of Dinah," *JBL* 110 [1991] 193–211). Also compare Susanne Scholz ("Was It Really Rape in Genesis 34? Biblical Scholarship as a Reflection of Cultural Assumptions," in *Escaping Eden: New Feminist Perspectives on the Bible* [ed. Harold C. Washington, Susan Lochrie Graham, and Pamela Thimmes; Washington Square, NY: New York University Press, 1999] 182–98) with Lyn M. Bechtel ("What if Dinah Is Not Raped? [Genesis 34]," *JSOT* 62 [1994] 19–36).

40. Frequently, evaluations from the narrator are more indirect—for example, they are spoken by characters within the story. At other times, they are missing altogether. Thus,

anger appears to be a natural response to what Shechem has done. The brothers cannot be faulted for becoming angry.

Did the brothers go too far, displaying irrationality in harming so many people? While many have joined Baloian and van Wolde in answering affirmatively, there are several reasons to be cautious about seeing the brothers' actions as fundamentally irrational.[41] First, Naomi Segal has questioned whether in fact one should "'automatically' judge rape as a much lesser crime than massacre." Such judgment, she asserts, reflects patriarchal assumptions that fail to do full justice to the degree of trauma involved in the act of rape, ignoring the abuse of autonomy, body, and will that this act entails for its sufferers.[42] Second, throughout the Hebrew Bible, many individuals, including God, maintain on a wide range of occasions that punishment must come not only against the evildoer but also against the entire community, presumably for its complacency in allowing the evildoing to occur.[43] Levi and Simeon appear to display the same type of logic. Third, it is obvious from Gen 34:30 that, if Simeon and Levi had killed only Shechem and not all the male inhabitants of the city, the two brothers would soon have faced bodily harm for their punishment of the Shechemites' chief prince.[44] If any retribution were to take place, then those who punished Shechem must be willing either to kill or be killed. Finally, the last verse of the chapter clearly suggests that, from Simeon and Levi's perspective, their actions are defensible. When Jacob scolds his sons and points to the life-threatening consequences, the two brothers remain steadfast, asking, 'Should he make a whore out of our sister?' (הַכְזוֹנָה יַעֲשֶׂה אֶת־אֲחוֹתֵנוּ). The narrator allows the episode to end with this question unanswered and unchallenged, suggesting that there was some degree of logic in what the

---

Sternberg refers to the "scarcity of evaluation on the narrator's part" (*The Poetics of Biblical Narrative*, esp. p. 54). See also Robert Alter, *The Art of Biblical Narrative* (New York: Basic Books, 1981) esp. p. 184.

41. Fewell and Gunn are not far removed from Baloian and van Wolde, describing the actions of Simeon and Levi as a "grossly disproportionate response" (Fewell and Gunn, "Tipping the Balance," 205). In favor of their interpretation is Deut 22:28–29 and "The Laws of Ur-Namma (Ur-Nammu)" (trans. Martha Roth; *COS* 2.153:408–410, esp. pp. 409–410, §§7–8). However, one should note that other texts on other occasions decree a strong punishment (such as execution) for the perpetrators of rape. See Deut 22:25; "The Code of Hammurabi" (trans. Martha Roth; *COS* 2.131:335–353, esp. p. 344, §130); and "The Middle Assyrian Laws (Tablet A)" (trans. Martha Roth; *COS* 2.132:353–360, esp. p. 354, §12).

42. Naomi Segal, "Review of Meir Sternberg, *The Poetics of Biblical Narrative: Ideological Literature and the Drama of Reading*," *VT* 38 (1988) 243–49, esp. pp. 245, 247.

43. Thus, in Gen 18:16–33, God is portrayed as having few qualms about destroying all of Sodom and Gomorrah. Even after God bartered with Abraham, the text implies (or at least leaves open the possibility) that nine innocent people could be killed with the guilty.

44. If there is any truth in Jacob's comment that the Canaanites and Perizzites may assemble against him in reaction to the slaughter, then certainly the Hivites, if they were not wiped out, would pose an even more likely threat.

brothers asserted.[45] It is thus questionable, if not doubtful, that the brothers have "lost all rational control," as van Wolde claims.[46]

The point of the preceding discussion is *not* that the just punishment for rape is the slaughter of an entire city. Rather, the point is that characterizing the brothers' response as irrational fails to do justice to the text. The chapter as a whole raises a series of challenging questions for readers that become obscured when the brothers' anger is quickly dismissed as irrational. At its heart, the text asks its readers, What is the proper response to sexual violence? What should one do when a family member has been disgraced, and there are no good options for punishing the wrongdoer? How does one exact justice in the absence of possibilities commensurate with the offense? If one sides with Jacob and does little or nothing, then how does one reply to the brothers' unanswered question? This chapter is more concerned with deep reflection on these types of questions than with tidy solutions. When readers dismiss the brothers' action as being driven by irrational anger, however, these enormously weighty and complex questions quickly lose their evocative power. Then the story merely tells Western readers what they already know: emotions are irrational.

When considering claims that biblical emotions are irrational, one should remember the words of Catherine Lutz: "In subtle ways, . . . the non-West has been constructed in the emotional image of the West—as emotionally almost indistinguishable from the West."[47] Edward Said makes similar points in describing the Western tendency to cast the Orient in its own image, seeing Oriental concepts as "repetitious pseudo-incarnations" of Western ideals.[48] Something quite similar takes place when biblical interpreters, rather than interpreting the text on its own terms with its own integrity, envision biblical anger under the darkness of Plato's long shadow. Biblical anger may be linked to sin, but it is not linked to false dichotomies invented by the West. Imposing Western categories on an ancient Near Eastern text adds more casualties to the already violent act of translation.

---

45. Granted, these words eventually are challenged in Gen 49:6–7, where Jacob condemns the anger of Simeon and Levi. Nevertheless, it is remarkable that Genesis 34 concludes with the brothers' question unanswered for much of the remainder of the book. Furthermore, one should note that, in Gen 49:6–7, the brothers' anger is condemned because of its intensity, not because of its irrationality.

46. Even van Wolde herself may now have some questions and doubts about this claim made in "Sentiments as Culturally Constructed Emotions," 14. In a publication that came out one year later (2009), she admits that, within the framework of the text, there is some justification for killing that results from what transpired between Shechem and Dinah (idem, *Reframing Biblical Studies*, 326). This more recent characterization makes better sense of the biblical evidence, particularly the brothers' point of view, and it supports the conclusions reached here.

47. Lutz, *Unnatural Emotions*, 218–19; see also p. 54.

48. Edward W. Said, *Orientalism* (25th anniversary ed.; New York: Vintage, 2003) 62; see also pp. 61, 63, 72. While Said is referring to characterizations of Islam, the implications of his argument extend to the discussion here.

Rather than embodying careful exegesis, it exemplifies the problems with Orientalist discourse characterized by Said. As we shall see in the next chapters, biblical anger clearly has its set of associated commonplaces, but irrationality is not among them.

3.4 Conclusion

When considering one's general orientation to language in the Hebrew Bible, Valentin Voloshinov provides a useful model. The Russian linguist boldly rejects both abstract objectivism and individualistic subjectivism. He also steers away from a golden mean between the two, calling instead for a "negation of both thesis and antithesis alike." He makes a case for a "dialectical synthesis" that sees language as a fundamentally social enterprise that cannot be abstracted from its context or reduced to the individual psyche. He asserts that "each and every word" fully integrates the ideological values and assumptions of its culture.[49]

This general approach to language is quite helpful when one considers the language used to express and describe emotion. Emotions are not objective entities, the qualities, divisions, and associative networks of which are self-evident to all peoples in all cultures. Nor are emotions so specific to individuals that interpreters must psychoanalyze particular characters. Rather, terms for emotions are given their meaning by the communities whose lives they characterize. They may have biological bases and individual groundings, but they are in many respects social constructions. Contexts—cultural, linguistic, and textual—imbue terms for emotion with an array of meanings, associations, and implications. Language, the lifeblood of culture, carries the values attached to emotions.

At times, different cultures and languages will have similarities in how they construct emotions (as will be seen in subsequent chapters). However, interpreters must avoid the trap of assuming that, because there are similarieties, one culture's conception of an emotion is identical to another's. The differences need to be respected. Failing to recognize the social function of language can quickly lead to disastrous consequences. When interpreters extract emotion concepts from one sociolinguistic context and simplistically transport them to another, then the source text becomes a hollow shell filled by the values and assumptions of the target audience. Words such as *irrational* enter commentaries, even though they do little more than distract readers from the text itself. Translators may never produce a casualty-free text—wounds and scarring will undoubtedly be present. At

---

49. V. N. Voloshinov, "'Language, Speech, and Utterance' and 'Verbal Interaction'," in *Bakhtinian Thought: An Introductory Reader* (ed. Simon Dentith; London: Routledge, 1995) 107–43. The first quotation in this paragraph is from p. 126, the second from p. 138. Key summaries are found on pp. 125, 139, and 140. See esp. p. 131 for a discussion that relates directly to emotion.

the same time, translators have the ethical responsibility of avoiding the destruction of key elements in the text they translate. The Hebrew Bible has much to teach audiences today, but these audiences will learn little if they do not understand the text on its own terms.

Chapter 4

The Hebrew Bible's Prototypical Understanding of Anger

If anger in the Hebrew Bible is not first and foremost a matter of irrationality, then what best characterizes this emotion? In what situations does it tend to arise? What is the normal range of outcomes? How is this emotion usually evaluated? This chapter answers these questions by drawing on the field of cognitive linguistics, particularly prototype theory. Although scholars have attempted to describe biblical anger along these lines, various errors have been committed. As with characterizations of biblical anger as irrational, individuals who use these approaches have tended to impose Western ideas about emotions onto the biblical text. This chapter presents an alternate approach to prototype theory, reaching conclusions that explain anger in the Hebrew Bible on its own terms.

4.1 Prototype Theory: An Introduction

Cognitive linguistics is a cross-disciplinary field that draws on both cognitive science and linguistics, as well as related fields such as psychology. One important area of cognitive linguistic research is prototype theory, which examines the processes of categorization that take place in the mind. Prototype theory owes much to Wittgenstein's discussion of 'family resemblances' (*Familienähnlichkeiten*). Wittgenstein, while explaining the category of "language," observes that frequently a mental category will not have a single defining quality that characterizes every member of the category. However, there are sufficient similarities between the various members to justify the categorization. In this sense, he observes, members of a category are much like members of a family: they may not all have the same "build, features, colour of eyes, gait, temperament, etc.," but these various characteristics "overlap and criss-cross in the same way" so that one can see clear resemblances between people in the same family.[1]

Building on this idea, prototype theorists argue that individuals do not always have sharp categories that include and exclude membership on the

---

1. Ludwig Wittgenstein, *Philosophical Investigations* (trans. G. E. M. Anscombe; New York: Macmillan, 1953) esp. p. 31. These ideas are also discussed in Ludwig Wittgenstein, *Preliminary Studies for the "Philosophical Investigations": Generally Known as the Blue and Brown Books* (New York: Barnes & Noble, 1969) esp. pp. 17–25.

basis of a definitive collection of essential and required characteristics.[2] Rather, the mind often operates with what have been called "fuzzy sets," that is, categories "without sharp boundaries, in which there is a gradual but specifiable transition from membership to nonmembership."[3] In these cases, the mind tends to see several types of members in a set:

1. *Prototypical Members*: These members are the most *central* and the most *representative* members of the class.
2. *Non-prototypical but Established Members*: These members are seen as *less central*. They lack key features that make them representative of the set, but they are still clearly within the category.
3. *Marginal members*: These members are deemed to have *peripheral* status, being considered members by some people but not by others.

Table 1 (p. 50) lists several examples of members within prototypical categories. As these examples illustrate, the prototypical members have key characteristics that allow them to be seen as the best representatives of a given category. When individuals are confronted with incomplete information about an object, they tend to assign to it features that are consistent with the prototypical members of its category.[4]

As the final example in the table suggests, prototype theory has proven especially useful for researchers working with emotions. The term *emotion* is a notoriously slippery term. As Fehr and Russell put it, "Everyone knows what an emotion is, until asked to give a definition."[5] Some have even called for a technical redefinition of *emotion* that admittedly stands at variance with current usage.[6] Scholars who work with prototype theory have come to recognize that the inability to define *emotion* by outlining a list of universal characteristics results from its constituting a fuzzy set. They have

---

2. An example of a sharp set would be *integers*. Numbers that are fractions or contain a fraction are excluded from this set, whereas numbers free from fractions are included. Many technical categories are sharp categories, having clearly marked boundaries. Many conceptual categories, on the other hand, are not governed by definitive characteristics.

3. James A. Russell, "A Circumplex Model of Affect," *Journal of Personality and Social Psychology* 39 (1980) 1165. See also Phillip Shaver et al., "Emotion Knowledge: Further Explorations of a Prototype Approach," *Journal of Personality and Social Psychology* 52 (1987) 1062–63.

4. René Dirven and Marjolijn Verspoor, eds., *Cognitive Exploration of Language and Linguistics* (Amsterdam: Benjamins, 1998) 16–17; James R. Averill, *Anger and Aggression: An Essay on Emotion* (New York: Springer, 1982) 330–31. See also Shaver et al., "Emotion Knowledge," 1062.

5. B. Fehr and J. A. Russell, "Concept of Emotion Viewed from a Prototype Perspective," *Journal of Experimental Psychology: General* 113 (1984) 464–86, esp. p. 464; see also Jerome Kagan, *What Is Emotion? History, Measures, and Meanings* (New Haven, CT: Yale University Press, 2007) esp. chaps. 1, 5.

6. Paul E. Griffiths, *What Emotions Really Are: The Problem of Psychological Categories* (Chicago: University of Chicago Press, 1997) 201, 228; James A. Russell, "In Defense of a Prototype Approach to Emotion Concepts," *Journal of Personality and Social Psychology* 60 (1991) 37–47, esp. p. 45.

Table 1. Members of Prototypical Categories

Category	Prototypical Member(s)	Less Central Member(s)	Marginal Member(s)
Chair[a]	Kitchen Chair	Reclining Armchair, Wheelchair, Highchair	Barstool
Sport[b]	Football, Baseball, Basketball	Volleyball, Wrestling	Bowling, Ping Pong, Jumping Rope
Canon[c]	Books of the Torah	Judges, Obadiah, Proverbs	The Apocrypha
Emotion[d]	Love, Anger, Sadness, Fear	Anxiety, Bliss	Discomfort, Nostalgia, Vanity

[a] Dirven and Verspoor, eds., *Cognitive Exploration of Language and Linguistics*, esp. pp. 16–17; Averill, *Anger and Aggression*, 330–31.

[b] Eleanor Rosch, "Cognitive Representatives of Semantic Categories," *Journal of Experimental Psychology: General* 104 (1975) 192–233.

[c] Cynthia L. Miller, "Response to Chapman," *ExAud* 19 (2003) 149–52. See also Stephen B. Chapman, "The Old Testament Canon and Its Authority for the Christian Church," *ExAud* 19 (2003) 125–48; idem, *The Law and the Prophets: A Study in Old Testament Canon Formation* (Tübingen: Mohr Siebeck, 2000) 284–86.

[d] Shaver et al., "Emotion Knowledge," 1061–72; Russell, "In Defense of a Prototype Approach to Emotion Concepts."

also come to see the basic emotions, such as *love, joy, anger, sadness,* and *fear,* as likewise constituting prototypical categories. Thus, a large range of experiences can be classified within the basic-level term *anger* (for example, *outrage, fury, aggravation, annoyance, abhorrence*), even if one has difficulty finding a definitive and complete list of characteristics that accounts for all of these types of experiences.[7] They bear a family resemblance to one another without meeting a single set of defining criteria.

Prototype theorists have taken another step, describing prototypical scenarios in which particular emotions arise, as well as less representative scenarios in which they may take place.[8] These prototypical scenarios are called *schemas, scripts,* or *stereotypes.*[9] While descriptions of these scenar-

---

7. Shaver et al., "Emotion Knowledge," 1063–72. See also Kagan, *What Is Emotion?* 122–26.

8. Shaver et al., "Emotion Knowledge," 1072–84; Catherine A. Lutz, *Unnatural Emotions: Everyday Sentiments on a Micronesian Atoll and Their Challenge to Western Theory* (Chicago: University of Chicago Press, 1998) 10.

9. Shaver et al., "Emotion Knowledge," 1061. For an excellent discussion of script theory, see James A. Russell, "Culture and the Categorization of Emotions," *Psychological*

ios vary, George Lakoff and Zoltán Kövecses have offered one of the most popular accounts of anger's prototypical script in American English.[10] They argue that, while there are many possible accounts of the way that anger operates, it prototypically has five stages:

Stage 1: The self is wronged.

Stage 2: The self experiences physiological symptoms and the desire for retribution.

Stage 3: The self attempts to control anger.

Stage 4: The self fails to control anger and exhibits angry behavior.

Stage 5: The self enacts retribution against the offender in order to assuage anger.[11]

Lakoff and Kövecses are not claiming that every instance of anger follows these five steps. Nor are they claiming that this account aligns with a universal psychosomatic process. Rather, they maintain that the above scenario is (perhaps on unconscious levels) understood within American culture as being the natural one against which other types of anger can be compared. It is the folk theory that is commonly assumed in usage of the American English language.

Lakoff and Kövecses argue that there are various terms that this language employs to describe deviations from the prototypical case. Thus, with *insatiable anger*, the variance from the prototypical scenario pertains to stage 5: an act of retribution takes place, but the anger does not dissipate. In contrast, with *explosive anger*, stage 3 (self-control) is bypassed, and the self moves directly from the physiological experience of anger (stage 2) to the exhibition of angry behavior (stage 4). To name a final example, with *cool anger*, there are no physiological effects (no stage 2), and anger is controlled (no stage 4).[12]

4.2 Anger and Prototype Theory in Biblical Scholarship

Ellen van Wolde has played a key role in appropriating this work to biblical studies.[13] She recounts Kövecses' model of anger in American English.

Bulletin 110 (1991) 426–50, esp. pp. 442–44. See also Zoltán Kövecses, "Introduction: Language and Emotion Concepts," in *Everyday Conceptions of Emotion: An Introduction to the Psychology, Anthropology and Linguistics of Emotion* (ed. James A. Russell et al.; Dordrecht: Kluwer Academic, 1995) esp. p. 10.

10. For alternate accounts, see Shaver et al., "Emotion Knowledge," 1073–80.

11. George Lakoff and Zoltán Kövecses, "The Cognitive Model of Anger Inherent in American English," in *Cultural Models in Language and Thought* (ed. Dorothy Holland and Naomi Quinn; Cambridge: Cambridge University Press, 1987) 211–14.

12. Ibid., 210–16.

13. Ellen van Wolde, "Sentiments as Culturally Constructed Emotions: *Anger* and *Love* in the Hebrew Bible," *BibInt* 16 (2008) 1–24; idem, "Language of Sentiment," *SBL Forum* 5 (2007), http://sbl-site.org/Article.aspx?ArticleID=660 (accessed April 11, 2007); idem,

Then she examines the prototypical model of anger in Japanese as an additional point of comparison. Drawing on the work of Keiko Matsuki, she describes how the Japanese language associates anger with various bodily locales: it begins in the belly, *hara* (not to be confused with the Hebrew *ḥārâ*), where it is controllable; can boil over into the chest, *mune*, where it can still be controlled; and reaches its height when it enters the head, *atama*, where control is lost.[14] Van Wolde turns next to the Hebrew Bible's prototypical account of anger. She argues that it consists of four stages:

> *Stage 1:* Report of an offence or offending event
> *Stage 2:* Anger takes over and burning heat immediately rises to the head
> *Stage [3]:* Loss of control and incontrollable fury
> *Stage [4]:* Act of retribution[15]

Van Wolde draws a sharp contrast between this script of anger and the Japanese model. Whereas there are Japanese terms like *hara* ('belly') and *mune* ('chest') to refer to controlled anger, van Wolde asserts that in Biblical Hebrew anger moves immediately to the head (אַף 'nose' and 'anger'). Consequently, she characterizes biblical anger as "an overflowing, incontrollable fury" that results in an "immediate response of a destructive nature."[16] Marshaling examples such as Genesis 34 (see §3.3), she claims that irrationality and uncontrollability are prototypical characteristics of anger in the Hebrew Bible.[17] She sees biblical anger's prototypical script as quite similar to American anger's, except that biblical anger is marked by an absence of control.[18]

While van Wolde's work moves in the right direction by seeking to apply the findings of prototype theory to the Hebrew Bible, there are several erroneous assumptions and interpretive moves. In particular, the notion of anger in the Hebrew Bible seems conflated with Japanese and American models. Simply because Japanese links facially located anger with a lack of control does not mean that Biblical Hebrew does. Cross-cultural studies

---

Reframing Biblical Studies: When Language and Text Meet Culture, Cognition, and Context (Winona Lake, IN: Eisenbrauns, 2009) 62–72.

14. K. Matsuki, "Metaphors of Anger in Japanese," in *Language and the Cognitive Construal of the World* (ed. J. R. Taylor and R. E. MacLaury; Berlin: de Gruyter, 1995) 137–51.

15. This is a quotation of van Wolde, "Sentiments as Culturally Constructed Emotions," 13. See also idem, "Language of Sentiment"; idem, *Reframing Biblical Studies*, 72.

16. The first quotation is from idem, "Language of Sentiment." The second quotation is from idem, *Reframing Biblical Studies*, 72. See also idem, "Sentiments as Culturally Constructed Emotions," 12–14.

17. Ibid., 12, 14, 16, 22; idem, "Language of Sentiment"; see also idem, *Reframing Biblical Studies*, 72.

18. Thus, her script of anger in the Hebrew Bible is the same as that offered by Kövecses for American anger, except that it lacks Kövecses's "stage 3," where the angry person attempts to control the emotion (van Wolde, "Sentiments as Culturally Constructed Emotions," 13; see also idem, *Reframing Biblical Studies*, 72).

have shown that many languages associate anger with the face and nose.[19] This association need not imply a lack of control simply because it does in Japanese. Moreover, van Wolde's use of biblical evidence is not comprehensive. Rather, it consists of illustrations that are not always compelling. For example, Genesis 34 is one of her chief examples, and it does not show subjects moving immediately from anger to violent actions. Rather, it shows characters willing to wait in order to carry out angry actions in carefully calculated ways. Interpreters need a different approach to biblical anger's prototypical script.

4.3 The Prototypical Understanding of Human Anger in the Hebrew Bible

To arrive at a better understanding of the prototypical script of human anger in the Hebrew Bible, we must examine (1) what tends to cause anger, (2) who tends to become angry, (3) with whom or what they tend to become angry, (4) what they tend to do while angry, and (5) how this emotion tends to be evaluated. The discussion below focuses primarily on human anger, rather than divine wrath, for the reasons stated in §1.6.[20]

4.3.1 Causes of Anger

A useful place to begin in order to discern the prototypical script of human anger in the Hebrew Bible is anger's causes. Many interpreters suggest that frustration is the primary reason for human anger in the Hebrew Bible. Thus, Baloian argues that frustration (along with pride and injustice) is a key cause.[21] Van Wolde does not use the word *frustration* but clearly refers to this concept when she argues, "The sentiment of anger [in the Hebrew Bible] arises when someone or something interferes with the deity's plans or with someone's plans or with His/his attainment of previously set goals."[22] Paul Krüger likewise sees frustration as the key cause of biblical

---

19. Ralph B. Hupka et al., "Anger, Envy, Fear, and Jealousy as Felt in the Body: A Five-Nation Study," *Cross-Cultural Research* 30 (1996) 243–64, esp. pp. 245, 250, 255. Mark S. Smith has appropriated this model with the Hebrew Bible ("The Heart and Innards in Israelite Emotional Expressions: Notes from Anthropology and Psychobiology," *JBL* 117 [1998] 427–36).

20. Furthermore, a number of studies have shown that emotion scripts vary depending on features like context. These studies include Julie Fitness, "Anger in the Workplace: An Emotion Script Approach to Anger Episodes between Workers and Their Superiors, Co-workers and Subordinates," *Journal of Organizational Behavior* 21 (2000) 147–62, esp. pp. 148–49; Griffiths, *What Emotions Really Are*, esp. p. 177; Zoltán Kövecses, *Metaphor and Emotion: Language, Culture, and Body in Human Feeling* (Cambridge: Cambridge University Press / Paris: Maison des Sciences de l'Homme, 2000) 13. Therefore, it makes sense to focus on contexts that involve human anger, rather than complicating matters by also examining contexts that pertain to divine wrath.

21. Baloian, "Anger," *NIDOTTE* 4.377–85, esp. pp. 379–80.

22. Van Wolde, "Language of Sentiment." Van Wolde's work displays some diversity of thought. In *Reframing Biblical Studies*, she comes closer to the conclusions here, associating

anger, particularly when plans are thwarted.[23] While these interpreters are not necessarily wrong in pointing to frustration as anger's prototypical cause, there is a problem here. *Frustration* is a vague word that can describe a variety of negative emotions. For example, one can feel *sad* or *ashamed* when something interferes with the fulfillment of a goal.[24] The suggestion that anger is caused by frustration does not add a great deal of clarity to our understanding of the prototypical script behind anger in the Hebrew Bible.

Can the interpreter be more specific? On the one hand, there are many texts where the cause of anger is unclear, such as a number of Proverbs that speak of anger on a generic level and do not reveal anger's precise cause.[25] Hence, Prov 16:14 says simply, "The anger of a king is a messenger of death. A wise person will appease it." Here, the discourse is not particularly concrete; it speaks of kings in general, not one king in particular. Amid these generalities, the cause of anger is unknown. On other occasions, the text is more concrete, but the cause of anger still remains unclear. For example, Amos 1:11 denounces the anger of Edom and seems to be alluding to a particular historical incident. However, the text does not state what specifically sparked Edom's anger. Even if biblical narrators are omniscient, they do not reveal all of their knowledge to readers.[26]

Although the cause of biblical anger is unknown in many cases, the majority of texts do explain the basis for anger. In these cases, nearly every instance bears a point of commonality: anger results from a perceived wrongdoing. Here, the word *perceived* is crucial. It suggests that one must consider the perspective of the individual who is angry, rather than adopting an exterior perspective. For example, Potiphar becomes angry with Joseph because he perceives that Joseph has done something wrong, even though he is innocent (Gen 39:19).

Within the broad category of *perceived wrongdoing*, there are many subtypes:

---

anger less with a blocked goal and more with "incorrect" action (p. 71).

23. Paul A. Krüger, "A Cognitive Interpretation of the Emotion of Anger in the Hebrew Bible," *JNSL* 26 (2000) 181–93, esp. p. 182.

24. Bryan J. Dik, Department of Psychology, Colorado State University, private communication, Aug. 6, 2007.

25. Several of these texts speak of individuals who generally are angry or who are quick to anger. A number of these texts also speak of fools who become angry. While internal factors such as foolishness can contribute to the likelihood of becoming angry, external environmental triggers also play a highly significant role, even if these texts do not always describe these triggers. For related matters, see Lutz, *Unnatural Emotions*, 102–3.

26. See Robert Alter, *The Art of Biblical Narrative* (New York: Basic Books, 1981) 158. Cases where the cause of human anger is unclear or not mentioned include Gen 49:23; Deut 32:27; 2 Kgs 19:27–28; Isa 7:4, 14:6, 16:6, 37:28–29, 41:11, 45:24, 51:13; Jer 48:30; Ezek 3:14, 35:11; Hos 7:16; Amos 1:11; Ps 4:5[4], 55:4[3], 76:11[10], 124:3, 138:7; Prov 12:16; 14:16–17, 29; 15:18; 16:14, 32; 19:3, 11–12, 19; 20:2; 21:14, 24; 22:8, 24; 24:19, 24; 25:15; 26:17; 27:3–4; 29:8–9, 22; 30:33; Job 5:2; 19:29; 36:13, 18; Song 1:6; Qoh 5:16[17], 7:9, 11:10; Esth 2:21; Dan 8:6; 11:20, 30, 44.

1. Many cases of anger stem from the perception of an *interpersonal wrong*, such as Jacob's stealing his brother's blessing (Gen 27:41–45).[27]

   • Within the category of interpersonal wrongdoing, much anger is caused by the perception of *insubordination*, such as Vashti's refusal to come to the king when ordered (Esth 1:12). In fact, biblical characters are so aware that perceived insubordination can cause anger that subordinates frequently request that their superiors not become angry when they initiate a line of conversation, as when Judah unwittingly approaches his brother in Egypt and asks that this high official not be angered by his speaking with him (Gen 44:18).[28]

2. On other occasions, the wrongdoing is less on the interpersonal level and more on the *intertribal* or *international* level, such as when Saul becomes enraged at Nahash's threat to gouge the eye of each male inhabitant of Jabesh-gilead (1 Sam 11:1–6).[29]

3. At times, people also become angry after perceiving *religious wrongdoing*, such as Moses' anger when he descends Mount Sinai (Exod 32:19, 22).[30]

4. On a number of other occasions, individuals become angry because they perceive some type of wrongdoing within the *divine economy*. An

---

27. The following are instances of human anger caused by perceptions of *interpersonal wrongdoings*: Gen 27:41, 44–45; 31:36; 34:7; 39:19; 45:5; 49:6–7; 50:15; 1 Sam 17:28, 20:34; 2 Sam 3:8, 12:5, 13:21; Prov 6:34, 15:1, 17:25, 25:23; Job 32:3, 5; Neh 5:6. See also Gen 45:24, 1 Sam 28:15. At times, more than one classification is possible. For example, the anger of Gen 49:6–7 pertains to Simeon and Levi's anger over what happens to their sister. Because it was caused by what one individual (Shechem) did to another (Dinah), I have classified it here with other instances of interpersonal wrongdoing. However, it would also be possible to classify it under "Wrongdoing between Peoples" because it involves the children of Israel and the people of Shechem.

28. Cases where human anger stems from perceptions of *insubordination* or *inappropriate requests* include: Gen 30:2, 31:35, 40:2, 41:10, 44:18; Exod 11:8*, 16:20; Lev 10:16; Num 16:15, 22:27, 24:10, 31:14; Judg 9:30; 1 Sam 18:8; 20:7, 30; 29:4; 2 Sam 11:20; 2 Kgs 5:11–12*, 13:19*; Jer 37:15*; Job 40:11; Esth 1:12, 18; 2:1; 3:5; 5:9; 2 Chr 16:10*, 26:19. See also Prov 14:35. Some individuals, especially prophets, are in an ambiguous position regarding issues of subordination. On the one hand, they represent God and therefore can expect others to be subordinate to them (for example, Moses' expectations with Pharaoh, Exod 11:8). On the other hand, those in positions of military or state authority sometimes see prophets as mere humans and therefore expect them to be subordinate (for example, Naaman and Elisha, 2 Kgs 5:12). Cases of ambiguous insubordination are marked with an asterisk (*).

29. Instances of human anger's resulting from perceived *intertribal* or *international wrongdoing* include: Num 23:7–8; Judg 14:19; 1 Sam 11:6; 2 Sam 19:43[42]; Esth 7:7, 10; Neh 3:33[4:1], 4:1[7]; 2 Chr 25:10. See also Gen 49:6–7; Isa 7:4, 14:6, 16:6, 51:13; Jer 48:30; Ezek 35:11; Amos 1:11; Ps 124:3; Dan 8:6; 11:20, 30, 44; 2 Chr 28:9. For more on the related idea of battle rage, see Baloian, *NIDOTTE* 4.379; idem, *Anger in the Old Testament* (American University Studies 7, Theology and Religion 99; New York: Peter Lang, 1992) 40–43.

30. Human anger results from perceptions of *religious wrongdoing* in Exod 32:19, 22; Job 32:2; 2 Chr 28:9. See also 1 Sam 15:11, Jer 15:17.

example would be David's anger at Yhwh for killing Uzzah after he touched the ark of the covenant (2 Sam 6:8, 1 Chr 13:11).[31]

While most known causes of anger fit within the prototypical category of *perceived wrongdoing* (and these subcategories), there are some texts that provide marginal examples that do not fit as well. For example, in Dan 11:30, Antiochus IV Epiphanes becomes enraged at "the holy covenant" after "ships from Kittim" come against him. In this instance, it is not clear how Antiochus perceives "the holy covenant" as being involved in wrongdoing. It may relate to perceiving wrongdoing within the divine economy, but the precise nature of this relation is not revealed. Prototypically, the cause of anger here is a more marginal example.

4.3.2 Objects of Anger

Given the preceding discussion, it is not surprising that nearly every instance of human anger involves anger at a person or group of people—namely, the individuals who have committed the perceived wrongdoing. Thus, biblical anger can be described as both transitive and personal.[32] Because most of the characters in the Hebrew Bible are males, anger tends to be directed toward males, though there are a few exceptions, such as Jacob's anger at Rachel for making an inappropriate request (Gen 30:2; see also Gen 31:35).

The instances in which individuals are said to be angry at something other than a person or people are quite rare and can be considered marginal members of this prototypical category. Dan 11:30 is again exceptional, where anger is directed toward the holy covenant rather than toward a person, specifically. Another exception is Num 22:27–30, where Balaam is angry at his disobedient donkey—though one should note that this donkey has some rather anthropomorphic qualities. There are also cases in which anger is directed toward God. Most of these imply rather than make explicit that God is the object (Gen 4:5–6; 2 Sam 6:8; Isa 8:21, 45:24; Jer 15:17; Jonah 4:1, 4, 9; 1 Chr 13:11).[33] On the whole, however, angry individuals in the Hebrew Bible tend to direct their anger at other humans.

---

31. Anger relating to perceived wrongdoings within the *divine economy* include Gen 4:5–6 (Yhwh ignoring offering); 1 Sam 15:11 (Yhwh rejecting Saul); 2 Sam 6:8 (Yhwh killing Uzzah); Isa 8:21 (inadequate provision by God and king); Jer 15:17 (Yhwh's deceptiveness); Jonah 4:1, 4, 9 (Yhwh's graciousness); Ps 37:1, 7–8 (evildoers prospering); Job 18:4 (innocent suffering); 1 Chr 13:11 (Yhwh killing Uzzah). See also 2 Kgs 19:27–28 and Isa 37:28–29 (Sennacherib's anger at Yhwh). Psalms of complaint would also be related to this category.

32. Van Wolde, "Language of Sentiment"; Krüger, "A Cognitive Interpretation of the Emotion of Anger in the Hebrew Bible," 182.

33. One should thus qualify the claim that "the OT never speaks of anyone becoming overtly angry towards God" (D. N. Freedman, J. R. Lundbom, and G. J. Botterweck, "חָרָה; חֲרִי; חָרוֹן," *TDOT* 5.171–76, esp. p. 176). In addition to the examples above, the complaint psalms obviously express anger toward God, at least on implicit levels. See also Prov 19:3.

In comparison with Western conceptions of anger, biblical anger has both similarities and differences. In both worlds, anger is frequently directed at other people, often over issues of right and wrong. However, Westerners regularly conceive of *anger* as being triggered by impersonal events, such as technological devices failing to operate the way one wishes they would. Perhaps ancient Israelites similarly became angry when their tools did not operate properly, but the Hebrew Bible gives virtually no evidence of this type of impersonal anger. Thus, anger as attested in Biblical Hebrew joins Western discourse in its portrayal of anger as interpersonal but does not go as far in connecting it with the malfunction of tools and devices. [34]

4.3.3 *Individuals Who Become Angry*

In the preceding discussion, I noted that biblical anger often arises in response to perceptions of insubordination. Not surprisingly, therefore, people who are angry in the Hebrew Bible frequently are those with power, status, and stature. There are even specific words for anger, primarily קצף and זעף, that are used almost exclusively for officials and other individuals with power. At the same time, the Hebrew Bible contains instances (albeit fairly small in number) where anger exists between equals, where inferiors are angry at their superiors, and where the power dynamics are unclear. [35] Thus, anger in the Hebrew Bible is prototypically associated with individuals who have power, but power is not an essential characteristic of anger.

In the Hebrew Bible, Yhwh, who obviously has more power than humans do, tends to become angry more frequently than people do. According to Baloian's calculations, roughly three-quarters of the references to

---

Regarding Gen 4:5–6, it seems likely that Cain is angry both at Yhwh for favoring Abel's offering and at Abel for being favored (J. Bergman and E. Johnson, "אָף; אֲנַף," *TDOT* 1.348–60, esp. p. 356). Regarding Jer 15:17—while it is possible that this verse refers to Jeremiah's being filled with Yhwh's wrath against the people, the accusations that Jeremiah launches at Yhwh in the following verse suggest that the prophet is filled with his own wrath against Yhwh.

34. In some respects, then, biblical anger may have more in common with the Ifaluk conception of anger (*song*), which has strong interpersonal qualities and is closely connected to issues of right and wrong (see esp. §2.2 above; Lutz, *Unnatural Emotions*, 155–82, esp. pp. 178–82). One should note, however, that there are important differences between *song* and anger in the Hebrew Bible. For example, the former is marked by nonaggression, whereas the latter is not.

35. Examples where the angry individuals seem to have roughly the same social standing as their objects include: Gen 45:5; Job 32:2, 3, 5. Instances where an inferior is angry at a superior include: Gen 31:36 and 1 Sam 20:34. These examples challenge the somewhat rigid language used by van Wolde, who claims, "[W]henever reference is made to human anger, the subject is someone in a higher social position who is angry with someone in a lower position" (*Reframing Biblical Studies*, 67; see also idem, "Sentiments as Culturally Constructed Emotions," 16–17). Furthermore, as noted above, a number of verses describe anger at Yhwh, particularly 2 Sam 6:8; Isa 8:21, 45:24; Jonah 4:1, 4, 9; Prov 19:3; 1 Chr 13:11; see also Gen 4:5–6, Jer 15:17.

anger in the Hebrew Bible envision divine anger.[36] In fact, some words for *anger* appear exclusively or nearly exclusively in reference to divine anger, such as חרון and אנף.[37] However, one should be cautious about assuming that these words function similarly to ברא ('create'), designating activity reserved for the divine. Although this may be the case, there are other words from the same roots that refer to human anger, whereas ברא in all its forms refers to divine activity.[38]

Throughout the Hebrew Bible, whenever an explicit reference is made to human anger, the person who is angry is always a male.[39] However, there are ways that the Hebrew Bible subtly allows for the expression of anger or anger-like emotion among women. Key examples from the book of Genesis are chaps. 16 and 21, which do not use the typical terms for anger but nevertheless describe several distressing interactions between Sarai/h and Hagar. Despite the missing terminology for anger, many of the fundamental characteristics of biblical anger are present here. Issues of wrongdoing (16:5; 21:9, 11), jealousy (21:10; see also 16:4–5; §5.1), authority and power (16:1–2, 9; 21:10), belittling (קלל, 16:4, 5), affliction (ענה, 16:6, 11), and mockery (צחק, 21:9) together result in separation (16:6; 21:10, 14), a very common outcome of anger (§4.3.4). While the text may thus imply that anger exists among women, this example is more on the margins of the prototypical category of biblical anger.

4.3.4 Outcomes of Anger

Although anger can elicit a range of different behaviors, there are some behaviors that are especially prominent in the Hebrew Bible:

1. Violence is one of the most common results of human anger.[40]

---

36. Baloian asserts that 518 of 714 references to anger in the Hebrew Bible are references to divine anger, which is 72.5% (*Anger in the Old Testament*, esp. p. 189). I disagree with some of the specifics of Baloian's calculations. For example, he sees רגז as referring to human anger only 2 times, whereas I believe it refers to human anger more frequently. Nevertheless, his numbers provide useful "ballpark" estimates.

37. Bergman and Johnson, "אָנֵף; אַף," *TDOT* 1.355–57; Baloian, *Anger in the Old Testament*, 189.

38. The reference here is to ברא meaning 'create' (homonym I in *HALOT*), not the other homonyms listed in lexicons.

39. Interpreters sometimes assert that 1 Sam 1:6, 7, and 16 refer to female anger in the Bible. The word used here is כעס. As shown below (§6.5, §15.1.3), this word means '(be) trouble(d)'. It is connected with anger only when a superior is troubled by an inferior. When Hannah, a barren woman, is troubled, she experiences not anger but anguish.

This differentiation between male and female expressions of emotion is by no means confined to the Hebrew Bible (Kagan, *What Is Emotion?* 152–66; Lila Abu-Lughod, *Veiled Sentiments: Honor and Poetry in a Bedouin Society* [Berkeley: University of California Press, 1999] passim; Arlie Russell Hochschild, *The Managed Heart: Commercialization of Human Feeling* [Berkeley: University of California Press, 1983] esp. pp. 172–73).

40. Cases in which human anger results in *violence* include: Gen 4:5–6; 27:41; 34:7; 49:6–7, 23; Exod 32:19, 22; Num 22:27; Deut 32:27; Judg 9:30, 14:19; 1 Sam 11:6, 18:8, 20:30; 2 Kgs 19:27–28; Isa 7:4, 14:6, 16:6, 37:28–29, 41:11, 51:13; Ezek 23:25, 35:11; Hos

2. Separation is also a very common outcome.[41]
3. Verbal confrontations also take place with a fair amount of frequency.[42]
4. Punishments (often imprisonment or death) emerge as a common outcome of anger as well.[43]
5. Other outcomes are more on the margins of this prototypical category, such as the odd reference to 'tearing oneself in anger' (טֹרֵף נַפְשׁוֹ בְּאַפּוֹ) in Job 18:4.[44]

In a number of these cases, more than one classification is possible. For example, nearly all of these outcomes involve an eventual separation of some sort, even if it is after violence takes place. There are also many cases in which the result of the anger is not mentioned or is unclear.[45] For example, in Gen 45:5, Joseph tells his brothers not to be angry that they sold him to Egypt. The text does not record whether the brothers felt lingering anger despite this plea—or if they did, what happened as a result of this anger.

Previously, I noted that Ellen van Wolde claims that a prototypical quality of human anger in the Hebrew Bible is its uncontrollability. She sees a direct movement from (1) the offense, to (2) "anger tak[ing] over," to (3) a loss of control, to (4) a retributive act.[46] Based on the evidence compiled here, the claims of anger's uncontrollability seem unfounded. Choosing to separate oneself from someone, deciding to engage someone in conversation (even if it is a harsh confrontation), or determining that someone deserves imprisonment is not the type of behavior that is typically associated with a lack of control.

7:16; Amos 1:11; Ps 55:4[3], 124:3; Job 5:2; Esth 2:21, 3:5, 5:9; Dan 8:6; 11:30, 44; Neh 4:1[7]; 2 Chr 28:9. See also Prov 6:34.

41. Human anger leads to *separation* in: Gen 27:44–45; Exod 11:8; Num 24:10; 1 Sam 20:34, 29:4; 2 Sam 3:8, 19:42[41]; 2 Kgs 5:11–12; Esth 1:12, 7:7; 2 Chr 25:10. See also 2 Sam 6:8, 1 Chr 13:11.

42. Instances in which human anger leads to *verbal confrontation* are: Gen 30:2, 31:36; Lev 10:16; 1 Sam 15:11, 17:28; 2 Sam 11:20; 2 Kgs 13:19; Isa 8:21; Jer 15:17; Jonah 4:1–9; Job 32:2–5; Neh 5:6. See also Num 23:7–8; 1 Sam 28:15; Prov 15:18; 29:9, 22; 30:33; Job 36:18; Neh 3:33[4:1].

43. Examples of human anger leading to *punishment* include: Gen 39:19, 40:2, 41:10, 50:15; Exod 32:19–22; Num 16:15, 31:14; 2 Sam 12:5; Jer 37:15; Job 19:29; Prov 14:35; 16:14; 19:12, 19; 20:2; Esth 1:12, 2:1, 7:10; 2 Chr 16:10, 26:19.

44. An additional example of human anger having a *nonprototypical result* is Song 1:6.

45. Cases in which the result of anger is marked by some level of *ambiguity* include: Gen 31:35; 44:18; 45:5, 24; Exod 16:20; 2 Sam 13:21; Isa 37:28–29, 41:11, 45:24; Jer 48:30; Ezek 3:14; Ps 4:5[4], 37:1–8, 76:11[10], 138:7; Job 36:13, 40:11; Prov 12:16; 14:16–17, 29; 15:1; 16:32; 17:25; 19:3, 11; 21:14, 19, 24; 22:8, 24; 24:19, 24; 25:15, 23; 26:17; 27:3–4; 29:8; Qoh 5:16[17], 7:9, 11:10; Esth 1:18; Dan 11:20. Included here are many cases where anger is potential (for example, when someone requests that another not become angry and the person obliges) or generic (for example, when a proverb states that anger leads to foolishness but does not specify the nature of the foolish activity).

46. Van Wolde, "Language of Sentiment"; idem, "Sentiments as Culturally Constructed Emotions," 13. See also the related points made in idem, *Reframing Biblical Studies*, 72.

Are the cases of violence marked by a lack of control? Interestingly, the Hebrew Bible tends *not* to portray violence as immediately following anger, as though the angry individuals have no control over their behaviors. Perhaps this is the case with the noun עברה and the verb עבר in the Hithpael, which usually refer to anger that displays a lack of restraint. However, these words are used only 11 times of human anger. In the Hebrew Bible as a whole, individuals who commit violence out of anger frequently exercise some level of control, rather than acting immediately. Thus, Esau decides to wait until after his father's death before enacting violence (Gen 27:41–45). Similarly, when Moses witnesses the golden calf, his smashing of the tablets is immediate and perhaps uncontrolled, but his killing of others comes after he confronts Aaron and is apparently in accordance with what God has ordered him (Exod 32:27–28).[47] Even with a despicable character such as Haman, the text says specifically that he did not lose control while enraged (Esth 5:9–10; see also 3:5–6).[48] Of the 40 verses mentioned above where anger results in violence, there are only 12 where the angry persons engage in behaviors that suggest a loss of control.[49] In roughly the same number of verses mentioning violence (13), the angry individuals display signs of contemplation, calculation, and/or confrontation prior to acting in violence.[50] (The other 15 cases involve some degree of ambiguity over whether a person has lost control.[51]) One can thus question van Wolde's claim that "anger seems always to have the instant effect of destruction."[52] In the Hebrew Bible, human anger prototypically results in confrontation, violence, and separation, but it is not prototypically uncontrollable.

4.3.5 Evaluation

Because anger frequently results in violence, the Hebrew Bible has a tendency to evaluate it negatively. These evaluations are most explicit in Gen

---

47. In fact, it is the idolatrous people—not the angry Moses—whom the text describes as out of control (Exod 32:25).

48. Thus, van Wolde is on shaky ground when she claims, "In the Hebrew Bible no mention is made of attempts to control the anger" ("Language of Sentiment"). She bases her comments on the fact that Biblical Hebrew often portrays anger as fire. Fire, as is commonly recognized, can become uncontrollable, but it is frequently something that humans can and do control (for example, for the purposes of cooking). Hence, it is best to disagree with van Wolde's argument that anger, by virtue of its metaphorical associations, should be seen primarily as uncontrollable.

49. Gen 49:6–7, 23; Exod 32:19; Num 22:27; Judg 14:19; Isa 7:4, 14:6; Amos 1:11; Ps 124:3; Esth 2:21; 2 Chr 28:9. Note that, in Gen 49:6–7, from the perspective of Jacob on his deathbed, Levi and Simeon's anger is considered uncontrolled. In Genesis 34, however, there are many clues that the anger is carefully calculated.

50. Gen 4:5–6, 27:41, 34:7; Exod 32:22; Judg 9:30; 1 Sam 11:6, 18:8, 20:30; Isa 51:13; Esth 3:5, 5:9; Neh 4:1[7]. See also Gen 50:15; Num 16:15, 31:14; Esth 7:7–10.

51. Deut 32:27; 2 Kgs 19:27–28; Isa 16:6, 37:28–29, 41:11; Ezek 23:25, 35:11; Hos 7:16; Ps 55:4[3]; Job 5:2; Dan 8:6; 11:30, 44.

52. Van Wolde, "Sentiments as Culturally Constructed Emotions," 12. See also the repeated references to anger resulting "immediate[ly]" in acts of vengeance in idem, *Reframing Biblical Studies*, 71–72.

4:6–7, Psalm 37, and Wisdom Literature, especially Proverbs.[53] Gen 4:6–7 will be treated in greater depth below (§9). Here, I simply note that, in the first post-Edenic episode, God warns Cain of anger's potentially disastrous consequences, associating it with sin (חטאת). Meanwhile, Psalm 37 exhorts readers to avoid wickedness and wait for Yʜᴡʜ, even when present circumstances may make alternatives seem better. In this context, the first eight verses deal particularly with anger over the prosperity of the wicked. These verses reach their culmination in v. 8, "Let go of anger (אף), and abandon wrath (חמה). Do not be upset (חרה, Hithpael). It leads only to evildoing (רעע, Hiphil)."

Several proverbs also associate anger with evildoing and wickedness.[54] Repeatedly, these sayings connect anger with foolishness (which is a moral/ethical quality in the Hebrew Bible), seeing it as a chief cause of strife.[55] Not surprisingly, therefore, Proverbs urges people to be slow to anger or to turn it away.[56] Echoing sentiments found in the wider ancient Near East, Proverbs such as 22:24 exhort individuals to avoid individuals who become angry.[57] Both the Hebrew Bible and other ancient Near Eastern texts understand anger not only to be caused by wrongdoing but also to result in additional wrongdoing (see the discussion of [ה/ע]רע in §5.2).

When the Hebrew Bible gives an explicit evaluation of human anger, therefore, it prototypically is negative. However, several qualifications need to be made. First, anger is not always seen negatively. For example, the anger of King Ahasuerus toward Haman appears justified and appropriate

---

53. Surprisingly, van Wolde asserts in her most recent publication about anger that the Hebrew Bible evaluates human expressions of anger in a positive or neutral light (*Reframing Biblical Studies*, 70–72). While it is good that she no longer associates it so closely with irrationality (as she did in "Language of Sentiment" and "Sentiments as Culturally Constructed Emotions," 14), she seems to miss these texts that give negative evaluations to anger because of its potentially catastrophic ethical consequences. The Hebrew Bible posits connections between anger and sin (but not irrationality), and therefore it prototypically considers this emotion negatively.

54. Prov 11:23, 22:8; see also Job 3:17, 36:13; Prov 24:19.

55. References to foolishness include Prov 12:16; 14:16, 17, 29; 17:25; 19:3; 27:3; 29:9; see also Job 5:2, Prov 29:8, Qoh 7:9. References to strife include Prov 15:18, 21:19, 26:17, 29:22, 30:33; see §5.6.

56. References to being slow to anger include Prov 16:32, 19:11, 25:15; see §5.8. References to turning it away include Prov 15:1, 29:8; see also Prov 21:14, 29:11; Qoh 11:10.

57. Like much of Proverbs 22–23, Prov 22:24 displays signs of borrowing from the *Instruction of Amenemope*. The Egyptian text, likely from the Ramesside period, speaks repeatedly of the "heated man," an angry individual who is portrayed as causing harm to himself and to people who come into contact with him (*COS*, 1.47:115–22; see esp. chaps. 2–4, 9–10, 12; for commentary, see Miriam Lichtheim, *Moral Values in Ancient Egypt* [OBO 155; Fribourg: University Press / Göttingen: Vandenhoeck & Ruprecht, 1997] 42–43).

While the *Instruction of Amenemope* presents a striking example, it is not alone in its attitudes toward anger. The *Instruction of Ptahhotep* specifically warns against anger on several occasions (*AEL* 1:61–80, esp. pp. 63–64, 70, §§2–4, §25). As Bergman and Johnson put it, "A quick temper is stigmatized from the earliest teaching . . . to the latest" (*TDOT* 1.349).

within the narrative framework of Esther (Esth 7:7–10).[58] Furthermore, the character most frequently angry in the Hebrew Bible is Yhwh, and a number of texts claim that, even if divine anger is horrifying, it is also an appropriate expression of justice.[59] Similarly, anger among rulers tends either to receive no explicit evaluation or to be seen positively.[60] It appears to fall into a different sort of category than typical human anger.[61] Last, the Psalter is of course filled with psalms of complaint that presuppose a level of anger among people who pray. While they are rarely left to wallow in their anger, the presence of such prayers suggests that anger, even when directed toward God, may not be entirely negative.

These points lead to a second qualification. While human anger tends to be seen negatively when an explicit evaluation is given, most texts do not give an explicit evaluation. Anger is presented, instead, as a typical part of human existence. It is an emotion that inevitably arises in the course of everyday experience. Hence, many of the texts that evaluate anger negatively do not advocate the outright eradication of anger but, rather, being slow to anger (for example, Prov 16:32, 19:11, 25:15) or guarding against the sin to which anger can lead (for example, Gen 4:6–7). Baloian correctly observes, "It is assumed that people will become angry in their daily experience; the clear admonition is against a quick response."[62]

One final qualification is in order. It is not always useful to categorize human anger with a simple *positive* or *negative* evaluation. Texts, particularly narratives, often communicate a great deal of complexity concerning the situations at hand. For example, consider Esau's anger toward Jacob. This anger clearly causes the older brother to plan fratricide (Gen 27:41–45), and murder is condemned throughout the Hebrew Bible, including several times in Genesis (for example, 9:5–6). In this sense, Esau's anger is obviously negative. But on the other hand, both Esau and his dying father have been deceived and robbed of what is most precious to them. Only someone who is morally numb would fail to feel some level of anger toward Jacob

---

58. K.-D. Schunck may overstate the case when asserting, "To the extent that a judgment is expressed, human *chēmāh* is always evaluated negatively" ("חֵמָה," *TDOT* 4.462–65, esp. pp. 463–64).

59. Ezek 7:8, Ps 7:12[11]. See also Bergman and Johnson, *TDOT* 1.359–60; van Wolde, *Reframing Biblical Studies*, 70–71.

60. Prov 14:35, 16:14, 19:12, 20:2; see also 1 Sam 11:6, 2 Sam 12:5; and ibid., 70–72.

61. As noted above (§4.3), a number of sources suggest that emotion scripts can vary, depending on factors such as context. See Fitness, "Anger in the Workplace," esp. pp. 148–49; Griffiths, *What Emotions Really Are*, esp. p. 177; Kövecses, *Metaphor and Emotion*, 13. In ancient Egypt, anger in interpersonal settings was perceived negatively (*COS* 1.47:115–22). When the king was angry, however, he was portrayed in a positive light as a lion enraged against his enemies, particularly in the Great Karnak Inscription and in texts associated with Ramesses III (Brent A. Strawn, *What Is Stronger Than a Lion? Leonine Image and Metaphor in the Hebrew Bible and Ancient Near East* [OBO 212; Fribourg: Academic / Göttingen: Vandenhoeck & Ruprecht, 2005] esp. p. 177).

62. Baloian, *NIDOTTE* 4.377.

and Rebecca for their actions.[63] In this sense, anger is a natural extension of one's moral sensitivities, which obviously are positive qualities. With situations such as this one, anger cannot be classified according to established dichotomies like *good* and *bad*, *right* and *wrong*, *positive* and *negative*. Although anger may prototypically be associated with evildoing and generate many proverbial warnings, it cannot be quickly dismissed as inherently evil without overlooking the complexities of life.

4.3.6 Conclusion: The Prototypical Script

To summarize the above findings, it is useful to recall the three types of membership in a prototypical category: prototypical members (such as a kitchen chair), established but nonprototypical members (such as a swivel chair), and marginal members (such as a barstool). Most of the components of anger have similar types of members:

- *Cause:* Anger is usually caused by a perceived wrongdoing.
  - Prototypically, these perceived wrongdoings occur in cases of interpersonal wrongdoing, including instances of perceived insubordination.
  - It is not unusual for these perceived wrongdoings to occur (1) between groups of people, (2) with respect to religious activities, or (3) regarding an aspect of the divine economy.
  - The case of Antiochus IV Epiphanes' anger toward the holy covenant (Dan 11:30) is a more marginal member of this category: it is not clear that his anger is caused by a perceived wrongdoing.
- *Object:* Anger is almost always directed toward the person(s) judged responsible for the perceived wrongdoing.
  - Prototypically, these people are males.
  - At times, women are also the objects of anger.
  - The case of Balaam's anger toward his donkey (Num 22:27–30) is closer to the margins of this category.
- *Subject:* Those who become angry are almost always male characters.
  - Prototypically, they possess a degree of power.
  - At times, however, they possess the same or even less power than those with whom they are angry.
  - Instances where the text hints that women are angry (Genesis 16, 21) are marginal members of this category.
- *Result:* Anger almost always entails a separation of some sort.
  - Prototypically, it results in violence and then separation.

---

63. For more on this topic, see Michael James Williams, *Deception in Genesis: An Investigation into the Morality of a Unique Biblical Phenomenon* (New York: Peter Lang, 2001) 18–19.

- It is not uncommon, however, for separation to take place without violence or for verbal confrontation and/or punishments to take place as well.
- Job 18:4 speaks of 'tearing oneself in anger' (טֹרֵף נַפְשׁוֹ בְּאַפּוֹ). While there is ambiguity about what this phrase means, it appears to suggest anger directed toward oneself rather than others, which would give this outcome a more marginal status.
- *Evaluation:* Anger almost always involves something negative.
  - Prototypically, texts with explicit evaluations of anger encourage individuals to dissociate themselves from anger and angry people when they can.
  - There are also many texts that suggest that anger is not entirely negative. For example, it can be and often is motivated by one's moral sensitivities. There are obvious ethical dimensions of anger, given its prototypical cause.
  - Kingly anger (like divine anger) appears to fall in a different category, in which anger is often seen as being appropriate.

Chapter 5

Biblical Anger's Associative Networks

As the previous chapter begins to illustrate, an emotion such as anger carries its own set of associations. In this chapter, I examine the types of ideas that are closely associated with anger in the Hebrew Bible. Particular attention is given to words that appear frequently with Biblical Hebrew's terms for anger. These words include: (1) קנא ('jealousy'); (2) words derived from the root רעע ('bad, evil, calamity'); (3) words related to extreme forms of violence, particularly, הרג ('kill'), שמד ('utter destruction'), חרם ('annihilate'), and כלה ('finish'); (4) אש ('fire') and various related terms; (5) שפך and נתך, both meaning 'pour out'; (6) ריב ('dispute') and דין ('judge, contend'); (7) שוב ('turn'); and (8) qualifiers such as מאד ('very'), גדל ('be great'), ארך ('long, length'), and קצר ('short, shortness').

5.1 Jealousy

One of the more significant concepts associated with biblical anger is *jealousy*, which is conveyed primarily with the words קנא, קנאה, and קנוא. The statistical evidence linking *jealousy* with *anger* in the Hebrew Bible is remarkable.[1] Of the 70 verses in which קנא, קנאה, or קנוא appears in the Hebrew Bible, 23 contain a word for anger.[2] Thus, in approximately one-third of the appearances of קנא and its cognates in the Hebrew Bible, anger is also explicitly mentioned. As a point of reference, consider צדקה/צדיק/צדק ('righteous[ness]') and משפט ('justice'), which many interpreters have recognized as being closely related to one another. The Hebrew Bible links קנא, קנאה, and קנוא with terms for anger with greater frequency (33% of the time) than it links צדק/צדיק/צדקה with משפט (21% of the time).[3] In fact, words from the root קנא are approximately 15 times more likely to appear in a verse that refers to anger than in a verse from the Hebrew Bible as a whole.[4]

---

1. See appendix A (pp. 185–192) for the way that statistics were calculated.

2. The terms for anger considered in these studies are: אף (nominal forms), אנף, זעם, זעף, חמה, חרה, חרון, חרי, כעס, כעש, עבר (Hithpael forms), עברה, קצף, רגז, and שטם. The individual meanings of these terms are discussed at the end of chap. 6 (§6.5) and in appendix B (pp. 193–201).

3. All percentage numbers in this chapter have been rounded, typically to the nearest whole number.

4. Although other scholars such as D. N. Freedman, J. R. Lundbom, and G. J. Botterweck have connected anger with jealousy, they do not offer the same degree of statistical evidence ("חָרָה; חָרוֹן; חֳרִי," *TDOT* 5.171–76, esp. pp. 173–74; see also Ellen van Wolde,

Table 2. Jealousy in the Hebrew Bible

Subject "[ ] is/are jealous . . ."	Object ". . . because [ ] . . ."	Reason ". . . has/ve received [ ]"	Verses
Yhwh	other gods	worship and allegiance	Exod 20:5, 34:14; Deut 4:24; 5:9; 6:15; 29:19[20]; 32:16, 21; Josh 24:19; 1 Kgs 14:22; Ezek 5:13; 8:3, 5; 16:38, 42; Zeph 1:18; Ps 78:58. See also Ezek 23:25, Zeph 3:8, Ps 79:5
Humans, on Yhwh's behalf	other gods	worship and allegiance	Num 25:11, 13; 1 Kgs 19:10, 14; 2 Kgs 10:16. See also Ps 69:10[9], 119:139
Yhwh, on Israel or Judah's behalf	God's people	unmerited or disproportionate harm	2 Kgs 19:31; Isa 9:6[7], 26:11, 37:32, 42:13; Ezek 36:5–6, 39:25; Joel 2:18; Nah 1:2; Zech 1:14, 8:2; see also Isa 63:15, Ezek 38:19
Individual(s)	other(s)	goods or property	Gen 26:14; 2 Sam 21:2; Isa 11:13; Ezek 31:9, 35:11; see also Qoh 4:4
Individual(s)	other(s)	power, honor, or status	Gen 37:11, Num 11:29, Ps 106:16
Individual(s)	other(s)	sexual encounters	Num 5:12–31, Prov 6:34; see also Gen 30:1, Ezek 16:38
Godly individuals	sinners	more than the Godly	Ps 37:1, 73:3; Prov 3:31; 23:17; 24:1, 19

Verses similar to Ps 79:5 are not uncommon: "Yhwh, how long? Will you be angry (תֶּאֱנַף) forever? Will your jealousy (קִנְאָתֶךָ) burn like fire?"

Why is קנא so closely related to words for anger in Biblical Hebrew? As shown above (§4.3.1), anger in the Hebrew Bible typically results from perceptions of wrongdoing. Jealousy, meanwhile, results from a particular type of wrongdoing: a perceived violation of who should receive or possess what. There are many variations on how this perception manifests itself, particularly with respect to who is jealous, with whom s/he is jealous, and the reason for her or his jealousy. Table 2 explains. Whether *jealousy* is related to idolatry (first row) or theodicy (last row), subjects see others as possessing what they should not possess.[5] Because anger in the Hebrew Bible also results from a perceived wrongdoing, one can consider *jealousy* to be a close cousin (if not a subset) of *anger*.

5.2 Evil / Calamity

Another set of words related to anger comprises terms from the root רעע, which often conveys the idea of 'evil'. Approximately 10% of the verses containing a word for anger also include the adjective רַע ('evil'), the noun רֹע ('evil'), the noun רָעָה ('evil'), or the verb רעע (homonym I in *HALOT*, meaning 'be evil'). The primary way that the idea of *evil* is connected with *anger* pertains to the cause of anger. These words are often used to refer to a perceived wrongdoing.[6] Thus, 2 Kgs 21:15 reads, "For they have done evil (עָשׂוּ אֶת־הָרַע) in my sight, making me angry (מַכְעִסִים אֹתִי) since the day their fathers left Egypt, even to this day."

Similarly, the words חטא ('sin' [verb]), חטאת ('sin' [noun]), חטא ('sin[ful]'), חטאה ('sin' [noun]), אָוֶן/עָוֹן ('iniquity'), and פֶּשַׁע ('crime') also appear more frequently in verses that mention anger than in verses that do not. The words נקמה/נקם ('take vengeance'/'vengeance'), נטר ('keep a grudge'), and עצב (homonym II in *HALOT* meaning '[be] harm[ed]') are also linked with terms for anger, pointing to ways that angry individuals see themselves as being wronged or harmed.[7] Anger's connection with עצב ('[be] harm[ed]') furthermore points to connections between anger and sorrow in Biblical Hebrew. Being harmed can lead to a mixture of sadness and anger.[8]

As students of Biblical Hebrew know, *evil* is not the only meaning for words from the root רעע. They can also refer to *calamity* or *destruction*. This meaning is also present in many verses that include terms for anger.[9] In these cases, words related to רעע are portrayed less as the cause of anger and more as the result. Jer 25:7 is exemplary of this type of connection: "'You have not obeyed me,' says Yнwн, 'in order to anger me (הַכְעִיסֵנִי, *Qere*)

---

5. There are also several verses that do not disclose the reason for jealousy, such as Isa 59:17; Job 5:2; Prov 14:30, 27:4; Qoh 9:6; Song 8:6.

6. Gen 50:15; Num 32:13; Deut 4:25, 9:18, 31:29; 1 Sam 17:28, 18:8; 1 Kgs 14:9, 16:7; 2 Kgs 17:11, 17; 21:6, 15; Isa 9:16[17]; Jer 4:4; 11:17; 21:12; 32:30, 32; 33:5; 36:7; 44:3; Jonah 4:1; Ps 37:1; Prov 24:19; Job 21:30; 2 Chr 33:6.

7. For נקמה/נקם, see Jer 15:15; Ezek 24:8; 25:14, 17; Mic 5:14[15]; Nah 1:2; Prov 6:34. For נטר, which is often used synonymously with נקם, see Lev 19:18; Jer 3:5, 12; Nah 1:2; Ps 103:9. For עצב, see Gen 34:7, 45:5; 1 Sam 20:34; Prov 15:1; 2 Chr 24:18.

8. Although some contend that עצב means to 'become angry', it most likely means to 'be hurt' or 'aggrieved' (see 2 Sam 19:2–3[1–2]), to which anger is a common response. Hence, this word may imply anger, but it need not denote this and should not be translated 'anger'. Contra Zacharias Kotzé, "Conceptual Metaphors for Anger in the Biblical Hebrew Story of the Flood," *Journal for Semitics = Tydskrif vir Semitistiek* 14 (2005) 149–64, esp. p. 162. If anything, the interrelationship between עצב and anger illustrates how sadness and anger are connected in the Hebrew Bible (see §2.2).

9. Jer 25:6–7, 49:37; Zech 1:15, 8:14; Ps 37:8, 78:49, 106:32; Neh 13:18.

with the work of your hands to your own destruction (לְרַע לָכֶם).'" Scholars such as Klaus Koch have spoken of a *level of moral causality* between "what one does and what happens in life" in the Hebrew Bible.[10] Anger is sometimes the mechanism of this causality: perceptions of *evildoing* cause anger, which in turn causes *calamity*. Gen 50:15 illustrates: "When Joseph's brothers saw that their father was dead, they said, 'What if Joseph is harboring anger against us (יִשְׂטְמֵנוּ) and returns (וְהָשֵׁב יָשִׁיב) to us all the evil (כָּל־הָרָעָה) that we did to him?'"

5.3 *Extreme Violence*

As seen above (§4.3.4), a prototypical outcome of anger is violence. The Hebrew Bible associates anger with levels of destruction and violence not seen in ordinary American English conversation about anger. Many words referring to extreme forms of violence appear frequently with terms for anger. This correlation is present not only with the word הרג 'kill'.[11] One also finds it with the terms שמד, חרם, and כלה, which can refer to utter destruction, the complete extermination of others, and the killing of people that leaves no survivors.[12] These terms have much in common with what today is called *genocide*. The first of these words, שמד, appears in its verbal forms approximately five times more frequently in verses mentioning anger than in verses from the Hebrew Bible as a whole.[13] It does not mean simply 'destroy', as it frequently is translated. Rather, it refers to 'utter destruction'. Those who suffer this fate are completely wiped out. The word appears in many military contexts and is not far removed from the second term, חרם (homonym I in *HALOT*), which means 'annihilate' but is also connected with ideas of holy war and sacrifice. This word also has strong connections with anger.[14] Dan 11:44 illustrates these interrelations: "With great wrath (בְּחֵמָא גְדֹלָה), he will go forth utterly destroying (לְהַשְׁמִיד) and completely annihilating (וּלְהַחֲרִים) many." The third term, כלה, has the basic

---

10. Klaus Koch, *The Prophets* (2 vols.; Philadelphia: Fortress, 1983–84) 1.64–65. John Barton has criticized Koch for overstating his case but admits that there is some truth in what Koch suggests (Barton, *Understanding Old Testament Ethics* [Louisville: Westminster John Knox, 2003] 40–42).

11. Words from the root הרג are approximately three times more likely to appear in a verse containing a word for anger than to appear in the Hebrew Bible as a whole. See Gen 27:41, 49:6; Exod 22:23[24], 32:12; Isa 10:4; Ps 78:31; Job 5:2; Lam 2:4, 21; 3:43; 2 Chr 28:9. In a Syrian inscription from 8th-century Zinjerli, 'anger' חמא, is also connected with 'killing' הרג ("Panammuwa I," *KAI* 214.33–34).

12. See 2 Chr 20:23, where שמד, חרם, and כלה appear together in immediate succession.

13. Deut 6:15; 7:4; 9:8, 19–20; Isa 13:9; Ps 106:23; Lam 3:66; Dan 11:44. For similar connections in Biblical Aramaic, see סתר in Ezra 5:12 and אבד in Dan 2:12.

14. Verses linking חרם with שמד are Josh 7:12, 11:20; Dan 11:44; 2 Chr 20:23. Verses containing a reference to both anger and חרם are Deut 13:18[17]; Josh 7:1, 22:20; Isa 34:2; Dan 11:44. Verses referring to anger are approximately three times more likely to contain a reference to חרם than verses in the Hebrew Bible as a whole.

meaning '(be) finish(ed)'. In many cases, this word is used to refer not to the completion of a task but to the ending of life. Like the English phrase "he finished him off," כלה can refer to killing, even massacres. It is approximately five times more likely to appear in a verse mentioning anger than in the Hebrew Bible as a whole. Most of the cases linking שׁמד, חרם, and כלה with anger posit a causal relationship, in that extreme violence results from anger.[15] This connection between anger and overwhelming violence has at least some contrasts with American English's use of words for anger. For example, within official discourse, Pentagon spokespersons rarely, if ever, portray themselves or their troops as angry with a bloodlust that seeks the total annihilation of another group of people. However, battle rage is found with some degree of frequency in both the Hebrew Bible and the inscriptions of the ancient Near East.[16]

5.4 Fire

Another key concept associated with biblical anger is אֵשׁ 'fire' (homonym I in *HALOT*). This word is approximately five times more likely to appear in a verse referring to anger than in the Hebrew Bible as a whole.[17] Biblical Hebrew contains many words related to אֵשׁ that likewise appear much more frequently in verses that also mention anger: כבה ('extinguish'), עשׁן ('smoke'), בערה/בער ('burn', 'burning'), דעך ('be extinguished'), קטרת/קטר/ מקטרת/מקטר/קיטור ('burn incense'/'smoke'/'dark smoke'/'incense'/'incense burner').[18] Of the 519 verses referring to anger, more than 10% contain אשׁ or one of these related words. Why are *anger* and *fire* so closely connected in the Hebrew Bible?

---

15. This statement is especially true of שׁמד, where there are no exceptions. With the case of חרם, there are also references to God's anger because the ban/annihilation, חרם, was not carried out (Deut 13:18[17]; Josh 7:1, 22:20). With כלה, most cases suggest this type of causal relationship: Exod 32:10, 12; Num 25:11; 1 Sam 20:7; Isa 10:25; Jer 49:37; Ezek 13:13, 22:31, 43:8; Zeph 1:18; Ps 59:14[13], 90:7; Job 4:9; Lam 2:22; Esth 7:7; Ezra 9:14; 2 Chr 12:12. Sometimes, however, כלה is used of the cessation of anger: Dan 11:36. Especially in Ezekiel, it can describe the expenditure of anger: Ezek 5:13; 6:12; 7:8; 13:15; 20:8, 13, 21; Lam 4:11. See also Jer 10:25, where God's anger is a response to the destruction (כלה) of Jacob. Although the anger causing this violence is frequently divine, it can be human (for example Dan 11:44).

16. See the Great Karnak Inscription and texts associated with Ramesses III, which link Pharaoh's anger with warfare (Brent A. Strawn, *What Is Stronger than a Lion? Leonine Image and Metaphor in the Hebrew Bible and Ancient Near East* [OBO 212; Fribourg: Academic Press / Göttingen: Vandenhoeck & Ruprecht, 2005] 177). For more on battle rage, see Baloian, "Anger," *NIDOTTE* 4.377–85, esp. p. 4.379; idem, *Anger in the Old Testament* (American University Studies 7, Theology and Religion 99; New York: Peter Lang, 1992) 40–43.

17. Verses connecting the two are: Num 11:1, 17:11[16:46]; Deut 32:22; 2 Sam 22:8–9; 2 Kgs 17:17, 21:6; Isa 9:18[19]; 30:27, 30; 65:5; 66:15; Jer 4:4, 7:18, 15:14, 17:4, 21:12, 32:29; Ezek 19:12; 21:36[31]; 22:20–21, 31; 23:25; 38:19; Nah 1:6; Zeph 1:18, 3:8; Ps 18:8–9[7–8], 21:10[9], 78:21, 79:5, 89:47[46]; Lam 2:3–4, 4:11; 2 Chr 33:6.

18. In Biblical Aramaic, Dan 3:19 also connects anger with words related to heat and burning.

The most likely reason for these connections between *fire* and *anger* is that both are related to heat. The most common verb for 'anger' in Biblical Hebrew is חרה (in the Qal, Niphal, and Hithpael stems; see also the nouns חרי, חרון). Both this root and its counterparts in Ugaritic, Akkadian, Arabic, and Aramaic carry the underlying meaning 'burn'.[19] Another very common word for 'anger' is חמה. The root from which this word most likely derives (יחם; see also חמם) and its Semitic counterparts refer to 'being warm' or 'being hot'.[20] Both חרה and חמה appear to be ways of metonymically referring to anger by mentioning a perceived physiological effect of this emotion, namely, feeling hot.[21]

Another reason for linking *anger* and *fire* is that the biblical text portrays both of them as destructive. A number of texts exploit this similarity, such as Jer 4:4: "Lest my rage (חֲמָתִי) spread like fire (כָאֵשׁ) and burn (וּבָעֲרָה) with no one to extinguish (מְכַבֶּה) it." This text makes clear with the -כ particle ('like') that God's anger is not literally seen as fire. There are other occasions, however, when the idiomatic expressions having to do with חרה and חמה are used with a degree of literalness that is not expected. The clearest example is probably Num 11:1–3. At the beginning of this passage, one reads, "[Yʜwʜ] grew angry [lit., 'his nose burned' וַיִּחַר אַפּוֹ], and the fire of Yʜwʜ raged against them (וַתִּבְעַר־בָּם אֵשׁ יְהוָה), consuming (וַתֹּאכַל) some of the outskirts of the camp." The context makes clear that the fire described is not merely a figurative way of speaking about divine anger but a literal way of describing the result of this anger.[22] As in this case, most verses referring to fire and anger use the former to describe the latter's effects.[23] There is also a smaller number of verses in which activities involving fire provoke Yʜwʜ's anger, particularly the sacrificial burning of one's child.[24] More will be said about the connections between *anger* and *fire* below when we discuss conceptual metaphors (chap. 6).

---

19. Freedman, Lundbom, and Botterweck, *TDOT* 5.171.

20. K.-D. Schunck, "חֵמָה," *TDOT* 4.462–65, esp. p. 462.

21. Many languages associate anger with heat (Ralph B. Hupka et al., "Anger, Envy, Fear, and Jealousy as Felt in the Body: A Five-Nation Study," *Cross-Cultural Research* 30 [1996] 243–64). Research has shown that angry individuals do experience a small increase in body temperature (Richard J. Davidson, Klaus R. Scherer, and H. Hill Goldsmith, eds., *Handbook of Affective Sciences* [Series in Affective Science; Oxford: Oxford University Press, 2003] 214). However, there is debate about whether this increase is significant enough for individuals to perceive it (D. Geeraerts and S. Grondelaers, "Looking Back at Anger," in *Language and the Cognitive Construal of the World* [ed. J. R. Taylor and R. E. MacLaury; Berlin: de Gruyter, 1995] 153–79, esp. p. 168).

22. Other passages, such as Exod 15:7, Ps 18:8–14[7–13] (2 Sam 22:8–13), and Isa 30:27–30 connect fire more directly with anger than one might expect.

23. This causation is seen in Deut 32:22; Isa 9:18[19], 66:15; Jer 4:4, 21:12, 32:29; Ezek 19:12; 21:36[31]; 22:20–21, 31; 23:25; 38:19; Nah 1:6; Zeph 1:18, 3:8; Ps 21:10[9]; Lam 2:3–4, 4:11. See also Jer 15:14, 17:4; Ps 78:21, 79:5, 89:47[46].

24. The cases where fire provokes Yʜwʜ's anger include 2 Kgs 17:17, 21:6; Jer 7:18; 2 Chr 33:6; and Isa 65:5. See also Num 17:11[16:46], where activity with fire curbs Yʜwʜ's anger.

5.5 *Pouring Out*

Two words closely associated with anger in the Hebrew Bible (particularly exilic and postexilic texts) are שפך and נתך. Both words can mean 'pour out'. Over 20 percent of the 112 verses containing a form of שפך also contain a reference to anger.[25] Meanwhile, the word נתך appears in only 19 verses in the Hebrew Bible, but over half of them (10) refer to some form of anger.[26] In fact, both words speak of pouring out anger more frequently than pouring out water.[27] Outside the Hebrew Bible, a Syrian inscription from Zinjerli dating to the 8th century B.C.E. refers to the pouring out (ליתכה from נתך) of anger (חרא) as well ("Panammuwa I," *KAI* 214:23).

There are several reasons why words for anger are associated with the terms שפך and נתך. First, both שפך and נתך frequently take objects related to the body or emotions.[28] Using שפך and נתך in conjunction with words for wrath aligns with other psychosomatic objects. Second, anger in Biblical Hebrew is often associated with *fire*, as seen above (§5.4). The word שפך can describe the pouring out of ashes (דשן, Lev 4:12), and נתך can describe the melting of metals (which obviously involves heat and fire; see especially Ezek 22:20–22). Some verses draw on this perceived interrelation between wrath, fire, and pouring out. For example, Zeph 3:8bcd reads, "For my judgment is to draw together nations, to gather kingdoms, in order to pour out (לִשְׁפֹּךְ) on them my wrath (זַעְמִי)—all my raging fury (כֹּל חֲרוֹן אַפִּי)—for all the land will be consumed (תֵּאָכֵל) with the fire of my jealousy (בְּאֵשׁ קִנְאָתִי)."[29] Third, in all of the cases where this association between *pouring* and *anger* is present (including the Zinjerli Inscription), the anger described is divine wrath. With divine beings envisioned in the heavens, a natural way to associate divine anger against humanity is to describe it as being *poured out*, which vividly connects the heavens and the earth. Finally, both שפך and words for anger are associated with killing and the shedding of blood. In fact, the most common object of שפך is דם 'blood' (the second

---

25. Isa 42:25; Jer 6:11; 10:25; Ezek 7:8; 9:8; 14:19; 16:38; 20:8, 13, 21, 33–34; 21:36[31]; 22:22, 31; 30:15; 36:18; Hos 5:10; Zeph 3:8; Ps 69:25[24], 79:6; Lam 2:4, 4:11.

26. Jer 7:20, 42:18, 44:6; Ezek 22:20–21; Nah 1:6; 2 Chr 12:7; 34:21, 25.

27. Only 3% of the time is מים ('water') the object of שפך: Exod 4:9; 1 Sam 7:6; Amos 5:8, 9:6. (There is also a small number of verses that contain שפך and refer to water as a point of reference but take a different object [Deut 12:16, 24; 15:23; Ps 22:15[14], 79:3; Lam 2:19; Hos 5:10; see also Judg 6:20, where the object is מרק ('broth')]). Meanwhile, there is only one occasion when מים ('water') is the object of נתך: 2 Sam 21:10; see also Exod 9:33, Job 3:24.

28. This observation is especially true of שפך, whose object can be נפש ('life', referring to sadness or distress: 1 Sam 1:15, Ps 42:5[4], Job 30:16, Lam 2:12; see also Ps 22:15[14]); רוח ('breath', referring positively to God's רוח: Ezek 39:29, Joel 3:1–2[2:28–29], Zech 12:10); לב(ב) ('heart', expressing sadness and distress: Ps 62:9[8], Lam 2:11); and שׂיחַ ('complaint'; Ps 102:1, 142:3[2]). The word נתך also refers to the pouring out of שאגה ('groanings') in Job 3:24.

29. For other verses connecting the pouring out of anger with fire, see Isa 42:25; Ezek 21:36[31], 22:31; Zeph 3:8; Lam 2:4, 4:11.

most-common object being a word for anger).[30] Some texts, especially in Ezekiel, draw out these connections, such as Ezek 14:19: "I will send a plague upon that land and pour out (וְשָׁפַכְתִּי) my wrath (חֲמָתִי) with blood (בְּדָם) upon it."[31] Whether as an act of intentional artistry or an unwitting use of preexisting connections in the Hebrew language, the words שפך and נתך are often used with terms for anger.

5.6 *Contend and Dispute*

As observed above (§4.3.4), one of the common outcomes of anger is verbal confrontation. When angry speech is in view, it is often depicted with words related to the roots ריב ('dispute') and דין ('contend'). Approximately 8% of the verses containing דין, מריבה, יריב, ריב, and מדון make explicit reference to anger.[32] Sometimes these words are used as rough synonyms for anger. For example, Isa 41:11 reads:

> Look! All who are angry (הַנֶּחֱרִים) with you
>   shall be ashamed and humiliated.
> Those who contend with you (רִיבֶךָ)
>   shall be as nothing and perish.

Words from the roots דין and ריב frequently involve angry conversation resulting from a perceived wrongdoing. Often, דין and ריב carry legal connotations (for example, Jer 21:12), but not always (for example, Prov 15:38). A verse containing a reference to anger is roughly four times more likely to contain at least one of these words than a verse randomly selected from the Hebrew Bible as a whole.

One can also note that the word למה ('why') often finds itself in the context of angry speech. There are several reasons. First, angry individuals who perceive a wrongdoing often ask why the wrongdoing occurred. Thus, when David arrives at the Israelite camp prior to slaying Goliath, his brother Eliab perceives that David has neglected his responsibility of shepherding the family flock. He grows angry (וַיִּחַר־אַף) and asks David, "Why (לָמָּה) have you come down? With whom have you left those few sheep in the wilderness?" (1 Sam 17:28).[33] Second, given the fact that people become angry not necessarily because of actual wrongdoing but because of perceived wrongdoing, other individuals sometimes challenge their rea-

---

30. The object of שפך is דם ('blood') in Gen 9:6, 37:22; Exod 29:12; Lev 4:7, 18, 25, 30, 34; 17:4, 13; Num 35:33; Deut 12:16, 24, 27; 15:23; 19:10; 21:7; 1 Sam 25:31; 1 Kgs 2:31, 18:28; 2 Kgs 21:16, 24:4; Isa 59:7; Jer 7:6; 22:3, 17; Ezek 16:38; 18:10; 22:3, 4, 6, 9, 12, 27; 23:45, 24:7, 33:25, 36:18; Joel 4:19[3:19]; Zeph 1:17; Ps 79:3, 10; 106:38; Prov 1:16, 6:17; Lam 4:13; 1 Chr 22:8, 28:3.

31. Ezek 36:18 is similar. Other verses, while not using the word דם ('blood'), also connect poured out anger with death and destruction (Ezek 9:8, 20:13, 21:36[31]).

32. Gen 31:36; Isa 41:11, 51:22, 57:16; Jer 21:12; Mic 7:9; Ps 106:32; Job 19:29; Prov 15:18, 21:19, 26:17, 29:22, 30:33; 2 Chr 19:10.

33. See also 1 Sam 28:15, 2 Chr 25:15.

sons for anger, asking *why* they are angry. This is the case with God's question to Cain (Gen 4:6).[34] Finally, anger can trigger a series of events that others seek to avoid. In a couple of instances, people ask *why* these sorts of events should take place. For example, when God is about to punish the people because of the golden calf, Moses makes the following plea with the angry deity: "Why (לָמָּה) should the Egyptians say, 'With evil intent (בְּרָעָה) he brought them out to kill (לַהֲרֹג) them in the mountains and to annihilate them (וּלְכַלֹּתָם) from the face of the earth? Turn (שׁוּב) from your raging anger (מֵחֲרוֹן אַפֶּךָ) and change your mind (וְהִנָּחֵם) from bringing harm (הָרָעָה) to your people" (Exod 32:12).[35] In all, the word למה appears approximately three times more frequently in verses such as Exod 32:12 that mention anger than in the entire Hebrew Bible. These data provide additional evidence that anger in the Bible does not automatically and immediately result in violence (see §3, §4.3.4, above) but instead may lead, for example, to verbal confrontation.

5.7 Turn

As just seen in Exod 32:12, the word שׁוּב is often used to describe turning from anger. Remarkably, over 10% of the 519 verses containing a word for anger also contain a form of שׁוּב. Although there are several ways that this word is used in conjunction with anger, the most common is to refer to the emotion's cessation.[36] Sometimes the context suggests that individuals have a degree of control over how angry they are, as in Exod 32:12. A number of texts suggest that other people can influence the dissipation of anger. Prov 15:1, for example, says, "A soft answer can turn away (יָשִׁיב) wrath (חֵמָה)" (see also Prov 29:8). There are also cases in which the text implies that anger will recede over time, as with Esau's anger (Gen 27:44–45). The tendency for a word such as שׁוּב to appear with words for anger suggests that individuals have some degree of control over anger. There are ways to turn this emotion back.[37]

5.8 Qualifiers

Four words, מאד, גדל, ארך, and קצר, frequently appear with terms for anger as a way of qualifying them. The word מאד ('very') is a fairly common word in the Hebrew Bible, making 300 appearances in 278 verses. Nearly

---

34. See also Exod 32:11, 2 Sam 19:43[42], Ps 74:1.

35. See also Gen 27:45.

36. The following texts make reference to the cessation of anger: Gen 27:44–45; Exod 32:12; Num 25:4, 11; Deut 13:18[17]; Josh 7:26; 2 Kgs 23:26; Isa 5:25; 9:11[12], 16[17], 20[21]; 10:4; 12:1; Jer 2:35, 4:8, 18:20, 23:20, 30:24; Ps 78:38, 85:4[3], 106:23; Job 9:13, 14:13; Prov 15:1, 24:18, 29:8; Dan 9:16; Ezra 10:14; Hos 11:9, 14:5[4]; Jonah 3:9; 2 Chr 12:12, 29:10, 30:8.

37. See also נחם in Exod 32:12; Jonah 3:9, 4:2; Zech 8:14. In these cases, this word is used to communicate changing one's mind concerning anger.

10% of these verses mention anger, usually with the adverb modifying the act of becoming angry. The words גדל ('be great') and גדול ('great') also appear more frequently with terms for anger than in the Hebrew Bible as a whole. Finally, the words ארך ('long, length') and קצר ('short, shortness') are often used with terms for anger (especially אף) to designate being slow to anger (that is, patient) and quick to anger (that is, short-tempered), respectively.[38] In fact, the adjective אָרֵךְ appears approximately 38 times more frequently in verses mentioning anger than in the Hebrew Bible as a whole. The adjective קָצֵר appears about 18 times more frequently.

5.9 *Conclusion*

Both differences and similarities emerge when one compares anger in Biblical Hebrew with anger in American English. One should not conflate the ways that the two cultures conceive of this emotion. At the same time, it would be erroneous to say that anger in the Hebrew Bible is so different from modern conceptions that readers today have little connection with the text. Both the Hebrew Bible and modern society tend to picture anger with strong interpersonal qualities. Although the Hebrew Bible may associate jealousy more closely with anger than moderns do, people today frequently understand some level of connection between these two emotions. Individuals in contemporary society may feel anger at the malfunction of technological devices, but they quite frequently join characters in the Hebrew Bible in growing upset over evil and wrongdoing committed by other individuals or groups. The Hebrew Bible may associate anger with battle rage more commonly than Westerners today who live outside war zones, but both societies understand that anger can result in violence. Modern society may not speak frequently of pouring out anger, but it joins the Hebrew Bible and many other cultures in conceiving of anger in terms related to heat and fire. For both readers today and the ancient text, anger can vary greatly, abate, or issue in an assortment of verbal confrontations. Therefore, while it is problematic to assume too much about the continuity between biblical and modern conceptions of anger, especially with regard to irrationality, readers today nevertheless share a common humanity with ancient writers.

---

38. מאד: Gen 4:5, 34:7; Num 11:10, 16:15; Deut 9:20; 1 Sam 11:6, 18:8; 2 Sam 3:8, 12:5, 13:21; 2 Kgs 17:18; Isa 64:8[9]; Lam 5:22; Esth 1:12; Neh 4:1[7], 5:6; 2 Chr 25:10. גדול/גדל: Exod 32:10–11; Deut 29:23[24], 27[28]; Josh 7:26; 1 Sam 17:28; 2 Kgs 3:27; 22:13; 23:26; Jer 21:5; 32:37; 36:7; Ezek 8:18; 16:26; 25:17; 38:19; Ps 145:8; Jonah 4:1; Nah 1:3; Zech 1:15; 7:12; 8:2; Dan 11:36, 44; 2 Chr 34:21. ארך: Exod 34:6; Num 14:18; Isa 48:9; Jer 15:15; Joel 2:13; Jonah 4:2; Nah 1:3; Ps 86:15, 103:8, 145:8; Prov 14:29, 15:18, 16:32, 19:11, 25:15; Neh 9:17. קצר: Prov 14:17, 29. In Biblical Aramaic, see the word שַׂגִּיא ('very') in Dan 2:12 and מלא ('be filled') in Dan 3:19.

Chapter 6

Biblical Anger and Conceptual Metaphor

As mentioned above (§5.4), many of the words for anger in Biblical Hebrew depict this emotion metaphorically by referring to a perceived physiological symptom. For example, חרה and חמה convey anger but are also related to ideas of *burning* and *heat*. A number of biblical scholars have examined the way that these words function by drawing on cognitive linguistic research into conceptual metaphor. This chapter shows that, while insights can be gained from this research, biblical scholarship again has not made the best use of findings in cognitive linguistics.

6.1 Conceptual Metaphor: An Introduction

Scholars working with conceptual metaphor analyze how metaphors work cognitively to organize and even create reality. Many of the studies in this area came as a result of George Lakoff and Mark Johnson's *Metaphors We Live By*, first published in 1980, although several thinkers in previous times helped lay the foundation for some of its basic postulates.[1] Lakoff and Johnson explore a spectrum of ways in which metaphors permeate language and guide thought processes. Their thesis is as follows: "We have found . . . that metaphor is pervasive in everyday life, not just in language but in thought and action. Our ordinary conceptual system, in terms of which we both think and act, is fundamentally metaphorical in nature."[2] Their work contains many examples that illustrate their point.

A key metaphor to which they devote considerable time is ARGUMENT IS WAR. They point to many examples of how this metaphor manifests itself in American English:

Your claims are *indefensible*.

He *attacked every weak point* in my argument.

His criticisms were *right on target*.

I *demolished* his argument.

I've never *won* an argument with him.

---

1. George Lakoff and Mark Johnson, *Metaphors We Live By* (Chicago: University of Chicago Press, 2003). On the precursors to this work, see Michael K. Smith, "Metaphor and Mind," *American Speech* 57 (1982) 128–34.

2. Lakoff and Johnson, *Metaphors We Live By*, 3.

You disagree? Okay, *shoot!*

If you use that *strategy,* he'll *wipe you out.*

He *shot down* all of my arguments.

Lakoff and Turner argue that this conceptual metaphor is not simply re-flected in our everyday manner of speaking. Rather, it also influences how we conceive of arguments and how we act in the midst of them. They write, "Argument is partially structured, understood, performed, and talked about in terms of war."[3]

Lakoff and his colleagues have extended the findings of this initial work to several other fields, including the study of emotions. A key work here is George Lakoff and Zoltán Kövecses' "Cognitive Model of Anger Inherent in American English," which examines the types of conceptual metaphors for *anger* that are reflected in American English. They examine several meta-phors, such as Anger is insanity, which is found in various idiomatic expres-sions of anger:

I'm *mad.*

You're *driving me nuts!*

He got so angry, he *went out of his mind.*

When my mother finds out, she'll *have a fit.*

He's about to *throw a tantrum.*

I just touched him, and he *went crazy.*[4]

The idiomatic expressions of this metaphor reinforce the perceived dichot-omy between reason and emotion among English speakers (a point that Lakoff and Kövecses could have better discussed).

Lakoff and Kövecses give attention to a variety of other conceptual metaphors for anger. They observe that these metaphors frequently entail the use of the perceived physiological effects of anger (that is, "increased body heat, increased internal pressure [blood pressure, muscular pressure], agitation") to represent metonymically the entirety of anger.[5] Thus, a com-mon conceptual metaphor is Anger is the heat of fluid in a container.[6] The examples they give include the following:

---

3. Ibid., 4–6, 77–86. This quotation comes from p. 5; the various examples in the list above are from p. 4.

4. These are all quotations taken from various locations in ibid., 204.

5. George Lakoff and Zoltán Kövecses, "The Cognitive Model of Anger Inherent in American English," in *Cultural Models in Language and Thought* (ed. Dorothy Holland and Naomi Quinn; Cambridge: Cambridge University Press, 1987) 196, capitalization re-moved. For a summary of what science has shown these physiological affects to be, see Richard J. Davidson, Klaus R. Scherer, and H. Hill Goldsmith, eds., *Handbook of Affective Sciences* (Series in Affective Science; Oxford: Oxford University Press, 2003) 214.

6. Lakoff and Kövecses, "The Cognitive Model of Anger," 195–202.

Keep *cool*.

They were having a *heated argument*.

You make my *blood boil*.

I was *fuming*.

I just needed to *vent*.

I could barely *keep it in* anymore.

When I told him, he just *exploded*.

She *blew up* at me. [7]

As they note, this metaphor is fairly well developed in the mind. It suggests that, as anger increases, so does heat and pressure in the body. Thus, anger can build to the point that it is described as explosive, which metaphorically corresponds to persons' losing control and causing harm to themselves or others. This metaphor also suggests that, if anger is kept inside too long and not properly released or "vented," it is dangerous to the individual. [8]

6.2 Attempts at Naming Biblical Anger's Conceptual Metaphors

Several additional studies show that metonymically depicting an emotion by its perceived physiological effects is a cross-cultural phenomenon. [9] A number of biblical interpreters have pointed to these sorts of features in Biblical Hebrew. In particular, Paul Krüger, Zacharias Kotzé, and Ellen van Wolde have appealed directly to the findings of cognitive linguists such as Lakoff and Kövecses. Other scholars such as H. Wheeler Robinson, A. R. Johnson, E. Dhorme, Mayer Gruber, and Mark Smith conducted earlier studies of the ways that emotions are depicted metonymically and metaphorically in the Hebrew Bible but without an explicit cognitive-linguistic framework. [10]

---

7. These expressions are quotations from throughout ibid., except the example of "I just needed to *vent*," which is a paraphrase.

8. Ibid. The notion that anger is dangerous unless it is vented has been challenged by Carol Tavris, *Anger: The Misunderstood Emotion* (rev. ed.; New York: Simon & Schuster, 1989).

9. Zoltán Kövecses, *Emotion Concepts* (New York: Springer, 1990); Ralph B. Hupka et al., "Anger, Envy, Fear, and Jealousy as Felt in the Body: A Five-Nation Study," *Cross-Cultural Research* 30 (1996) 243–64.

10. H. W. Robinson, "Hebrew Psychology," in *The People and the Book* (ed. A. S. Peake; Oxford: Claredon, 1925) 353–82; A. R. Johnson, *The Vitality of the Individual in the Thought of Ancient Israel* (Cardiff: University of Wales Press, 1949); E. Dhorme, *L'emploi métaphorique des noms de parties du corps en hébreu et en akkadien* (Paris: Librairie Orientaliste, 1963); Mayer I. Gruber, *Aspects of Nonverbal Communication in the Ancient Near East* (Studia Pohl 12; 2 vols.; Rome: Pontifical Biblical Institute, 1980); see also Mark S. Smith, "The Heart and Innards in Israelite Emotional Expressions: Notes from Anthropology and Psychobiology," *JBL* 117 (1998) 427–36.

Paul Krüger has played a key role in applying this cognitive linguistic ap-proach to emotion in the Hebrew Bible. An important study of anger came in 2000 with his publication "A Cognitive Interpretation of the Emotion of Anger in the Hebrew Bible."[11] It reviews in detail the work of Lakoff and Kövecses described above. Then Krüger asserts that many of the conceptual metaphors for anger found in American English are also present in Biblical Hebrew. He draws special attention to the metaphor ANGER IS THE HEAT OF FLUID IN A CONTAINER, citing the following passages to claim that Biblical Hebrew conceives of anger with this metaphor as well (the translations are his):

> *Deut 19:6*: "Lest the avenger of blood pursue the slayer, while his heart is *hot* (חמם)."
>
> *Isa 30:27*: "He (his lips) is/are *filled* (מלא) with anger."
>
> *Ezek 38:18*: "My fury shall *come up* (עלה) in my face."
>
> *2 Sam 22:9*: "*Smoke went up* (עלה עשן) from his nostrils."
>
> *Jer 42:18*: "My anger and my wrath *were poured out* (נתך) upon the inhabitants of Jerusalem."
>
> *Prov 29:11*: "A fool gives vent (יצא) to all his anger [רוח]; a wise man *stills* (שבח) it."[12]

Based on examples such as these, Krüger concludes that many expressions of anger in the Hebrew Bible use essentially the same conceptual meta-phors as American English.[13]

Several scholars, particularly Zacharias Kotzé and Ellen van Wolde, have drawn on Krüger's findings in their own work. Kotzé, in a number of his works published before 2006, makes similar arguments and outlines a methodology for the study of conceptual metaphor in the Bible.[14] Pub-lications by van Wolde in 2007 and 2008 also appropriate Krüger's work, summarizing him, quoting him, and even taking his conclusions a step farther.[15] For example, she does more than Krüger to emphasize the explo-siveness and uncontrollability of anger in Biblical Hebrew.[16]

---

11. Paul A. Krüger, "A Cognitive Interpretation of the Emotion of Anger in the Hebrew Bible," *JNSL* 26 (2000) 181–93.

12. Ibid., esp. pp. 187–89.

13. Ibid., 191.

14. His methodological essay is: Zacharias Kotzé, "A Cognitive Linguistic Methodol-ogy for the Study of Metaphor in the Hebrew Bible," *JNSL* 31 (2005) 107–17. Additional conceptual metaphors for biblical anger are explored in idem, "Metaphors and Meton-ymies for Anger in the Old Testament: A Cognitive Linguistic Approach," *Scriptura* 88 (2005) 118–25; idem, "Conceptual Metaphors for Anger in the Biblical Hebrew Story of the Flood," *Journal for Semitics = Tydskrif vir Semitistiek* 14 (2005) 149–64.

15. Ellen van Wolde "Language of Sentiment," *SBL Forum* 5 (2007), http://sbl-site .org/Article.aspx?ArticleID=660 (accessed April 11, 2007); idem, "Sentiments as Culturally Constructed Emotions: Anger and Love in the Hebrew Bible," *BibInt* 16 (2008) 1–24, esp. pp. 9–10.

16. With respect to explosiveness, Krüger admits that the examples he gives may refer instead to an overflowing ("A Cognitive Interpretation of Anger," 188). Van Wolde, on the

6.3 Problems with Scholarship on Conceptual Metaphor

Although these approaches take initial steps in the right directions, there are several key problems. First, the examples that these authors give do not always fit especially well with the conceptual metaphor from which they allegedly derive. Most of the texts cited as examples of explosive anger in fact refer to the *pouring out* of anger described above (§5.5).[17] *Pouring out* need not entail any type of explosion. In fact, one wonders how frequent *explosions* were in the ancient Near East.[18] Second, Lakoff and Kövecses refer to established, idiomatic expressions in the English language, such as "Keep cool," and "You make my blood boil." They argue that these established, idiomatic expressions reflect pervasive conceptual metaphors that guide American thinking about anger. Biblical scholars, on the other hand, fail to give sufficient evidence that their examples are widespread, at least with the more elaborate metaphors such as ANGER IS AN EXPLOSION and ANGER IS THE HEAT OF FLUID IN A CONTAINER.[19] Without a demonstration that these metaphors are widespread, one can easily question whether they guide the thinking of a culture and truly are *conceptual* metaphors.

---

other hand, claims that the metaphor of "anger as explosion" is "very frequently used" in the Hebrew Bible ("Language of Sentiment"; however, see also idem, *Reframing Biblical Studies: When Language and Text Meet Culture, Cognition, and Context* [Winona Lake, IN: Eisenbrauns, 2009] 72).

Regarding whether anger can be controlled, Krüger makes a brief comment about this topic ("A Cognitive Interpretation of the Emotion of Anger in the Hebrew Bible," 189). Meanwhile, van Wolde speaks of the uncontrollability of anger on many occasions ("Sentiments as Culturally Constructed Emotions," 11–14, 16–17, 22; "Language of Sentiment"; *Reframing Biblical Studies*, 72).

17. Admittedly, certain verses refer to anger as *going up* (עלה). However, these verses often have more similarities with the military idiom of *rising up against* someone than with anger rising within a person's body (2 Sam 11:20; Ezek 38:18; Ps 78:31; Prov 15:1; 2 Chr 28:9, 36:16). The evidence that van Wolde cites as referring to a person exploding with intense anger is likewise questionable. Two verses describe anger as *overflowing* (שטף; Isa 30:27–28, Prov 27:4), but these may invoke water imagery more than explosiveness. Similarly, other examples that she mentions describe anger as being *poured out* (שפך, נתך), which need not imply any type of explosion (Jer 42:18, 44:6; Nah 1:6; Job 40:11; 2 Chr 12:7, 34:25). Probably the clearest examples of explosiveness are Isa 30:27–30 and Ps 78:21. If anger was commonly conceived in terms of this type of rising and exploding, one would expect a greater number of examples than these two.

18. Zacharias Kotzé, "In Response to van Wolde," *SBL Forum* (2007), http://www.sbl-site.org/Article.aspx?ArticleID=671 (accessed May 31, 2007).

19. Regarding the second of these metaphors, van Wolde argues that עבר (Hithpael) and עברה refer to anger in terms of an overflowing container ("Sentiments as Culturally Constructed Emotions," 8; see also her *Reframing Biblical Studies*, 65). However, it is not clear that these words are related to the meaning 'cross over', as she assumes (Schunck, *TDOT* 10.426). Even if 'cross over' is valid, the etymological roots of this metaphor may relate to crossing over restraint, not crossing over the brim of a container that metaphorically represents the body. For additional discussion, see G. Sauer, "עֶבְרָה *'ebrâ* wrath," *TLOT* 2.835.

Several publications on conceptual metaphors for biblical anger rely on the work of Lakoff and Kövecses, but they do not adequately address the ways that Lakoff and Kövecses have been criticized. Ronald Butters faults Lakoff and Kövecses' use of evidence, which consists more of a series of examples than a sustained empirical analysis.[20] Butters furthermore suggests that, even if individuals routinely employ particular metaphors, these metaphors are not taken seriously for very long.[21] Naomi Quinn, meanwhile, criticizes Lakoff and his colleagues for failing to examine the cultural models that may underlie common metaphorical expressions.[22]

Dirk Geeraerts and Stefan Grondelaers attack specifically the work that Lakoff and Kövecses have done with *anger*. In a move analogous to Butters's and Quinn's, they argue that the metaphors in American English describing anger as THE HEAT OF FLUID IN A CONTAINER are not particularly significant on their own. Rather, they are vestiges of the Classical and Medieval doctrine of the four humors, which posited a close relation between one's emotional displays and bodily fluids, particularly between anger and hot yellow bile. Much of the language for anger in American English, they conclude, reflects this outdated model and is used primarily for its functional value, the same way that *sunrise* and *sunset* are used without endorsing pre-Copernican models of the universe.[23] Others have made similar points, such as Gerard Steen and Raymond Gibbs, who observe that common metaphors may be evident in the speech patterns of people who neither understand what gave rise to these metaphors nor "have all the full-blown conceptual metaphors uncovered by linguistic analysis."[24]

In more recent publications, Ellen van Wolde and Zacharias Kotzé have taken note of many of these criticisms and changed course. Van Wolde has backed away from approaches associated with George Lakoff, turning

---

20. Ronald R. Butters speaks of the evidence as "amazingly scanty and weak" ("Do 'Conceptual Metaphors' Really Exist?" *The SECOL Bulletin* 5 [1981] esp. p. 111). While Butters here is refuting Lakoff's work (written with Mark Johnson) *Metaphors We Live By*, the same type of evidence is used in this work by Lakoff and Kövecses. This evidence is not based on empirical studies but the listing of a few examples. In Lakoff's, Johnson's, and Kövecses' defense, however, one can note that the examples they list are salient, more so than some of the examples mentioned by biblical scholars.

21. Butters, "Do 'Conceptional Metaphors,'" 111, 115.

22. Naomi Quinn, "The Cultural Basis of Metaphor," in *Beyond Metaphor: The Theory of Tropes in Anthropology* (ed. J. W. Fernandez; Stanford: Stanford University Press, 1991) esp. pp. 65–72. See also idem, "'Commitment' in American Marriage: A Cultural Analysis," *American Ethnologist* 9 (1982) 775–98.

23. D. Geeraerts and S. Grondelaers, "Looking Back at Anger," in *Language and the Cognitive Construal of the World* (ed. J. R. Taylor and R. E. MacLaury; Berlin: de Gruyter, 1995) 153–79, esp. p. 155.

24. Gerard J. Steen and Raymond W. Gibbs Jr., "Introduction," in *Metaphor in Cognitive Linguistics: Selected Papers from the Fifth International Cognitive Linguistics Conference, Amsterdam, July 1997* (ed. Raymond W. Gibbs Jr. and Gerard J. Steen; Amsterdam: Benjamins, 1999) 1–8, esp. p. 4.

to other medthods within cognitive linguistics.[25] Meanwhile, Zacharias Kotzé has shifted positions, giving particular attention to the criticisms that Geeraerts and Grondelaers make regarding humoral doctrine. However, the new path that Kotzé takes is problematic as well. He argues that, as the English language reflects a doctrine of the humors in its metaphors for emotion, so does the Hebrew Bible.[26] He does not believe it is the same doctrine of the humors, but he does contend that bodily fluids are closely related to emotion in the Hebrew Bible. Thus, he argues that *saliva* plays an especially significant role in the Hebrew conception of anger. He claims that חמה, קצף, and זעם "have as their basic meaning 'foam' or 'froth,'" and he argues, "these designations make metonymic allusion to a perceived symptom of anger, i.e. the emotion of anger is accompanied by foam (at the mouth)."[27] It is doubtful that Kotzé is correct here. First, it is not clear that these three words refer to *foaming*.[28] Second, *saliva* plays a very insignificant role in the Hebrew Bible, and one would expect greater evidence if it was foundational to the Israelite understanding of anger.[29] Third, it is not apparent that foam at one's mouth would have been a perceived symptom of anger among the communities that gave rise to the Hebrew Bible. The clearest account of someone foaming at the mouth is 1 Sam 21:14[13], where it is associated with *insanity* not *anger*.

---

25. She takes an approach closely related to Ronald Langacker's Cognitive Grammar (van Wolde, *Reframing Biblical Studies*, 30–34; see Langacker, *Foundations of Cognitive Grammar*, vol. 1: *Theoretical Prerequisites* [Stanford, CA: Stanford University Press, 1987]).

26. Zacharias Kotzé, "Humoral Theory as Motivation for Anger Metaphors in the Hebrew Bible," *Southern African Linguistics and Applied Language Studies* 23 (2005) 205–9. See also idem, "In Response to van Wolde." While Kotzé has gone the furthest in arguing for the existence of a humoral theory embedded in the Hebrew Bible, others use language borrowed from humoral theory to describe emotion in the Hebrew Bible. See, for example, Hans Walter Wolff, *Anthropology of the Old Testament* (trans. Margaret Kohl; Philadelphia: Fortress, 1981) esp. pp. 36–37.

27. Kotzé, "Humoral Theory," 206. He also asserts that *anger* is closely connected to *bile* in the Hebrew Bible, appealing to cases where *anger* is related to words from the root מרר (pp. 206–7). Here, his moves are questionable as well. The connection between מרר and anger in Ezek 3:14, for example, is a creative combination of words for *anger* and *bitterness*, not a reflection of a widespread theory that anger is related to *bile* and *gall*. Simply because מררה refers to 'gall' on two occasions (Job 16:13, 20:25), one should not assume that all words from the root מרר refer to 'bile'. As Robinson puts it, "The liver, so important for Babylonian psychology, takes little place in the Hebrew" ("Hebrew Psychology," esp. p. 364).

28. Gruber is one of the few to make such a claim, and he does so primarily with regard to חמה, on the basis of the Akkadian *imtu* (*Aspects of Nonverbal Communication*, esp. 2.538–50). There are, however, many other Semitic cognates, and so most lexicographers tend to connect חמה less with *foaming* and more with *heat* (BDB, 404–5; HALOT [study ed.], 1.326; Schunck, *TDOT* 4.462; Gale B. Struthers, "חֵמָה," *NIDOTTE* 2.170–71).

29. While a few texts speak of spitting on someone as a potential expression of anger (Num 12:14, Deut 25:9; see also "The Story of Sinuhe" [*AEL* 1:222–35, esp. p. 225, §B, 40–43]), they do not indicate a perception of anger's being fundamentally linked with saliva.

6.4 Reassessing Biblical Anger's Conceptual Metaphors

Although the approaches described above have their problems, one should not abandon the study of metaphors and emotion altogether. Instead, one needs to begin at the most basic level. When one considers the foundational meaning of each of the terms for anger in the Hebrew Bible, it quickly becomes apparent that many of them are dead metaphors or dead metonyms:[30]

ANGER IS A BURNING NOSE (חרה אף).

ANGER IS A NOSE (אף).

ANGER IS HEAT (חמה, חרה).

ANGER IS A SHAKING (רגז).

ANGER IS A DISTURBANCE (זעף).

Unlike the elaborate metaphor ANGER IS THE HEAT OF FLUID IN A CONTAINER, these metaphors pervade and even constitute Biblical Hebrew's terminology for anger.[31] Frequently, these basic metaphors are dead; they are understood by readers as straightforward references to anger without evoking a moment of *Gestalt* (so Ricoeur) wherein both contradictions and similarities are seen between the metaphorical referents.[32] The beginning of Gen 27:45, for example, is best translated 'until the anger (אף) of your brother subsides (שוב)'. There is no need for readers in this case to see אף as a reference to 'nose'. Rather, the metaphor ANGER IS A NOSE has reached such a degree of currency that אף simply means 'anger'. Thus, one can debate the extent to which a dead metaphor such as this influenced everyday thinking or what the significance would be if it did.[33] Just as the etymological origins of a

---

30. Like *dead metaphors*, *dead metonymies* are expressions that have gained such currency that they are no longer recognized as tropes.

31. Kotzé, van Wolde, and Krüger pay some attention to the basic metaphors outlined here. The chief problem is not their work with these basic metaphors but, rather, their work with metaphors that are more elaborate, particularly, ANGER IS AN EXPLOSION and ANGER IS THE HEAT OF FLUID IN A CONTAINER.

32. Paul Ricoeur, *The Rule of Metaphor: Multi-disciplinary Studies of the Creation of Meaning in Language* (trans. Robert Czerny, Kathleen McLaughlin, and John Costello; Toronto: University of Toronto Press, 1977) 212–14.

33. When the metaphors or metonyms at hand are so worn out that their figurative qualities are not usually recognized, then they most likely do not exert powerful influence on one's thinking. For example, one can use the word *armchair* without having one's thinking heavily influenced by the anthropomorphic qualities that such chairs possess. Thus, there are problems with those who claim that חרה אף should not be translated 'became angry', because this translation does not reveal metaphorical qualities. See, for example, S. Schroer and T. Staubli, *Body Symbolism in the Bible* (trans. Linda M. Maloney; Collegeville, MN: Liturgical Press, 1998) 95–96. Because the metaphor was dead in Biblical Hebrew, translators engage in questionable moves by bringing the metaphorical qualities to light.

word may not figure prominently in its present usage, so the figurative meaning of a dead metaphor may not have much bearing on everyday speech.[34] Moreover, one need not assume that each reference to אַף, חרה, or חמה (as dead metaphors) meant that the angry person literally felt heat or redness in the face.[35] People do not consistently perceive the same physiological symptoms of particular emotions (even within the same culture).[36] Although the perception of warmness in the face was probably prototypical among the perceived physiological symptoms of anger, there is no reason to see it as being universal.[37]

Paul Ricoeur observes that sometimes dead metaphors are revived or rejuvenated, particularly when writers expand their implications or employ them in fresh ways.[38] There are several instances in the Hebrew Bible where writers appear to reanimate dead metaphors for anger. As discussed above (§5.4), אֵשׁ ('fire') is often used to express vivid imagery about anger that points to its destructive nature, among other things. These instances can be seen as cases where writers took the dead metaphor ANGER IS HEAT and breathed into it new life, allowing readers to understand afresh the dynamic connections between *anger* and *fire*. At the same time, one should be cautious about seeing all such connections between anger and fire as merely reviving dead metaphors. One needs also to be aware of underlying cultural models. In this case, texts portraying YHWH as breathing smoke and fire (2 Sam 22:9 [Ps 18:9(8)]; Isa 30:27, 33; 33:11; 65:5) may have less to do with extending a dead metaphor and more with appealing to motifs in ancient Near Eastern mythology, where some deities (for example, Huwawa) were portrayed with fire imagery, frequently using it as a weapon in battle.[39]

The preceding discussion leads to the following conclusions. First, on the basic level, there are some similarities between how *anger* is metaphorically depicted in American English and Biblical Hebrew. Both languages engage in a larger cross-cultural phenomenon of metonymically depicting

---

34. On the etymological fallacy, see James Barr, *The Semantics of Biblical Language* (London: SCM, 1961) esp. pp. 102–3.

35. Contra Lytta Basset, *Holy Anger: Jacob, Job, Jesus* (Grand Rapids, MI: Eerdmans, 2007) 21–22.

36. As Martha C. Nussbaum points out, researchers have faced fundamental problems correlating particular emotions with particular physiological states, essentially abandoning the quest to find connections of this sort (*Upheavals of Thought: The Intelligence of Emotions* [Cambridge: Cambridge University Press, 2001] 95–100, esp. p. 97).

37. Thus, when referring to Gale B. Struthers's argument that אַף "is the type of anger in which the face may turn red and the passions are aroused" (*NIDOTTE* 1.463), one should emphasize the word *may*. Just because heat in the face is part of the prototypical experience of anger, not everyone always experiences it this way.

38. Ricoeur, *The Rule of Metaphor*, 291–95.

39. "The Epic of Gilgamesh" (*ANET*, 72–99, esp. p. 79 [III iii 18–20]); W. G. E. Watson, "Fire אֵשׁ," *DDD* 332; Patrick D. Miller, "Fire in the Mythology of Canaan and Israel," *CBQ* 27 (1965) 256–61.

an emotion by referring to a perceived physiological symptom.[40] Second, while American English has fairly well-developed metaphors such as ANGER IS THE HEAT OF FLUID IN A CONTAINER, one should be hesitant about assuming that Biblical Hebrew routinely develops the metaphor ANGER IS HEAT in the same way. For example, there are many idiomatic expressions in American English that suggest that the metaphorical fluid in this container (that is, the body) can rise and explode, resulting in a loss of control and harm to oneself or others. When one turns to Biblical Hebrew, however, there are not many unambiguous, idiomatic examples to suggest that anger was routinely conceived this way. One should not conflate the American English model of anger with the Hebrew Bible's, even when there are similarities. Third, many of Biblical Hebrew's routine depictions of anger are dead metaphors that sometimes were revived for particular purposes. Thus, the metaphor ANGER IS FIRE extends and vivifies the dead metaphor ANGER IS HEAT, pointing particularly to anger's dangerous consequences (especially its consuming nature). Although dead metaphors obviously influence their vivification, they do not necessarily influence everyday thinking in decisive ways. Finally, cultural factors can play a role in metaphorical formulations. Just as the Classical and Medieval doctrine of the four humors surfaces in many American English expressions for anger, so the depiction of an angry deity fuming with smoke and fire may derive from motifs in ancient Near Eastern mythology. One need not commit Kotzé's error of assuming that, because English language for emotion reflects a humoral understanding, Biblical Hebrew does likewise. The text needs to be understood on its own terms, not ours. Only in this way can violence against the text be minimized.

6.5 *The Nuances and Meanings of Terms for Anger*

Before concluding this discussion of the Hebrew Bible's language for anger, I will comment briefly on the specific terms used to convey this emotion. Biblical scholars have tended to see anger in the Hebrew Bible as a complex albeit unified concept that a variety of words can convey.[41] There are compelling reasons for doing so, such as the ways that various terms for anger can be used interchangeably (for example, Ps 78:49). Nevertheless, there are discernible differences between the various terms for anger,

---

40. Hupka et al., "Anger, Envy, Fear, and Jealousy," passim. See also Smith, "Metaphor and Mind," 132; Krüger, "A Cognitive Interpretation of the Emotion of Anger in the Hebrew Bible," 183; Smith, "The Heart and Innards in Israelite Emotional Expressions," 432; Johnson, *The Vitality of the Individual*, 88–89; Schroer and Staubli, *Body Symbolism in the Bible*, 94–96; Gruber, *Aspects of Nonverbal Communication*, 2.550.

41. See Bruce Edward Baloian, *Anger in the Old Testament* (American University Studies 7, Theology and Religion 99; New York: Peter Lang, 1992) 5; J. Bergman and E. Johnson, "אַף; אָנַף," *TDOT* 1.348–60, esp. p. 356; van Wolde, *Reframing Biblical Studies*, 64, 67–70.

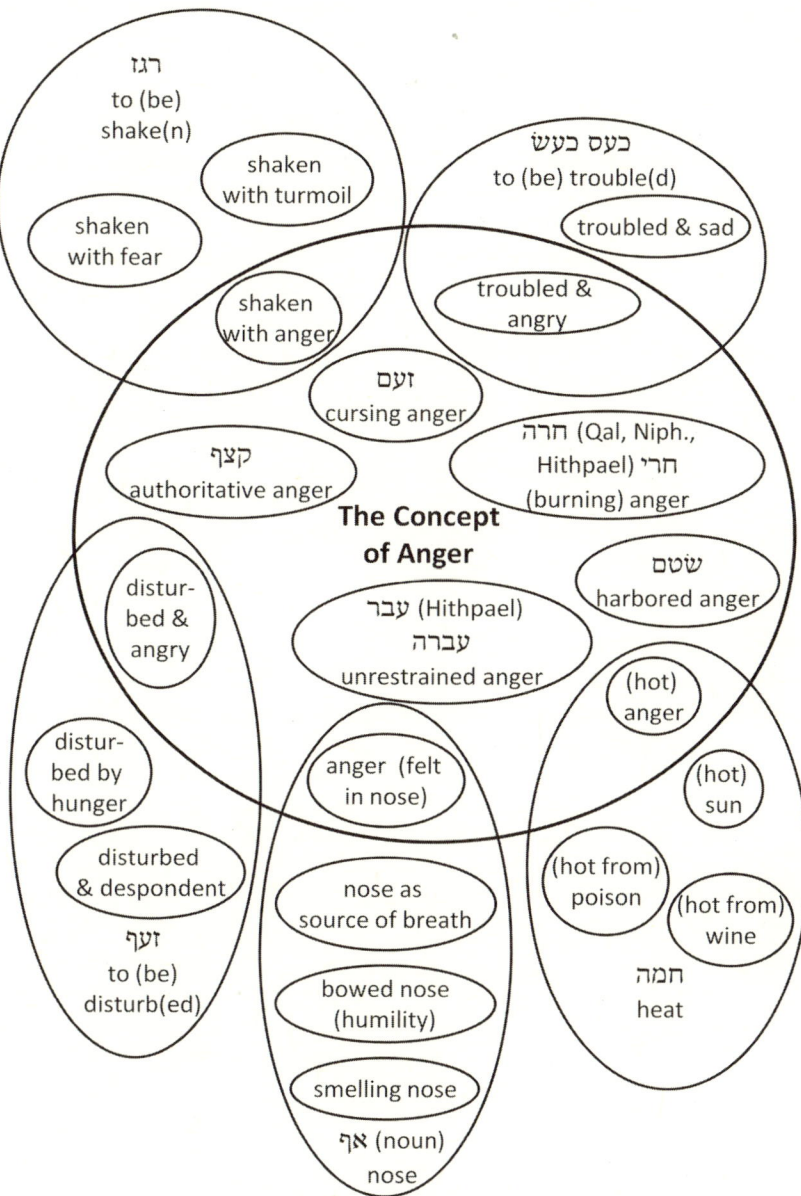

Figure 1. The interrelation of terms for anger.

which constitute the final focus of this chapter. A brief explanation of the words for anger is provided here, and a more detailed analysis is found in appendix B (pp. 193–201).

Figure 1 begins to explain the meanings of terms for anger in Biblical Hebrew. Although it has limitations, this diagram illustrates that many words for anger have meanings that extend beyond *anger*.[42] As this diagram illustrates, three words refer to *more than one type of emotion*: זעף, רגז, and כעש/כעס:

1. The word רגז means basically to 'shake'. Although it can be used to refer to a literal shaking (such as an earthquake), it frequently refers to an emotional shaking, particularly with anger or fear.
2. The word זעף means 'greatly disturbed' or 'in an uproar'. It tends to refer to anger, although it is also used to speak of hunger and despondency on a few occasions. Individuals who experience this sort of disturbance tend to have authority.
3. The word כעס (spelled כעש in Job) carries the meaning of being 'troubled'. It conveys anger when someone in a hierarchical position is described with this word, but interestingly it refers to anguish or sadness when describing a subordinate.

Three other words for anger have basic meanings that relate to *perceived physiological symptoms* of anger: אף, חרה, and חמה:

1. The word אף can mean not only 'anger' but also 'nose'. Most lexicographers see the two meanings as related, suggesting that anger is often felt in the face. The most common word for anger in the Hebrew Bible, אף, has a fairly generic meaning.
2. The word חרה is related to the meaning 'burn', most likely playing off the perceived physiological symptom of feeling hot while angry. Whereas אף is the most common noun for anger in the Hebrew Bible, the word חרה is the most common verb. It similarly has a broad meaning that can refer to a variety of different types of anger.

---

42. This diagram does not point to all the spheres of semantic overlap (for example, חרה and אף). Nor is it drawn to scale. Thus, חרה represents a relatively small portion of the diagram, though it is one of the most common words for anger.

The words for anger that appear here are the same words that Baloian (*Anger in the Old Testament*, 5–7) and Bergman and Johnson (*TDOT* 1.351–56) classify as "Words for 'Anger' in the Old Testament" with two exceptions. First, רוח is not included here. Although there are cases in which it has connections with anger (esp. Prov 16:32), רוח is not innately connected with anger. Like נפש and לב(ב), רוח refers to a component of one's personhood. Sometimes, these words are connected with anger (Job 18:4, Prov 19:3) but not typically. Second, the word שׂטם is included here. Although it is quite rare (appearing only in Gen 27:41, 49:23, 50:15; Job 16:9, 30:21; Ps 55:4[3]), it appears to refer to *harbored anger*, particularly with the desire to harm someone.

3. The word חמה has the underlying meaning of 'heat', presumably for similar reasons. This word typically refers to fierce anger that involves at least the possibility of deadly violence.

Finally, there are four words that tend to designate particular types of anger: קצף, זעם, עבר/עברה (Hithpael), and שטם.

1. The root קצף signifies 'authoritative anger'. Individuals who experience this type of anger are almost always those with power.
2. The word זעם refers to 'angry speech'. 'Cursing' is often conveyed with this word.
3. The noun עברה and the Hithpael forms of עבר point to 'unbridled' emotion, most commonly 'unchecked anger'. Like the term חמה, these words are used to describe harsh anger that frequently has violent results.
4. The term שטם conveys 'buried anger' or 'harbored anger', that is, anger that 'bears a grudge'. In some respects, this word is an antonym of עברה, meaning bridled anger that is marked (at least temporarily) by restraint.

6.6 Conclusion to Part 1: From Conflation to Incorporation

Neither the Hebrew Bible's concept of anger nor the various words that express it always have precise equivalents in the English language. There are obvious connections: for example, both languages connect anger with heat, violence, and matters of wrongdoing. However, these connections break down as soon as they are taken too far. The prototypical script of anger in the Hebrew Bible needs to be understood not in terms of an American or Japanese model but on its own terms. It arises in response to perceived wrongdoings more than mere frustrations over daily affairs. It is concerned with ethical issues and is communal, directed not toward things but toward people. It almost always results in some form of estrangement and frequently leads to violence. Consequently, it tends to be evaluated negatively but, because of its moral dimensions, it also has positive qualities. The associative networks of biblical anger pertain to the concepts of *jealousy, fire, evil, extreme violence,* and *pouring out*—far more than to the Western associations with *being mad, inner fluids rising,* or *explosiveness.* The Hebrew terms reveal connections between anger and sadness (רגז, זעף, and כעס), between feeling angry and feeling warm (אף, חרה, and חמה), and between anger and authority (קצף), speech (זעם), restraint (שטם), and a lack thereof (עברה). For many of these terms, there are no precise equivalents in the English language. Inevitably, translating these terms involves casualties, particularly as elements of the source language are lost and elements of a target language are imposed on the text. Translators and interpreters have a responsibility to minimize these casualties and avoid conflating past and modern conceptions of emotion.

However, George Steiner, who speaks at length about the violence of translation, maintains that translation is not merely negative. It entails not only aggression but also incorporation—that is, the importation and embodiment of new concepts, insights, and world views not fully manifest within the sociolinguistic confines of the target language. Thus, Steiner uses the metaphors of "sacramental intake" and "incarnation" to describe the act of translation.[43] Von Humboldt grasps a similar idea when he observes that translators have the opportunity of helping their target audience awaken values and concepts that "slumber" in their native language, opening themselves to new ways of speaking, thinking, and being.[44] While interpreters would not want to incorporate all of the Hebrew Bible's conceptualization of anger (such as its masculine bias), studying how another culture conceives of anger may facilitate freedom from the problematic conceptions of emotions in Western discourse. Despite all the intricate differences between biblical anger and modern anger, the humanity shared by ancient writers and contemporary readers allows us to forge connections, gain insights, and be shaped anew. By understanding the text on its own terms, readers can enter new worlds and envision alternate modes of existence.

---

43. George Steiner, *After Babel: Aspects of Language and Translation* (Oxford: Oxford University Press, 1975) 299.

44. Wilhelm von Humboldt, "From the Introduction to His Translation of *Agamemnon*," in *Theories of Translation: An Anthology of Essays from Dryden to Derrida* (ed. Rainer Schulte and John Biguenet; Chicago: University of Chicago Press, 1992) 56–57.

Part 2

Daybreak after the Dim Glow of the Enlightenment: Approaching the Ethics of Genesis

Chapter 7
Advances in Old Testament Ethics

In this chapter, I survey the field of Old Testament ethics, focusing not only on important scholarly works but also on the reasons that this field has grown dramatically in recent decades, whereas previously it received little attention. One of the key arguments offered here is that the most important advances have occurred as biblical scholars have embraced alternatives to the Enlightenment's narrow approach to ethics. This chapter outlines these advances and then evaluates them, examining their suitability for understanding Genesis' message about anger.

7.1 The Rise of Works on Old Testament Ethics

The last 25 years have seen a marked increase in works on the ethics of the Hebrew Bible.[1] Only a handful of works on this topic were written during the first three-quarters of the 20th century.[2] Thus, Cyril Rodd refers to ethics as being a "non-subject" for biblical scholars in the middle of the century, a topic assumed to have "no future."[3] Similarly, Christopher Wright explains that, when he planned a dissertation on Old Testament ethics in 1970, John Sturdy told him "nobody had written anything on [the topic] in English for fifty years."[4] In the same year, Brevard Childs observed, "In spite of the great interest in ethics, to our knowledge, there is no outstanding modern work written in English that even attempts to deal adequately with the Biblical material as it relates to ethics."[5] As many of these authors go on to acknowledge, the state of Old Testament ethics is now quite different. A variety of works have been published on the topic.[6]

---

1. For an excellent bibliographical essay, see Christopher J. H. Wright, *Old Testament Ethics for the People of God* (Leicester: Inter-Varsity, 2004) 415–40, see also pp. 65–66.

2. These earlier works include: Hinckley G. Mitchell, *The Ethics of the Old Testament* (Chicago: University of Chicago Press, 1912); Max Weber, *Ancient Judaism* (trans. Hans H. Gerth and Don Martindale; Glencoe, IL: Free Press, 1952); John Murray, *Principles of Conduct: Aspects of Biblical Ethics* (Grand Rapids, MI: Eerdmans, 1957); Johannes Hempel, *Das Ethos des Alten Testaments* (2nd ed.; Berlin: Alfred Töpelmann, 1964).

3. Cyril S. Rodd, *Glimpses of a Strange Land: Studies in Old Testament Ethics* (Edinburgh: T. & T. Clark, 2001) ix.

4. Wright, *Old Testament Ethics for the People of God*, 13.

5. Brevard S. Childs, *Biblical Theology in Crisis* (Philadelphia: Westminster, 1970) 124.

6. See also John Rogerson, *Theory and Practice in Old Testament Ethics* (JSOTSup; London: T. & T. Clark, 2004) 1.

There are several reasons why Old Testament ethics received relatively little attention until the 1980s. First, for much of the 20th century, source criticism and form criticism were the prevailing areas of concern. Compared with literary and rhetorical approaches, which did not come on the scene prominently until the late 1970s and the 1980s, source and form criticism did not lend themselves easily to theological or ethical exploration.[7] They tended to focus on reconstructing the hypothetical authors and Sitz im Leben of a given text. Literary and rhetorical approaches, on the other hand, were more concerned with the messages that texts convey and the means by which they convey them. The focus on content in these approaches facilitated a focus on the ethical dimensions of a passage's content.

A second reason for a lack of concern about Old Testament ethics prior to the 1980s pertains to biblical theology, of which biblical ethics is often considered a subset. In preceding decades, especially the 1950s and 1960s, the enterprise of biblical theology appeared increasingly problematic and faced an uncertain future. At the time, Brevard Childs characterized these problems as a "crisis," while John J. Collins later used stronger language, asserting that the biblical theology movement "died of its own contradictions in the late 1960s."[8] With the broader field of biblical theology in a state of crisis (if not demise) in the middle of the 20th century, biblical ethics not surprisingly received relatively little attention.[9] However, when biblical theology resurged in the 1980s and beyond, works on biblical ethics flourished as well.

There is a third, broader reason why biblical ethics received much more attention in the 1980s and following: this period brought freedom from many assumptions that had been taken for granted since the Enlightenment. As is well known, the Enlightenment exalted reason as the ultimate authority, rejecting appeals to tradition and ideas of the supernatural. It assumed that reason could articulate a universally valid morality (and thus prevent a freefall into moral relativism in a world free from the constraints of traditional authority). The project of articulating this morality gave priority to abstractions, generalizations, and universals over the concrete, the particular, and the contingent. To achieve the universality for which

---

7. For an account of how historical approaches failed to reckon with the "text as such," see Hans W. Frei, *The Eclipse of Biblical Narrative: A Study in Eighteenth and Nineteenth Century Hermeneutics* (New Haven, CT: Yale University Press, 1974) 134–36.

8. Childs, *Biblical Theology in Crisis*, passim, esp. chap. 3; John J. Collins, "Historical Criticism and the State of Biblical Theology," *ChrCent*, July 28–Aug 4, 1993, 743.

9. On a related note, one wonders if Barth's influence is partially to blame for this lack of attention to ethics in biblical theology during this period. Barth has obviously exerted great influence on many biblical theologians. However, his work on ethics was not as enthusiastically received. See John Webster, *Barth's Ethics of Reconciliation* (Cambridge: Cambridge University Press, 1995) esp. p. 1.

it strove, the Enlightenment project placed great emphasis on impartiality, objectivity, and neutrality. Taking cues from science and mathematics, it strove to locate the laws and formulas that lay at the heart of things. It exhibited a strong tendency toward monism, preferring singularity over plurality, systematization over fragmentation, unity over diversity, consistency over variety, commensurability over difference, commonality over irreducibility, and certainty over ambiguity. It focused more on the metaphysical and transcendental than the material and immanent.

In comparison with classical ethical theories, the Enlightenment took an approach that was more Platonic than Aristotelian, emphasizing first principles over practical wisdom.[10] Reason was esteemed over the emotions, theory reigned over particular experience, and propositional discourse took priority over narrative and poetic genres. John Rawls, in *A Theory of Justice*, articulates a modernist vision of what an ethical theory must encompass in order to be valid. In a summary statement, he writes, "a conception of right is a set of principles, general in form and universal in application, that is to be publicly recognized as a final court of appeal for ordering the conflicting claims of moral persons."[11] By equating ethics with principles, Rawls excludes a number of other possible priorities for ethical theory, such as paradigms, virtues, ethos, wisdom, perception, and learned experience. By emphasizing generality and universality, he sidelines the particular and concrete.[12] The major ethical theories of the Enlightenment, Kantianism (in which Rawls participates) and utilitarianism, fit Rawls's criteria, upholding in typical monistic fashion a single guiding principle for all.[13]

---

10. Gavin D'Costa, "Postmodernity and Religious Plurality: Is a Common Global Ethic Possible or Desirable?" in *The Blackwell Companion to Postmodern Theology* (ed. Graham Ward; Oxford: Blackwell, 2001) 136.

11. John Rawls, *A Theory of Justice* (Cambridge: Belknap Press of Harvard University Press, 1971) 135. For a discussion of these criteria and their shortcomings, see Martha C. Nussbaum, *Love's Knowledge: Essays on Philosophy and Literature* (New York: Oxford University Press, 1990) 175, esp. n. 22. Rawls has since restated some of his positions in *Justice as Fairness: A Restatement* (Cambridge: Belknap, 2001). This work displays some evolution while still retaining a focus on the importance of principles (see esp. pp. 42–50).

12. Although I am critical of the Enlightenment approach on the whole, there is some value in universal ethics. Reaching across cultures to reach a minimum consensus about upright moral behavior, for example, has led to advances in human rights. The Hebrew Bible at times participates in something quite similar, as I have argued in "Teaching the Hebrew Bible amid the Current Human Rights Crisis: The Pedagogical Opportunities Presented by Amos 1:3–2:3," *SBL Forum* 4 (2006), http://sbl-site.org/Article.aspx?ArticleId=478 (accessed July 31, 2008).

13. Traditional Kantianism is driven by the categorical imperative: "Act only according to that maxim whereby you can at the same time will that it should become a universal law" (Immanuel Kant, *Grounding for the Metaphysics of Morals; with, On a Supposed Right to Lie Because of Philanthropic Concerns* [trans. James W. Ellington; 3rd ed.; Indianapolis: Hackett, 1993] 30, §421). Utilitarianism, meanwhile, seeks to answer the architectonic question, "What brings the most good to the most people?"

7.1.1 Biblical Ethics along the Lines of Modernity?

On occasion, biblical scholars have attempted to articulate an ethics of the Hebrew Bible that fits within this type of Enlightenment model. Perhaps the best example is Walter Kaiser's *Toward Old Testament Ethics*, published in 1983, which attempts to describe the ethics of the Hebrew Bible by focusing on legal materials.[14] Kaiser argues that the ethics of the Old Testament are unified, consistent, universal, and comprehensive—all qualities that modernists such as Rawls uphold.[15] Further reflecting the aspirations of modernity, Kaiser argues that Old Testament ethics can be summarized with a single principle, that of holiness.[16]

Although Kaiser provided a valuable service in initiating an important conversation about Old Testament ethics, his work has significant flaws. The diverse, organic qualities of ethical material in the Hebrew Bible simply do not fit within the rigid framework of the Enlightenment.[17] Like the failed attempts at recognizing a single theological center of the Old Testament, Kaiser's focus on holiness has multiple problems.[18] Clay Libolt's critique of Kaiser in 1985 is revealing:

> In the end the most significant thing that can be learned from this book is that it is a bad project. "Old Testament ethics" is a strange mixing of categories, rather like "Old Testament philosophy" or "Old Testament botany." We do ethics. The writers of the Old Testament did law or prophecy, or they told stories, some of which are, by our standards, hardly ethical. To put this in another way, the Old Testament prompts reflection, but, with the exception of Proverbs (which Kaiser scarcely mentions), it rarely does the sort of thing that counts for ethics in our culture. The differences should be respected. The texts should be read as they were written.[19]

When ethics are understood in Enlightenment terms—that is, as a set of general, universal, and consistent principles—one cannot but agree with

---

14. Walter C. Kaiser, *Toward Old Testament Ethics* (Grand Rapids, MI: Zondervan, 1983). Murray makes similar moves in *Principles of Conduct*.

15. Kaiser, *Toward Old Testament Ethics*, 3, 11, 22, 26–28, 64–67.

16. Ibid., 139, 301, see also "Part III: Content of Old Testament Ethics." Note, however, that on pp. 20–21, he is more open to a plurality of governing ideas, speaking about several "central concepts" (obedience, divine will, holiness, and creation).

17. For related remarks, see Waldemar Janzen, "Review of Walter Kaiser, *Toward Old Testament Ethics*," *Int* 39 (1985) 424.

18. Furthermore, it makes little sense for Kaiser to claim that the call to holiness is central to Old Testament ethics and is what distinguished Israel from the nations (*Toward Old Testament Ethics*, 140–41), while also claiming, "Old Testament ethics are *universal*, embracing the same standard of righteousness for all the nations of the earth as it does for Israel" (p. 11).

19. Clay Libolt, "Review of Walter Kaiser, *Toward Old Testament Ethics*," *CTJ* 20 (1985) 106. One should note that there are some problems with this characterization of the Old Testament. For example, the concept of "Old Testament philosophy" is not so unusual when one interacts with texts such as Job and Qoheleth.

Libolt that Old Testament ethics is a fundamentally flawed enterprise. As long as modernity sets the terms and definition of the ethical enterprise, interpreters face extreme difficulties in articulating the ethics of the Hebrew Bible.

However, in the 25 years since the publication of Kaiser's work, biblical scholars have developed a much broader understanding of ethics that has led to a wide variety of new analyses. This broader understanding stemmed from changes in philosophical and related fields. Moral philosophers began to question traditional Enlightenment priorities. For example, as early as 1958, Elizabeth Anscombe's "Modern Moral Philosophy" argued, "The concepts of obligation, and duty—*moral* obligation and *moral* duty . . . ought to be jettisoned." She called instead for attention to moral psychology.[20] Many of her emphases were picked up and later popularized, especially in the 1980s with a variety of publications by Alasdair MacIntyre and Martha Nussbaum, who argued in favor of a more Aristotelian virtue-centered approach to ethics. At roughly the same time, postmodernity came prominently on the scene, undermining many of the Enlightenment's aims and assumptions, particularly those related to authority, hegemony, rationality, certainty, and language. With renewed interest in Aristotelian virtue ethics and the advent of postmodernity, biblical scholars began to think about ethics in a broader sense than scholars such as Kaiser had envisioned. In many cases, they retained strong connections with modernity. But by and large, they no longer had the concerns that Kaiser did, of focusing on legal materials, extrapolating its principles, locating its center, and arguing for its unity, consistency, and universality. Rather than abandoning the project of Old Testament ethics, biblical scholars reformulated what a project of this sort might entail.

Many interpreters have observed that the Old Testament contains (1) texts that appear morally problematic (such as the *ḥērem* texts), (2) texts that are morally ambiguous (for example, is Jacob's trickery praised or condemned?), and (3) texts that are very diverse, potentially in conflict with one another.[21] Dynamics of this sort make it nearly impossible to formulate a *modernist* vision of Old Testament ethics—that is, a vision that is unified, consistent, systematic, and focused on moral principles. However, these textual dynamics do not present insurmountable problems for articulating a more *postmodern* vision of Old Testament ethics. Postmodernity has brought an awareness of the value of diversity and particularity, as well as an awareness that morality is about far more than ethical rules. These insights have led to various shifts in assumptions, and at least five broad, creative advances have resulted in the field.[22]

---

20. G. E. M. Anscombe, "Modern Moral Philosophy," *Philosophy* 33/124 (1958) 1–19.

21. John Barton, *Understanding Old Testament Ethics* (Louisville: Westminster John Knox, 2003) 2–3.

22. In addition to the five areas listed here, one could also mention ideological criticism. This type of approach tends to be particularly concerned with power relations,

7.1.2 Old Testament Narratives as Ethical Resources

First, rather than focusing on legal materials as Kaiser did (which prima facie share a greater affinity with abstract principles than a number of other genres), several works appeared arguing that narratives provide tremendous ethical resources.[23] Especially noteworthy here are several essays by John Barton and *Story as Torah: Reading Old Testament Narrative Ethically* by Gordon Wenham.[24] Both authors rely heavily on the work of Martha Nussbaum and Wayne Booth to argue that narratives are particularly suited to addressing the complexities and difficulties of moral decision-making. Their work has inspired many interpreters. For example, Mary Mills's *Biblical Morality: Moral Perspectives in Old Testament Narratives* and Robin Parry's *Old Testament Story and Christian Ethics: The Rape of Dinah as a Case Study* spring from Barton's and Wenham's suggestive proposals.[25]

7.1.3 The Diversity of Biblical Ethics

A second creative advance pertains to the Hebrew Bible's polyvocality. Moving beyond the modernist tendency toward monism, several works in the last decade stress the diversity of Old Testament ethical teachings.[26] Rather than attempting to find a single center, they either examine multiple centers or abandon this type of approach altogether, stressing the plurality of perspectives in the Hebrew Bible. John Barton's work points to multiple centers in Old Testament ethics. He argues that there are three

---

marginalization, and treatment of "the Other." While perspectives differ (for example, taking a feminist approach versus a postcolonial approach), these studies share in common a general posture that seeks to expose how particular works serve (or in some cases counteract) the interests of hegemonic forces. For further discussion, see my "Biblical Studies and Rhetorical Criticism: Bridging the Divide between the Hebrew Bible and Communication," *Review of Communication* 7 (2007) 244–75, esp. pp. 253–54, 269–72.

Ideological criticism could play a fruitful role in subsequent discussions of how Genesis' message about anger relates to the experiences of Jewish communities in the exilic and postexilic periods (see §1.5). Does Genesis' largely negative portrayal of anger serve hegemonic interests and lead to a preservation of the status quo, squelching anger that may serve as an agent of change? Or does Genesis' message about the dangers of anger serve to prevent marginalized groups from becoming violent toward one another amid imperial pressures?

23. The phrase *prima facie* is an important qualification in this sentence. On close inspection, legal materials are not as congruent with abstract principles as one might assume (Rogerson, *Theory and Practice in Old Testament Ethics*, 17).

24. Barton, *Understanding Old Testament Ethics*, esp. chap. 4; see also chap. 5; idem, *Ethics and the Old Testament* (1st North American ed.; Harrisburg, PA: Trinity Press International, 1998); Gordon J. Wenham, *Story as Torah: Reading Old Testament Narrative Ethically* (Grand Rapids, MI: Baker Academic, 2000).

25. Mary E. Mills, *Biblical Morality: Moral Perspectives in Old Testament Narratives* (Aldershot: Ashgate, 2001) vii, 1; Robin Allinson Parry, *Old Testament Story and Christian Ethics: The Rape of Dinah as a Case Study* (Milton Keynes: Paternoster, 2004).

26. Even some earlier works display an awareness of the ethical diversity of Old Testament materials, such as Hempel, *Das Ethos des Alten Testaments*, and idem, "Ethics in the OT," *IDB*, esp. 2.154–57.

primary categories of ethical norms in the Old Testament: (1) norms that
God explicitly commands, (2) norms that conform to the moral qualities
present in the created order, and (3) norms that can be seen as ways of
imitating God.[27]

Other authors have gone much further in stressing the diversity of Old
Testament ethical materials, abandoning the search for a center or centers.
Cyril Rodd maintains on a general level the vast diversity of Old Testament
ethics. In *Glimpses of a Strange Land: Studies in Old Testament Ethics*, he "deliberately reject[s] an overall scheme, model, paradigm, dominant theme,
underlying principle, or any other attempt to discover a unifying motif
by means of which the ethics [of the Old Testament] can be packaged."[28]
David Pleins's *Social Visions of the Hebrew Bible* makes similar moves with
respect to social ethics. Explicitly seeking a postmodern understanding of
biblical social ethics, he argues that the Hebrew Bible is less a single system
of ethics and more "an anthology of theological diversity."[29]

Mary Mills also stresses the diversity of Old Testament ethics. However,
she does so not by focusing on the differences between the sources and
books of the Old Testament, as Rodd and Pleins do, but by arguing for the
multiplicity of meaning in a given text. When she examines the Abraha-
mic narrative, for example, she argues that the patriarch's moral life can be
interpreted in a variety of ways: as a pious individual, a comic character, a
trickster, a tragic figure, a savage parent, and an unworthy husband.[30] She
furthermore argues against a single interpretation trumping the others. She
writes, "morality, in any given text, is not a single message but consists of
a plethora of interpretations, some contradictory to others."[31] Obviously,
approaches such as those taken by Rodd, Pleins, and Mills are far removed
from the unifying tendencies seen with Kaiser.

7.1.4 Paradigmatic Approaches

A third creative advance pertains to the primary concern of ethics. A
number of biblical interpreters have argued against the modernist assumption that ethics is primarily an issue of outlining moral principles. Waldemar Janzen and Christopher Wright have, in their own ways, made the case
that the Old Testament imparts ethical resources less by offering abstract
principles and more by providing paradigms and models.[32] Throughout

---

27. Barton, *Understanding Old Testament Ethics*, esp. chaps. 1–3.

28. Rodd, *Glimpses of a Strange Land*, 3–4; see also pp. 159, 272.

29. J. David Pleins, *The Social Visions of the Hebrew Bible: A Theological Introduction* (Louisville: Westminster John Knox, 2000) 21.

30. Mills, *Biblical Morality*, 32–47. The above summary is a very close paraphrase of
Mills's language on various occasions.

31. Ibid., 243. Although Mills does not draw heavily on the writings of Mikhail
Bakhtin (pp. 258–59 contain one of the few references to him), her approach has some
similarities with his thoughts about polyvocality.

32. John Rogerson's *Theory and Practice in Old Testament Ethics* does not use the language of paradigms and models as prominently as Janzen's and Wright's works, but it is

Old Testament Ethics: A Paradigmatic Approach, Janzen argues that focusing on ethical principles is an incomplete exercise.[33] Instead, he turns to five loci of concern, which he terms "paradigms." He asserts that, although no particular character in the biblical text may serve as a perfect example, readers form in their minds ideal images with respect to various spheres of life. Thus, he examines "Israel's inner image" of the following:

1. "a loyal family member," that is, the familial paradigm;
2. "a dedicated worshiper," that is, the priestly paradigm;
3. "a wise manager of daily life," that is, the wisdom paradigm;
4. "a just ruler," that is, the royal paradigm; and
5. "an obedient proclaimer of the prophetic word," that is, the prophetic paradigm.[34]

Christopher Wright in his work *Old Testament Ethics for the People of God* also takes a paradigmatic approach but focuses on a single paradigm, Israel, rather than Janzen's five paradigms. He understands the term "paradigm" in a somewhat different sense than Janzen, seeing it as referring to both "the total conceptual matrix of Israel's faith" and "the concrete model by which Israel was to be an exemplar to the nations."[35] Wright argues that, just as grammatical paradigms provide a pattern that can be used in a nearly infinite variety of contexts, so the Old Testament provides the paradigm of Israel, which can be drawn on for ethical decisions in a vast variety of situations.[36]

7.1.5 Virtue in the Old Testament

Focusing on paradigms is not the only alternative to a focus on principles. A fourth advance in Old Testament ethics occurred as John Barton and Gordon Wenham, taking cues from Alasdair MacIntyre, argued that certain biblical texts, particularly narratives, provide ethical instruction by upholding virtues for readers to emulate.[37] Barton's essay "Virtue

---

worth mentioning here because it emphasizes repeatedly that the Old Testament offers resources less by providing principles and more by offering insightful examples. Paul Hanson also promotes a paradigmatic approach to the Old Testament. Hanson understands paradigms as events in the Bible that reveal the divine nature and are "treasured by the tradition through retelling, reinterpretation, and in special cases such as the Passover *sēder* or the Lord's Supper, through re-enactment that takes on sacramental significance" (Hanson, *The People Called: The Growth of Community in the Bible* [San Francisco: Harper & Row, 1986] 529–30).

33. Waldemar Janzen, *Old Testament Ethics: A Paradigmatic Approach* (Louisville: Westminster John Knox, 1994) 20.

34. Ibid.

35. Wright, *Old Testament Ethics for the People of God*, 431; see also pp. 66–70.

36. Ibid., 65–66.

37. Alasdair MacIntyre argues in favor of virtue ethics over against an Enlightenment approach to ethics (*After Virtue: A Study in Moral Theory* [2nd ed.; Notre Dame, IN: University of Notre Dame Press, 1984]).

in the Bible" raises the question whether the Bible displays concern for anything analogous to the interest in virtue ethics in recent times, which Barton nicely summarizes as (1) sometimes emphasizing being and dispositions more than a set of decisions, (2) stressing moral formation and development over time, (3) seeing moral rules "more as a distillation from many good decisions made by virtuous people than as laws operating in an abstract way," and (4) understanding the necessity of a moral vision for virtuous living.[38] Barton contends that, while books such as Proverbs and Deuteronomy display little affinity with this sort of approach to ethics, there are deeper resonances with the Bible's complex narratives, such as 1–2 Samuel. This essay by Barton is suggestive rather than comprehensive. For example, he does not undertake a full examination of the books of Samuel.[39] Wenham, meanwhile, goes further by developing a methodology and applying it. He posits three criteria for determining what an implied author of a given narrative upholds as a virtue: (1) a repeated behavior pattern, (2) appearance in a positive context, and (3) confirmation from legal codes, psalms, and wisdom books.[40] In *Story as Torah*, Wenham applies this method to Genesis.[41]

7.1.6 *Examining Ethos*

In line with this broader understanding of ethics as pertaining to more than principles, a fifth advance in Old Testament ethics occurred as biblical interpreters turned attention to the question of ethos—that is, the type of atmosphere envisioned by texts that is most conducive to right living.[42]

---

38. Barton, *Understanding Old Testament Ethics*, chap. 5, pp. 65–74. See pp. 65–66 for the quotation.

39. One should note that he does treat the David and Bathsheba narrative (2 Samuel 11–12) more fully in idem, *Ethics and the Old Testament*, 19–36.

40. Wenham, *Story as Torah*, 88–89.

41. Wenham also gives some attention to the book of Judges. Others have studied virtues in the book of Proverbs, including William P. Brown, *Character in Crisis: A Fresh Approach to the Wisdom Literature of the Old Testament* (Grand Rapids, MI: Eerdmans, 1996) esp. pp. 22–49 (see also pp. 134–43 for a discussion of Qoheleth); and Ellen F. Davis, "Preserving Virtues: Renewing the Tradition of the Sages," in *Character and Scripture: Moral Formation, Community, and Biblical Interpretation* (ed. William P. Brown; Grand Rapids, MI: Eerdmans, 2002) 183–201. Richard S. Briggs has also concerned himself with the Old Testament and virtues, although he does so with a primary interest in the virtues one brings to the act of reading the biblical text (*The Virtuous Reader: Old Testament Narrative and Interpretive Virtue* [Studies in Theological Interpretation; Grand Rapids, MI: Baker Academic, 2010]).

42. Some of the authors mentioned in the discussion of paradigmatic approaches also deal with the question of ethos. Janzen maintains that legal materials point beyond themselves to a more comprehensive ethos (*Old Testament Ethics*, 91). Rogerson is more reticent to use the language of "ethos," and yet, his appropriation of Habermasian discourse ethics, especially with respect to issues of *Lebenswelt*, has obvious points of continuity, such as the creation of an atmosphere most conducive to ideal living (*Theory and Practice in Old Testament Ethics*, 54–57).

Here, William Brown has played a significant role in his book *The Ethos of the Cosmos*, which examines five creation texts (Gen 1:1–2:4a, 2:4b–3:24; 2 Isaiah; Prov 8:22–31; and Job 38:4–41:26[34]), studying how creation is ordered in these texts and how an ordering of this sort relates to faithful living.[43] Works by Eckart Otto also move in this direction.[44]

7.2 Principles in Conflict

Understanding the ethical message of Genesis requires building on and qualifying these advances in Old Testament ethics. To begin, it is useful to turn to the matter of principles. While Genesis does give attention to ethical principles on explicit and implicit levels, it displays considerable awareness of their shortcomings. It tends to present ethical principles in conflict with one another, and it does not always offer easy solutions for resolving these conflicts (contra Rawls's emphasis on ordering ethical principles so that these conflicts can be easily resolved). The text of Genesis suggests that, while ethical principles are necessary, they are fairly obvious and often insufficient. Within the imperfect world it envisions, making a moral decision is frequently more difficult than simply following a moral maxim. One is hard pressed to extrapolate universal moral principles from this text that are always binding regardless of context.[45]

At times, the text of Genesis explicitly names commands that may sound initially as though they are universal moral principles. For example, the prohibition of bloodshed in Gen 9:6 is issued by God to all living humans, which suggests it has a universal appeal. Furthermore, the rationale given for this prohibition likewise has a broad appeal: bloodshed is prohibited because humanity is created in God's image. The rationale is not particular to Israel or another subset of humanity. Rather, it appeals to a characteristic assumed to be present among all humans. Because of who issues the com-

---

43. William P. Brown, *The Ethos of the Cosmos: The Genesis of Moral Imagination in the Bible* (Grand Rapids, MI: Eerdmans, 1999). He also discusses "the ethos of instruction" in Proverbs 1–9 in *Character in Crisis*, 30–33.

44. Eckart Otto, *Theologische Ethik des Alten Testaments* (Stuttgart: Kohlhammer, 1994). See also Hempel, *Das Ethos des Alten Testaments*; Wolfgang Richter, *Recht und Ethos: Versuch einer Ortung des weisheitlichen Mahnspruches* (Munich: Kösel, 1966). However, with these works, one must keep in mind that *Ethos* in German has a broader meaning than Brown's use of the English word *ethos* in his work. Whereas Brown is concerned with the settings conducive to moral formation, the German term *Ethos* refers to "the lived, embodied set of convictions and virtues and also customs/laws that characterize a particular moral community," which should not be confused with the German term *Ethik*, which refers to the discipline of reflecting on moral principles and the like without necessarily embodying them (Reinhard Huetter, private communication, Apr. 8, 2008).

45. As Jacqueline E. Lapsley puts it, "In the narrative worlds of the Old Testament easy moral judgments are elusive and most often miss the mark" (*Whispering the Word: Hearing Women's Stories in the Old Testament* [Louisville: Westminster John Knox, 2005] 11).

mand, who receives it, and the rationale undergirding it, the text appears to portray this prohibition as universally binding.[46]

Yet, in the course of Genesis, the universality of this prohibition is called into question. For example, when Lot is taken captive (14:12), Abram leads 318 trained soldiers against the captors to recover Lot and his goods. Using the verb נכה ('strike down', 14:15), the text leaves little doubt that the attack by Abram and his soldiers involved bloodshed.[47] However, rather than portraying Abram and his soldiers negatively, the text portrays the patriarch as motivated by the bonds of kinship (14:14a) and not by the prospect of personal gain (14:21–24).[48] Immediately following the battle, Abram does not receive condemnation but a blessing (14:18–20). The next narrative begins with YHWH's promising Abram "an exceedingly great reward" and descendents without number (15:1, 5). So, in this framework, the prohibition of bloodshed appears to conflict with the principles *Care for one's kin* and *Punish wrongdoing*. Abram, adhering to the last two principles, is blessed for his actions. At least in the final redacted form of Genesis, the seemingly universal command not to shed another's blood (9:6) is subject to qualification when it conflicts with other principles.[49]

One sees similar dynamics in Gen 18:17–33. Here, the deity does not issue eternally valid prescriptions that are binding in all situations and contexts. Rather, one reads about a bartering match between YHWH and Abraham over the fate of Sodom and Gomorrah. Uncertain about the ethics of YHWH's plan for extermination, Abraham raises a series of risky questions about what the deity has planned. Both parties in this dispute assume that the exceptionally grave sin of these cities merits punishment (assuming that it is verified by firsthand observation, 18:20–21). The text thus implies that both parties agree with the principle *Punish wrongdoing*.[50] However, when one moves to the specifics of punishment, there is disagreement. In 18:23, Abraham perceives a potential conflict between this principle and

---

46. Another example is the divine command given to all humans to be fruitful, multiply, and fill the earth (Gen 1:28; 9:1, 7). It is interesting that, with Abram and Sarai, readers encounter protagonists who are unable to fulfill this command—not because of their lack of willingness but because of forces beyond their control. This narrative qualifies the extent to which this command should be understood as universal. Beyond its second chapter, Genesis does not so much present an ideal world always conducive to ethical living as portray an imperfect world where characters encounter difficulties fully embodying moral principles.

47. The verb רדף ('pursue', 14:14–15) may also suggest the presence of bloodshed, because it frequently connotes an aggressive, military pursuit resulting in violence.

48. Hermann Gunkel, *Genesis: Translated and Interpreted* (Macon, GA: Mercer University Press, 1997, 1901) 281–82.

49. See the related points made by Harry Lesser, "'It's Difficult to Understand': Dealing with Morally Difficult Passages in the Hebrew Bible," in *Jewish Ways of Reading the Bible* (ed. George J. Brooke; JSSSup 11; Oxford: Oxford University Press, 2000) 298–302.

50. Victor P. Hamilton, *The Book of Genesis: Chapters 18–50* (NICOT; Grand Rapids, MI: Eerdmans, 1994) 25.

the principle *Do not punish the righteous*: "Will you actually sweep away the innocent with the wicked?" Like one uttering a complaint psalm (Psalms 6, 10, 13, 22, 35), Abraham essentially rebukes the deity, raising questions about YHWH's future actions and asking the deity to abide by the highest standards of human morality:[51] "Far be it from you to do such a thing—to kill the innocent with the wicked, to treat the innocent and wicked alike! Far be it from you! Shall not the judge of all the earth act justly?" (18:25). After several similar requests, YHWH eventually agrees to spare the city if it contains ten righteous individuals.

The passage illustrates, among other things, the complexity of enacting justice, even when the actors are none other than YHWH and Abraham. It shows that, while consensus can sometimes be reached about general principles (here, *Punish wrongdoing*), there are divergent understandings about how these principles are concretely enacted. The passage furthermore illustrates that two fairly obvious moral principles (*Punish wrongdoing* and *Do not punish the righteous*) can quickly come into conflict with one another amid the concrete realities of an ethical decision (see Gen 20:3–4 for an analogous scenario). This narrative does not offer a system that orders particular principles so that one knows which to follow when they are in conflict. Rather, this text offers a conversation between a mortal and the immortal, a conversation that displays, not so much an outright aversion to ethical principles but, rather, an awareness of their shortcomings and limitations.[52] It enters the difficult terrain where moral decisions lack easy resolution. It portrays ethical action not in terms of a straightforward implementation of right principles but, rather, in terms of a confrontation that takes place in an imperfect world.

Genesis is not an Enlightenment text, and so it may not be surprising that it has little continuity with an Enlightenment program of ethics. What is surprising, however, are the ways that Genesis resonates with thinkers in the last century who have criticized the Enlightenment. For example, Martha Nussbaum's *Love's Knowledge* conducts a thoroughgoing critique of rule- and principle-based ethical theories. Appealing to both classical thinkers (especially Aristotle) and modern writers (especially Henry James), she describes "the ethical crudeness of moralities based exclusively on

---

51. See the discussion in James L. Crenshaw, "The Sojourner Has Come to Play the Judge: Theodicy on Trial," in *God in the Fray: A Tribute to Walter Brueggemann* (ed. Tod Linafelt and Timothy K. Beal; Minneapolis: Fortress, 1998) 87; idem, *Defending God: Biblical Responses to the Problem of Evil* (New York: Oxford University Press, 2005) 89; R. N. Whybray, "'Shall Not the Judge of All the Earth Do What Is Just?' God's Oppression of the Innocent in the Old Testament," in *Shall Not the Judge of All the Earth Do What Is Right? Studies on the Nature of God in Tribute to James L. Crenshaw* (ed. David Penchansky and Paul L. Redditt; Winona Lake, IN: Eisenbrauns, 2000) 1–19, esp. p. 6.

52. As argued below (§8.3.4), conversation can play a key role in moral development. See also Rogerson, *Theory and Practice in Old Testament Ethics*, 7–8, 37–38, 46, chaps. 5–7, 15.

general rules." She maintains that ethical theories need to empower actors with greater freedom to improvise and respond to situations as they arise. Pre-formulated ethical rules, she maintains, fail to do justice to the complexities of particular situations. For example, they cannot account for what is new and unanticipated in given situations.[53] One sees similar limitations in Gen 18:17–33. The simple principle *Punish wrongdoing* is, at least in Abraham's mind, potentially insufficient for the particularities of the actual situation.

Mikhail Bakhtin's *Toward a Philosophy of the Act*, not unlike Nussbaum's work, displays great awareness of the shortcomings of basing one's ethics exclusively on rules and principles. Although this study has received surprisingly little attention by biblical scholars, it has some interesting points of continuity with a text like Gen 18:17–33.[54] This work undertakes a thorough critique of Kant's approach to ethics (and those undertaking similar enterprises). For Bakhtin, focusing exclusively on general ethical principles has problems because actual ethical decisions are never made on the plane of abstract generalities. Such a realm, Bakhtin maintains, is "not that unique Being in which we live and die, in which our answerable acts or deeds are performed; it is fundamentally and essentially alien to living historicity." This realm, Bakhtin avers, is an uninhabited, disembodied, and ultimately artificial world where it makes little difference whether one exists.[55] Bakhtin thinks that while there may be some limited value in general principles, they represent neither the fullest nor the ultimate focus of ethical concern. He maintains that a general ethical principle should be seen as "a rough draft of a possible actualization or an unsigned document that does not obligate anyone to do anything."[56] Rather than focusing on generalities, Bakhtin fixes his gaze on the concrete, unique, never-repeatable situations in which individuals have the responsibility to act as only they can act.[57]

While the book of Genesis may not go as far as Bakhtin in stressing the uniqueness of human experience, it joins him in displaying an awareness of the limitations of ethical principles. Instead of operating on the abstract level, it focuses on the concrete and often complicated cases in which individuals face a variety of limitations. This is clearly the case when one looks at texts pertaining to anger. The book of Genesis does little to offer

---

53. Nussbaum, *Love's Knowledge*, 37–40.

54. Mikhail Bakhtin, *Toward a Philosophy of the Act* (trans. Vadim Liapunov; Austin: University of Texas Press, 1993) 8. Barbara Green is one of the few to interact with this work, and even then the interaction is sparse and rather generic (*Mikhail Bakhtin and Biblical Scholarship* [Atlanta: Society of Biblical Literature, 2000] 13, 30 n. 6, 32 n. 9, 33 n. 11, 40, 45).

55. Bakhtin, *Toward a Philosophy of the Act*, 43.

56. Ibid., 44.

57. Ibid., 40. See also Gary Saul Morson and Caryl Emerson, *Mikhail Bakhtin: Creation of a Prosaics* (Stanford, CA: Stanford University Press, 1990) 25.

universal principles about this emotion. In Gen 49:5–7, Jacob condemns the anger of Simeon and Levi. However, as shown in §3.3 above, there is ambiguity about whether the brothers' anger and subsequent deeds have some justification, given both the narrator's condemnation of Shechem in 34:7 and the chapter's ending without challenging the brother's defense of their actions. As in Gen 18:17–33, Genesis 34 portrays a conflict between the principles *Punish wrongdoing* and *Do not punish the righteous*. If the brothers agree to Shechem's offer, then evildoing goes unpunished. Their alternative of killing the entire city appears to conflict with the principle *Do not punish the righteous*. Genesis does not offer a foolproof system of ordered principles that resolve complex situations of this sort. Instead, it is acutely aware of the ways that ethical norms have the potential to conflict amid life's events.

While there are texts within the Hebrew Bible that imply a bare minimum of ethical norms binding on all peoples, it frequently presents ethical ideas of a different type, viewing norms as bound to particular peoples and situations, not as general and universally binding.[58] Perhaps the most obvious example is Prov 26:4–5.[59] There, one finds two maxims with almost identical language. The first instructs the reader *not* to answer a fool in folly, while the second instructs the reader *to* answer a fool in folly. There is a logical contradiction when these words of advice are understood to be universal principles. However, it seems likely that the redactor(s) placed these proverbs beside one another not so they would cancel each other out but to show that such maxims need to be understood contextually. There are some times when it would be appropriate to answer fools according to their folly and others when it would be inappropriate to do so. The book of Proverbs, when viewed as a collection, is less about offering readers an enormous set of universal ethical principles than the collective wisdom of communities whose members participate in a shared humanity while displaying considerable variation. In some circumstances, a maxim can offer sound guidance—but not in all. A level of practical wisdom, what Aristotle called φρόνησις, but what the Hebrew Bible calls תבונה, is necessary to know which maxims can best guide one on particular occasions.[60] Their validity depends in no small part on their context.

---

58. Roland E. Murphy, *The Tree of Life: An Exploration of Biblical Wisdom Literature* (3rd ed.; Grand Rapids, MI: Eerdmans, 2002) 124–25. On texts that appear to imply a universal standard of morality, see Schlimm, "Teaching the Hebrew Bible amid the Current Human Rights Crisis;" Rogerson, *Theory and Practice in Old Testament Ethics*, 27.

59. For a useful discussion, see Peter Enns, *Inspiration and Incarnation: Evangelicals and the Problem of the Old Testament* (Grand Rapids, MI: Baker Academic, 2005) 76.

60. Aristotle, *Eth. nic.* 6.5; Michael V. Fox, "Words for Wisdom," *ZAH* 6 (1993) 149–69, esp. p. 153; Davis, "Preserving Virtues," esp. pp. 189–92. See also the important discussion of propriety in James L. Crenshaw, *Old Testament Wisdom: An Introduction* (rev. ed.; Louisville: Westminster John Knox, 1998) 11–12; as well as idem, "The Acquisition of Knowledge in Israelite Wisdom Literature," *WW* 7 (1987) esp. p. 248.

The importance of context is obvious not only with wisdom texts such as proverbs but also with law codes. The biblical evidence makes clear that legal materials are to an extent context-dependent, being reinterpreted in various ways and on various occasions.[61] Although there are obviously points of continuity between the various law codes of the Hebrew Bible, it is also clear that different circumstances at times called for different norms. On a micro-level, one sees that, while Exod 20:13 prohibits murder on a general level, other passages such as Exod 21:13 and Num 35:9–34 display an awareness of different circumstances' meriting a different punishment for individuals who kill another person.[62] On a macro-level, many have argued that some of the Hebrew Bible's law codes are reinterpretations of earlier ones. Thus, Eckart Otto sees Deuteronomy as a "modernizing interpretation of the Covenant code with cultic centralization as its hermeneutical key" and the Holiness Code (Leviticus 17–26) as "an exegetical harmonization of the Priestly Code, the Decalogue, the Covenant Code, and Deuteronomy."[63]

Turning more specifically to anger in Genesis—perhaps the closest Genesis comes to offering a guiding principle about anger is in Yhwh's words to Cain in Gen 4:7. When Cain becomes upset following the rejection of his offering, Yhwh speaks directly to him, asking why he is angry. Yhwh then utters the words, "Is it not true that if you do good, then a lifting up? But if you do not do good, then at the entryway to sin is a creature crouching down. Its craving is for you, but you can rule over it."[64] Unfortunately, this text is exceptionally difficult. A thorough treatment and interpretation appears below (§9.1). Here, however, it is obvious that the ethical instruction contained in this verse (when considered in isolation from context) is fairly vague. If the verse contains a universal principle, this principle would be essentially *Do what is right* or *Watch out for sin*. Truisms of this sort, placed on an abstract plane, are not of great value to individuals who are facing ethical decisions. As I will show, the words in this verse actually display considerable literary artistry and ethical richness. This richness is not evident, however, when the verse is reduced to generalities or is considered independently of the particularities of the book of Genesis.

The ethical concerns of Genesis, therefore, do not match the concern for universal principles found with the Enlightenment project. Occasionally, there may be a similarity (such as the prohibition of bloodshed), but the

---

61. Brevard S. Childs, *Biblical Theology of the Old and New Testaments: Theological Reflection on the Christian Bible* (Minneapolis: Fortress, 1992) 680–81; M. Gilbert, J. L'Hour, and J. Scharbert, *Morale et Ancien Testament* (Louvain-la-Neuve: Université Catholique de Louvain, 1976) 46, 78.

62. Rogerson, *Theory and Practice in Old Testament Ethics*, 8, 27; see also p. 19.

63. Eckart Otto, "Of Aims and Methods in Hebrew Bible Ethics," *Semeia* 66 (1994) 161–72, esp. pp. 163–64.

64. This translation presupposes a slight repointing of the MT, which is explained in §9.1.

text of Genesis is keenly aware of the shortcomings of ethical principles and their potential to conflict with one another. The narratives of Genesis are far removed from Aesop's fables. That is to say, their primary purpose is not to illustrate a single moral point. This option was available to the authors and redactors of Genesis. The literature of the ancient Near East, for example, includes some stories that resemble the genre for which Aesop is so well known. The Hittite myth of "Appu and His Two Sons" provides an excellent case in point (*COS*, 1.58:153–55). This narrative contains a number of parallels with the text of Genesis. However, it exhibits a simplistic understanding of moral principles in contrast to the more complex treatment found in Genesis. In this story, the wealthy but childless Appu is visited by a god and promised offspring (compare Abram in Gen 15:2). His wife conceives while he is intoxicated (compare Lot in Gen 19:31–36). She gives birth to a son who is named Wrong and later becomes pregnant again, giving birth to a second son named Right (compare Cain and Abel in Gen 4:1–8). These two have disputes over land and decide to settle in different locations (compare Abram and Lot in Gen 13:7–12). The two brothers divide their cattle, with Wrong taking a healthy ox and giving an unhealthy cow to his brother. Although Brother Right receives the unhealthy animal, divine forces heal his sick animal and cause him to prosper (compare Jacob and Laban in Gen 30:25–31:12). Next, the brothers appear before the Sun God, seeking justice. The Sun God awards judgment to Brother Right. Brother Wrong in turn curses, so the Sun God refers the matter to Šawuška.[65] The episode involving this final arbitration has been lost.

The *proemium* of this story is particularly noteworthy for our discussion of principles: "He/she it is (i.e., some deity) who always exonerates just men, but chops down evil men like trees, repeatedly striking evil men on their skulls (like) . . .s until he/she destroys them." In this prologue, one sees the morals and main points of the entire story: the divine will *punish wrongdoing* and *exonerate the righteous*, so humans should *avoid wrongdoing* and *pursue righteousness*. The prologue is quite similar to the moral-filled epilogues found at the end of Aesop's fables. One senses that, while the story of Appu illustrates these principles, the principles are of primary importance. The story serves the secondary role of exemplifying them. The principles *Punish wrongdoing* and *The righteous should be exonerated* are not shown to be in conflict with one another. Nor are they shown to have many shortcomings. In the book of Genesis, by contrast, one sees greater complexity. Although similar *theological* points are made by Genesis and the myth of Appu,[66] texts such as Gen 18:17–33 present a more complex *ethical* picture, demonstrating that these same two principles (*Punish wrong-*

---

65. For more on Šawuška, see M. Hutter, "Shaushka," *DDD* 758–59.
66. For example, divine forces cause both Right and Jacob (Gen 30:25–31:12) to prosper even though human forces seek to undermine them.

doing and *Exonerate the righteous*) have the potential to conflict in ways that are not easily resolvable.[67]

7.3 The Problems with Paradigms, Models, Virtues, and Ethos

If Genesis is not primarily about offering its readers clear-cut ethical principles, then how does it offer ethical guidance? Do the paradigmatic approaches implemented by Waldemar Janzen and Christopher Wright provide the answer? Is the virtue-oriented approach upheld by John Barton and Gordon Wenham preferable? Should one instead follow in the footsteps of William Brown, focusing on ethos? While all of these works made significant advances in moving beyond the Enlightenment's preoccupation with moral principles, they also display weaknesses and shortcomings, particularly when applied to Genesis.[68]

7.3.1 Paradigms Revisited

The paradigmatic approach has several problems. First, although Janzen and Wright are aware of the Hebrew Bible's diversity, their writings sometimes do not go far enough to acknowledge this diversity.[69] Janzen, for example, speaks of the familial paradigm (as though there is only one), giving insufficient attention to the way that different texts display different ethical presuppositions about how family members should behave.[70] Wright arguably does better in exhibiting an awareness of the Hebrew Bible's historical and theological diversity.[71] Nevertheless, he makes questionable moves at

---

67. One wonders whether the book of Genesis is not in some way parodying "Appu and His Two Sons," making obvious parallels with the story while also presenting a far more complex moral understanding.

Incidentally, one can note that the book of Job displays something quite similar to Genesis: it assumes that the principle of divine retribution is a universal principle, but then this assumption is called into question throughout the ensuing dialogues (Crenshaw, *Old Testament Wisdom*, 95–109). Likewise, the book of Joshua appears at first glance to take for granted the principles of Deuteronomy (such as Deut 7:1–2), but then it subjects these principles to various questions and qualifications (Ellen F. Davis, "The Poetics of Generosity," in *The Word Leaps the Gap: Essays on Scripture and Theology in Honor of Richard B. Hays* [ed. R. Wagner, K. Rowe, and A. K. Grieb; Grand Rapids, MI: Eerdmans, 2008] 626–45, esp. pp. 630–39).

68. These problems are less prominent in other books of the Bible. For example, paradigms and models can help one understand the interrelation of laws in Leviticus.

69. See, by contrast, Pleins, *The Social Visions of the Hebrew Bible*, passim.

70. For example, whereas Exod 20:12 commands one to honor one's parents, a narrative such as 1 Sam 19:11–17 illustrates the complexities of following such a command, particularly when one's father is attempting to murder one's spouse. For more on the conflict between "filial devotion and erotic attachment," see the excellent discussion in James L. Crenshaw, *Samson: A Secret Betrayed, A Vow Ignored* (Atlanta: John Knox, 1978) esp. chap. 2. The Hebrew Bible does not present a single, unified familial paradigm so much as it presents several varying examples.

71. For example, in examining Israel as a political model, he admits that interpreters need to wrestle with the question "which Israel and when?" as well as the "apparently

times. Thus, many might agree with him that Israel, at its best moments in the textual world of the Old Testament, is exemplary. However, a great number of scholars would disagree with the ways Wright affirms that Israel's "whole concrete existence in history is paradigmatic."[72] Wright could do much more to acknowledge the difference between the textual world of the Old Testament and the historical practices of ancient Israel.

Second, if a book such as Genesis provides ethical instruction by imparting paradigms and models to its readers, why does it not provide clearer paradigms and models? Admitting that characters such as Abraham, Moses, and David are not in themselves models to emulate, Janzen maintains that their right actions collectively contribute in the minds of readers to an image of what ideal ethical living entails.[73] There is, however, a qualitative difference between what Janzen seeks to do and what a text like Genesis seeks to do. The narratives of Genesis appear less concerned with presenting ideals and more concerned with portraying human beings who are never ideal. Even though Genesis occasionally labels individuals righteous (Noah, 6:9, 7:1; Abraham, 15:6; Tamar, 38:26), these people are certainly not perfect. Moreover, the text nowhere suggests that, if readers saw the image of an ideal family member, they would somehow gain the capacity to act in ideal ways themselves. Gen 18:19, for example, says that Abraham will guide his descendents toward righteousness and justice by his commands, not by his example.

Likewise, Wright's upholding of Israel as a model has problems. Although he admits, "Israel failed to be all they believed themselves called to be in terms of their own covenant, law and social institutions," his primary emphasis is on the positive ways that Israel's faith serves as a model.[74] The Hebrew Bible, by comparison, tends to present Israel's faith as falling far short of divine expectations.[75] In this sense, the Hebrew Bible is concerned with ethics in a much broader sense than Janzen and Wright emphasize. It focuses on not only right actions but also the limitations and temptations that impede ethical living. In other words, taking an approach to the Old Testament that focuses on positive examples (and turns negative

---

contradictory viewpoints" between various texts (Wright, *Old Testament Ethics for the People of God*, 219).

72. Ibid., 68. For example, Otto states explicitly, "The actual behavior of Israelites and Judeans cannot be the subject matter of an ethics of the Hebrew Bible" ("Of Aims and Methods in Hebrew Bible Ethics," 162).

73. Janzen, *Old Testament Ethics*, 8–9, 27–28.

74. This quotation comes from Wright, *Old Testament Ethics for the People of God*, 68.

75. The most common theme in the Latter Prophets is the sinfulness of Israel and Judah. Similarly, the Deuteronomistic History condemns the majority of Israel's and Judah's kings. Late liturgical prayers often mention the sinfulness of the people. Even a text such as Joshua arguably displays a level of "disquiet" with the ethics of slaughtering the indigenous population, as astutely pointed out by Lawson Stone, "Ethical and Apologetic Tendencies in the Redaction of the Book of Joshua," *CBQ* 53 (1991) 25–35.

examples into positive ones by negation [see Janzen's account of "models and countermodels"[76]]) is an incomplete treatment of the ethics of the Hebrew Bible. Among other things, scholars who expound biblical ethics need to do more to acknowledge the extent of human and circumstantial evil, which obviously is a chief concern of many texts.[77] The Hebrew Bible instructs readers not only about how one should live but also about the limitations that individuals face in pursuing ethical goals.

Finally, although both Janzen and Wright stress that biblical ethicists must be concerned with much more than principles, their paradigms sound, at times, very much like a set of principles. Wright defines a paradigm as "a model or pattern that enables you to explain or critique many different and varying situations by means of some single concept or set of governing principles."[78] Janzen quotes Wright's principle-focused definition of paradigms, offering only relatively minor qualifications.[79] Though Janzen and Wright strongly oppose focusing only on principles, contending that their paradigms offer an improvement, readers of their works are at times left wondering how their paradigms guide moral living other than through the paradigms' constituent principles.[80]

7.3.2 Virtues Revisited

Gordon Wenham's approach to virtues displays many of the same types of problems, while Barton's work is fairly incomplete.[81] At times, Wenham appears insufficiently aware of the Hebrew Bible's ethical diversity. For example, one of the methodological steps that he proposes for determining the virtues upheld by a narrative is turning to nonnarrative texts elsewhere in the canon for confirmation.[82] This step presupposes that different texts uphold the same virtues, which is not necessarily the case.[83] Second, his

---

76. Janzen, *Old Testament Ethics*, 36.

77. This is not to say that these authors are ignorant of the grim picture that the Bible paints about evil and sin (see, for example, Wright, *Old Testament Ethics for the People of God*, 150–53). Rather, the point is that these negative emphases do not, on the whole, receive sufficient attention.

78. Ibid., 63.

79. Janzen actually quotes an earlier work by Wright that emphasizes the role of principles in paradigms even more: "A paradigm is something used as a model or example for other cases where a basic principle remains unchanged, though details differ" (Christopher J. H. Wright, *An Eye for an Eye: The Place of Old Testament Ethics Today* [Downers Grove, IL: InterVarsity, 1983] 43, quoted in Janzen, *Old Testament Ethics*, 26–27).

80. Wright seems aware of this problem, but he does not offer a fully satisfactory solution (*Old Testament Ethics for the People of God*, 70).

81. Barton's work offers suggestive proposals but not a full treatment that includes a textual application of these proposals. Barton moves in this direction by treating 2 Samuel 11–12 (*Ethics and the Old Testament*, 19–36). Although his treatment is quite rich, this particular narrative (David and Bathsheba) has some fairly obvious ethical implications. One wishes he would engage the ethical dimensions of many other texts.

82. Wenham, *Story as Torah*, 88–89.

83. Pleins thoroughly illustrates this point in *The Social Visions of the Hebrew Bible*.

compilation of the virtues upheld by Genesis seems flat, one-dimensional, and markedly different from what one finds in the text itself. Summarizing the virtues of Genesis, he writes:

> [The righteous person] is pious, that is prayerful and dependent on God. Strong and courageous, but not aggressive or mean. He or she is generous, truthful and loyal, particularly to other family members. The righteous person is not afraid to express emotions of joy, grief or anger, but the last should not spill over into excessive revenge, rather he should be ready to forgive. Finally righteousness does not require asceticism: the pleasures of life are to be enjoyed without becoming a slave to them.[84]

Although Wenham argues that narratives such as Genesis can do justice to the complexities of the moral life, his account of virtues in the Bible's first book does not.[85] Just as there is a sharp contrast between the ideal image of a family member posited by Janzen and the family members of Genesis, so there is a marked difference between Genesis' complex characters and the catalog of virtues upheld by Wenham. A final problem with Wenham's work is that on occasion he also reduces complex narratives to ethical principles. For example, he indicates that the Jacob cycle (25:19–35:29) and the Joseph story (37:2–50:26) suggest to readers "that they too should forgive even their long-term enemies, if they show sincere contrition."[86] As I will shown in chap. 12, the moral message of these two massive sections of texts is much more complex than this moral cliché put forward by Wenham.[87] One should not criticize Wenham too much for making these types of comments, which are summaries (not comprehensive totalities) of what he finds in the texts. At the same time, one wonders if there are ways of doing greater justice to the complexities of moral living.[88]

7.3.3 Ethos Revisited

In comparison with the paradigmatic and virtue approaches by Janzen, Wright, and Wenham, analyses of ethos in the Old Testament tend to do

---

84. Wenham, *Story as Torah*, 100.

85. See ibid., 13–14.

86. Ibid., 38.

87. See also Theo L. Hettema, *Reading for Good: Narrative Theology and Ethics in the Joseph Story from the Perspective of Ricoeur's Hermeneutics* (Kampen: Kok Pharos, 1996) 312–14.

88. One should also note that there are other obvious differences between virtue ethics as advanced by MacIntyre (who influenced Wenham) and the key emphases of the Hebrew Bible. For example, virtue ethics is concerned with issues of "selfhood" and "identity" (MacIntyre, *After Virtue*, 216–17; Robert C. Roberts, "Narrative Ethics," in *A Companion to Philosophy of Religion* [ed. Philip L. Quinn and Charles Taliaferro; Cambridge, MA: Blackwell, 1997] 473–80, esp. p. 474; Stanley Hauerwas, "Character, Narrative, and Growth in the Christian Life," in *Toward Moral and Religious Maturity: The First International Conference on Moral and Religious Development* [Morristown, NJ: Silver Burdett, 1980] 461). At least explicitly, the Hebrew Bible does not share this same concern. When writers and narrators express concern for one's נפש, the text usually has in mind the preservation of life, not the integrity of the self.

better. William Brown recognizes the diversity of Old Testament texts. For example, he does not speak at times as though there is one ethos reflective of the entire Old Testament. Furthermore, in turning to the issue of ethos, he clearly has a much broader understanding of ethics than the principle-based approach seen in Kaiser or even the paradigmatic and virtue-oriented approaches seen in Janzen, Wright, and Wenham. Moreover, it is clear that Brown is examining a topic with which the texts themselves are concerned. The issue of ethos is, for example, of great importance to Genesis 1–2.

Nevertheless, in terms of the role of anger in the book of Genesis, there is something missing in Brown's work. Brown defines *ethos* as "the setting that is conducive for the formation of a community's character."[89] However, most of Genesis is concerned with a world and setting that does not appear particularly conducive to forming character. His examination of the type of ethos presupposed by Gen 1:1–2:4a and 2:4b–3:24 is appropriate, given that these texts (at least chaps. 1–2) do portray worlds conducive to moral living, the former being called "very good" and the latter displaying utopian characteristics.[90] However, most of Genesis is concerned with a realm very different from the relatively ideal visions found in the opening chapters. Humanity is expelled from Eden to inhabit a world of fratricide. The evil of humanity is so great that even a worldwide flood cannot wash it away, as Gen 9:18–29 and 11:1–9 vividly illustrate. Rather than portraying humanity with the freedom to design and achieve their own moral excellence, Genesis presents people inhabiting a world they did not create and do not fully comprehend or control. While the book of Genesis does not present moral formation as impossible, it does present a world with serious moral obstacles and ethical dilemmas. Character formation does not come easily, and many fail along the way. Strife is a topic that the text returns to time and again. Although Brown does not ignore texts such as Genesis 3–4 (or even 9:18–29), he does give insufficient attention to some questions.[91] In particular, how do individuals make morally laudable decisions when they are not in settings conducive to doing this? It is possible to build on the work of Brown by examining the challenges of the world envisioned by the text.

The issue of ethos is essential to determining the approach one takes to ethics. If one presupposes that the world is consistently ordered in a way that is transparent to human beings, then it makes sense to view ethics as an exercise in determining this order and formulating moral principles based on this order. On the other hand, if one presupposes an imperfect world, then a rule-based approach makes little sense, and one must turn

---

89. Brown, *The Ethos of the Cosmos*, 11.

90. Steven James Schweitzer, "Utopia and Utopian Literary Theory: Some Preliminary Observations," in *Utopia and Dystopia in Prophetic Literature* (ed. Ehud Ben Zvi; Helsinki: Finnish Exegetical Society, 2006) 15 nn. 7, 9.

91. Brown, *The Ethos of the Cosmos*, 144–74, 179–81.

to other ways of approaching ethics. Bernard Williams draws this type of distinction when comparing the ethics of Greek philosophy and its heirs with the ethics of Greek tragedy:

> Plato, Aristotle, Kant, Hegel are all on the same side, all believing in one way or another that the universe or history or the structure of human reason can, when properly understood, yield a pattern that makes sense of human life and human aspirations. Sophocles and Thucydides, by contrast, are alike in leaving us with no such sense. Each of them represents human beings as dealing sensibly, foolishly, sometimes catastrophically, sometimes nobly, with a world that is only partially intelligible to human agency and in itself is not necessarily well adjusted to ethical aspirations.[92]

On the whole, the moral vision of the world offered by Genesis has more affinity with Sophocles and Thucydides than with their philosophical counterparts. Though its opening chapters present a carefully ordered world, the chapters that follow present a world that humans struggle to understand and master ethically. With the loss of Eden, the world's order has become partially undone, and humanity's capacity for perceiving this order has been impaired. This sort of world calls not for a relentless focus on principles but, rather, a reflection on the complexity and difficulty of the moral life.

7.4 Conclusion

Many works on Old Testament ethics have made progress by moving beyond the narrowness of the Enlightenment's vision of ethics. At the same time, they have focused on questions that may not be the best suited for examining the teachings of Genesis about anger. Biblical ethicists such as Janzen have wanted to know:

> *What is the* ideal *ethical image (singular) put forth by the text?*

However, a better question for Genesis is:

> *What are the* realistic *ethical images (plural) put forth by the text?*

Interpreters such as Janzen, Wright, and Wenham have focused on questions of this sort:

> *What positive models and virtues does the text uphold for emulation?*

However, one needs to inquire more broadly:

> *How does the narrative equip readers with a better understanding of the world's ethical dynamics, wherein goodness and evil are frequently intertwined?*

One cannot stop with merely asking Brown's question about ethos:

---

92. Bernard Williams, *Shame and Necessity* (Berkeley: University of California Press, 1993) 163–64.

What type of environment does the text presuppose is conducive to moral formation?

Genesis invites readers also to ask:

What factors, internal and external, impede the realization of moral goodness by characters?

Attending to these alternate and additional questions allows interpreters to come closer to understanding the ethical message of Genesis on its own terms.

Chapter 8

Ethics, Emotion, and Experience: The Power of Stories

The preceding discussion has examined approaches that are not necessarily the best for understanding the ethical message of Genesis. Although the questions posed at the end of the last chapter move toward positive ways of understanding this message, it is possible to be more specific and articulate clearly the ways in which Genesis instructs readers ethically. Turning to a variety of literary, philosophical, and critical theorists, I will now make the case that a complex narrative such as Genesis is particularly suited for treating a topic such as the ethics of anger. Some of the most useful resources for understanding the ethical message of Genesis are the works of Mikhail Bakhtin, Paul Ricoeur, Jean-François Lyotard, Martha Nussbaum, Wayne Booth, and Kenneth Burke. While none of these thinkers offers an approach to narrative or ethics that aligns perfectly with the ways that ethics are conceived in Genesis, their alternatives and modifications to traditional Enlightenment emphases provide useful heuristic models that resonate in different ways with this text.

8.1 Mimesis: Fictive Reality

I begin with the foundational concept of *mimesis*.[1] The fundamental idea is that narrative is essentially an imitation of life.[2] Thus, individuals in narrative converse in the way that they do in real life; they act as actual people act; they experience the same things that readers experience; they confront problems in the ways that most sensible individuals confront problems.[3] Building on this idea and drawing on the work of Paul Ricoeur, Robin Parry speaks of the "proto-narrative structure" of human life, maintaining that lived experience "calls out to be narrated."[4]

---

1. For a classic account of mimesis, which includes a discussion of Genesis 22, see Erich Auerbach, *Mimesis: The Representation of Reality in Western Literature* (trans. Willard R. Trask; fiftieth-anniversary ed.; Princeton: Princeton University Press, 2003) esp. pp. 3–23.

2. Bruce C. Birch, *Let Justice Roll Down: The Old Testament, Ethics, and Christian Life* (Louisville: Westminster John Knox, 1991) 53–65. See also the account of what is typical of narrative in D. M. Gunn and Danna Nolan Fewell, *Narrative in the Hebrew Bible* (Oxford Bible Series; Oxford: Oxford University Press, 1993) chap. 1.

3. Barbara Hardy, "Towards a Poetics of Fiction: 3) An Approach through Narrative," *Novel: A Forum on Fiction* 2 (1968) 5.

4. Robin Allinson Parry, *Old Testament Story and Christian Ethics: The Rape of Dinah as a Case Study* (Milton Keynes: Paternoster, 2004) 11. See also Alasdair MacIntyre, *After*

Elaborating on the concept of mimesis, Paul Ricoeur undermines the common assumption that fiction is unreal. This assumption is true on the level of first-order reference—that is, referring to events that happened in history. However, it is not true, Ricoeur maintains, on the level of second-order reference. There, fictional narratives refer to reality less by describing particular people and more by describing and redescribing the logical structure of human experience.[5] Thus, whether a narrative reflects historical events or is completely imaginative, it can mimic real life. Some fantasies, as Bakhtin and Dostoevsky have noted, are the most realistic and most truthful works we will ever encounter.[6] In fiction, even exaggerations and things that are blatantly unreal can serve to illuminate human nature.[7]

The book of Genesis, by participating in narrative, functions not as *mere fiction*, but rather as a collection of realistic depictions of the types of events that can and do take place in life.[8] Attempts to see Genesis as historically accurate quickly run into problems.[9] However, the ethical value of this work is tied less to its accuracy as history and more to its function as mimesis. To use Ricoeur's language, its degree of second-order referentiality (that

---

Virtue: A Study in Moral Theory (2nd ed.; Notre Dame, IN: University of Notre Dame Press, 1984) 211.

5. Paul Ricoeur, "The Narrative Function," *Semeia* 13 (1978) 177–202. See also Aristotle, *Poet.* 6, §1450a15; H. Richard Niebuhr, "The Story of Our Life," in *Why Narrative? Readings in Narrative Theology* (ed. Stanley Hauerwas and L. Gregory Jones; Eugene, OR: Wipf & Stock, 1997) 21–44.

6. Mikhail Bakhtin, *Problems of Dostoevsky's Poetics* (Minneapolis: University of Minnesota Press, 1984) 55. One is reminded here of Wayne Booth's comment that some texts "will be, *as* fictions, the most precious truths we ever know" (*The Company We Keep: An Ethics of Fiction* [Berkeley: University of California Press, 1988] 345).

7. Robert C. Roberts, "Narrative Ethics," in *A Companion to Philosophy of Religion* (ed. Philip L. Quinn and Charles Taliaferro; Cambridge, MA: Blackwell, 1997) 474.

8. Granted, there are sections of Genesis that clearly depict a different time that has less commonality with the present realm. One thinks not only of texts such as the Eden narrative, but also Gen 6:1–4, which clearly belongs to a different age with its remark, 'These were the heroes *of old*' (הֵמָּה הַגִּבֹּרִים אֲשֶׁר מֵעוֹלָם, italics mine, v. 4). While such differences exist, there are many areas of commonality. Eden may be lost, as well as the antediluvian world, but as their names suggest, אדם (Adam, meaning 'humanity') and חוה (Eve, meaning 'life') are representations of *humanity* as a whole, not bygone figures of a past age (see §8.3.1 below).

9. Genesis obviously reflects the time period when its texts were written and compiled, and it appears to offer some glimpses into historical features of the ancestral period (see Ronald S. Hendel, *Remembering Abraham: Culture, Memory, and History in the Hebrew Bible* [New York: Oxford University Press, 2005] 45–55, 135–39). It may even align with ancient ways of writing history (John Van Seters, *Prologue to History: The Yahwist as Historian in Genesis* [Louisville: Westminster John Knox, 1992]). However, there are problems with the notion that, in order for Genesis to be meaningful or sacred, it must be a historically accurate account of everything that happened in and before the second millennium. There is no reason Scripture needs to be confined to *history* in the modern sense of the word. Its sacred value depends more on how well it characterizes humanity and divinity than how well it aligns with historical details.

is, how well it depicts human nature) is of greater ethical significance than its degree of first-order referentiality (that is, how well it recounts historical occurrences). By persuasively portraying archetypal features of human nature, Genesis invites its readers to envision themselves within its textual world and to make transferences from this world to their own.[10]

Understanding a narrative such as Genesis to function mimetically is not to say that all readers experience events just as the characters in the narrative. It is, however, to say that there are sufficient points of commonality that readers can forge relationships between what they read and what they experience.[11] Although each individual life is unique, it bears points of continuity with other lives, actual and imagined. As Booth puts it, life stories fit within various genres that are not limitless in number.[12] Or, as Kenneth Burke describes in his work "Literature as Equipment for Living," narrative functions much like proverbial sayings: it seeks to chart social situations that are common and recurrent, providing strategies by instructing readers in matters such as what to expect and when to be cautious. He writes that literature "singles out a pattern of experience that is sufficiently representative of our social structure, that recurs sufficiently often *mutatis mutandis*, for people to 'need a word for it' and to adopt an attitude towards it."[13] Readers will certainly perceive differences between what they read and what they actually encounter, but they will also discover sufficient similarities for narratives to provide guidance of various types, including moral instruction.

Because of the narrative contours of human experience, many theorists make epistemological claims about the power of narrative. In rhetorical criticism, Walter Fisher describes "narrative rationality," which he sees as broader than traditional logics, providing warrants for beliefs and action. Affirming Alasdair MacIntyre's characterization of the human being as essentially a "story-telling animal," Fisher maintains that humanity is always pursuing a narrative logic: "all forms of discourse can be considered stories, that is, interpretation of some aspect of the world occurring in time and shaped by history, culture, and character."[14]

---

10. See Paul Ricoeur, *The Symbolism of Evil* (trans. Emerson Buchanan; New York: Harper & Row, 1967) 235–36.

11. Martha C. Nussbaum, *Love's Knowledge: Essays on Philosophy and Literature* (New York: Oxford University Press, 1990) 95; Mary E. Mills, *Biblical Morality: Moral Perspectives in Old Testament Narratives* (Aldershot: Ashgate, 2001) 11.

12. Booth, *The Company We Keep*, 289.

13. Kenneth Burke, "Literature as Equipment for Living," in *The Philosophy of Literary Form* (rev. ed.; New York: Vintage, 1957) 253–62, esp. pp. 254–56, 259.

14. Walter R. Fisher, "Narration, Knowledge, and the Possibility of Wisdom," in *Rethinking Knowledge: Reflections across the Disciplines* (ed. Robert F. Goodman and Walter R. Fisher; Albany: State University of New York, 1995) 170; see also MacIntyre, *After Virtue*, 216.

In philosophical circles, Jean-François Lyotard makes similar claims, distinguishing scientific knowledge from narrative knowledge and asserting, "Narration is the quintessential form of customary knowledge."[15] He explains that, although science has achieved a place of prominence in the modern world, influencing for example the shape of ethical and political discourse, it has many limitations and never represents the totality of knowledge. Lyotard sees knowledge as much broader, encompassing such topics as justice, happiness, and beauty. In sharp contrast to scientific knowledge, which is incapable of adequately addressing such matters, narrative knowledge is particularly suited for dealing with these subjects.[16]

Narratives provide so many valuable ethical resources that individuals at times fall into the danger of exaggerating their importance.[17] Thus, the point to stress is that narrative has an essential role to play in ethics—not that it has the solitary role.[18] After all, stories do not always lead readers on to admirable ends.[19] For this reason, Booth suggests that readers neither naïvely trust the text nor skeptically retain a distance, but rather "pursue a two-stage kind of reading, surrendering as fully as possible on every occasion, but then deliberately supplementing, correcting, or refining our experience with the most powerful ethical or ideological criticism we can manage."[20] An approach of this sort allows one to appreciate the value of narrative without being misguided about its shortcomings.

8.2 Narrative and Anger

Even with its limitations, narrative is particularly useful for tackling the topic of the ethics of anger. There are several reasons. First, emotions themselves tend to have a narrative structure.[21] Consider, for example, the

---

15. Jean-François Lyotard, *The Postmodern Condition: A Report on Knowledge* (trans. Geoff Bennington and Brian Massumi; Minneapolis: University of Minnesota Press, 1984) 18; see also pp. 7–8.

16. Ibid., 60.

17. There are reasons for having reservations about Stanley Hauerwas's claim that "Narrative is the form of God's salvation" (*The Peaceable Kingdom: A Primer in Christian Ethics* [Notre Dame, IN: University of Notre Dame Press, 1983] 28), as well as the thesis "Scripture is rightly understood . . . as a coherent dramatic narrative" (Ellen F. Davis and Richard B. Hays, eds., *The Art of Reading Scripture* [Grand Rapids, MI: Eerdmans, 2003] 1). One can affirm the necessity of narrative for framing and understanding human experience without elevating it to an all-encompassing level that displays insufficient awareness of its shortcomings and limitations. There is no need for dissolving the idea of narrative into something so broad it encompasses the entire Bible or all of human experience.

18. Genesis is joined with various legal materials within the Pentateuch, and this union can be seen as a complimentary pairing rather than a violent clash. The narrative and legal materials qualify and clarify each other in a variety of ways.

19. Booth, *The Company We Keep*, 159–67.

20. Ibid., 280–81. See also the excellent discussion in ibid., chaps. 6–8.

21. Parry, *Old Testament Story and Christian Ethics*, 37–38. See also Stanley Hauerwas and L. Gregory Jones, eds., *Why Narrative? Readings in Narrative Theology* (Eugene, OR: Wipf & Stock, 1997) 13.

prototypical account of anger in the Hebrew Bible outlined in chap. 4: one can fairly easily speak about the cause of anger, the subject who becomes angry, the object toward whom the anger is directed, and the result of anger. More specifically, one can describe anger as prototypically having a narrative-like genre, or at least common plot elements: someone perceives that a wrongdoing has taken place and experiences anger toward the party deemed responsible, which typically results in verbal confrontation, violence, or separation. Because of this narrative structure, stories are particularly useful media for instructing readers about the nature of emotion. Martha Nussbaum explains:

> [T]he evaluative beliefs that ground our emotional life are not learned in logical arguments. . . . They are learned through exposure—usually very early and very habitual—to complex social forms of life, in which these beliefs and the related emotions are housed, so to speak, and by which, for the individuals who learn them, they are constructed. A child does not learn its society's conception of love, or of anger, by sitting in an ethics class. It learns them long before any classes, in complex interactions with parents and society. . . . And, since we are all tellers of stories, and since one of the child's most pervasive and powerful ways of learning its society's values and structures is through the stories it hears and learns to tell, stories will be a major source of any culture's emotional life. . . .
> . . . [T]he whole story of an emotion, in its connections with other emotions and forms of life, requires narrative form for its full development.[22]

Because of the narrative structure of emotions, stories play an indispensible role in teaching readers and listeners about them.

Second and related, narrative is useful for engaging a topic such as the ethics of anger because it can give readers the opportunity to experience anger and other emotions in the course of their reading.[23] Although readers of fiction know that they are not reading of events that historically occurred, they also sense, because of the mimetic function of narrative, that the events about which they read are realistic possibilities for human beings. Hence, they can experience powerful emotions even while reading

---

22. Nussbaum, *Love's Knowledge*, 293, 296; see also p. 287. For more on how stories concretely teach the scripts undergirding emotions, see Peter Stearns's excellent account of Victorian children's books (*American Cool: Constructing a Twentieth-Century Emotional Style* [New York: New York University Press, 1994] chap. 2).

23. As Martha C. Nussbaum puts it, "Literature is in league with the emotions. Readers of novels, spectators of dramas, find themselves led by these works to fear, to grief, to pity, to anger, to joy and delight, even to passionate love. Emotions are not just likely responses to the content of many literary works; they are built into their very structure, as ways in which literary forms solicit attention" (*Poetic Justice: The Literary Imagination and Public Life* [Boston: Beacon, 1995] 53). See also the thesis advanced by Karl Allen Kuhn that "Affective appeal in varying forms is the means by which narratives compel us to enter their storied world and entertain the version of reality they present" (*The Heart of Biblical Narrative: Rediscovering Biblical Appeal to the Emotions* [Minneapolis: Fortress, 2009] esp. pp. 4, 10, 63, 131, italics removed).

about events that they know never took place.[24] They thus are able to reflect on these emotions, not from the distant realm of abstraction, but as they concretely experience them through the events of the story.

It is one thing to speak abstractly about the level and type of anger one should feel toward one's kin. It is another thing to be a silent observer as Laban catches up with a fleeing Jacob, hurling repeated accusations, while Jacob defends himself and launches his counterattacks. Narrative, by realistically depicting the types of events that may take place in life, brings its readers into a more immediate encounter with what it depicts.

Third and finally, narrative is especially suited for addressing the ethics of anger because of the attention it can give to the complexities and limitations of moral living.[25] Anger presents difficulty for the moral life because it urges individuals to enact the principle *Punish wrongdoing* (§4.3.1), even though individuals are rarely in a position to enact this sort of principle flawlessly.[26] This principle does not, for example, explain who bears the responsibility for punishing, how to verify wrongdoing, how much punishment is appropriate, or the many other perplexing issues involved in the execution of justice. When one recognizes (as Genesis does) the limitations of these sorts of principles, ethics becomes a complicated matter. Rather than appealing to a singular good (as most Enlightenment approaches do with their monistic focus on a primary guiding principle), actors must wrestle with a plurality of goods that are not always commensurate.[27] Simultaneously, they must make moral decisions in a world that they do not fully control and where they never know all the facts—a world filled with unforeseeable occurences, many of which are disastrous.[28] Narrative is particularly suited for tackling these sorts of surprises, in marked contrast to most philosophical discourse, which has tremendous difficulty depicting the unexpected nature of life's events.[29]

Narratives such as Genesis can also point to the complexities of the moral life by showing that blessing does not always follow on the heels of right action. Whether one considers Cain's desire to win Yʜwʜ's approval by sacrifice (Genesis 4), Isaac's and Esau's simple desire to abide by custom and transfer a blessing (Genesis 27), or Joseph's helping his prison mate,

---

24. Martha C. Nussbaum, *Upheavals of Thought: The Intelligence of Emotions* (Cambridge: Cambridge University Press, 2001) 242–45; idem, *Love's Knowledge*, 296.

25. See Booth, *The Company We Keep*, 266, 284–88; Gunn and Fewell, *Narrative in the Hebrew Bible*, 49.

26. Several texts suggest that even Yʜwʜ has difficulty enacting this principle, such as Jer 31:15–20 and Hos 11:8–9.

27. Martha C. Nussbaum, *The Fragility of Goodness: Luck and Ethics in Greek Tragedy and Philosophy* (Cambridge: Cambridge University Press, 2001) xxix.

28. Ibid., 25.

29. See Jean-Paul Sartre, *Existentialism and Human Emotions* (New York: Philosophical Library, 1957) 47; Nussbaum, *Love's Knowledge*, 3.

only to be forgotten himself (Genesis 40), Genesis makes clear that blessing is not an immediate result of right actions.[30] It thus offers qualifications to the presentation of the divine economy that one sees in nonnarrative texts such as Deuteronomy 27–28.[31] Furthermore, Genesis makes clear, as many narratives do, that undeserved disaster can strike individuals so hard that their capacity for moral living is seriously impaired.[32] Thus, Genesis never points to reconciliation and forgiveness as simple activities easily achieved following severe wrongdoings. Rather, it suggests that sometimes decades must transpire before individuals are again in the position to offer even partial forgiveness, as one sees with Esau and Jacob, as well as Joseph and his brothers.[33]

In addition to its value in addressing these specific moral complexities, an extended narrative such as Genesis is useful for dealing with anger because, on a more general level, the ethical truth about this emotion is too complex to nail down with a single principle or solitary illustration. Rather, readers need to return to it in different circumstances from alternate perspectives before gaining a sense of wisdom for handling it. Presenting readers with a dozen episodes involving anger, the texts of Genesis begin to do justice to the manifold perspectives necessary for approximating the truth about this emotion. Bakhtin describes how Dostoevsky "transfers onto the plane of literary composition the law of musical modulation from one tonality to another. . . . These are different voices singing variously on a single theme. This is indeed 'multivoicedness,' exposing the diversity of life and the great complexity of human experience."[34] The various episodes featuring anger in Genesis operate similarly to Dostoevsky's polyphony: they present a variety of perspectives on this emotion in order to promote a greater understanding of its complexity. Thus, Genesis does not so much offer hackneyed solutions to ethical dilemmas as present the manifold moral difficulties of this emotion with richness and depth.

---

30. See Nussbaum, *The Fragility of Goodness*, 334; Aristotle, *Eth. Nic.* 1.8.15–16; MacIntyre, *After Virtue*, 176, 213–15.

31. For more on the contrast between Genesis and Deuteronomy, see John Van Seters, "The Theology of the Yahwist: A Preliminary Sketch," in *"Wer Ist wie Du, Herr, unter den Göttern?" Studien zur Theologie und Religionsgeschichte Israels für Otto Kaiser zum 70. Geburtstag* (ed. Ingo Kottsieper et al.; Göttingen: Vandenhoeck & Ruprecht, 1994) 219–28, esp. p. 228.

32. Nussbaum, *The Fragility of Goodness*, 338–39.

33. Nussbaum describes how people who suffer have been "denied at least some ethically significant elements of human flourishing. Such people are not only unhappy: they also do and exchange fewer of the things that make for a completely good human life" (ibid., xvi).

34. Bakhtin, *Problems of Dostoevsky's Poetics*, 42. While there is a fruitful comparison here, one should note that Genesis does not go as far as Dostoevsky with respect to polyphony and multivoicedness.

8.3 *How Genesis Provides Ethical Guidance*

In elaborating on the mimetic function of narrative, I have described in the preceding discussion key reasons *why* readers can receive ethical guidance about anger from Genesis. In the remainder of this chapter, I outline *how* readers can receive this guidance, mapping four intersecting avenues: engaging in metaphoric transference, acquiring imaginative experience, being shaped by the second persona, and participating in formative conversations. These possibilities present a way forward to receiving the ethical resources that Genesis offers.

8.3.1 *Metaphorical Transference*

Wayne Booth has argued that one of the requisite tasks of gleaning ethical insight from narratives is forging metaphorical connections between the world of the text and the world of lived experience. The continuities between narrative and human experience described above (§8.1) facilitate this metaphor-making. Booth argues that in narratives one encounters "a vast articulated network of interrelated images, emotions, propositions, anecdotes, and possibilities."[35] This network, Booth maintains, functions to present the world in a particular way, giving readers a view of the world that they can, at least in part, metaphorically adopt as their own.[36]

In the field of biblical studies, Richard Hays has made similar proposals with respect to New Testament ethics. He launches a full, frontal attack on approaches to New Testament ethics that attempt to extract timeless truths from the Bible and disregard the culturally conditioned elements. This sort of Kantian enterprise, he contends, is fundamentally at odds with the text itself, all of which is culturally conditioned. Rather than dismissing the particularities of the text, Hays calls for valuing them by seeing how they may metaphorically illuminate the lives of readers. He also distinguishes between metaphors and allegories. Whereas the latter posit a point-by-point connection between story and referents, metaphors allow readers to "sustain the tension of simultaneous likeness and unlikeness between the semantic fields that are joined metaphorically."[37] In this way, he maintains, the foreign world of the Bible can illumine the ethical practices of its subsequent readers.

Appropriating the work of Booth and Hays, one enjoys several benefits from understanding metaphor-making as an essential task of Old Testament ethics. First, approaching narratives metaphorically provides a non-

---

35. Booth, *The Company We Keep*, 336–37; see also chaps. 10–11.

36. See also Paul Ricoeur, "Metaphor and the Main Problem of Hermeneutics," *New Literary History* 6 (1974) 95–110, esp. pp. 103–6; idem, *Interpretation Theory: Discourse and the Surplus of Meaning* (Fort Worth: The Texas Christian University Press, 1976) 92–93.

37. Richard B. Hays, *The Moral Vision of the New Testament: Community, Cross, New Creation; A Contemporary Introduction to New Testament Ethics* (San Francisco: HarperSanFrancisco, 1996) 303; see also pp. 6, 298–306, 310–12.

reductive way of seeing continuity between the textual world and the reader's world. As many theorists of metaphors have emphasized, metaphors are irreducible.[38] One cannot pinpoint a set of similarities between the metaphorical referents and assume, on the basis of such a set, that one has exhausted the rich and various meanings of the metaphor. The old substitution view of metaphors, which claimed that metaphors are merely ornamental and can be replaced by essential definitions, has been abandoned by nearly everyone working in the field.[39]

When narratives are considered metaphors for life, they potentially intersect with experiences in innumerable ways that one cannot reduce to a single set. To put this point differently, approaching narratives metaphorically allows readers to avoid the tendency toward extrapolation and abstraction present in rule-based and even paradigm-based and virtue-based approaches. The full integrity of the narrative is preserved, and readers can never say that they have arrived at a text's definitive, singular meaning. The "surplus of meaning" inherent in biblical texts is not dismissed by reducing the text's meaning to a formula or model.[40]

I mentioned above that Genesis addresses anger by giving attention to the complexities presented by this emotion. Were one to boil Genesis' message about anger down to a set of propositions, these complexities would likely be lost in the transference to generality, or else the set of propositions would probably become too complicated to be useful. However, by forging metaphorical connections with particular texts, readers can retain a focus on these complexities. In short, metaphor-mapping allows closer attention to the particularities of the text itself.

Another advantage of seeing narratives as providing metaphors for life is their flexibility. Moral principles and rules do not inherently entail a great deal of flexibility in their application. Even the focus on paradigms and virtues can be inflexible at times, failing to address the unique specifics of a given situation. However, seeing texts as offering metaphorical guidance gives readers freedom in application. For example, readers sensing a strong metaphorical connection between their situation and the situation depicted in a text may see the need for relying closely on the ethical

---

38. Janet Martin Soskice, *Metaphor and Religious Language* (Oxford: Clarendon, 1985) 93; Monroe Beardsley, "Metaphor," in *The Encyclopedia of Philosophy* (ed. Paul Edwards; New York: Macmillan and Free Press, 1967) 5.287.

39. See Soskice, *Metaphor and Religious Language*, 10–14.

40. Ricoeur, *Interpretation Theory*, esp. pp. 54–57. See also Daniel W. Hardy, "Reason, Wisdom and the Interpretation of Scripture," in *Reading Texts, Seeking Wisdom: Scripture and Theology* (ed. David F. Ford and Graham Stanton; Grand Rapids, MI: Eerdmans, 2003) 69–88; William Stacy Johnson, "Reading the Scriptures Faithfully in a Postmodern Age," in *The Art of Reading Scripture* (ed. Ellen F. Davis and Richard B. Hays; Grand Rapids, MI: Eerdmans, 2003) 122; Jacqueline E. Lapsley, *Whispering the Word: Hearing Women's Stories in the Old Testament* (Louisville: Westminster John Knox, 2005) passim; David C. Steinmetz, "The Superiority of Pre-critical Exegesis," *ThTo* 37 (1980) 27–38.

guidance offered therein, while readers sensing only a loose metaphorical connection have the freedom to improvise and adapt the metaphorical image to the specifics of their situation.[41]

A hidden assumption (or at least a logical corollary) of rule-based ethics is that individuals are fairly ignorant of right and wrong and therefore need very specific direction. While there are obviously times in life when people are in fact ignorant of what is best and need the specific guidance provided by rules and principles, there are also times when a focus on rules and principles can feel paternalistic—even suspicious of individuals' abilities to make creative decisions amid their concrete situations. In such circumstances, a metaphor-based approach to ethics can feel more affirming of the moral capabilities of individuals. Rather than telling them what *must* be done, this approach provides them with ethical resources that they can appropriate in the unique situations that they alone encounter. By appropriating a variety of narratives metaphorically, individuals can find themselves empowered to use their ethical resources in their unique contexts.

A final advantage to a metaphor-based approach is that metaphors already play an important role in ethical decision-making. As described in chap. 6, metaphors can influence how one thinks and speaks. The power of metaphor exerts itself not only with specific concepts such as *anger*, but also with broader frameworks governing our perceptions of the world and how we act within it. Thus, Kenneth Burke in his *Attitudes toward History* contends that every world view has a metaphor, implicit or explicit, that serves as its organizational base. For example, understanding the human being to function metaphorically as a *machine* leads to a host of philosophical presuppositions, whereas metaphorically envisioning individuals as *gods* or *apes* leads to quite different views of the world and its inhabitants.[42] Richard Rorty joins Burke in pointing to the importance of metaphors, writing, "It is pictures rather than propositions, metaphors rather than statements, which determine most of our philosophical convictions."[43] Meanwhile, in *Moral Politics*, George Lakoff argues that metaphors provide the baseline orientations that guide people in making moral decisions in the political realm.[44]

A variety of evidence suggests that, since its earliest receptions, readers of the Bible mapped metaphors between their worlds and the world evoked by the text itself, forging connections that provide ethical and theological

---

41. For more on connections between improvisation and ethics, see Nussbaum, *Love's Knowledge*, 37–38, 94; Samuel Wells, *Improvisation: The Drama of Christian Ethics* (Grand Rapids, MI: Brazos, 2004).

42. Kenneth Burke, *Attitudes toward History* (Berkeley: University of California Press, 1984) 262.

43. Richard Rorty, *Philosophy and the Mirror of Nature* (Oxford: Blackwell, 1980) 12.

44. George Lakoff, *Moral Politics: How Liberals and Conservatives Think* (2nd ed.; Chicago: University of Chicago Press, 2002) passim, esp. pp. x, 99–101, 135–40.

guidance.[45] Understanding biblical narratives to function in this way is an extension of what we already know about the earliest interpretations of the Bible.

Fundamental to all of Genesis, and to the discussion below, is the driving metaphor WE ARE EXPELLED FROM PARADISE.[46] No reader of Genesis has literally been expelled from the Garden of Eden. No reader has seen firsthand the cherubim and whirling, flaming sword east of the tree of life. And yet, Genesis clearly invites its readers to adopt Adam and Eve as metaphorical representations of themselves. In fact, it is a casualty of translation that the Hebrew אדם and חוה are typically rendered 'Adam' and 'Eve', when in fact their names literally are 'Humanity' and 'Life'. Few readers of the English Bible are aware of this connection, and thus they fail to realize how the text itself invites them to see these characters less as historical figures and more as metaphorical representations of the human race. Once one understands the driving metaphor WE ARE EXPELLED FROM PARADISE, however, suddenly the remainder of Genesis and even our own lives make much more sense.

Then, one can begin to understand why Abraham, for example, would have multiple wives. It is not that he inhabited a morally ideal universe, or even a morally neutral universe, and then elected to have sexual relations with his wife's slave. Rather, he lived in the land outside Eden—a place where individuals do not always know exactly what God expects or how to conform oneself to these expectations. In the barren land outside the garden, he and Sarah attempt to find a way beyond their childlessness. They make a decision that in the end causes great distress to themselves, to Hagar, and to Ishmael—and was not at all what God had in mind. But even Abraham does not have direct access to the mind of God. He does not live in a place where he can stroll with the deity during the cool of the day. While Abraham does have some close encounters with the divine, he

---

45. For example, the phrase תֹהוּ וָבֹהוּ in Jer 4:23 appears to be a metaphorical appropriation of Gen 1:2 (although the dating of the texts is a complex matter here). It seems that the poet takes the chaos and confusion prior to creation (Gen 1:2) as a metaphor for the chaos and confusion of the destruction of the land and subsequent exile. See, for example, the excellent discussion in Jack R. Lundbom, *Jeremiah 1–20: A New Translation with Introduction and Commentary* (AB 21; New York: Doubleday, 1999) 356–59. Similarly, the writers of the *Damascus Document* metaphorically appropriate Adam to speak about eternal life: המחזיקים בו לחיי נצח וכל כבוד אדם להם הוא ('Those who remain steadfast in it will live forever, and all the glory of Adam will be theirs'; CD-A III 20 [= 4Q269 2]). Hays describes ways that New Testament writers also forged these metaphorical connections (for example, 1 Cor 10:1–5; *The Moral Vision of the New Testament*, 303).

46. Some interpreters, such as David Penchansky, have challenged whether Eden should accurately be characterized as a paradise or a utopia ("God the Monster: Fantasy in the Garden of Eden," in *The Monstrous and Unspeakable: The Bible as Fantastic Literature* [ed. G. Aichele and T. Pippin; Sheffield: Sheffield Academic Press, 1997] 43–60, esp. p. 54). While there may be some truth in what Penchansky and others claim, there does appear to be a drastic difference between the relatively ideal life in the garden and the chaos and murder beyond it.

does not always know the ways that God's promises will reach fruition. He has to make do with the limited resources he has. And like all of us, he makes decisions that seem wise at the time, but in the end lead to nothing but tears.

Although WE ARE EXPELLED FROM PARADISE is a driving metaphor that nearly all of Genesis' readers can metaphorically adopt, the text of Genesis also provides a wide range of more-particular metaphors that are useful for the unique situations individuals face. Most of Genesis' narratives about anger fall into this category of more-particular metaphors. Thus, Genesis does not give readers one story about anger that is useful for all people in all situations. Instead, it presents a dozen stories about anger, providing readers with a realistic range of metaphorical possibilities for intersection with their lives. Because of the diversity of Genesis' texts and the diversity of reading communities, it is difficult to lay out in detail how narratives metaphorically connect with various readers. Ultimately, it is the task of preachers and interpretive communities to find imaginative ways that the text metaphorically relates to the particularities of their lives. Thus, in the discussion of Genesis below, I am not concerned with outlining "one-size-fits-all" metaphorical connections between narratives about anger and readers. Rather, I will show that Genesis presents a variety of examples for engaging anger that can be appropriated in ways that best fit the particular needs and demands of interpretive communities.

8.3.2 *Imaginative Experience*

A second, complementary way of understanding how narratives provide moral guidance about anger is by focusing on the gift of imaginative experience that narratives provide readers. Through the mimetic function of narrative, readers vicariously experience what characters within the narrative experience. These experiences instruct readers in the concrete and complex moral dynamics of the world. The modernist infatuation with science has deceived many into thinking that, if one knows all the formulas and rules, one can always arrive at the right solution. However, as workers in most nonscientific fields know well, formulas and rules can only guide novices so far; they also need to gain experience in the field.[47] Narratives help equip readers with the type of field experience required for moral competence.

A number of key theorists speak of the importance of narratives in equipping readers with experience. Hence, Jean-François Lyotard describes narratives as "apprenticeships." He contends that stories instruct readers in moral capacities and real-world standards, teaching individuals how to operate within society.[48] Paul Ricoeur makes similar remarks, speaking of narrative as the "laboratory" of ethics. Through storytelling, readers exchange experiences and thus allow one another to acquire practical wisdom about

---

47. See Aristotle, *Eth. Nic.* 6.8.5.
48. Lyotard, *The Postmodern Condition*, 18–23.

how the world works. Ricoeur contrasts this practical wisdom (which Aristotle calls φρονησις [*Eth. Nic.* 6.5]) with scientific observation, asserting that the former is of much greater value to individuals in their everyday lives.[49] Walter Fisher makes similar points, maintaining that the world in which we live abounds in knowledge but is surprisingly short on wisdom. Narrative, he contends, allows readers to regain wisdom and incorporate ethical value into thought processes.[50] When individuals turn to the Hebrew Bible, they encounter texts that resonate more with the idea of practical wisdom than scientific or abstract knowledge.[51] Many of its narratives presuppose an integral connection between life experience and the wisdom required for making sound ethical decisions.[52]

While it is certainly true that narratives have their limitations and that some literature negatively influences the moral life (see §8.1 above), many reasons exist for seeing the imaginative experience provided by literature as being as valuable as, if not more valuable than, "real-life" experience. First, as Wayne Booth has astutely pointed out, fiction gives its readers a "relatively cost-free offer of trial runs."[53] As laboratories (so Ricoeur), narratives provide controlled environments where readers can test out experiments without fearing too greatly the consequences. They can learn, for example, something of how seemingly benign decisions lead to moral catastrophe, or of the human capacity to hurt and be hurt by those we love the most. Second, and this is a point also made by Booth, stories allow one to acquire more experience than one could in real life. He writes, "In a month of reading, I can try out more 'lives' than I can test in a lifetime."[54] Nussbaum makes a similar point in explaining why narrative experience is a necessary supplement to life experience: "We have never lived enough. Our experience is, without fiction, too confined and too parochial."[55] Third, as Nussbaum hints, there is not only a *quantitative* but also a *qualitative* difference in the experiences that narratives provide. Literature allows readers to enter situations they have not and could not have previously encountered.[56] It can foster compassion and respect for others and moreover

---

49. Paul Ricoeur, *Oneself as Another* (trans. Kathleen Blamey; Chicago: University of Chicago Press, 1992) 163–66. See also Parry, *Old Testament Story and Christian Ethics*, 26–29; and Theo L. Hettema, *Reading for Good: Narrative Theology and Ethics in the Joseph Story from the Perspective of Ricoeur's Hermeneutics* (Kampen: Kok Pharos, 1996) 108–9.

50. Fisher, "Narration, Knowledge, and the Possibility of Wisdom," esp. pp. 187–88.

51. See the excellent essay by Merold Westphal, "Phenomenologies and Religious Truth," in *Phenomenology of the Truth Proper to Religion* (ed. Daniel Guerrière; Albany: State University of New York Press, 1990) 105–25, esp. pp. 107–8.

52. For example, see Job 12:12.

53. Booth, *The Company We Keep*, 485. Speaking specifically of Genesis, Booth adds, "If you try out a given mode of life in life itself, you may, like Eve in the garden, discover too late that the one who offered it to you was Old Nick himself."

54. Ibid.

55. Nussbaum, *Love's Knowledge*, 47.

56. Idem, *Poetic Justice*, 5, 45.

prepare individuals for situations they will later encounter in life. Finally, narrative has the capacity to focus attention in ways that are not always available in life as it is actually encountered. Literature can allow readers to reflect and contemplate on subjects they would be unable to consider amid the flux of everyday life.[57] This last point is particularly important for our study: anger may be too painful a topic to withstand extended reflection as it is encountered in everyday experiences. However, when anger is readers' first encounter outside Eden, and when they see it leading to nothing less than fratricide, they are called to reflect on this emotion in ways that they cannot consider when they are in the middle of their personal experiences of it.[58]

8.3.3 Second Persona

A third avenue by which narratives such as Genesis guide readers ethically is what Edwin Black calls "the second persona." If the first persona is the persona put forward by the author of a work (that is, the implied author), then the second persona refers to a "model of what the rhetor would have his real audience become."[59] The idea here is that, when authors choose the various elements of narrative—a genre, a vocabulary, a type of discourse, particular focal points, a sort of plot, and a kind of resolution—they shape their readers in subtle but profound ways by controlling, to an extent, what readers experience. In this sense, reading is a vulnerable and risky business. It entails an act of submission to the experiences and means of experience the author offers.[60] In a variety of ways, readers have their desires shaped by what they read.[61]

Consider, for example, the function of genre. Kenneth Burke explains, "Form is the creation of an appetite in the mind of the auditor and the adequate satisfying of that appetite."[62] In other words, when readers encounter a particular genre, they naturally come to expect particular things. Narrators may tempt readers with the illusion of filling their appetites, only to leave them hungry for more. In so doing, they shape the desires, hopes, and expectations of readers. Obviously, some works will shape readers' de-

---

57. Robert Alter, *The Art of Biblical Narrative* (New York: Basic Books, 1981) 156. See also Booth, *The Company We Keep*, 223.

58. As Nussbaum puts it regarding the imaginative experience found in literature, "We are free from some of the distortions that come with the vulgar heat of everyday life" (*Love's Knowledge*, 47–48). See also idem, *Poetic Justice*, 5–6.

59. Edwin Black, "The Second Persona," *Quarterly Journal of Speech* 56 (1970) 111–19, esp. p. 113. See also Gordon J. Wenham, *Story as Torah: Reading Old Testament Narrative Ethically* (Grand Rapids, MI: Baker Academic, 2000) 7–15.

60. Wayne C. Booth, *The Rhetoric of Fiction* (Chicago: University of Chicago Press, 1961) 137–38.

61. Idem, *The Company We Keep*, 201–6.

62. Kenneth Burke, "Psychology and Form," in *Counter-Statement* (Los Altos, CA: Hermes, 1953) 31. See also Nussbaum, *Love's Knowledge*, 5–6.

sires in life-giving ways, while others will pattern readers' desires toward what is unedifying.[63] One should note, nevertheless, that this patterning of desire sometimes works differently from what one may initially assume. Some openly pious works lead readers toward selfish desires, while others that appear aggressive on the surface may in fact lead readers on to admirable ends.[64]

Readers of Genesis have their desires shaped in a variety of ways. Concerning anger, when readers encounter this emotion in the first episode beyond the fire-protected garden, an appetite is whetted. As Cain rises up against his brother in the field, readers begin to desire not only the Edenic community that has been shattered but also alternatives to anger and fratricide. On the surface of things, Genesis' account of murder in its opening chapters is neither uplifting nor inspiring. But something happens as readers witness Abel's blood pouring out onto the ground. Their perspective on the world shifts. Anger is no longer a mere emotion. It is something so powerful that divine words (which just a couple of chapters ago created the universe) are powerless to stop. With anger, readers encounter the driving force behind the Bible's first recorded sin. Cain's murderous rage is something that cries out for resolution—if not in his own life, then at least in the generations that follow. One longs to find someone who, in marked contrast to Cain, can serve as his brother's keeper.

Narrative patterns desires. It summons attitudes. It instills values. It evokes a view of the world. It shows readers what truly matters, what is worth considering and reflecting on, what people are truly like, and what hazards and opportunities the environment has in store. In different ways, literature serves as a screen through which reality is viewed. It does not merely reflect reality but selects and even deflects reality.[65] Particular features come to the fore, while others are obstructed. Narrative has the potential to offer readers nothing less than an outlook on life, a posture toward humanity, a way of being in the world.[66] Narrative certainly serves a descriptive function, but this is never all that it does. It also prescribes ways of living and being for its readers.[67]

---

63. Booth, *The Company We Keep*, 201.

64. Ibid., 206.

65. Burke and Black use similar ideas to explain the function of language and metaphors, respectively (Kenneth Burke, *Language as Symbolic Action: Essays on Life, Literature, and Method* [Berkeley: University of California Press, 1966] 45; Max Black, *Models and Metaphors: Studies in Language and Philosophy* [Ithaca, NY: Cornell University Press, 1962] 40–44). Their ideas are applicable to literature as well.

66. Paul Ricoeur, *Figuring the Sacred: Religion, Narrative, and Imagination* (trans. David Pellauer; Minneapolis: Fortress, 1995) 41–42; idem, *Interpretation Theory*, 92. See also Nussbaum, *Poetic Justice*, 2.

67. Ricoeur, *Oneself as Another*, 152. See also idem, "The Narrative Function," 193; Gunn and Fewell, *Narrative in the Hebrew Bible*, 191.

8.3.4 *Formative Dialogue*

A fourth and final avenue by which narratives provide ethical instruction is by evoking discussions about morality among their readers.[68] While such discussion is hardly all that is necessary for ethical development, it can serve several important functions. The dialogue prompted by the text can be understood in two senses: a reader's dialogue *with the text* and a reader's dialogue *with other readers* about the text. Concerning the former, one might object, asserting that true dialogue cannot exist with a text, only a monologue. However, Bakhtin suggests that the act of reading is more dialogic than one might presume.[69] He understands particular novels (and one could transfer his point to include the complex narratives of Genesis) to be polyphonic, expressing a variety of independent and unmerged perspectives interacting dialogically.[70] This type of dialogic interaction can be greatly beneficial to the moral life, as readers consider a variety of perspectives and gain a better understanding of both others and themselves.

Bakhtin makes other remarks that reinforce this idea of conversing with a text. He contends that any utterance anticipates the perspective of its intended audience and seeks to respond both to objections raised by the readers and to the types of voices that the audience encounters in its wider world.[71] As Newsom puts it in her appropriation of Bakhtin, "No matter how monologic the form of the utterance, one can inquire about the way in which it is implicitly dialogized by its orientation to the already said and the yet to be said."[72] With this sort of understanding of utterances, it is possible to see texts like Genesis as serving the essential function of interacting with readers and thus constituting a moral conversation partner.

This idea of conversing with a text is not far removed from Booth's argument that reading can be fruitfully understood through the metaphor of *people meeting*.[73] The author implied by a text has the potential to serve as a friend, one who interacts with readers and invites them to a richer life than would otherwise be experienced.[74] Luis Alonso Schökel makes a similar point when describing specifically readers' ability to enter into dialogue

---

68. See John Rogerson, *Theory and Practice in Old Testament Ethics* (JSOTSup; London: T. & T. Clark, 2004) 7–8, 37–38, 46; chaps. 5–7, 15.

69. Mikhail Bakhtin, *The Dialogic Imagination* (trans. C. Emerson and M. Holquist; Austin: University of Texas Press, 1981, 1935) 45. See also Baltasar Gracián y Morales, *The Art of Worldly Wisdom* (trans. Christopher Maurer; New York: Doubleday, 1991) 129–30, §229.

70. Bakhtin, *Problems of Dostoevsky's Poetics*, 6–7. Carol A. Newsom has made this type of transference to several biblical books including Genesis ("Bakhtin, the Bible, and Dialogic Truth," *JR* 76 [1996] 302–4).

71. Bakhtin, *The Dialogic Imagination*, 281.

72. Newsom, "Bakhtin, the Bible, and Dialogic Truth," 302–3.

73. Booth, *The Company We Keep*, passim, esp. p. 170. Nussbaum (*Love's Knowledge*, chap. 9) draws on Booth's points and extends them in several ways.

74. Booth, *The Company We Keep*, 223.

with Genesis. As he puts it, "Those who want to familiarize themselves with Genesis, so to speak, incorporate themselves into its family."[75]

Texts provide ethical guidance not only by eliciting conversations *with* their readers but also by eliciting conversations *between* their readers. A point made well by both Wayne Booth and Martha Nussbaum is that reading is most conducive to moral formation when it takes place in a community that can reflect together on their textual encounters.[76] Because of the rich imaginative experience provided by narrative, it can be an especially useful forum for dialogue among readers, leading to their moral edification. There is ample evidence to suggest that the Hebrew Bible has been used in communal settings of this sort for almost all of its existence. To some extent in the biblical text itself and certainly in the rabbinic and early Christian commentaries, one sees communities gathered before the text, awaiting ethical instruction while recognizing that instruction frequently comes through conversation and interaction with the text and with one another.[77]

The Enlightenment taught interpreters to approach Scripture as an object with a single meaning available for extraction.[78] The Hebrew Bible, however, stubbornly refused to elicit a singularity of meaning. Its ambiguities defied resolution. Although individuals who continue to hold onto Enlightenment ideals have contended that these ambiguities are grounds for objecting to the enterprise of Old Testament ethics, there is another way of understanding them. These ambiguities serve the essential function of prompting deep reflection and formational dialogue. Rather than rejecting the ethical value of texts like Genesis 34 that contain their share of ambiguity, one can understand these texts as (1) realistically presenting the ambiguities inherent to the moral life and (2) inviting the audience to draw its own conclusions about how individuals should act in similar situations.[79] Lacking resolution, these texts invite readers both to discussion with the multiple perspectives they present and to ethical conversation with each other.[80]

---

75. Luis Alonso Schökel, *Dónde está tu hermano? Textos de fraternidad en el libro del Génesis* (Valencia: Institución San Jerónimo, 1985) 9–10, translation mine.

76. Booth, *The Company We Keep*, 72; Nussbaum, *Poetic Justice*, 76.

77. For example, Exod 24:7, Nehemiah 8. David Pleins, in outlining his postmodern approach to the diverse social ethics of the Hebrew Bible, notes the continuity between his work and the discussion found among the early rabbis (*The Social Visions of the Hebrew Bible: A Theological Introduction* [Louisville: Westminster John Knox, 2000] 21).

78. Johnson, "Reading the Scriptures Faithfully in a Postmodern Age," 118–19.

79. See Parry, *Old Testament Story and Christian Ethics*, 178.

80. The idea of a text's presenting ambiguities to readers and evoking questions among them has much in common with Sternberg's concept of "gapping" in the Hebrew Bible (*The Poetics of Biblical Narrative: Ideological Literature and the Drama of Reading* [Indiana Studies in Biblical Literature; Bloomington: Indiana University Press, 1985] chap. 6). At times, however, Sternberg tends to minimize the amount of ambiguity left by the texts, as his discussion of Genesis 34 illustrates (ibid., chap. 12).

8.4 Conclusion to Part 2:
What to Expect in Genesis

Readers who approach Genesis hoping to gain a formula, rule, or paradigm to help them handle anger will be disappointed. However, it is not
apparent that rules are what one should be looking for in the first place.
Rules and formulas work very well in science, but they are at best half-
truths in a complex and imperfect world containing a plurality of conflicting goods. Iris Murdoch writes, "You may know a truth, but if it's at all
complicated you have to be an artist not to utter it as a lie."[81] Through
the artistry of Genesis' narratives, readers gain experience and wisdom for
engaging anger. They acquire within their ethical repertoire a collection of
"metaphors for life" that are adaptable to the particularities they encounter. They gain conversation partners for thinking about this emotion. They
receive training in small and large ways to envision the world differently.
Their desires and longings are patterned anew. They long for alternatives
to anger's worst outcomes, while being sensibly cautious about what to
expect.

---

81. Iris Murdoch, *An Accidental Man* (London: Chatto and Windus, 1971) 90.

Part 3

In Search of A Brother's Keeper: Anger and Its Antitheses in Genesis

Chapter 9

Ethics outside Eden:
Cain and Abel

Genesis has approximately one dozen narratives in which human anger appears on either an explicit or an implicit level. Each of these narratives speaks clearly in its own voice about this emotion. Although particular themes emerge and reemerge, the text does not repeat a solitary message about this emotion. Rather, these narratives form a conversation about the multiple dimensions of anger. They qualify, amplify, and build on one another. Thus, readers who experience these narratives view anger from a variety of perspectives and in different lights, gaining wisdom for diverse encounters with anger that they may face. As a whole, these narratives display a deep sensitivity to human frailty, an acute awareness of anger's power, and a realistic range of possibilities for engaging this emotion.

9.1 The Appearance of Anger, Sin, and Death

Readers of Genesis first encounter anger as soon as humanity is forced out of Eden (4:1–16). This initial account of the world's post-paradise realities is an exceptionally laconic text that leaves much unsaid. Like Genesis 22, the style here is, to borrow Auerbach's oft-quoted phrase, "fraught with background."[1] Its language is more suggestive than explanatory, pointing more to possibilities than to definitive answers. Readers gain little knowledge about Cain and Abel's upbringing, their character traits, or their religious life. The audience receives no certainty about why God gives more attention to Abel's sacrifice than to Cain's. Even the murder itself is retold with exceptional brevity, revealing nothing about whether Abel put up a struggle, how Cain committed the murder, what happened to the body, or when and how Adam and Eve learned of the death.

What readers do learn is precisely the reason that Cain becomes angry, God's response to this emotion, and the life-shattering events that this anger causes. The text says specifically that Cain becomes very angry because God has regard for his brother's offering but not his own (4:3–5).[2]

---

1. Erich Auerbach, *Mimesis: The Representation of Reality in Western Literature* (trans. Willard R. Trask; fiftieth-anniversary ed.; Princeton: Princeton University Press, 2003) 3–23, esp. p. 12. There are a number of parallels between Genesis 22 and this text, such as the (near) death of a family member and repeated references to 'brother' (אח) and 'son' (בן).

2. Many correctly translate the *waw* at the outset of 4:5b in a resultative or consequential sense. Hence, the NRSV reads, "*So* Cain was very angry."

135

Interpreters have debated whether Cain could have done more to win God's approval.[3] The text itself is ambiguous, possibly reflecting the liminal world outside Eden, where old realities are gone and new realities are not yet apparent. Perhaps God would have accepted the offering if Cain had had a better disposition or if he had brought a better offering. Perhaps it would have made no difference at all. In any event, Cain is understandably upset. Although God has not commanded that he bring sacrifices, Cain does so. He offers fruits from the ground, presumably resulting from his own sweat and toil (3:17–19). Yet, God ignores this gift. If Cain has somehow violated the divine will, he is never told what he did wrong. In this world outside Eden, he has reached toward God and experienced nothing in return. When his younger brother brings an offering, however, God looks at it favorably. Consequently, Cain experiences jealousy and anger. The terminology depicting Cain's emotion is וַיִּחַר לְקַיִן מְאֹד, which stresses the intensity of Cain's anger. Even Cain's name, קַיִן, sounds strikingly similar to the Hebrew word for jealousy, קִנְאָה.[4]

---

3. Some have claimed that there was a problem with Cain's attitude or character (Heb 11:4; 1 John 3:12; Jude 11; Josephus [*Ant.* 1:52–62]; *Targum Pseudo-Jonathan*; or, much more recently, J. C. de Moor, "The Sacrifice Which Is an Abomination to the Lord," in *Loven en geloven: Opstellen van collega's en medewerkers aangeboden aan Prof. Dr. Nic. H. Ridderbos ter gelegenheid van zijn vijfentwintigjarig ambtsjubileum als hoogleraar aan de Vrije Universiteit te Amsterdam* [Amsterdam: Bolland, 1975] 211–26). Others have found the problem not in Cain's disposition but his sacrifice (Katharina Heyden, "Die Sünde Kains: Exegetische Beobachtungen zu Gen 4,1–16," *BN* 118 [2003] 85–109, esp. pp. 92–95; Sigmund Mowinckel, *The Two Sources of the Predeuteronomic Primeval History [JE] in Gen. 1–11* [Oslo: Dybwad, 1937] 32; Frederick E. Greenspahn, *When Brothers Dwell Together: The Preeminence of Younger Siblings in the Hebrew Bible* [New York: Oxford University Press, 1994] 91–92; E. A. Speiser, *Genesis: Introduction, Translation, and Notes* [AB 1; Garden City, NY: Doubleday, 1964] 30; Bruce K. Waltke, "Cain and His Offering," *WTJ* 48 [1986] 368–69). Still others assert that God acts arbitrarily (Claus Westermann, "Kain und Abel, die biblische Erzählung," in *Brudermord: Zum Mythos von Kain und Abel* [ed. Joachim Illies; Munich: Kösen, 1975] 17–20, esp. p. 20; Joseph P. Klein, "How Job Fulfills God's Word to Cain," *BR* 9 [1993] 40–43, esp. p. 41; Walter Brueggemann, *Genesis* [IBC; Atlanta: John Knox, 1982] 56). The approach here is essentially one of agnosticism—that is, a healthy skepticism about how sure interpreters can be when the text tells us so little. A similar approach is taken by Dennis T. Olson, "Untying the Knot? Masculinity, Violence, and the Creation-Fall Story of Genesis 2–4," in *Engaging the Bible in a Gendered World: An Introduction to Feminist Biblical Interpretation in Honor of Katharine Doob Sakenfeld* (ed. Linda Day and Carolyn Pressler; Louisville: Westminster John Knox, 2006) 73–86, esp. p. 81.

4. Cain's name is significant for several other reasons as well. First, while Cain's name initially refers to the gaining, acquisition, and creation of life (see 4:1), he ironically is responsible for the losing, taking, and destruction of life. Second, his name is quite similar to both the verb קִין, which in the Polel means 'sing a funeral song', and its related noun קִינָה, which refers to a 'dirge'. It is striking that words closely associated with death are quite similar to the name of the individual who brings death into the world. Finally, it may not be accidental that Cain's name has a homonym used in 2 Sam 21:16 to describe one of the weapons with which Ishbi-benov intends to kill David. Although readers are never told the means by which Cain strikes down his brother (Gen 4:8), the fact that Cain's name sounds like an instrument of death does not bode well for Abel.

Although Cain's sacrifice is ignored by God, his anger is not. Yhwh confronts Cain about this emotion, which is highly significant, given that the divine word in Genesis is reserved for the most important of events: the creation of the world, the making of several promises, and the forging of numerous covenants. Yhwh begins his conversation with Cain by asking him to express his anger:[5] "So Yhwh said to Cain, 'Why are you angry? Why has your face fallen?'" (4:6). These questions appear to be an invitation to the types of complaints found in the Psalms, Job, and many of the Latter Prophets. Yhwh asks Cain to vocalize his anger lest it continue unabated and result in life-devastating consequences.[6]

However, Cain turns down this invitation, remaining silent. Yhwh continues: "Is it not true that if you do good, then a lifting up? But if you do not do good, then at the entryway to sin is a creature crouching down.[7] Its craving is for you, but you can rule over it" (4:7). Although interpretations of this verse differ considerably, it is best understood as presenting to Cain two options that can result from his anger.[8] He can do what is good, and in turn experience a "lifting" (4:7a). In the immediate context of chap. 4, this refers to a lifting of Cain's face, which 4:5b–6 has described as falling in conjunction with his anger.[9] Cain is thus told that his anger can abate, particularly if he does what is right. At the same time, this reference to a

---

5. Kenneth M. Craig incorrectly maintains, "Yhwh allows no time for answers to [these] two questions about anger and a fallen countenance" ("Questions outside Eden [Genesis 4.1–16]: Yahweh, Cain and Their Rhetorical Interchange," *JSOT* 86 [1999] 107–28, esp. p. 115). To the contrary, the text portrays Yhwh as interested in conversing with Cain— exercising care and concern for what Cain says, even after he commits murder (4:13–15).

6. André LaCocque, *Onslaught against Innocence: Cain, Abel, and the Yahwist* (Eugene, OR: Cascade, 2008) 38–39, 118; Elie Wiesel, *Messengers of God: Biblical Portraits and Legends* (trans. Marion Wiesel; New York: Random, 1976) 63–64; Arthur I. Waskow, "Brothers Reconciled," *Sojourners* 28 (1999) 42–46, esp. p. 42; Lytta Basset, *Holy Anger: Jacob, Job, Jesus* (Grand Rapids, MI: Eerdmans, 2007) 22, 24, 35.

7. I here depart slightly from the MT, repointing לַפֶּתַח חַטָּאת רֹבֵץ to read לְפֶתַח חַטַּאת רֹבֵץ so that פתח is in construct with the noun that follows. The reason is twofold. First, this interpretation resolves a question that has troubled interpreters for centuries: why does חַטָּאת ('sin'), which is typically a feminine noun in Hebrew, fail to agree with both the masculine participle רֹבֵץ ('croucher') in 4:7b and the masculine pronouns in 4:7c? This perplexing question is not an issue if one understands a construct chain to be at work because חַטַּאת ('sin') then modifies פֶּתַח ('door'), rather than serving as the subject of רֹבֵץ. Second, in the 164 times that the noun פֶּתַח appears in the Hebrew Bible (not counting Gen 4:7), the immediate context always specifies the type of door that is envisioned. Repointing the MT thus allows this noun to function in the same way it is always used in the Hebrew Bible. Otherwise, this reference to a "door" is out of place and referentially unclear.

8. The literature on this verse is extensive. For a useful overview of many key issues and positions, see Claus Westermann, *Genesis* (3 vols.; Minneapolis: Fortress, 1984–2002) 1.298–301.

9. Although some suggest that this "lifting" is a reference to forgiveness (see Gen 50:17), in the immediate context, Cain has not yet committed any known sin. More likely, it is a reference to Cain's face (see Gen 19:21, 32:21[20]; Heyden, "Die Sünde Kains," 97; Giorgio Castellino, "Genesis 4:7," *VT* 10 [1960] 442–45; Speiser, *Genesis*, 33; Edward A.

"lifting" looks beyond the immediate context to other encounters with anger. In the broader scope of Genesis, there are other instances of different types of liftings that result from individuals' doing what is good in conjunction with anger (as described in the chapters below).

Here in Genesis 4, Cain's emotion has brought him to a morally dangerous place. YHWH tells him that if he fails to do what is good, there is a "crouching creature" (רֹבֵץ) beside "a doorway to sin" (לְפֶתַח חַטָּאת; 4:7b).[10] Readers in the ancient Near East would likely have understood the reference to this creature at a door as an allusion to a sin-punishing demon, a life-threatening lion, or perhaps both.[11] Cain thus is warned that his anger brings with it the possibility of sin and peril. He cannot approach the entryway to sin without ominous consequences. Should he fail to do good, he will be like one facing a lion or demon. Punishment will ensue, and his life will become endangered.

God's word of warning concludes with a restatement of the two possibilities that lie before Cain (4:7c). On the one hand, the menacing, punishing creature "desires" him. The Hebrew text here uses a word for desire (תשוקה) that in this context probably refers to the attraction of a beast to its prey.[12] This imagery suggests that escaping the worse effects of anger will not be easy. At the same time, Cain is not damned to doing evil. He is told that he can rule, מָשַׁל, over this beast. The word suggests that Cain will need a kingly, perhaps even a divine, power to overcome the threat to his life.[13]

Mangan, "A Discussion of Genesis 4:7," *CBQ* 6 [1944] 91–93, esp. p. 92; Gerhard von Rad, *Genesis* [rev. ed.; OTL; Philadelphia: Westminster, 1972] 105).

10. On this slight repointing of 4:7b, see n. 7 above.

11. Again, the literature discussing the meaning of רֹבֵץ is quite extensive. The position taken here is similar to the position taken by Westermann, "Kain und Abel," 20–21; André Wénin, "Adam *et* Éve: La jalousie de Caïn, 'semence' du serpent: Un aspect du récit mythique de Genèse 1–4," *RevScRel* 73 (1999) 3–16, esp. pp. 15–16; Brueggemann, *Genesis*, 57–58. Literature and iconography from the ancient Near East portray both demons and lions as crouching at doors. On demons, see Hans Duhm, *Die bösen Geister im Alten Testament* (Tübingen: Mohr [Siebeck] 1904) 9; "rābiṣu," *CAD* 14.23; M. L. Barré, "Rābiṣu רבץ," *DDD* 682–83; Jeremy Black, Anthony Green, and Tessa Rickards, *Gods, Demons and Symbols of Ancient Mesopotamia: An Illustrated Dictionary* (Austin: University of Texas Press, 1992) 63. On lions, see Brent A. Strawn, *What Is Stronger Than a Lion? Leonine Image and Metaphor in the Hebrew Bible and Ancient Near East* (OBO 212; Fribourg: Academic / Göttingen: Vandenhoeck & Ruprecht, 2005) 217–28, figs. 4.290–315, esp. figs. 4.290, 293, 295, 300, and 314; as well as Gen 49:9, Ezek 19:2, Ps 104:22; see also Isa 11:6, Hos 13:7.

12. Some interpreters assert that this word refers to Abel's desire for Cain (Benno Jacob, *The First Book of the Bible: Genesis* [trans. Ernest I. Jacob and Walter Jacob; New York: Ktav, 1974] 35; see also Heyden, "Die Sünde Kains," 99–100). However, Abel has not been mentioned since v. 4, making it unlikely that he is the antecedent of the possessive pronoun attached to this noun. Furthermore, when the Hebrew Bible uses the word תשוקה, it refers to bodily attraction. It is unclear why Abel would have this type of craving for his older brother. Thus, it is preferable to see this word as referring to the beast's (not Abel's) ravenous attraction to Cain.

13. A "divine" power is mentioned because a fair amount of ancient Near Eastern iconography depicts gods as standing or sitting on animals such as lions (compare the

Whereas the divine word previously in Genesis has incredible power, creating the world out of primeval chaos, in this episode it falls flat. Cain's anger continues unhindered by Yhwh's speech. Unable to kill God, Cain kills God's favorite.[14] In the field, he rises up and strikes down Abel (4:8). As mentioned above, the text is exceptionally brief, giving virtually no details of this climactic event. What the text does stress repeatedly is that Abel is none other than Cain's brother. Six times in four verses (4:8–11), the text uses the word אח ('brother'). The purpose of this repetition is to drive home the devastating power of anger within families. The readers who witness Cain's murder see that even the people who are closest by blood and by birth can fall prey to the worst effects of this emotion. Neither God's warning nor the bonds of kinship stop the devastating emotion that Cain experiences.

Anger brings death into the world. Readers expected Adam and Eve to die after eating the forbidden fruit (2:16–17, 3:3–4). Death was delayed. Instead of God killing Adam and Eve for their sins, Cain slays Abel for receiving God's favor. Various parallels exist between Adam and Eve's act of disobedience in the garden and Cain's act of murder outside the garden. In each case, God brings a warning (2:16–17, 4:6–7), which humans refuse to heed (3:1–7, 4:8). In response, God initiates a series of questions that begin 'Where are you?' (אֶיֶּכָּה, 3:9) or 'Where is Abel, your brother?' (אֵי הֶבֶל אָחִיךָ, 4:9a). The humans reply by denying responsibility (3:10–12, 4:9b) before Yhwh asks, "What have you done?" (מֶה־[זֹאת] עָשִׂית, 3:13, 4:10). Next, Yhwh issues various punishments pertaining to both the disobedient humans and the ground (אדמה) that contain the words 'Cursed are you from/more than' (אָרוּר אַתָּה מִן, 3:14–19 and 4:11–12). Finally, both episodes conclude with an expulsion from previous locales, making reference to what is east (קדם) of the Garden of Eden (3:22–24, 4:16).[15] These manifold parallels suggest that the narrative of Cain and Abel clarifies and amplifies the initial account of Adam and Eve's disobedience.[16] If Genesis 2–3 shows humanity disobeying God in a nearly ideal environment, then Genesis 4 shows humanity sinning amid the concrete realities of the world.[17] Collectively, the

---

"croucher" of v. 7b), ruling with authority. See Othmar Keel and Christoph Uehlinger, *Gods, Goddesses, and Images of God in Ancient Israel* (trans. Thomas H. Trapp; Minneapolis: Fortress, 1998) 190; *ANEP*, figs. 470–73, 486, 522, 526, 530, 534; Strawn, *Stronger Than a Lion*, 189–200, figs. 4.94, 186, 221–73, 289.

14. LaCocque, *Onslaught against Innocence*, 85, 143.

15. On these parallels, see esp. Heyden, "Die Sünde Kains," 103–4; Gordon J. Wenham, *Genesis* (2 vols.; WBC; Nashville: Thomas Nelson, 1987) 1.99–100; Alan J. Hauser, "Linguistic and Thematic Links between Genesis 4:1–16 and Genesis 2–3," *JETS* 23 (1980) 294–305; Donald E. Gowan, *From Eden to Babel: A Commentary on the Book of Genesis 1–11* (ITC; Grand Rapids: Eerdmans, 1988) 65.

16. S. McKnight, "Cain," in *Dictionary of the Old Testament: Pentateuch* (ed. T. Desmond Alexander and David W. Baker; Downers Grove, IL: InterVarsity, 2003) 107. See also Wénin, "Adam *et* Éve," esp. pp. 5, 10.

17. These parallels also suggest that Gen 2:4b–3:24 is not devoid of teaching about disobeying God and the consequences of disobedience. The traditional "sin and fall"

stories describe in archetypal terms the fundamentals of human nature and experience, underscoring humanity's capacity for evil.[18] Remarkably, of all the ways that the narrator could have portrayed primal disobedience and sin outside Eden, anger is the one chosen. Genesis names this emotion as one of the most fundamental threats to moral living and human existence. It endangers one's ability to do what is right and can lead to both the destruction of community and the slaughter of the innocent.

Cain's anger is portrayed in prototypical terms, inviting readers to see his anger as not far removed from their own. As pointed out in §4.3.1, anger is prototypically caused by a perceived wrongdoing in the Hebrew Bible. Given that Yhwh pays no attention to Cain's sacrifice, the human obviously has reason to be angry (4:3–5). Cain's anger appears to be directed both toward God (to whom he does not respond, 4:6–7) and toward his brother Abel (against whom he acts, 4:8). This God-directed anger is less prototypical but not unheard of with accounts of human anger (§4.3.2).[19] Those who become angry in the Hebrew Bible are prototypically male with some degree of power (§4.3.3), as Cain appears to be (with his age and power over his younger brother, 4:1, 8). The normal outcomes of anger are violence and separation (§4.3.4), which clearly match Cain's experience with respect to both his murder and his exile in the "Land of Wandering" (4:8, 16). In the Hebrew Bible, anger is often evaluated as a part of life that, while inevitable, should be avoided and held in check when possible (§4.3.5). This evaluation matches God's words of warning in Gen 4:6–7 quite nicely. Little differs from the prototypical account of anger that I inductively compiled from the Hebrew Bible in §4.3.[20] Thus, the narrator presents Cain's emotion

---

interpretation of this passage may not have gotten everything right, but it was not baseless either. On this topic, see Lyn M. Bechtel, "Rethinking the Interpretation of Genesis 2.4b–3.24," in *A Feminist Companion to Genesis* (ed. Althalya Brenner; Princeton: Princeton University Press, 1993) 77–117; idem, "Genesis 2.4b–3.24: A Myth about Human Maturation," *JSOT* 67 (1995) 3–26; Carol Meyers, *Discovering Eve: Ancient Israelite Women in Context* (New York: Oxford University Press, 1988) 87.

18. Some have understood Cain less as a representative of humanity and more as the legendary progenitor of a Bedouin tribe mentioned in the Hebrew Bible a dozen times as the Kenites (קֵינִי; Westermann, "Kain und Abel," 13–14, esp. p. 24). Although this text may at one point have described the origination of the Kenites, the present form of Genesis does not present Cain this way. For example, Genesis does not divide humanity into tribes or groups of people until its 10th chapter. See esp. LaCocque, *Onslaught against Innocence*, 3, 14–15, 89–90, 119; Gowan, *From Eden to Babel*, 62–63.

19. It is striking that the one place where Cain's anger appears less prototypical is its object. In this symbolic depiction of the world's post-paradise realities, the text appears to imply that God bears some level of responsibility for the difficulties and inequalities that humanity faces. It suggests that humanity has reasons to become angry with the divine.

20. Some interpreters, such as Mayer Gruber, claim that Cain is not so much angry as depressed (Mayer I. Gruber, "The Tragedy of Cain and Abel: A Case of Depression," *JQR* 69 [1978] 89–97; idem, "Was Cain Angry or Depressed?" *BAR* 6/6 [1980] 34–36; idem, *Aspects of Nonverbal Communication in the Ancient Near East* [Studia Pohl 12; 2 vols.; Rome: Pontifical Biblical Institute, 1980] 1.370–71). Although the Hebrew Bible does see stronger links

as a common form of anger, allowing readers to see connections between Cain and themselves. The text is thus particularly open to the type of metaphoric transference described above (§8.3.1). For everyone, anger possesses the potential for great harm, particularly within families.

9.2 Desiring Alternatives

Anger is harmful not only to those like Abel who experience the worst effects of someone else's anger, but also to those like Cain who experience this emotion themselves. After telling of Abel's death, the narrative spends its remaining verses discussing God's punishment of Cain, which causes him to fear for his life, renders the soil worthless, and forces him to wander alone east of Eden (4:11–16). While there is an element of grace in God's punishment (4:13–15), Cain's way of life is irreversibly changed. His brother is forever gone. He must leave those he knows. His occupation must change. Once a sedentary farmer, he now is a restless wanderer. The text portrays Cain as estranged even from God (4:16).[21] In Cain's descendants, violence becomes fruitful and multiplies, particularly in Lamech, who boasts not only of killing a child but also of vengeance far more destructive than even God's (4:23–24).[22] The violence mobilized by Cain's anger becomes humanity's greatest threat (see 6:11–13).

In presenting the grave danger and consequences posed by anger, the narrative creates the desire for an alternative to how Cain engages this emotion. When readers see anger resulting in death and punishment, they desire an antidote. Anger has led to the irreparable. Abel is forever gone. The human community has been irreversibly impoverished. As J. Robert Cox insightfully observes, rhetorical occurrences of the irreparable lead to shifts in attitudes and thinking among audiences.[23] By tying anger to death, Genesis focuses heightened attention on this emotion, generating a desire for more information about it and its ethical implications. Readers want to know ways it can be handled that avoid irreversible damage. They wonder what other options are available.[24]

---

between anger and sadness than are commonly assumed in Western society (see §5.2, §6.5, and §15.1), it would be incorrect to see Cain as primarily experiencing depression. His behavior not only matches the prototypical script for anger, but Cain also fails to engage in behavior that the Hebrew Bible associates with sadness and depression, such as lamentation, "psychomotoric retardation," eating and sleeping disorders, and thoughts of one's own death (Paul A. Krüger, "Depression in the Hebrew Bible: An Update," *JNES* 64 [2005] 187–92, esp. pp. 190–92).

21. LaCocque writes, "The first sacrificer in human history is also, paradoxically, the first 'excommunicated'" (*Onslaught against Innocence*, 101).

22. Luis Alonso Schökel, *Dónde está tu hermano? Textos de fraternidad en el libro del Génesis* (Valencia: Institución San Jerónimo, 1985) 323.

23. J. Robert Cox, "The Die Is Cast: Topical and Ontological Dimensions of the Locus of the Irreparable," *Quarterly Journal of Speech* 68 (1982) 227–39.

24. The earliest audiences of Genesis likely inhabited a culture of honor and shame that placed a significant emphasis on retribution and "getting even" (see Victor H.

Two times, the text hints at alternatives to anger-driven violence. The first occurs when God warns Cain about his anger. The deity makes clear that Cain, though he is angry, can still do good (4:7a). Cain obviously does not take this path, but the text leaves open the possibility that other characters will come in Genesis who will respond to anger in ways that are markedly different from Cain. Readers want to encounter one who will do good (Hiphil of יטב, Gen 4:7a)—a brother who will find the strength to rule over (מָשַׁל, Gen 4:7c) the menacing, punishing creature (רֹבֵץ, Gen 4:7b) at the doorway to iniquity (לַפֶּתַח חַטָּאת, Gen 4:7b). Readers desire to know more about the type of lifting (נשׁא, 4:7a) that can take place even after anger enters the scene.[25]

A second hint about alternatives to Cain's anger-inspired violence is found in Cain's response to God's inquiry about the murder: "Am I my brother's keeper (שֹׁמֵר)?" The key word is שֹׁמֵר ('keeper'), which is often associated with shepherding.[26] It refers to watching over someone or something, providing sustenance and security.[27] Obviously, being Abel's keeper is the polar opposite of being his murderer. The former protects Abel from harm; the latter harms him unto death. By mentioning his own opposite, Cain alludes to the possibility that there may be alternatives to the path he himself has taken. His words hint that he may be a foil to other, greater characters, yet to come.

As Cain's disastrous life unfolds, readers long for one who will serve as an anti-Cain, fulfilling the role of being a keeper for his brothers, providing security and sustenance for family members in a harsh world (see §8.3.3 on the shaping of readers' desires). The audience will receive a glimpse of someone serving this role in Abram (§10.1), but they will need to wait until the end of Genesis before encountering Joseph, who truly fulfills this role and provides in a variety of ways for his brothers, even after a long history of anger, jealousy, and abuse (§12.2).

Matthews and Don C. Benjamin, eds., "Honor and Shame in the World of the Bible," *Semeia* 68 [1994] 1–161; for an example of the desire for retribution, see the Samson narrative, as well as the commentary by James L. Crenshaw, *Samson: A Secret Betrayed, a Vow Ignored* [Atlanta: John Knox, 1978] esp. pp. 122–24). By creating in readers the longing for alternatives to violence, the book of Genesis subtly challenges the value placed on retribution, upholding nonviolence as a higher good.

25. This sort of lifting will be mentioned in the stories of Abram and Lot (§10.1; Gen 13:6, 10, 14), Sarah and Hagar (§11.1; Gen 21:18), Jacob and Esau (§12.1; Gen 32:21[20]), and Joseph and his brothers (§12.2; Gen 50:17).

26. Gen 30:31, 1 Sam 17:20, Jer 31:10.

27. The standard lexicons (BDB, *HALOT*) connect שׁמר with providing protection. On the connections between this verb and providing sustenance, see Gen 28:20, 30:31, 41:35; F. García López, "שָׁמַר; שֹׁמְרִים; שְׁמֻרָה; שָׁמְרָה; מִשְׁמָר/מִשְׁמֶרֶת; אַשְׁמוּרָה/אַשְׁמֹרֶת," *TDOT* 15.279–305, esp. p. 288.

9.3 Conclusion

Gen 4:1–16 presents anger as a grave danger to the moral life. It brings death into the world. It is linked to the Bible's first explicit mention of "sin" (חטאת, 4:7). It shatters what community existed beyond Eden. It wreaks havoc on Cain and destroys humanity's first family. By presenting anger as a grave moral problem, the text whets readers' appetites for alternatives to Cain's way of handling his anger. As readers engage the plots of Genesis, they desire to meet characters who will bring anger's deadly force to an end. They look for individuals who will respond to anger by doing good, providing for and protecting their family.

Chapter 10

A Land of Limitations:
Anger among Shepherds

Abel is the first shepherd of Genesis. In the chapters that follow, Genesis returns to shepherds repeatedly and often recounts angry episodes among them. These narratives show how anger can arise in a land of limited resources. Though each episode contains the potential for great violence, the characters seem to be haunted by the murder of Abel—aware of anger's deadly dangers and determined to avoid violence, even if it means great personal sacrifice. In the present chapter, I focus on three narratives involving angry shepherds: Genesis 13, where anger arises among the shepherds of Abram and Lot; Genesis 26, an analogous narrative depicting jealousy between the shepherds of Isaac and the Philistines; and Genesis 31, where Jacob and Laban angrily confront one another.

10.1 A Glimpse of a Keeper: Abram and Lot

The next time that Genesis portrays anger, readers witness the continuing reverberations of Yнwн's curse of the ground, which occurred in response to the disobedience and sin of Adam and Cain (Gen 3:17, 4:11). The readers learn that the land is unable to sustain (lit., 'lift') both Abram and Lot (וְלֹא־נָשָׂא אֹתָם הָאָרֶץ לָשֶׁבֶת יַחְדָּו; 13:6). In a land of insufficient resources, conflict breaks out between Abram's and Lot's shepherds. The text speaks specifically of 'contention' (מריבה, ריב), which as noted above (§5.6) is a term closely associated with anger in the Hebrew Bible. This sort of strife apparently was quite common among shepherds of the ancient Near East.[1] The earliest readers of this text most likely would have been familiar with occurrences such as this.

Abram takes the initiative in response to this conflict by appealing to the bonds of brotherhood. Although Abram and Lot are technically uncle and nephew, the Hebrew word אח is broad enough to encapsulate this relationship as well.[2] The text reads:

---

1. Roland de Vaux, *Ancient Israel: Its Life and Institutions* (trans. John McHugh; New York: McGraw-Hill, 1961) 7; Claus Westermann, *Genesis* (3 vols.; Minneapolis: Fortress, 1984–2002) 2.172–74, 426–27. Note also that land disputes recur in Genesis (Gen 21:22–34, 26:12–33).

2. Luis Alonso Schökel, *Dónde está tu hermano? Textos de fraternidad en el libro del Génesis* (Valencia: Institución San Jerónimo, 1985) 61–62.

144

[13:8] So Abram said to Lot, "Let there be no strife between me and you, or between my shepherds and your shepherds, for we are brothers.[3] [13:9] Is not the entire land before you? Separate yourself from me. If to the left, then I will go to the right. If to the right, then I will go to the left."

On close examination, these verses and their broader context have many connections with the narrative of Cain and Abel. On a thematic level, both stories deal with the limitations of the land (4:11, 13:6), the emotion of anger (4:5–6, 13:7–8), the significance of brotherhood (4:2, 8–11; 13:8), and the necessity of relocation (4:12, 14, 16; 13:9–12). On a semantic level, one finds parallels regarding particularities such as moving *eastward* (words related to קֶדֶם; 3:24, 4:16, 13:11), the *Garden of Eden*/Yhwh (גַּן, עֵדֶן, or both; 3:24, 4:16, 13:10), and a *lifting* (נשׂא; 4:7; 13:6, 10, 14). Syntactically, Abram's הֲלֹא question ('Is not . . . ?') in 13:9 is followed by an exceptionally concise אִם . . . וְאִם . . . ('If . . . , and if . . . ?') construction depicting opposites—much like God's question to Cain in 4:7.

These various parallels serve the purpose of shuttling readers back to the Cain and Abel narrative, particularly Gen 4:7: "Is it not true that if you do good, then a lifting up? But if you do not do good, then at the entryway to sin is a creature crouching down." Abram faces these same options that Cain did. But unlike his predecessor, Abram chooses to do what is good. Although he inhabits a world of limited resources, Abram acts with generosity, humility, and even self-sacrifice, offering Lot first choice of land. Instead of giving priority to his own needs and exercising the prerogatives of the *paterfamilias*, he gives priority to his relationship with Lot and yields to his nephew's wishes.[4] His generosity counteracts the strife and anger between himself, his nephew, and their shepherds, introducing an alternate logic, a different means of relating that diffuses the anger and conflict. This theme of generosity's ameliorating anger will reappear many times in Genesis, presenting itself in each of the following generations (Isaac's actions with the Philistines in Genesis 26, Jacob's actions with Esau in Genesis 33, and Joseph's and his brothers' interactions in Genesis 43 and 50).

This pregnant text looks not only forward but also backward. God's words to Cain in 4:7 tell him that, if he does good, then there will be a "lifting." Here in Genesis 13, both Lot and Abram experience a lifting. The text

3. Literally, Abram says, 'For we are men—brothers'. The Hebrew words אֲנָשִׁים and אַחִים are clearly in apposition, with the latter (אַחִים) clarifying the type of men that they are (GKC §131b). In English, it is preferable on an idiomatic level to say simply, "We are brothers" (Gordon J. Wenham, *Story as Torah: Reading Old Testament Narrative Ethically* [Grand Rapids, MI: Baker Academic, 2000] 1.293, 297).

4. Victor P. Hamilton, *The Book of Genesis: Chapters 1–17* (NICOT; Grand Rapids, MI: Eerdmans, 1990) 392. In a contrasting interpretive move, Walter Vogels suggests that Lot was stronger than his uncle and that Abram gave up land simply so that Lot would not seize it from him ("Lot in His Honor Restored: A Structural Analysis of Gen 13:2–18," *EgT* 10 [1979] 5–12). However, this claim does not fit especially well with the textual evidence. As Genesis 14 illustrates, Abram appears much stronger than Lot.

says that Lot, in response to Abram's offer, *lifted* his eyes (וַיִּשָּׂא־לוֹט אֶת־עֵינָיו) and saw the valley of the Jordan, which looked 'like the garden of YHWH' (כְּגַן־יְהוָה, 13:10). He chooses this land and moves eastward (מִקֶּדֶם, 13:11).[5] Abram, meanwhile, settles in Canaan (13:12), and it is there that YHWH tells him to *lift* his eyes (שָׂא נָא עֵינֶיךָ, 13:14) and to behold the land, which shall be given to his countless descendents (13:15–17). The beginning of this pericope presented the crucial problem of the narrative by saying that the land could *not* "lift" (or "support") Abram and Lot living together (וְלֹא־נָשָׂא אֹתָם הָאָרֶץ לָשֶׁבֶת יַחְדָּו, 13:6). By its conclusion, however, there *is* a lifting for both Lot and Abram. The difficulty has been resolved, thanks to Abram's generosity.

Above (§9.2), I mentioned that being a brother's keeper entails providing both sustenance and security. Here in Genesis 13, Abram gives sustenance for his "brother" (see 13:8), acting like a shepherd and providing green pastures and fresh waters (see esp. 13:10). In the next chapter, Genesis 14, Abram provides security for Lot. When Abram learns that 'his brother' (אָחִיו, 14:14) has been taken captive, he leads 318 soldiers to rescue Lot from harm. After a long pursuit, Abram is able to bring back not only Lot but also his nephew's family and possessions. He fulfills the shepherd's role, rescuing Lot from danger.[6] The text stresses that Abram again displays generosity. It says specifically that Abram 'emptied out' (Hiphil of ריק) the trained men from his house (14:14), essentially leaving his immediate family and possessions vulnerable to attack and plunder. The text also emphasizes that after victory Abram took none of the possessions for himself—not 'a thread or even a sandal strap' (מִחוּט וְעַד שְׂרוֹךְ־נַעַל, 14:21–24, esp. v. 23). Because he has done what is good, Abram receives both a blessing from Melchizedek (14:18–20) and a promise of "great reward" from YHWH (15:1).[7]

In Abram, then, readers glimpse a clear alternative to Cain. They encounter someone who, at least on these occasions, responds to anger by doing what is good, serving as a 'keeper' (שֹׁמֵר) for his nephew Lot. There are, of course, shortcomings to the ways that Abram provides for Lot. Most notably, the two have separated, and they never live together again. What community the "brothers" once had has been lost. Genesis makes clear that, even for a figure like Abram, the limitations of this world often disal-

---

5. Moving eastward is significant, given that numerous parties in Genesis are seen moving to the east as a result of separation (Mark McEntire, *The Blood of Abel: The Violent Plot in the Hebrew Bible* [Macon, GA: Mercer University Press, 1999] 27–28; Devora Steinmetz, *From Father to Son: Kinship, Conflict, and Continuity in Genesis* [Literary Currents in Biblical Interpretation; Louisville: Westminster John Knox, 1991] 90–91). These include Cain (4:16), Isaac (26:17–23), Jacob (27:43, 28:10, 29:1), Laban (32:1[31:55]), and Esau (36:6–8).

6. Amos 3:12 says that, when a flock is attacked by a lion, a shepherd will snatch from the lion's mouth only an ear or a pair of legs. Abram, however, goes even further, bringing back not a remnant of what was taken but 'all the possessions' (כָּל־הָרְכֻשׁ, 14:16).

7. Alonso Schökel, *Dónde está?* 72.

low brothers' living together, no matter how good and pleasing that sort of unity may be.[8] Thus, while this text begins to satisfy readers' desire to see an alternative to Cain, it leaves them hungry for more.

10.2 Land Limitations Revisited: Isaac and the Herders of Gerar

Genesis 26 is one of the few chapters in the Bible that depicts the character Isaac as an adult. Verses 12–33 describe conflict and strife between Isaac and the herders of Gerar. The narrative interacts in various ways with Genesis 13.[9] In each text, anger emerges after the patriarch (Abram in Genesis 13, Isaac in Genesis 26) has an awkward encounter with the rulers of another land regarding his wife (passed off as his sister). Either during this encounter or after it, the patriarch becomes wealthy and numerous. The land, however, does not expand with the increase in wealth and possessions.[10] With insufficient resources, anger and jealousy break out, particularly among shepherds. In Genesis 13, Abram deals with strife by appealing to the bonds of brotherhood, relinquishing power, and acting with generosity.

In Genesis 26, however, Isaac does not have the same options that his father had. The strife and jealousy he faces come not from a family member but from the Philistines in whose land he lives. He cannot appeal to the bonds of kinship in the hope of making peace, as Abram did. Furthermore, he is not in a position to approach the Philistines, asking them which land they would like. The Philistines have already approached him, demanding that he vacate their land. He can either comply with their wishes or respond with force. Verses 12–16 (see also vv. 28–29) make clear that Isaac has the numbers and wealth at least to put up a fight with the Philistines.

He does not. Isaac responds to the Philistine's anger, jealousy, and strife by vacating whatever land they ask him to leave. Several times, the text uses anger-related words, including קנא ('be jealous', 26:14; see §5.1) and ריב ('contend', 26:20, 21; see §5.6). After each encounter, Isaac agrees to what the Philistines want, rather than holding onto land at the cost of intensifying anger and bloodshed. He moves farther away from the Philistines and relinquishes both the wells his father dug and those he dug by himself. Isaac finally settles at Beer-sheba (26:23–25), where he is subsequently approached by Abimelech, the Philistine king, and two of his officers (26:26).

---

8. Ps 133:1; Benno Jacob, *The First Book of the Bible: Genesis* (trans. Ernest I. Jacob and Walter Jacob; New York: Ktav, 1974) 92.

9. See the useful discussion in Wenham, *Genesis*, 2.187.

10. The text points not only to the limitations of the land (that is, a reaffirmation of the curse of the soil in Genesis 3–4) but also to what Thomas L. Brodie calls "the ambiguity of riches," where wealth brings not only an abundance but also various troubles (*Genesis as Dialogue: A Literary, Historical, and Theological Commentary* [Oxford: Oxford University Press, 2001] 301–2).

When they arrive, Isaac appears upset, confronting Abimelech and his officials about their past wrongdoings (26:27). Although Isaac had agreed to vacate the land as the Philistines had demanded, he did not believe that their demands were fair. He voices his complaints against them, observing that they have 'hated' (שָׂנֵא) him and 'sent [him] away' (שׁלח).[11] He asks why they have even come to meet with him in Beer-sheba. The Philistines respond by requesting peace, although the presence of Phicol, Abimelech's military commander, suggests that they are prepared for alternatives. The Philistines note that, when they sent Isaac away, they did so without violence. Isaac agrees to make peace, and the two parties form a nonaggression pact with one another, sharing in a feast and exchanging vows (26:30–31).

In this rare glimpse of Abraham and Sarah's grown son, the text sets forth its drama on a limited stage. There is not enough to go around. Water is in short supply. Peoples compete. Characters' actions are limited. They must make do with what they have, rather than awaiting an ideal opportunity in which they can act in perfect ways. Isaac never has the opportunity to take the initiative in making peace as his father did. He can vacate land even though it seems unjust or else ignite anger and violence.

Although Isaac believes he has been wronged, he finds peace more attractive than fostering anger and violence. He relinquishes land, including land he could claim as his family's (see Abraham's covenant with Abimelech in 21:22–34).[12] When confronted by Abimelech and his officials at the end of this narrative, Isaac has the opportunity to hold onto past wrongdoings and dismiss the Philistines from his presence at Beer-sheba. Instead, he makes peace. Isaac responds to the limited options he faces by avoiding violence whenever possible.

If Genesis 13 points to the importance of seeking peace in response to anger when family members are involved, then Genesis 26 points to the importance of seeking peace when outsiders are involved. In both cases, the text suggests that it is better to relinquish land than to foster anger—a particularly bold message given the value and limited nature of fertile land in Palestine. Although YHWH has promised land to the patriarchs, this text

---

11. Some have characterized Isaac as among the most fearful, timid, and passive of the patriarchs (Wenham, *Genesis*, 2.192–93). While there may be some truth in such an assertion, it should not be taken too far. Many of Isaac's actions have close parallels in the life of his father (chaps. 13, 20, 21), and his bold interchange with Abimelech at Beer-sheba (26:27) suggests that he is not afraid to confront rulers when he deems it necessary.

12. Gen 21:22–34 has clear parallels with Gen 26:12–33 (such as Beer-sheba, wells, Abimelech, Phicol, covenant, and vows), although terms for anger and related concepts (such as ריב) are missing in the prior story. Like several others, E. A. Speiser argues that one event lies in the background that was "differently reported in two independent sources" (*Genesis: Introduction, Translation, and Notes* [AB 1; Garden City, NY: Doubleday, 1964] 203). Those taking a more literary approach, on the other hand, see Gen 26:12–33 as the "sequel" to Gen 21:22–34 (Victor H. Matthews, "The Wells of Gerar," *BA* 49 [1986] 118–26, esp. p. 122).

does not advocate the seizure or even retention of land through violent means.[13] With the death of Abel lurking in the background, readers see characters who place the highest value on the preservation of life, no matter how limited the options before them. They take anger quite seriously, particularly its potential for great harm. Abram and Isaac respond to this emotion by doing what is right, finding a path that leads to שׁלוֹם ('peace', 26:29, 31), even though doing so involves personal sacrifice and hardship.

In *The Curse of Cain: The Violent Legacy of Monotheism*, Regina Schwartz reflects at length on the limitations portrayed by Genesis and other texts of the Hebrew Bible. She argues that the scarcity it envisions provides the impetus for violence in the Bible. On this point, she is essentially correct. In this narrative, the scarcity of land has the potential to result in great violence. However, what she does with this exegetical observation is fundamentally flawed. Schwartz calls for her readers to abandon the Hebrew Bible's portrayal of a world of limitations, maintaining that they should instead embrace a utopian ideal of plenitude, which she believes will foster generosity and counteract greed and violence.[14]

There are three key problems with Schwartz's ideal of plenitude. First and foremost, it is no more than wishful thinking. The ancient writers and readers of Genesis knew how difficult it is simply to survive. They knew the potential for death in every birth, every famine, and every conflict. They appropriately observed that God allows no reentry into paradise (3:24). Second, Schwartz ignores the ways that Genesis is concerned precisely with the problem she outlines. She misses how Genesis zeroes in on anger, which serves as a crucial link between scarcity and violence. Though the writers of Genesis did not believe much could be done about the inherent scarcity of the world, they did believe that individuals could prevent the resultant anger from erupting into violence. Third, Schwartz never makes clear why generosity would be necessary in the world of abundance that she envisions. There is no reason to share when everyone has more than enough. Genesis, on the other hand, presents things quite differently. It envisions generosity as a necessity precisely because there is not enough to go around. In Genesis, generosity flows not from whimsical notions of abundance but as a concrete means of ameliorating anger and preventing it from causing violence.

---

13. Many have understood Isaac to be a representation of the people of Israel (Westermann, *Genesis*, 2.429). If so, this story has nonviolent implications for not only individuals but also the people of Israel as a whole, particularly with regard to land holdings. Voices in the Bible advocating the seizure of land by force are at least partially counteracted by texts such as this one.

14. Regina M. Schwartz, *The Curse of Cain: The Violent Legacy of Monotheism* (Chicago: University of Chicago Press, 1997) 34, 77–83, 176.

10.3 Keeping a Safe Distance:
Jacob and Laban

Genesis 31 picks up on several themes found in previous episodes involving anger. In many ways, it offers a more in-depth treatment of hardships that transpire between shepherds, as well as the fierce anger that can
result. It also picks up on previous themes of brotherhood. Although Jacob
and Laban are technically nephew and uncle, the Hebrew word for brother,
אח, is used several times here to describe their relationship, just as it was
with Abram and Lot (29:12, 15; see also 31:54). Jacob and Laban interact
with one another over the course of three chapters (Genesis 29–31), and
several injustices transpire during the 20 years they live together. Most notably, Laban deceives the deceiver, giving Leah to Jacob as a bride rather
than the expected Rachel (29:20–25).[15] The wages for which Jacob works
are also a persistent concern. Jacob believes that Laban has robbed his family (31:6–7), while Laban's sons feel it is Jacob who has robbed their family (31:1). Faced with a history of wrongdoing that does not appear easily
rectified, Jacob and his wives decide to depart. When they do so, Rachel
steals Laban's teraphim, while 'Jacob steals Laban's mind' (וַיִּגְנֹב יַעֲקֹב אֶת־לֵב
לָבָן; 31:19–20), that is, Jacob leaves Laban clueless about their departure.[16]

When Laban realizes they have left, the text uses words with military
connotations to describe Laban's actions. He 'pursues' (רדף, 31:23) and
eventually 'overtakes' (נשׂג, 31:25) Jacob. However, God intervenes. Just as
Yʜᴡʜ warned Cain in order to protect Abel (4:6–7), so God here confronts
Laban in order to protect Jacob (31:24).[17] These divine words curb violence,
but anger nevertheless erupts when Laban and Jacob finally meet. The two
family members hurl accusations at one another in one of Genesis' most
detailed accounts of verbally expressed anger. Laban demands to know why
Jacob left without a farewell, why Jacob carried away his daughters 'like
captives of the sword' (כִּשְׁבֻיוֹת חָרֶב; 31:26), and why his idol (the teraphim)

---

15. See the excellent characterization of Laban's deception of Jacob in comparison
with Jacob's deception of Isaac in Victor P. Hamilton, *The Book of Genesis: Chapters 18–50*
(NICOT; Grand Rapids, MI: Eerdmans, 1994) 261–62.

16. The purpose of stealing the teraphim has been the subject of much debate. See the
overview of various explanations in Anne-Marie Korte, "Significance Obscured: Rachel's
Theft of the Teraphim—Divinity and Corporeality in Gen. 31," in *Begin with the Body:
Corporeality Religion and Gender* (ed. Jonneke Bekkenkamp and Maaike de Haardt; Leuven:
Peeters, 1998) 147–82. One possibility, significant for the discussion here, is that the theft
is an expression of Rachel's anger toward her father (Sharon Pace Jeansonne, *The Women
of Genesis: From Sarah to Potiphar's Wife* [Minneapolis: Fortress, 1990] 81).

17. In both cases, God sides primarily with the one who has less power (see 31:42).
Westermann observes, "It is surprising that already in the patriarchal stories the God of
the fathers is the one who stands by the weak and the one to whom the weak can have
recourse when oppressed by the powerful" (*Genesis*, 2.501).

was stolen (31:26–30). [18] Fokkelman describes Laban's accusations as "a psychological portrait of thirteen sentences, in which rage and resignation, castigation and sweetness contend for mastery and eventually achieve an unstable equilibrium. Honest indignation here enframes the whole." [19]

Jacob denies wrongdoing and asks Laban to substantiate his accusation concerning the teraphim (31:31–32). Laban rummages through Jacob's possessions, hoping to find the stolen god. At a key point, Laban comes to Rachel, who has placed the idol beneath the saddle on which she sits. In a particularly rich and multivalent statement, Rachel says, "Let not my lord be angry (אַל־יִחַר בְּעֵינֵי אֲדֹנִי) that I cannot rise before you, for I have the way of women" (31:35). Jacqueline Lapsley interprets these words as an instance of what Bakhtin calls "double-voiced discourse." [20] To Laban, it appears that his daughter is requesting that he not become angry that she cannot arise and show the proper respect because of menstruation. Rachel's words, however, testify on another level to the marginalized status of women, who could not stand and express their anger toward men in that culture (see §4.3.3). Though Laban has treated his daughters as though they were slaves (31:14–16), they lack the means of confronting him directly. However, Rachel's words "constitute a discourse of resistance, a subtle protest against the patriarchal discourse and social structures that attempt to silence her." [21] One could also note that Rachel's voice is perhaps the closest to the voice of God in this narrative. When she asks that Laban not be angry, she joins her voice with the deity who has pleaded with Laban not to harm Jacob.

Unable to substantiate his accusation, Laban now faces Jacob's anger (חרה, 31:36; see §6.5, §15.2.2). Like other episodes involving quarreling shepherds, Jacob contends (ריב; see §5.6) with Laban. [22] Jacob begins by asking his uncle what he has done wrong, demanding that Laban explain the nature of his 'crime' פשע, and 'sin' חטאת (31:36). Laban is unable to answer. Jacob then moves beyond the immediate wrongdoings to describe a long

---

18. On translating תְּרָפִים in the singular, see 1 Sam 19:13, 16 (although Zech 10:2); ibid., 2.493.

19. J. P. Fokkelman, *Narrative Art in Genesis: Specimens of Stylistic and Structural Analysis* (2nd ed.; Sheffield: JSOT Press, 1991) 166.

20. Jacqueline E. Lapsley, *Whispering the Word: Hearing Women's Stories in the Old Testament* (Louisville: Westminster John Knox, 2005) 21–34.

21. Ibid., 22. (See §§11.1–2 below for more on how Genesis challenges cultural assumptions regarding women and anger.)

22. Some commentators have overstated the way this episode resembles a legal proceeding (Westermann, *Genesis*, 2.490; Alonso Schökel, *Dónde está?* 186–87; and esp. Charles Mabee, "Jacob and Laban: The Structure of Judicial Proceedings [Genesis XXXI 25–42]," *VT* 30 [1980] 192–207). The key word is ריב, which refers to 'strife', particularly when wrongdoings have taken place. Naturally, strife between parties will involve accusations and the seeking of justice. But the concept need not take on legal associations, particularly when the setting has no judges in sight. As Wenham observes, it is not clear that this word ever refers to a 'lawsuit' in the Pentateuch (*Genesis*, 2.277). In the text at hand, there is no judge—or if there is, it is God, who has already rendered judgment (Gen 31:42).

history of injustices. Jacob speaks in detail of the harsh material conditions he has endured while living with Laban (31:36–42). Jacob accuses his uncle of unfairly forcing him to bear the loss of animals himself (31:38–39). He also accuses Laban of failing to pay him properly (31:41). Both accusations portray Laban as engaging in behavior forbidden by biblical and ancient Near Eastern law.[23] Jacob finishes his counterattack by providing his own spin on God's words of warning to Laban, asserting that God was rendering judgment in his own favor, siding with the afflicted (31:42).

In this anger-charged context, Laban recognizes that he and Jacob have reached a point in their relationship marked by limited possibilities. There is the potential for physical harm and violence, should these two remain in the same community (31:31, 42).[24] Rather than an intensification of anger and ensuing violence, Laban proposes that they legally separate, establishing a border between them. Jacob agrees, and he sets up a stone pillar (31:45), while Laban and his company (whom the text calls Jacob's *brothers* [אֶחָיו]) make a mound of stones (31:46–47). They covenant not to see one another again, and Jacob promises not to harm Laban's daughters. They all share a meal, stay the night together, then exchange kisses, and split apart.

The narrative does not shower praises on this permanent separation of family members, but it does suggest that this sort of "divorce" is preferable to additional anger and violence.[25] Faced with limited options, as characters in Genesis typically are, Laban and Jacob agree to something that is not an ideal solution but is a realistic resolution for moving forward. The characters do not overestimate their own abilities to bring good out of a difficult situation. They are acutely aware of the threat that anger poses to them both. They do whatever they can to blunt the worst effects of this emotion. Characters accept their moral limitations and act accordingly. The narrative as a whole suggests that it may be better to separate than to try to force good out of a situation that is beyond rectification.

10.4 Conclusion

These stories involving anger among shepherds reinforce the message of Genesis 3. Humanity is expelled from Eden. Whimsical notions of plentitude are mere fantasy. In the present world, anger carries the threat of

---

23. On bearing the loss of animals, see Exod 22:9–12[10–13]; "The Code of Hammurabi," translated by Martha Roth (*COS* 2.131:335–353, esp. 2.131:350, §266); Hermann Gunkel, *Genesis: Translated and Interpreted* (Macon, GA: Mercer University Press, 1997) 338; Wenham, *Genesis*, 2.277. On failing to pay properly, see Lev 19:13; Deut 15:13–14, 24:14–15; Jer 22:13; Mal 3:5; compare "The Code of Hammurabi," translated by Martha Roth (*COS* 2.131:335–53, esp. 2.131:350, §261). See also Westermann, *Genesis*, 2.496–97.

24. The use of 'pursue' (רדף) and 'overtook' (נשׂג) carry military connotations (31:23, 25).

25. David L. Petersen makes this point persuasively ("Genesis and Family Values," *JBL* 124 [2005] 5–23, esp. pp. 19–20). On similar practices in the ancient Near East, see the useful overview in Gunkel, *Genesis*, 341–42.

making life miserable, if not ending it all together. At times, survival hinges on one's ability to relinquish goods and even land, regardless of how un-fair these deeds may be. These narratives suggest that peace apart is better than conflict together. Although Genesis affirms the importance of family, it does not uphold familial togetherness as the highest ideal. In a world of competing and incommensurate goods, nonviolence is, at least on these occasions, preferable to community.

Chapter 11

Anger at the Margins

Genesis includes several texts that involve anger among the marginalized, particularly women and slaves. In this chapter, I explore these narratives. I look first at instances in which two women appear angry, (1) Sarai/h in Genesis 16 and 21 and (2) Rachel in Genesis 30. Attention then shifts to the episode involving Dinah in Genesis 34. Next, I turn to anger involving slaves, particularly the episodes involving Potiphar and Joseph in Genesis 39 and Pharaoh and two of his servants in Genesis 40–41. In subtle ways, many of these narratives push dominant cultural understandings involving anger. Regarding women, Genesis invites readers to see at least some women as having similar emotional experiences as men, in contrast to dominant cultural expectations. Regarding slaves and servants, Genesis shows that power differentials can lead to great injustices.

11.1 Sarai/h's Anger toward Hagar

The Hebrew Bible never explicitly portrays anger among female characters (§4.3.3). It most likely reflects cultural assumptions that associated anger primarily with males.[1] The book of Genesis, however, depicts Sarai/h and Rachel in ways that subtly push cultural assumptions about anger, inviting readers to see similarities between male and female experiences of emotion. These characters have striking similarities with one another, as well as with male characters who experience anger in Genesis. A common humanity, of which anger is an integral component, underlies them all.

Sarai/h is not explicitly called angry, and yet, in Genesis 16 and 21, most prototypical elements of anger are present. Power dynamics play

---

1. There may be some truth in Carol Meyers's argument that the situation on the ground in premonarchic Israel differed from the situation presented in the Hebrew Bible (*Discovering Eve: Ancient Israelite Women in Context* [New York: Oxford University Press, 1988]; see p. 181 for a concise summary). However, it seems unlikely that the entire Hebrew Bible, most likely written by many diverse people in many different contexts, would present only male figures as angry in all 519 of its explicit references to anger, were there not some cultural basis for doing so. As Lila Abu-Lughod points out, Bedouin societies today have very strict associations between gender and emotion (*Veiled Sentiments: Honor and Poetry in a Bedouin Society* [rev. ed.; Berkeley: University of California Press, 1999]). One suspects something similar took place in the cultures that gave rise to the Hebrew Bible. For additional discussion, see Ellen van Wolde, *Reframing Biblical Studies: When Language and Text Meet Culture, Cognition, and Context* (Winona Lake, IN: Eisenbrauns, 2009) 69–70, 72.

an important role, as is frequently the case with anger (16:1–2, 9; 21:10; §4.3.3). There are various perceptions of wrongdoing (16:5; 21:9, 11; §4.3.1) relating to belittling (קלל, 16:4, 5), affliction (ענה, 16:6, 11), and mockery (צחק, 21:9). Sarah furthermore seems jealous (21:10; see also 16:4–5; §5.1). In the end, these dynamics lead to separation (16:6; 21:10, 14), a very common outcome of anger in the Hebrew Bible (§4.3.4). Sarai/h appears angry, even if the text does not specifically say that she is.[2]

Genesis 16 presents Sarai as a barren elderly woman with few good options. According to Gen 15:3, it appears that, when she and her aged husband die, their goods will be given to a steward of the house. Rather than let this happen, Sarai gives Hagar to Abram that he might have children by her (16:2–4). Sarai appears to have the best of intentions, trying to bring what good she can out of an immensely difficult situation.[3] However, things go awry when the concrete realities of her sacrifice are set in motion (16:4–5). When Hagar becomes pregnant, she also becomes insubordinate, displaying contempt toward Sarai. The Hebrew verb used to describe this display of contempt, קלל, means to 'make light' or 'small' (16:4–5). Sarai, who already knows too well how small her womb is, receives further belittlement from Hagar. Sarai naturally becomes upset.[4] She explains to Abram what has transpired; he tells her to do whatever seems good in her eyes (16:6). Sarai afflicts (ענה) Hagar until the slave flees toward Egypt, her homeland (16:6).[5] A messenger of YHWH meets Hagar in the desert, presenting a mixed message. On the one hand, Hagar is told to return and submit to Sarai's affliction.[6] On the other, the celestial being promises Hagar countless descendants—the only time that a woman in the Hebrew Bible receives a promise of this sort. The text also says that she converses with God, who "hears her suffering" (16:11). Furthermore, Hagar becomes the only person in the Hebrew Bible to name the deity.[7] She is at once told to suffer and to prepare for blessings.

---

2. Many modern interpreters understand the text as implying that Sarai/h is angry (Thomas L. Brodie, *Genesis as Dialogue: A Literary, Historical, and Theological Commentary* [Oxford: Oxford University Press, 2001] 237; E. A. Speiser, *Genesis: Introduction, Translation, and Notes* [AB 1; Garden City, NY: Doubleday, 1964] 155).

3. Alice Ogden Bellis, *Helpmates, Harlots, and Heroes: Women's Stories in the Hebrew Bible* (Louisville: Westminster John Knox, 1994) 70–71; André LaCocque, *Onslaught against Innocence: Cain, Abel, and the Yahwist* (Eugene, OR: Cascade, 2008) 45.

4. Indeed, the Code of Hammurapi can be interpreted as forbidding Hagar's type of behavior (so Speiser, *Genesis*, 117, 119–21; *COS* 2.131:335–353, esp. p. 345, §146).

5. The word used to describe this affliction, ענה, could be translated 'abuse' (Speiser, *Genesis*, 116, 118). However, it may refer to something less severe, namely, "bring[ing] Hagar back from her exalted position as a temporary wife of Abram into her former low position of maidservant" (van Wolde, *Reframing Biblical Studies*, 288).

6. This command raises disturbing ethical issues pertaining to the character of God, as observed by Phyllis Trible, *Texts of Terror: Literary-Feminist Readings of Biblical Narratives* (Philadelphia: Fortress, 1984) 16.

7. Ibid., 16, 18.

Hagar returns to the house, but not all is well. In Genesis 21, Sarah recapitulates her past actions during the feast to celebrate Isaac's weaning. When she sees Ishmael 'playing' (מְצַחֵק, 21:9), she becomes disturbed and confronts Abraham, commanding him to cast out Hagar and Ishmael.[8] Sarah appears jealous, telling her husband to drive them out because she does not want Isaac to share Abraham's inheritance with his older half-brother (21:9–10). The text says that Sarah's "speech was exceedingly wicked in the eyes of Abraham" (21:11). Abraham's reaction is quite understandable. In essence, Sarah has asked Abraham both to become estranged from his son and to jeopardize Hagar's and Ishmael's lives.[9] As the subsequent narrative shows, Sarah's command approximates a death sentence for them both (21:14–21), hardly an appropriate punishment for a young person who engages in play or even mocking with his younger brother.[10] The text makes clear that anger can have unfair and disastrous consequences for those with little or no power.[11]

---

8. Interpreters have understood מְצַחֵק in 21:9 in three primary ways. First, some have suggested that Isaac is sexually abusing his brother (see how this verb is used in Gen 26:8). Second, some understand the text as saying that Isaac is mocking his brother. Finally, some see Ishmael as acting like his brother, that is, "Isaacing" Isaac (מְצַחֵק plays on the name יִצְחָק 'Isaac'). Key to interpreting this word is Gen 21:10, where Sarah says that she does not want Ishmael to share in Isaac's inheritance. These words suggest that Sarah has perceived Ishmael acting as though he were either equal to Isaac or superior. They do not suggest something so serious as sexual abuse (Amanda Benckhuysen, private communication, Oct. 29, 2008). Thus, it seems reasonable to see Ishmael's actions as involving either the amusement or mocking of Isaac, nothing that would merit a potentially deadly banishment. See also the insightful points made by Speiser, *Genesis*, 155; Jo Ann Hackett, "Rehabilitating Hagar: Fragments of an Epic Pattern," in *Gender and Difference in Ancient Israel* (ed. Peggy L. Day; Minneapolis: Fortress, 1989) 12–27, esp. pp. 20–21; and Victor P. Hamilton, *The Book of Genesis: Chapters 18–50* (NICOT; Grand Rapids, MI: Eerdmans, 1994) 79.

9. Claus Westermann, *Genesis* (3 vols.; Minneapolis: Fortress, 1984–2002) 2.340. See also Tikva Simone Frymer-Kensky, "Patriarchal Family Relationships and Near Eastern Law," *BA* 44 (1981) 209–14, esp. pp. 211–12; Victor P. Hamilton, *The Book of Genesis: Chapters 1–17* (NICOT; Grand Rapids, MI: Eerdmans, 1990) 443–46.

10. The text speaks of the expectation of death in a variety of ways, including Hagar's prayer in 21:16 and the language of 'leaving' [שלך] Ishmael under a shrub, which is terminology used in the Hebrew Bible to describe leaving someone to die (Hamilton, *The Book of Genesis: Chapters 18–50*, 83). Hagar and Ishmael have come nowhere near the sin of Cain, and yet they are forced to share his fate, driven out (גרש; 4:14, 21:10) to wander in the dangerous wilderness.

11. J. Cheryl Exum asserts, "The biblical narrator manages the reader's sympathy with Hagar and Ishmael, keeping it at a minimum" ("The Accusing Look: The Abjection of Hagar in Art," *Religion and the Arts* 11 [2007] 143–71, esp. p. 151). While it is true that the narrator gives virtually no access to Hagar and Ishmael's point of view, Exum's characterization is not exactly accurate. First, giving little attention to a key element in the plot is quite common for this narrator. It is not evidence that she or he is attempting to influence the readers against seeing it as significant (see Genesis 4, 22). Second, the events themselves speak sufficiently to elicit sympathy; one need not know the inner workings of Hagar and Ishmael's psyches to know they are distressed. Third and finally, much of the art that Exum discusses in this article illustrates that interpreters and artists have felt

Surprisingly, God tells Abraham not to be troubled by the matter and to do what Sarah commands because "through Isaac [Abraham's] descendants shall be named" (21:12–13).[12] While the deity's speech may contain a degree of capriciousness toward Hagar and Ishmael (compare 16:9), the deity's actions also display a degree of care for them. God does not have Abraham send them into the wilderness to die. Rather, the deity reiterates for Abraham the promise made previously to Hagar: Ishmael will become a "nation" (21:13; see also 16:10–12). Furthermore, the subsequent narrative shows God personally caring for Hagar and Ishmael in the desert (21:14–19).[13] The word נשׂא ('lift'), which was a key word in Gen 4:7 and 13:6, 10, 14, appears again in this anger-charged episode. Hagar lifts her voice (נשׂא, 21:16), and God provides both by opening her eyes to a spring of water and by telling Hagar to 'lift up' (נשׂא) her dying son because he will become a great nation (21:18). The text concludes by suggesting that this divine encounter was no anomaly: "God was with the boy as he grew" (21:20).

Although God tells Abraham to follow Sarah's command, God is actively involved in softening the blows of Sarah's anger, caring for the individuals who lack the power to defend themselves. This text joins others in Genesis (esp. 4:6–7 and 31:24, 42) in portraying God as attempting to help weaker parties endangered by the anger of someone with more power. The present narrative is not monologic, and it by no means offers a definitive statement of liberation from slavery or patriarchy.[14] However, it does bear witness to the unfair hardships that can result from anger in disproportionate power relationships. As Gerald West has pointed out, simply describing the problems resulting from inequalities may itself constitute a significant act of resistance.[15] The text testifies that not all is right when individuals

---

sympathy toward the slave and her son. Exum does not sufficiently explain where this consistent element of sympathy comes from if it is not elicited by the text.

12. Gerhard von Rad notes, "One could call vs. 12 f. the 'tense moment' in the structure of the narrative, for the reader has not expected that God would be on Sarah's side, but rather on Abraham's" (*Genesis* [rev. ed.; OTL; Philadelphia: Westminster, 1972] 233). See also Gerald O. West, *Genesis: The People's Bible Commentary* (Oxford: Bible Reading Fellowship, 2006) 119.

13. One aspect of this personal care is that, in the words of Hemchand Gossai, "Yahweh does what Abram and Sarai fail to do, namely to enter into conversation with Hagar" (*Power and Marginality in the Abraham Narrative* [Lanham, MD: University Press of America, 1995] 14).

14. As Margaret D. Kamitsuka puts it, "It goes without saying that Sarah and Hagar are 'sinned against' structurally in ways that cry out for an insurrection of subjugated knowledges" ("Toward a Feminist Postmodern and Postcolonial Interpretation of Sin," *JR* 84 [2004] 179–211, esp. p. 205). The point of the commentary above is not to deny the ways Sarai/h and Hagar are trapped in patriarchal systems. Rather, it is to highlight one small way that Genesis displays an openness to assigning similar emotional experiences to women and men. For more on the complex power dynamics at work in these narratives, see Gossai, *Power and Marginality*, 1–33.

15. Gerald O. West, *The Academy of the Poor: Towards a Dialogical Reading of the Bible* (Sheffield: Sheffield Academic Press, 1999) 45.

lack equal power.[16] Slaves who have done little or nothing wrong may find themselves suffering unjustly because of their masters' anger—something readers see later with Joseph and Potiphar (Gen 39:17–20; see §11.4 below).

Elsewhere, texts in Genesis uphold separation as the best way to deal with anger when other solutions are not available. This text, however, adds some qualifications. The narratives of Abram and Lot, Isaac and the Philistines, and Jacob and Laban suggest that separation can prevent anger from erupting into violence, but here with Sarai/h and Hagar, separation borders on being an act of violence in itself. Even though Yhwh allows and even helps the separation to happen, the text makes clear that Sarah's word was evil in the eyes of Abraham, requiring an act of God to prevent the deaths of Hagar and Ishmael. The text thus illustrates once again the dangerous nature of anger. It can quickly become violent and lead to the splintering of families.

Although elements in the text fault Sarah's anger, the narrative does so similarly to the way that it faults most male characters who become angry—that is, by showing the disastrous consequences to which their anger can lead. By hinting that Sarah is angry, the text takes an important step forward to challenge cultural assumptions and to acknowledge Sarah's humanity—even if particular elements of this humanity are morally problematic.

11.2 Rachel's Jealousy of Leah

Sarah is not the only woman that Genesis implies is angry.[17] In the character of Rachel, the text comes even closer to associating a woman with this emotion. As §5.1 explains, jealousy is related to anger in the Hebrew Bible. It may even be considered a subset of anger. Gen 30:1 says specifically that Rachel is jealous, and in so doing, it constitutes the only verse in the Hebrew Bible where a female character is explicitly described with this emotion. The verse reads, "When Rachel saw that she bore no children for Jacob, Rachel became jealous (וַתְּקַנֵּא) of her sister. So she said to Jacob, 'Give me children, or if there will be nothing, then I shall die.'"[18] Like Sarai/h's

---

16. See Nussbaum's account of Aeschylus (*The Fragility of Goodness*, 49–50). Note in particular Nussbaum's point that there are times when "the only thing remotely like a solution . . . is to describe and see the conflict clearly and acknowledge that there is no way out" (ibid.).

17. Ellen van Wolde claims that "the Hebrew Bible pays no attention at all to the sentiment of anger with reference to women" (*Reframing Biblical Studies*, 72). Although she is correct with respect to explicit references to anger, she could have given more attention to ways that the text subtly imples that females are angry.

18. Ironically, it is when Rachel gives birth that she dies (35:16–19; Athalya Brenner, "Female Social Behaviour: Two Descriptive Patterns within the 'Birth of the Hero' Paradigm," *VT* 36 [1986] 257–73, esp. p. 263). Commenting on 30:1, Christiana De Groot remarks, "Her cry reflects the doubly precarious position of women valued primarily for childbearing. If they don't have children, they have no life; and if they have children,

anger, Rachel's jealousy stems from her barrenness vis-à-vis another woman who has children by her husband.

Elsewhere in Genesis, readers see that sibling relations often lead to anger, particularly with sets of brothers: Cain and Abel, Jacob and Esau, and Joseph and his brothers.[19] In Genesis 30, anger and jealousy emerge among sisters. Here, Rachel remains barren while she watches Leah give birth four times (29:31–35). One is reminded of Cain's receiving no attention from Yₕwₕ while Abel obtains God's favor. After the text characterizes Rachel as jealous, it says that she demands children from her husband. Jacob, in turn, experiences anger himself (וַיִּחַר־אַף יַעֲקֹב, a common expression for anger; see §6.5; §15.2.2). He asks Rachel, "Am I in the place of God, who withheld from you the fruit of the womb?" Rachel then repeats the actions of Sarai in Genesis 16, giving her husband her slave to impregnate. Here in Genesis 30, however, one does not read of the type of conflict that Sarai/h experienced with Hagar. Instead, Rachel interprets Bilhah's births as signs that God has vindicated her and that she has prevailed over Leah (30:5–8).

Although this text is brief, it provides insights into anger with its focus on the inner workings of family life.[20] Rachel responds to the limitations of her barrenness the best that she can, giving Jacob her slave in the hope, as she puts it, "that [Bilhah] will give birth on my knees" (30:3).[21] Although God will later open Rachel's womb (Gen 30:22–24, 35:16–18), Rachel has no crystal ball or diviner's cup to predict the future. Like other characters in Genesis, she needs to make decisions amid her present realities, where no miracles are in sight. She does the best that she can in the barren land outside the Garden of Eden. Genesis never reveals ideal solutions to life's most difficult problems. It does, however, give readers a realistic picture of the hardships and limitations of a cursed world, so that they at least know what they might face. They become more aware of anger, its causes, and its attendant moral difficulties.

In the broader scope of Genesis, barrenness is related to God's word of punishment to Eve in Gen 3:16.[22] In the following verses (3:17–19; see also

---

they risk losing their life" ("Genesis," in *The IVP Women's Bible Commentary* [ed. Catherine Clark Kroeger and Mary J. Evans; Downers Grove, IL: InterVarsity, 2002] 20).

19. One could perhaps add Ishmael and Isaac, although the primary focus in Genesis 16 and 21 is on their mothers. Note also that Abram and Lot, as well as Jacob and Laban, are referred to as "brothers" or "kin" (אח).

20. Westermann observes that this brief text is the only glimpse readers receive of Rachel and Jacob interacting as a married couple: "To think that after the beautiful, gentle love story of 29:1–20 this angry exchange between the two is our first and only experience of their marriage!" (*Genesis*, 2.474).

21. This act refers to adoption (Gen 50:23; *COS*, 1.58:153–55, esp. p. 154).

22. Although עצבון and עצב in 3:16 have traditionally been associated with the pains of actually giving birth (1 Chr 4:9), they can carry emotional connotations (Prov 15:1, as well as instances of the verb עצב in Gen 6:6, 34:7, 45:5). Thus, this verse may be about not only the toil of labor but also the emotional pain of barrenness. The same is true of עצבון in 3:17. Its primary sense pertains to the physical labor, exertion, and suffering associated

4:11), God issues a word of punishment to Adam, which pertains to the soil. Interestingly, the limitations of womb and soil lead to much of the anger in Genesis.[23] One sees Sarah and Rachel as being implicitly angry over issues stemming from their barrenness. Likewise, readers see Abram and Lot, as well as Isaac and the Philistines, angry over issues stemming from the inability of the land to provide for all. Famine, an overwhelming failure of the land, appears frequently enough in Genesis that some interpreters name it as one of the book's motifs.[24] Although modern readers may not closely associate the barrenness of womb and soil, readers in the ancient Near East certainly would have. For example, numerous myths focus on fertility and portray a god such as Enki as impregnating the soil with rain.[25] The narratives of Genesis are also concerned with soil, wombs, and fertility, but rather than explaining barrenness in polytheistic terms, Genesis portrays a world that God has cursed because of the disobedience of humans. The limitations of womb and soil described at the outset of Genesis reverberate throughout the rest of the book, causing deep distress and often sparking anger.

11.3 When There Are No Good Options: Dinah's Brothers

A consistent element in Genesis' stories about anger is that characters do not face limitless possibilities but often are forced to make the best out of situations that are exceptionally difficult. Genesis 34 continues this line of the book's conversation about anger, affirming that there are cases when anger presents no good options for those who experience it. This passage has been analyzed a number of times above (§3.3; §7.2), so it needs only to be summarized here. Shechem rapes (or at least disgraces) Dinah, which enrages her brothers and leads to their killing the residents of Shechem's city.[26] The narrator describes their anger as intense (וַיִּחַר לָהֶם מְאֹד; 34:7),

---

with working the ground, but the larger context (for example, the reference to death in 3:19) makes clear that realities like famine have connections with this passage (see also the expulsion in 3:24 from a garden, presumably to a land less fertile).

23. See the related point made by Luis Alonso Schökel, *Dónde está tu hermano? Textos de fraternidad en el libro del Génesis* (Valencia: Institución San Jerónimo, 1985) 323.

24. Westermann, *Genesis*, 3.36–37; see also Katie M. Heffelfinger, "From Bane to Blessing: The Significance of Food in Genesis 37–50," in *Rounded Stones: Literary Readings of Genesis Narratives* (ed. Dennis Olson and Diane Sharon; SBLSymS; Atlanta: Society of Biblical Literature, forthcoming).

25. David Leeming, *Jealous Gods and Chosen People: The Mythology of the Middle East* (Oxford: Oxford University Press, 2004) 43–44.

26. As noted above (§3.3), I agree with Susanne Scholz, who argues that the text depicts rape ("Was It Really Rape in Genesis 34? Biblical Scholarship as a Reflection of Cultural Assumptions," in *Escaping Eden: New Feminist Perspectives on the Bible* [ed. Harold C. Washington, Susan Lochrie Graham, and Pamela Thimmes; Washington Square, NY: New York University Press, 1999] 182–98). At the same time, I do recognize a degree of ambiguity in the text, which makes possible other interpretations, such as are offered by Lyn M.

while Jacob characterizes it as overwhelmingly fierce, using the term אַף repeatedly, then switching to the term עברה (which refers to unrestrained anger), and furthermore using the adjective עז ('fierce') and the stative verb קשה ('be severe', Gen 49:5–7).[27]

Many condemn the brothers' anger and what they do with it, including Jacob when he uses these various terms (Gen 34:30, 49:6–7). But as shown above (§3.3), the text itself is much more ambiguous, presenting anger as a complex emotion that does not always have easy solutions. Although the brothers clearly have reason to be angry, it is not clear what they should do with this sort of rage. Shechem's people appear ready to make some level of reparations. In fact, Shechem's father, Hamor, makes Jacob and his family the most generous offer in Genesis, essentially agreeing to whatever they ask (34:9–12). While generosity frequently assuages the worst effects of anger in Genesis (see §§10.1–2 above, §§12.1–2 below), it does not have this effect here; the text makes clear that generosity is not a magic solution to anger's worst problems. For Dinah's brothers, there is nothing that can be done to rectify the outrage that has occurred. They agree to Hamor's offer only so that they can slaughter all the inhabitants of Hamor's city, grossly distorting the rite of circumcision in the process.

The narrative refuses to speak monologically about the brothers' response. It gives voice to Jacob's perspective, who condemns them in both Gen 34:30 and 49:5–7. However, it does not allow this voice to triumph over the brothers, who are given the last word in the narrative (but not the last word in the book). When confronted by their father in 34:30, they ask, "Should he make a whore out of our sister?" (34:31). Neither the narrator nor Jacob is able to answer this question directly. It lingers for readers to wrestle with, unanswered and perhaps unanswerable. It is wrong to slaughter the innocent, but it is also wrong to pretend that Shechem is guiltless. Amid the limited world that characters in Genesis inhabit, the brothers' desire for justice (punishing Shechem) ironically leads to injustice (punishing all the other inhabitants of his city as well). Characters inhabit a broken world, where the right course of action with anger is not always apparent or even possible. Genesis does not place a veneer over the difficulties of the moral life or present a world in which moral perfection is still possible. In the cursed land outside Eden, humans often face few possibilities and must deal with anger's deadly force even when all options are morally troublesome.[28]

Bechtel, "What if Dinah Is Not Raped? (Genesis 34)," *JSOT* 62 (1994) 19–36; and van Wolde, *Reframing Biblical Studies*, 283–96.

27. See §5.8, §6.5, §15.2.1, §15.3.3.

28. At times, commentators do not do justice to the realities and difficulties of moral living in Genesis. For example, Benno Jacob writes, "All conflicts in the story of the patriarchs end in harmony and reconciliation" (*The First Book of the Bible: Genesis* [trans. Ernest I. Jacob and Walter Jacob; New York: Ktav, 1974] 176). This claim is certainly not true of

11.4 Exposing the Plight of the Powerless:
Anger toward Slaves

The beginning of this chapter discussed the narratives of Sarai/h and Hagar. It showed that individuals without power can be placed in extremely difficult situations—situations they do not appear to deserve—because of anger on the part of their superiors. This sort of message is reaffirmed in Genesis 39, where Joseph encounters the anger of Potiphar. The story entails power, sex, and injustice. Potiphar's wife repeatedly attempts to seduce Joseph, who resists her advances. On one occasion, when the two are alone in the house, she physically seizes him. Joseph manages to flee but without his garment (39:7–12). When Potiphar returns home, his wife claims that Joseph tried to seduce her, presenting the garment as evidence against Joseph (39:16–19). Thus, for the second time (see 37:31–33), a garment is used deceitfully to cover a crime against Joseph.[29] In response to his wife's allegations, Potiphar becomes angry (וַיִּחַר אַפּוֹ in 39:19 is a common, somewhat nondescript expression for anger; see §6.5, §15.2.2) and has the slave imprisoned (39:20). Joseph first suffered at the hands of his brothers, then faced sexual harassment amid slavery, and now is the victim of false accusations and wrongful imprisonment.[30]

When Genesis 39 is read alongside Genesis 16 and 21, several interesting patterns emerge. Joseph and Hagar may not initially appear to be similar characters, given their differences in origin, gender, power, and status with respect to election. However, there are striking analogies. One of them is a slave *from* Egypt *in* the house of Abraham, while the other is a slave *in* Egypt *from* the house of Abraham. Both Hagar and Joseph are asked to become involved in sexual acts by superiors with little regard for their own will. Both characters face anger from their superiors. Both suffer as a result of this anger, facing banishment. Neither deserves this punishment. However, as slaves, they are unable to defend themselves. Nevertheless, even in their places of banishment, both Hagar (along with Ishmael) and Joseph experience God's presence. Gen 21:20 says, "God was with the boy [Ishmael]." Similarly, Gen 39:21 says, "Yhwh was with Joseph" (see also 39:23).

With these various parallels centering on injustices resulting from anger, the text provides at least subtle critiques of disproportionate power

---

the conflict between Dinah's brothers and the Shechemites, where there is no harmony and reconciliation, only bloodshed and violence. One can also question whether Genesis truly envisions harmony and reconciliation as following on the heels of conflict between patriarchs. Aside from Joseph and his brothers, there may be peaceful agreements, but there is frequently estrangement and lasting separation.

29. Nelly Furman, "His Story versus Her Story: Male Genealogy and Female Strategy in the Jacob Cycle," *Semeia* 46 (1989) 141–49.

30. On Joseph as a victim of sexual harassment and violence, see West, *Genesis*, 188; Heather A. McKay, "Confronting Redundancy as Middle Manager and Wife: The Feisty Woman of Genesis 39," *Semeia* 87 (1999) 215–31, esp. pp. 226–28.

relationships, exposing some of the moral problems inherent with slavery and servitude. Again, it is worth noting that simply describing the problems of unequal power relations may constitute a significant act of resistance.[31] Moreover, these texts portray God as actively concerned for marginalized individuals who suffer unduly. Although it is easy to fault Genesis for not doing more to counteract unequal social relations, resistance literature can (and often does) work in subtle ways to question the status quo.[32] This is the case both with Genesis' texts that subtly affirm the emotional experience of women and with texts that show that unequal power relations lead to mistreatment of the powerless, particularly around issues of anger. Elements within Genesis counteract some of the more problematic cultural features of its time.

Indeed, Genesis 39 gives a word of warning to individuals who read from the perspective of Potiphar. The narrative shows that the human desire to punish the guilty and to free one's home from immorality may in fact have the opposite effects when anger is involved. When Potiphar receives news that his servant Joseph has attempted to seduce his wife, he naturally becomes angry, and he acts in a way that from his perspective seems just and reasonable. He takes care of the matter not by physically harming his slave but by imprisoning him.[33] However, the readers of this narrative know something Potiphar does not: Joseph is innocent; the allegations are false. The narrative shows that, even when characters act carefully in their anger in order to bring about justice, injustice can instead occur.[34] The problem appears to be compounded by differences in power. Potiphar acts unilaterally, while Joseph is unable to defend himself.

The same sort of problem may be signaled by Pharaoh's anger toward his two officials in Gen 40:2 and 41:10, which is conveyed by the term קצף, a term used exclusively of people in power (§6.5, §15.3.1).[35] The exact

---

31. West, *The Academy of the Poor*, 45.

32. Ibid., 44–55; Daniel L. Smith-Christopher, *A Biblical Theology of Exile* (OBT; Minneapolis: Fortress, 2002) 23–24; Mark G. Brett, *Genesis: Procreation and the Politics of Identity* (Old Testament Readings; London: Routledge, 2000) 44; see also James C. Scott, *Weapons of the Weak: Everyday Forms of Peasant Resistance* (New Haven, CT: Yale University Press, 1985) 28–41, 284–89; idem, *Domination and the Arts of Resistance: Hidden Transcripts* (New Haven, CT: Yale University Press, 1990) passim.

33. As Speiser observes, this punishment is "surprisingly mild" (*Genesis*, 304).

34. One is reminded of Aristotle's teaching about anger: "Any[one] can become angry—that is easy . . . but to [do this] to the right person, and to the right amount, and at the right time, and for the right purpose, and in the right way—this is not within every[one]'s power and is not easy; so that to do these things properly is rare, praiseworthy, and noble" (*Eth. Nic.*, esp. 2.9.2 [trans. H. Rackham; LCL; Cambridge: Harvard University Press, 1934]).

35. In Gen 40:6, it is possible that the cupbearer and baker were angry (זעף) because of what happened to them (van Wolde, *Reframing Biblical Studies*, 68). However, it seems more likely that they were distressed over their troubling dream. In addition to referring to anger, זעף can refer to being disturbed and despondent (see §15.1.2).

circumstances surrounding this anger are not revealed in the text. However, it is clear that Pharaoh imprisons two of his servants, only to restore one to his previous position while killing the other. This course of events raises questions about whether Pharaoh rightfully imprisoned them both in the beginning. Was the cupbearer innocent all along and imprisoned only by mistake (like Joseph)? Were the breadmaker's actions so problematic that he really deserved death? Why does Pharaoh initially give these servants the same punishment, only to reverse course suddenly, freeing one and killing the other? The text does not answer questions of this sort, but it leaves open the possibility that Pharaoh's anger leads to undue suffering by his servants, much like the suffering experienced by Hagar and Joseph.

11.5 Conclusion

Genesis is not a remedy to all social evils, and it is certainly possible for readers to dwell on the most morally problematic features of Genesis, such as 16:9 and 21:12. However, Gerald West reminds interpreters that it is not their responsibility to magnify the Bible's problems in hopes of abolishing its sacred status. Rather, he argues, our duty is to amplify the most edifying voices in the text. Echoing Gustavo Gutiérrez, West writes, "The question is not whether the Bible will survive but whether it will bring life or death and how we can ensure that it does indeed bring life."[36] Jacqueline Lapsley makes a similar point: "The question is not, then, *can* the Bible be understood as making any positive contribution to ethical and theological reflection, even on gender issues, but *how* do we read in such a way that we are open to those contributions?"[37] The above discussion of Genesis 16, 21, 34, 39–41 offers possibilities for reading Genesis' accounts of anger in ways that are open to the life-giving voices in the text. Although Genesis is no feminist manifesto, it takes steps toward affirming the emotional equality of men and women in a culture that apparently did not. Even though Genesis never shows readers how to achieve a society free from sexual abuse and mistreatment, it does present an honest account of how vexing these matters can be. While the Bible's first book is no emancipation proclamation, it shows the types of problems inherent to disproportionate power relations such as slavery.

---

36. Gerald O. West, "Review of R. S. Sugirtharajah, ed., *Voices from the Margin: Interpreting the Bible in the Third World*," *RBL* (2007) 5, http://www.bookreviews.org/pdf/5534_5829 .pdf (accessed June 13, 2008).

37. Lapsley, *Whispering the Word*, 10.

Chapter 12

Attempting Reconciliation:
Brothers at the End of Genesis

In the last two generations of Genesis, brothers become fiercely angry and nearly kill one another. However, the fate of Abel is averted, and the narrative explores what the future may hold for siblings in the decades following brushes with fratricide. Although the final chapter of Genesis presents resolutions for a family torn apart by anger and jealousy, the Bible's first book never loses its realistic focus on the dangers and difficulties of engaging this emotion.

12.1 A Short-Lived Reunion: Jacob and Esau

Separation is a common outcome of anger (§4.3.4). In the narratives involving Jacob and Esau, Genesis explores whether the estrangement caused by anger can be overcome. It does so in ways that poignantly depict the difficulty and pain that can accompany attempts at reconciliation. The exchanges between Esau and Jacob bear witness to the limitations that humans face and the difficulty for all parties in rebuilding the community that anger and its attendant issues have previously driven apart. The text comes close to envisioning forgiveness and reconciliation, but ultimately it stops short, testifying to the lasting impact of anger.

The hostilities between the two brothers begin in Rebecca's womb (25:21–26). In Gen 25:29–34, they sharpen when Jacob forces his own brother to sell his birthright in exchange for lentil stew. Many Western commentators who have probably never experienced life-threatening hunger quickly condemn Esau's actions.[1] However, the text depicts Esau as a person facing limitations and restraints on a variety of levels. He inhabits a world in which the soil has been cursed, and the land does not always provide the sustenance one needs. Facing a hunger that he sees as imperiling his own life (25:32), the famished (and obviously unsuccessful) hunter

---

1. Hermann Gunkel, *Genesis: Translated and Interpreted* (Macon, GA: Mercer University Press, 1997) 291–93; Judah Goldin, "The Youngest Son or Where Does Genesis 38 Belong?" *JBL* 96 (1977) 36; see also Devora Steinmetz, *From Father to Son: Kinship, Conflict, and Continuity in Genesis* (Literary Currents in Biblical Interpretation; Louisville: Westminster John Knox, 1991) 97–98, 150; Joel S. Kaminsky, *Yet I Loved Jacob: Reclaiming the Biblical Concept of Election* (Nashville: Abingdon, 2007) 45, 56.

enters his brother's kitchen, only to find his sibling exploiting his desperate situation, willing to share food only in exchange for his birthright. Confronted with difficulties and limitations on every level, Esau sells his birthright in this episode, which foreshadows the loss of his father's blessing to the same conniving brother. Nussbaum describes how Greek tragedy "shows good people doing bad things, things otherwise repugnant to their ethical character and commitments because of circumstances whose origin does not lie with them."[2] One sees something quite similar here with Esau. Narratives such as this one illustrate vividly the constraints that individuals face and the ways that they do not make decisions in a moral vacuum or an ideal world; they make them while they are subject to the often-harsh gusts of fortune and luck.

In Genesis 27, the strife between these brothers reaches a pinnacle as Jacob, operating under Rebecca's direction, deceives his father, Isaac, and robs his brother, Esau, of his blessing. In Gen 27:41–42, Esau appears poised to recapitulate the sin of Cain. The text uses the verb שׂטם to signal that Esau 'harbored anger' against Jacob and desired to harm him (see §6.5, §15.3.4). It also mentions the verb 'kill' (הרג; 27:41, 42), the same word used to depict Cain's murder in 4:8. Also like Gen 4:1–16, this text uses the word 'brother' (אח) several times in an exceptionally short amount of space (five appearances in as many verses, 27:41–45). Esau yearns for the days of his father's mourning to draw near, so he may then kill his brother. However, Rebecca intervenes, again looking out for Jacob's well-being while thwarting Esau's plans. She warns Jacob of Esau's intentions, telling her younger son to flee to her brother Laban until Esau's anger subsides.[3] She describes Esau's emotion both with the generic term for anger אף and with the term חמה, which is often used of grave anger that has the potential for deadly violence (§6.5, §15.2.1, §15.2.3).

Twenty years pass. When Jacob is forced back home, Esau initially appears ready to kill him. In two places, the text makes clear that Esau approaches Jacob with 400 men (32:7[6], 33:1). If Abram was victorious in rescuing Lot from several armies with 318 trained men in Genesis 14, then Esau's 400 men appear more than enough to exact vengeance on Jacob and his family here in Genesis 32–33. The younger brother naturally fears for his life. He does all that he can to counteract his past actions. Foremost, he follows in the footsteps of his grandfather, Abram, and his father, Isaac, acting with generosity to diffuse an anger-charged situation. Jacob offers

---

2. Martha C. Nussbaum, *The Fragility of Goodness: Luck and Ethics in Greek Tragedy and Philosophy* (Cambridge: Cambridge University Press, 2001) 25.

3. In Genesis, Jacob's movement from one location to another frequently signals a change in character. For more on this literary device of linking personal and geographical transformation, see the discussion of *chronotopes* in Mikhail Bakhtin, *The Dialogic Imagination* (trans. C. Emerson and M. Holquist; Austin: University of Texas Press, 1981) 84, 111–15, 120.

droves of animals (550 total) to Esau as a gift (32:14–22[13–21], 33:8–11). The Hebrew word מנחה ('gift') is highly significant, appearing here for the first time since it was used in the narrative of Cain and Abel (32:14[13], 19[18], 21[20], 22[21]; 33:10; see 4:3, 4, 5). Whereas Cain's and Abel's gifts to God led eventually to a rage-filled murder, Jacob's gifts to Esau serve the opposite purpose, preventing fratricide. It is clear that Jacob has robbed Esau of what was rightfully the older brother's. Now, in an act of significant sacrifice, Jacob offers Esau something akin to reparations. Jacob specifically commands Esau to take his ברכה ('blessing', 33:11), the very thing that he stole from Esau in Genesis 27.[4] Jacob shows that he is no longer someone who steals from Esau but someone who gives to Esau. This act of generosity alters Esau's perception of Jacob and of past wrongdoings, facilitating an alleviation of Esau's prolonged anger.[5] Esau sees that Jacob has changed.

In addition to giving significant possessions, Jacob's gestures and speech illustrate a willingness to give up the power he has taken from Esau. This relinquishing of power is particularly evident when one compares Isaac's blessing of Jacob with the text at hand. In 27:29, Isaac blessed Jacob by saying, "May your mother's children bow down to you." Here in 33:3, 6–7, however, Jacob and his family bow down to Esau.[6] Isaac's blessing of Jacob also contained the words "Be lord over your brothers" (27:29), but here, Jacob repeatedly refers to Esau as "my lord" (32:5[4], 6[5], 19[18]; 33:8, 13, 14, 15), while calling himself "your servant" (32:19[18], 21[20]).[7] In speech and deed, Jacob is giving back what he previously took from Esau, voiding the blessing that he received through deceit. The younger brother who

---

4. See 27:12, 35, 36 [2x], 38, 41; see also ברך ('bless') in 27:4, 7, 10, 19, 23, 25, 27 [2x], 29 [2x], 30, 31, 33, 34, 38, 41. For commentary, see Michael Fishbane, *Text and Texture: Close Readings of Selected Biblical Texts* (New York: Schocken, 1979) 52; Frederick E. Greenspahn, *When Brothers Dwell Together: The Preeminence of Younger Siblings in the Hebrew Bible* (New York: Oxford University Press, 1994) 127.

5. Giving is presented as a way of alleviating anger and hostility, not only here in Genesis (see also §10.1, §12.2), but also in other biblical texts (Prov 21:14, 25:21–22), the ancient Near East ("The Story of Idrimi, King of Alalakh," *ANET*, 557–58; "Emesh and Enten: Enlil Chooses the Farmer-God," in S. N. Kramer, *Sumerian Mythology: A Study of Spiritual and Literary Achievement in the Third Millennium b.c.* [Memoirs of the American Philosophical Society; Philadelphia: American Philosophical Society, 1944] 49–51; "Horus and Seth," *AEL* 2:214–23, esp. 215, 222]; "Counsels of Wisdom," in W. G. Lambert, *Babylonian Wisdom Literature* [Winona Lake, IN: Eisenbrauns, 1996] 96–107, esp. 101, lines 41–45), and different parts of the modern world (Catherine A. Lutz, *Unnatural Emotions: Everyday Sentiments on a Micronesian Atoll and Their Challenge to Western Theory* [Chicago: University of Chicago Press, 1998] 175; David L. Petersen, "Genesis and Family Values," *JBL* 124 [2005] 5–23, esp. p. 20).

6. The Amarna letters attest to the sevenfold bowing depicted in this text (James B. Pritchard, ed., *The Ancient Near East: An Anthology of Texts and Pictures* [Princeton: Princeton University Press, 1958] 262–77, §234, 244, 250, 254, 270, 271, 280, 286, 287, 288, 289, 290, 297, 298, 320).

7. While a different Hebrew word lies behind 'lord' in 27:29 (גְּבִיר) and 'lord' in chaps. 32–33 (אָדוֹן), there are obvious conceptual similarities.

once demanded his brother's birthright now asks only to receive grace in his brother's eyes (33:8, 10, 15).

Jacob's generosity and humility have a profound impact on Esau. Although the elder brother appeared poised to kill the younger in a Cain-like act of anger, Esau instead embraces Jacob, kisses him, and together the two brothers weep (33:4).[8] In Gen 32:21[20], the night before Jacob and Esau confront one another, the younger brother says that he hopes Esau, in response to his generosity, will 'lift my face' (יִשָּׂא פָנָי). The phrase refers to acceptance, perhaps even forgiveness. Esau's actions in chap. 33 suggest that Jacob experiences exactly what he had hoped. In this sense, there is a fulfillment of God's words to Cain: 'If you do what is good, then a lifting' (אִם־תֵּיטִיב שְׂאֵת; 4:7a).

Not only does Esau embrace and kiss Jacob; he also demonstrates his acceptance of Jacob by inviting him to journey with him (33:12), in marked contrast to Jacob's solitary journey in Gen 27:45. The invitation appears to be an offer for the two to live together in community.[9] Readers are thus offered a glimpse of anger overcome—a case in which brothers live in unity despite the grave transgressions that their relationship once endured.

The glimpse, however, is fleeting. Jacob turns down his brother's offer, saying that he would not be able to keep pace with Esau if they traveled together. Jacob's words appear primarily to be a ploy, giving him an excuse for not staying with Esau. Nevertheless, there is some truth in his assertion. Jacob is still limping after his wrestling match in Genesis 32. He is in a weak, vulnerable, and humbled position. He wants distance, not togetherness. Jacob says that he would like to meet with his brother later at Seir, something that never occurs in the text (33:13–14). In response, Esau offers essentially to be like a keeper (שֹׁמֵר) for Jacob, saying that he would like to leave soldiers with him, presumably to protect him (33:15).

Jacob again refuses Esau's offer, perhaps out of fear that Esau is secretly planning to kill him or else out of a sense of shame and guilt for past wrongs. Although readers were concerned that Esau's anger would prevent reconciliation between the brothers, Esau's anger is not the final problem. In a poignant twist of the narrative, it is fear, shame, and guilt on Jacob's part that prevent a lasting reunion. The conclusion of the episode says that

8. The BHS apparatus suggests that reference to Esau's kissing Jacob is perhaps an addition, based on the *puncta extraordinaria* (see also the LXX). It also suggests that one read וַיֵּבְךְ ('he wept') instead of וַיִּבְכּוּ ('they wept'). However, it is unclear that one needs to deviate from the MT (Claus Westermann, *Genesis* [3 vols.; Minneapolis: Fortress, 1984–2002] 2.523). Literarily, this act of kissing echoes Jacob's making of peace with Laban (32:1[31:55]), and it foreshadows the subsequent forgiveness between Joseph and his brothers (45:15).

9. Thus, there is the reference to "until I come to my lord at Seir" in 33:14. As Westermann puts it, "Esau takes it for granted that they will now go on together. He does not name the destination; but when he says he will go on ahead, he can mean only (and this is confirmed by v. 14) that Jacob will live in the place where he is now living" (ibid., 2.526).

Jacob and Esau lived in separate places (33:16–17). Much later, after the narrative says the two brothers came together momentarily for their father's funeral (35:29), the text echoes Gen 13:6 and says that Esau separated himself from Jacob because the land could not 'lift' (or 'support' נשׂא) the two of them together (Gen 36:6–8).[10]

In these accounts of Jacob and Esau, readers encounter variations on previous themes. Anger is presented as a deadly and ominous force that is particularly dangerous within families. Genesis 33 shows readers that the estrangement resulting from anger need not be permanent, although it makes clear that sacrifices are required to find a way beyond past wrongdoings. At the cost of many possessions, intense fear, and great risk to himself and his family, Jacob gains some sense that he has favor in the eyes of his brother. But the reconciliation is short-lived at best. The brothers soon go their separate ways. While there is a moment of forgiveness here, the narrative is painfully realistic about the difficulty, demands, and dangers of attempting to assuage anger. Genesis does not portray anger or forgiveness in simplistic terms. It minimizes neither the force of anger nor the prolonged impact that it can have on human lives. The desire patterned in readers for someone to provide sustenance and protection for family members again comes up short, as individuals' limitations along with the limitations of the land prevent the possibility of brothers dwelling together.

12.2 Joseph, a Brothers' Keeper

Only in Joseph and his brothers do readers finally see characters overcoming the worst effects of anger. These prolonged narratives provide a capstone to the preceding episodes of anger in Genesis. As Brodie puts it, the Joseph story "is not a special pearl, different from the rest of Genesis. . . . It is Genesis breaking into full bloom, a blossoming that builds on all that precedes."[11] These accounts of Joseph expound on many ideas mentioned previously. Specific words and phrases are echoed, while particular events are recapitulated. Through these echoes and recapitulations, these narratives reinforce and qualify what previous episodes teach about anger, drawing attention to both common motifs and the broader ethical

---

10. As Kaminsky mentions, scholars have debated whether Jacob and Esau are reconciled (*Yet I Loved Jacob*, 54–56). Kaminsky aims for a middle ground, asserting that some level of reconciliation takes place. In contrast, Petersen interprets this passage as Jacob engaging in "a verbal jousting match" to disarm Esau, who seeks to kill him ("Genesis and Family Values," 21). While Petersen on the whole does very important work with this passage, his emphasis on Esau's continually trying to kill his brother does not match well with Gen 33:4, where he embraces Jacob.

11. Thomas L. Brodie, *Genesis as Dialogue: A Literary, Historical, and Theological Commentary* (Oxford: Oxford University Press, 2001) 351; see also James G. Williams, "Number Symbolism and Joseph as Symbol of Completion," *JBL* 98 (1979) 86; Kaminsky, *Yet I Loved Jacob*, 72–78.

significance of the matter at hand.[12] In many ways, these narratives involving Joseph and his brothers offer resolutions to the problems encountered earlier. It is only here that brothers find a way to regain the community that anger and jealousy previously tore apart.

While Genesis thus presents a sort of resolution in these narratives, it never loses sight of how difficult the moral life is. Although solutions to prior problems are found in the Joseph narratives, so are the harsh realities found elsewhere in Genesis. There is no return to Eden. Contrary to what some claim, the narrative never attempts to portray Joseph as a saint.[13] As Visotzky astutely points out, readers of Genesis encounter something far more "adult" than any biography of ancient saints:

> It is not the niceness of Genesis that makes it attractive to generation after generation of readers. Quite the contrary, it's the gut-wrenching quiddity of the narrative that draws us in year after year. Genesis is all those dirty little secrets we know about one another strung into a "family" narrative. This family is so "nuclear" it's fissile. Genesis is R, it's NC-17. Genesis is what spouses hide from the neighbors, hide from the children, hide from each other. The narratives of Genesis are roiling in repressions we refuse to tell our therapists. It's not pretty, it's not nice, it's not for polite company—and it's canonical Scripture for hundreds of millions of Jews and Christians, the background for a revelation to hundreds of millions more Muslims, and the inspiration to zillions more secular folks who just happen to enjoy reading Western literature.[14]

Like the rest of Genesis, the stories of Joseph and his brothers portray fundamentally flawed characters who struggle to prevent evil from erupting into utter chaos. Joseph and his brothers eventually move beyond anger, but they all display morally problematic behavior with this emotion along the way. The text explains that anger can subside but only after great difficulties.

---

12. Both Sommer and Hays provide excellent discussions of allusions and echoes within texts (Benjamin D. Sommer, *A Prophet Reads Scripture: Allusion in Isaiah 40–66* [Stanford, CA: Stanford University Press, 1998] esp. pp. 6–31; Richard B. Hays, *Echoes of Scripture in the Letters of Paul* [New Haven, CT: Yale University Press, 1989] esp. pp. 29–32). These insights inform the discussions below about how Genesis 37–50 forms a capstone to previous narratives about anger, although some of the specifics of Sommer's and Hays's works (for example, Sommer's technical definition of "echo") are not retained.

13. Some interpreters have attempted to portray Joseph (and other characters of Genesis) in this light, such as Benno Jacob, *The First Book of the Bible: Genesis* (trans. Ernest I. Jacob and Walter Jacob; New York: Ktav, 1974) 249, 253, 284, 287, 296, 302. These characterizations do not fit easily with the ways that the text portrays Joseph's multiple moral shortcomings (37:2; 42:7, 9, 12, 14, 16, 17, 30; 44:1–15). More accurate portrayals of this patriarch can be found in Gunkel, *Genesis*, 424; Aaron Wildavsky, "Survival Must Not Be Gained through Sin: The Moral of the Joseph Stories Prefigured through Judah and Tamar," *JSOT* 62 (1994) 37–48, esp. p. 38.

14. Burton L. Visotzky, *The Genesis of Ethics* (New York: Crown, 1996) 9–10.

The narrative begins in Genesis 37 by recounting Jacob's favoritism toward Joseph (v. 3).[15] Much like God's favoritism toward Abel, Jacob's preferential treatment results in hatred and jealousy among the brothers who are less favored (שׂנא in 37:4, 5, 8; קנא in 37:11; see §5.1). This ill feeling is compounded when Joseph boasts of dreams that depict himself as superior to his older brothers and even his parents (37:5–10). As with Cain, jealousy leads Joseph's brothers to thoughts of fratricide. When they see the "master dreamer" approaching from a distance, they plan to "kill" him (37:18–19; the word is הרג, the same word as 4:8; 27:41, 42).[16] The individuals who were responsible for killing Shechem and his people now appear ready to kill their own brother. However, first Reuben and then Judah persuade the others to take alternate courses of action, which they do by throwing Joseph into a cistern and later selling him into slavery.

Both Reuben and Judah mention the word דם ('blood') in their appeals for the brothers to desist from killing Joseph. Reuben urges his brothers, "Pour out no blood!" (37:22), while Judah asks his brothers, "What is the profit if we kill our brother and cover his blood?" (37:26). Here the book of Genesis, like much of the Hebrew Bible, upholds the basic conviction that blood is no mere bodily fluid. Rather, it is an intensely powerful and precious substance containing life itself (see Lev 17:11), a substance that is wrapped up in goodness, evil, and the fates that befall people. Much of the Bible suggests that innocent blood stains those who shed it, releasing forces that demand vengeance. These forces are drawn to and endanger the perpetrator of violent acts, much like the beast at the entryway to sin described in Gen 4:7. Indeed, in Gen 4:11–12, Abel's blood cries out from the ground, bringing an angry deity to punish Cain. Similarly, the Noahic covenant forbids the shedding of human blood, with particular reference to one's brother, describing how God seeks out individuals who shed it (9:4–6). Here in Genesis 37, Reuben and Judah have at least some awareness of these explosive and volatile forces released when blood is shed. They appeal to blood to convince their brothers to sell Joseph rather than kill him. However, it is remarkable that, later in Genesis 42, when the brothers face

---

15. The opening lines of this story include the words יוֹסֵף (37:2) . . . הָיָה רֹעֶה אֶת־אֶחָיו בַּצֹּאן. On the surface, it appears that this sentence should be translated 'Joseph . . . was a shepherd with (= אֵת) his brothers among the flocks'. However, as Duane L. Christensen, points out, the syntax leaves open the possibility that it could be rendered 'Joseph was shepherding (אֵת = marker of the definite direct object) his brothers among the flocks' ("Anticipatory Paronomasia in Jonah 3:7–8 and Genesis 37:2," *RB* 90 [1983] 261–63, esp. p. 263). Given that Joseph later acts as a shepherd for his brothers, providing them with nourishment and security, it is possible to understand this verse in terms of anticipatory paronomasia, foreshadowing what is to come. (See also §9.2 on the connections between shepherding and acting as a keeper [שׁמר].)

16. The translation 'master dreamer' is borrowed from Victor P. Hamilton, *The Book of Genesis: Chapters 18–50* (NICOT; Grand Rapids, MI: Eerdmans, 1994) 417.

a series of frightening events in Egypt, they suspect that these events are not a stretch of bad luck but, rather, a reckoning for Joseph's blood (42:22).[17] Vengeance comes for individuals whose anger leads to bloodshed, or in this case, even forced separation.

Before examining the details of Genesis 42, however, we should note what happens in the intervening chapters. After Joseph's brothers sell him into slavery for 20 pieces of silver (37:25–30), readers encounter a variety of subplots involving Judah and Tamar (chap. 38), Joseph and Potiphar's wife (chap. 39), and Joseph's imprisonment and eventual rise to power (chaps. 40–41). Then, at the beginning of chap. 42, the brothers who were flung apart by jealousy come back into each other's presence. The limitations of land are once more quite obvious. Amid famine and drought, Joseph's brothers face starvation and go to Egypt for food (without Benjamin; 42:1– 5). Joseph, who is in charge of food distribution, recognizes his brothers but pretends that he does not (42:6–8). They fail to recognize him, and Joseph deals very harshly with his hungry brothers, much as his father, Jacob, did when approached by *his* starving brother (42:7–17; see 25:29–34).

Unlike the last interchange between Joseph and his brothers, Joseph now holds all the power. His brothers bow before him (42:6), referring to themselves as "your servants" (42:10) and to Joseph as "lord" (42:10). Although Jacob's humility ameliorated Esau's anger in chap. 33, humbleness is not so efficacious this time. Joseph is unmoved by their actions, and he begins to inflict great retributive harm on them. At the outset of the Joseph narratives, the text says that Joseph's brothers 'were unable to speak to him peaceably' (וְלֹא יָכְלוּ דַּבְּרוֹ לְשָׁלֹם, 37:4).[18] With calculated revenge, Joseph now speaks harshly with them (וַיְדַבֵּר אִתָּם קָשׁוֹת, 42:7). He falsely accuses them of being spies several times, despite the brothers' pleas to the contrary (42:9, 12, 14; see also 42:16, 30). Just as Potiphar imprisoned Joseph following false accusations (39:17–20), so now Joseph imprisons his brothers on fraudulent allegations (42:17). After letting them suffer for a period of time, Joseph releases his half-brothers (except Simeon) on the condition that they bring back his sole full brother, Benjamin, who is in Canaan with their father (42:18–20, 24–26). The brothers, unaware of who this Egyptian ruler actually is, nevertheless suspect that the hardships befalling them result from how they treated Joseph many years ago (42:21–22). They are more correct than they realize. As Alter puts it, "The entire dialogue between Joseph and his brothers is remarkable for the way that words, creating the fragile surface of speech, repeatedly plumb depths of moral relation of which the brothers are almost totally unaware and which even Joseph

---

17. For more on the magical, ethical, and theological significance of blood in the Hebrew Bible, see B. Kedar-Kopfstein and J. Bergman, "דָּם," *TDOT* 3.234–50, esp. p. 242.

18. On the unusual use of the suffix in דַּבְּרוֹ, see GKC §115c. The BHS textual apparatus proposes (following the LXX) the reading (לְ)דַבֵּר לוֹ.

grasps only in part."[19] The brothers assume that Joseph has died (42:22), but he ironically controls their lives.[20]

When Joseph hears the brothers refer to their treatment of him, he turns away and weeps (42:23–24). Once his composure is regained, he returns, gives them grain, and secretly returns the money they used to purchase the grain (42:25). While this act may foreshadow Joseph's subsequent generosity (43:16–44:3; 45:10–11, 21–23; 47:11–12; 50:15–21), his returning the brothers' silver is best understood in the immediate context as another way that he unsettles and disturbs his siblings.[21] Indeed, when the brothers discover the money, the text says that their heart sank, they trembled, and they asked each other, "What is God doing to us?" (42:28; see also 42:35). Joseph's brothers once sold him into slavery for financial gain (37:26–28). In an act of symmetrical retribution, Joseph strikes fear into their hearts by giving them silver that they do not deserve and should not rightfully possess. The brothers, who have already been falsely accused, now fear what will happen next. Money once led the brothers to harm Joseph, and now Joseph uses money to harm them.

When the brothers return to their father, they explain what transpired. The text focuses initially on Reuben and then on Judah, the same brothers that the text focused on when describing Joseph's harsh treatment and enslavement in Genesis 37. After their return, Reuben urges their father to let them go back to Egypt with Benjamin, offering his own sons as surety for Benjamin. But Jacob, who has lost both Joseph and now Simeon, is unwilling to part with Benjamin. Time passes. When the family is again on the verge of life-threatening starvation (43:8), Judah steps forward, requesting that they go to Egypt. He offers himself as surety for Benjamin (43:9–10).

Jacob reluctantly agrees, and he encourages his brothers to respond to the situation with a tactic that alleviated the anger of his brother, Esau, years earlier: the offering of gifts. As 43:11 puts it, "Then their father Israel said to them, 'If it must be so, then do this: take some of the best products of the earth (מִזִּמְרַת הָאָרֶץ) in your bags. Bring them to the man as a gift (מִנְחָה).'" The language of this verse calls to mind other references to מנחה ('gift'), which appear in Genesis only in narratives describing the possibility of fratricide—that is, the stories of Cain and Abel (4:3, 4, 5) and Jacob and Esau (32:14[13], 19[18], 21[20], 22[21]; 33:10). The narrative signals to readers that, in anger-filled contexts with great potential for bloodshed,

---

19. Robert Alter, *The Art of Biblical Narrative* (New York: Basic Books, 1981) 164.

20. Gerald O. West, *Genesis: The People's Bible Commentary* (Oxford: Bible Reading Fellowship, 2006) 199.

21. Gunkel takes a position similar to the mine here (*Genesis*, 426). There is, nevertheless, an element of ambiguity in Joseph's actions that probably reflects the ambiguity that he feels toward his brothers (Mignon R. Jacobs, "The Conceptual Dynamics of Good and Evil in the Joseph Story: An Exegetical and Hermeneutical Inquiry," *JSOT* 27 [2003] 309–38, esp. pp. 324–25; Westermann, *Genesis*, 3.111).

gifts have the opportunity to introduce an alternative set of dynamics that can facilitate the diffusion of anger. This appears to be the case especially when the gifts are lavish, like Jacob's droves of animals for Esau and the brothers' 'best products of the earth' (זִמְרַת הָאָרֶץ) for Joseph.[22]

In addition to gifts from the land, Jacob also tells his sons to take double the money needed: "Take in your hand twice (מִשְׁנֶה) the silver, and return in your hand the silver that was returned in the mouth of your sacks. Perhaps there was a mistake (מִשְׁגֶּה; 43:12)." The word משגה ('mistake') is carefully chosen. It is a rare word that serves several functions. It forms an audible and visual pun with the word משנה ('twice') earlier in the verse. It also carries a variety of shades of meaning. On the most literal level, the phrase אוּלַי מִשְׁגֶּה הוּא ('perhaps there was a mistake') suggests that the Egyptian viceroy or his officials may have made a mistake when money was placed in their sacks. In the passage's broader context, however, the reference to money's being a mistake alludes to the grave error that the brothers committed previously in selling Joseph for 20 pieces of silver.[23]

The brothers follow their father's command, returning to Egypt with both gifts and Benjamin. When Joseph sees his brothers, he immediately arranges for a meal (43:16). The brothers, however, do not know of Joseph's intentions. They approach the steward of Joseph's house at the door (43:18–19; פתח), fearful that punishment may be coming.[24] The steward comforts them (43:23), in contrast to their fearful expectations. He greets them with the words שָׁלוֹם לָכֶם ('peace to you'), which is significant because Gen 37:4 says that the brothers were unable to speak 'peaceably' (לְשָׁלם) to Joseph. As Joseph approaches his brothers for the meal, they present their gifts from home, bowing down before him, just as Jacob did with Esau (33:3, 6–7; 43:26, 28). Although the brothers face extreme famine, they give away what little food they have (honey, spices, nuts) as gifts for Joseph. After being deeply moved upon seeing his brother Benjamin (43:29–31), Joseph eats with them, providing food from his own table and allowing them to eat and drink freely (43:34).

Elsewhere in Genesis, episodes involving anger frequently depict people sharing in a meal just prior to some sort of separation (the separation of Hagar and Ishmael from Sarah and Abraham in 21:8, 14; Isaac and Abimelech from one another in 26:30; Jacob, Rachel, and Leah from Laban in

---

22. In contrast to Cain, who brought only 'some fruit from the ground' (מִפְּרִי הָאֲדָמָה), Joseph's brothers are instructed to bring 'some of the best products of the earth' (מִזִּמְרַת הָאָרֶץ). This contrast gives readers a hint that the outcome may be different from what happened with Cain. Giving may, on this occasion, lead to reconciliation rather than violence.

23. Although this word can refer to a simple error or mistake, it can also refer to more significant moral wrongdoing. The verbal form of this word is used, for example, in Saul's (second) confession of sin for seeking to kill David (1 Sam 26:21).

24. This text may allude to Gen 4:7, where God's words imply that punishment comes to those who approach the פתח 'door' of iniquity.

31:54; Joseph and his brothers in 37:25).[25] Here in chap. 43, this glimpse of the brothers reunited in fellowship appears about to give way to another separation. Joseph seems interested in a long-term reunion only with Benjamin, not with his abusive half-brothers (44:10, 17). He sends them on their way, placing his divination cup with Benjamin's belongings so that he has an excuse for keeping Benjamin with him.[26] The reference to this cup as being "silver" is highly significant. Joseph was sold for silver (37:28). Joseph tormented his brothers by returning silver to them (42:25, 28, 35). Here in chap. 44, silver leads to their (potential) re-arrest. Concerning these repeated episodes involving silver, Brodie memorably writes, "Ever since [selling Joseph into slavery], the silver seems to stick to [the brothers]. Like Lady Macbeth, unable to get the blood of the murdered king off her hands, they cannot get away from the bloody silver."[27]

Joseph's plan appears to be working. After the brothers depart, his officials catch up with them and locate the cup in Benjamin's possessions. The brothers return to Egypt, where Joseph asks them, 'What is this deed that you have done?' (מָה־הַמַּעֲשֶׂה הַזֶּה אֲשֶׁר עֲשִׂיתֶם, 44:15). The words are a close echo of God's words to Eve in 3:13 and to Cain in 4:10. Like God's words there, Joseph's question is a call for reflection on the moral significance of all that has transpired, both in the immediate and in the distant past. Thus, Joseph's question uses a plural verb, addressing all of his brothers, even though Joseph claims that he is only interested in the one who took the cup (44:15).

Amid this tense moment, Judah approaches Joseph with a confession: "God has found the guilt of your servants" (44:16). He appears to be confessing wrongdoing regarding the "stolen" cup, but his words can also be understood as referring to the iniquity of selling Joseph into slavery. Judah says that he and all his brothers will become Joseph's servants. Joseph refuses. He wants only Benjamin to stay with him. Judah then begins the longest speech in Genesis, and he does so by urging Joseph not to be angry (וְאַל־יִחַר אַפְּךָ, 44:18).[28] Like Rachel's word to her father in 31:35, this plea not to be angry is typical when an inferior speaks to a superior (see 18:30, 32; §§4.3.1, 3). However, given the theme of anger throughout this book, as well as Judah and Joseph's past, Judah's words take on a broader

---

25. For an insightful analysis of food as a *leitmotif* in Genesis, see Katie M. Heffelfinger, "From Bane to Blessing: The Significance of Food in Genesis 37–50," in *Rounded Stones: Literary Readings of Genesis Narratives* (ed. Dennis Olson and Diane Sharon; SBLSymS; Atlanta: Society of Biblical Literature, forthcoming).

26. Somewhat surprisingly, the text stresses that this cup was used in divination (44:5, 15). As West notes, this emphasis may serve to frighten the brothers further, showing that they have offended not only a political but also a religious ruler (*Genesis*, 206; see also Gerhard von Rad, *Genesis* [rev. ed.; OTL; Philadelphia: Westminster, 1972] 391–92).

27. Brodie, *Genesis as Dialogue*, 387.

28. On these words' constituting the longest speech in Genesis, see Westermann, *Genesis*, 3.134.

significance than what the common idiom normally conveys. They express the desire of Judah (and readers), who long to see an ending to anger and a peaceful resolution.

Judah recounts his father's deep concern for Benjamin—who he thinks is Rachel's only surviving son (44:19–31).[29] Next, Judah offers himself in Benjamin's place (44:32–34). In so doing, Judah unwittingly reveals to Joseph that he is not the same person that he was many years ago. The brother who once sold Joseph into slavery (37:26) is willing to become a slave himself to prevent a recurrence of past evils. In this poignant moment, Joseph reveals his identity (45:3–4). As he does so, he urges his brothers not to be dismayed or angry with themselves on account of their wrongdoing (וְעַתָּה אַל־תֵּעָצְבוּ וְאַל־יִחַר בְּעֵינֵיכֶם, 45:5).[30] He offers them land so that they may live together (45:10) and provisions lest they become dispossessed (45:11). Then Joseph embraces and weeps over them the same way that Esau wept over their father.[31] Gen 45:15 reads, "He kissed all of his brothers and wept upon them, and afterward his brothers spoke with him." The reference to the brothers' speaking serves two purposes. First, the narrative said earlier that the brothers were stunned to silence when Joseph first revealed his identity to them (45:3). The text signals that they are finally able to speak. Second, on a broader level, this reference to the brothers' speaking with Joseph is significant because Joseph and his brothers were previously unable to speak peacefully with one another (37:4, 42:7; see also 37:2).

News of the brothers' reunion reaches Pharaoh, who offers to give the brothers good land so that they may eat well (45:18). Joseph sends his brothers back to retrieve their father, giving them provisions, vehicles, clothing, and money for the journey (45:21–23). As they depart, Joseph encourages them, on a literal level, not to 'shake on the journey' (אַל־תִּרְגְּזוּ, 45:24). The word used for 'shake' here is רגז. It is often used of emotions, including not only anger but also fear and turmoil (§6.5, §15.1.1). Given the conflict that brothers have been prone to elsewhere in Genesis, it is appropriate to understand Joseph's words as encouraging them not to be angry with one another, just as he did in 45:5. However, his words may also contain overtones that signal that he does not want them to be afraid or in turmoil. Overtones of this sort also match Joseph's words elsewhere (45:5; 50:19, 21) and furthermore signal an awareness of the emotional difficulties that can persist even after a reunion has been attempted among previously estranged parties (see Jacob and Esau in Genesis 33).

---

29. The speech contains 14 references to their אב 'father' (Gordon J. Wenham, *Genesis* [2 vols.; WBC; Nashville: Thomas Nelson, 1987] 2.425). As noted above, Genesis at times refers repeatedly to a family member in a short amount of space, such as the references to אח 'brother' in 4:8–11, 27:41–45 and בן 'son' in 22:1–19.

30. On the central significance of this verse (and the verses immediately following it) to the Joseph narratives, see Jacobs, "The Conceptual Dynamics," 309–38, esp. pp. 313–16.

31. The linguistic connections between 45:14–15 and 33:4 are striking (see also 46:29).

The brothers return with their father, receiving land and provisions from Joseph (46:31–47:12). However, the brothers live in fear. After Jacob dies, Joseph's brothers are afraid that Joseph has harbored anger against them, waiting until this moment to exact vengeance, just as Esau planned to do to Jacob following Isaac's death (27:41, 50:15). Indeed, the word used to describe Joseph's harbored anger also describes Esau's anger just prior to the death of Isaac (שׂטם; see §6.5, §15.3.4).[32] Although the Joseph narratives have previously described reunions between the brothers, they never specifically mentioned forgiveness. This changes in 50:16–17. Joseph's brothers claim in a message, perhaps deceptively, that their father has ordered Joseph to 'forgive' (נשׂא) their 'crime' (פשׁע) and 'sin' (חטאת).[33]

When Joseph hears their words, he weeps (50:17). The brothers, who heard their father, Jacob, offer himself as Esau's servant in 32:19[18], 21[20], now offer themselves as Joseph's servants (50:18). Joseph responds by telling them not to be afraid (50:19, 21). Readers recall that fear probably played a key role in Jacob's decision not to reunite with his brother (chap. 33; §12.1). Joseph, unlike Esau, assures and reassures his brothers that they need not fear. He makes clear that he is no threat to them. He asks, 'Am I in the place of God?' (הֲתַחַת אֱלֹהִים אָנִי; 50:19). This question was asked by Jacob when Rachel demanded that he give her children (30:2). The implication then was that God is ultimately responsible for fertility. The implication here is that God is ultimately responsible for punishing wrongdoers (see Lev 19:18, Deut 32:35).[34] The text suggests that Joseph has not harbored anger against his brothers precisely because he has entrusted God with the responsibility of vengeance.[35] Although Joseph has been appointed with power over all of Egypt (Gen 41:39–45), he sees retribution as God's responsibility, not his own. He leaves the angry impulse to punish others in the hands of God. He has borne witness to ways that God has brought good out of the wickedness that the brothers committed (50:20).

---

32. Amid Jacob's words of blessing to his sons, Gen 49:23 also uses the word שׂטם, speaking of archers who intend to harm Joseph. The verse is textually difficult and referentially unclear. If it refers to the person Joseph, then the archers presumably are figurative depictions of his brothers, who felt jealousy and anger toward him. If it refers to the tribe of Joseph, then the archers presumably are a group that attacked Ephraim at some point in its existence (possibly mentioned in Judges 12 or Judges 19–21). See the useful discussion in Hamilton, *The Book of Genesis: Chapters 18–50*, 684.

33. These words for 'crime' and 'sin' were used in tandem by Jacob in his angry confrontation with Laban in 31:36 (Wenham, *Genesis*, 2.277).

34. Indeed, many of the sins in Genesis can be understood as ways that humans (and the "sons of God" in Gen 6:1–4) attempt to take on divine responsibilities. Thus, the serpent in Eden says that God does not want Eve and Adam to eat from the tree lest they "become like God, knowing good and evil" (3:5). Cain takes human life (4:8), which God alone should do. Similarly, the tower of Babel is condemned because through it humanity attempted to reach the heavens (where God resides) and make a great name for themselves (11:4). See the useful discussion in Hamilton, *The Book of Genesis: Chapters 18–50*, 705.

35. Ibid.; see also Jacobs, "The Conceptual Dynamics," 316.

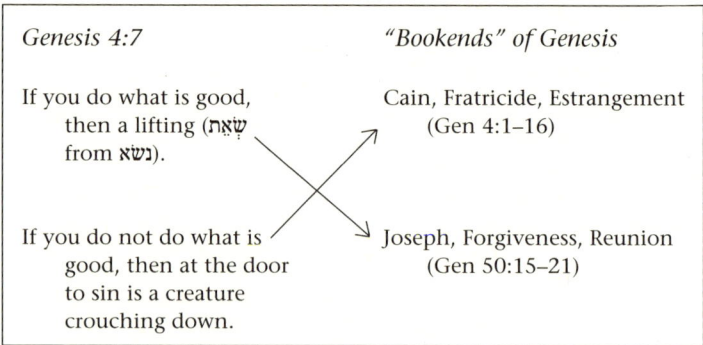

Figure 2. Genesis 4:7 and the Macrostructure of Genesis.

Joseph also knows that the brothers have suffered, and he has witnessed their changed character. He comforts and speaks graciously with them (50:21; in sharp contrast to 37:4, 42:7). For the third time in these narratives, Joseph reassures his brothers that he will provide both for them and for their children (50:21; see also 45:11, 47:12). It is a moment of reconciliation offered just before the book closes, allowing readers to see Joseph as an anti-Cain—a brother who has all the power and all the reasons to harm his brothers but instead turns away from anger and, despite the inherent difficulties, offers forgiveness.[36] After a long history of jealousy, anger, sin, and violence, Joseph and his brothers are reconciled. Whereas Cain implied that he never was and never should have been his brother's keeper, Joseph shows himself in precisely the role of שֹׁמֵר אָחִים ('a brothers' keeper'), providing sustenance and protection for his family in a foreign land.[37]

At the outset of Genesis, God told an angry Cain, "If you do what is right, then a שְׂאֵת, *lifting*." In that context, as well as in many other episodes about anger, the verb נשׂא refers to the lifting of one's face.[38] However, the narrator of Genesis uses this word because it provides something akin to what Mikhail Bakhtin calls "a loophole"—that is, a literary construction that allows one to alter a word's meaning at a later point in time.[39] The word נשׂא

---

36. See Brodie, *Genesis as Dialogue*, 359–60; Theo L. Hettema, *Reading for Good: Narrative Theology and Ethics in the Joseph Story from the Perspective of Ricoeur's Hermeneutics* (Kampen: Kok Pharos, 1996) 212–14.

37. P. J. Berlyn suggests that Judah is actually the person who serves as a keeper for his brothers in this narrative, given his role in bringing the family back together again ("His Brothers' Keeper," *JBQ* 26 [1998] 73–83, esp. p. 83). Judah does not, however, provide for his brothers the same way that Joseph does on multiple occasions (45:11, 47:12, 50:21).

38. Gen 13:10, 14; 21:18; 32:21[20]; 33:1, 5; 37:25; 43:29.

39. Mikhail Bakhtin, *Problems of Dostoevsky's Poetics* (Minneapolis: University of Minnesota Press, 1984) 233.

can also refer to 'forgiveness', and here, at the conclusion of the book, after many episodes dealing with anger in many ways, readers are able to see the truth of God's word to Cain in a new light: "If you do what is good, then forgiveness (שְׂאֵת)" (4:7). After nearly killing their brother and then selling him off into slavery, Joseph's brothers have committed evils that cry out to be punished. Joseph appears willing to act on his anger and pay back his brothers evil for evil (Gen 44:4). The brothers, however, do what is good. They are willing to give back silver that they do not rightfully deserve. They offer gifts of food though they face grave famine. The brothers who once dominated Joseph now kneel in submission, calling him "my lord." Judah is willing to become a slave himself instead of allowing a younger brother to be enslaved wrongfully. Joseph, in return, also does what is good. He is reluctant at first. Gradually, however, he begins speaking graciously to them. He provides nourishment for them. He urges them not to be angry or afraid. He offers them food, land, and protection in a harsh world. As a result of doing what is right, the brothers experience forgiveness (נשׂא; 50:17). Cain did not do what is right, but Joseph and his brothers eventually do, and they experience forgiveness just before the book closes. There is thus a chiastic interplay between Gen 4:7 and the book of Genesis as a whole, moving from fratricide to forgiveness (fig. 2).

God's first words in a post-Edenic world lay the framework for all that follows. From Cain killing his brother to Joseph forgiving his brothers, Genesis shows the grave dangers of anger while realistically depicting ways that its worse effects can be counteracted. Readers encounter not only dramatic and compelling stories. They also gain vicarious experience in handling anger, witnessing both its worst and its best possible outcomes. They walk away from the text with a better understanding of the immense threat that anger presents for all parties involved, and they have encountered a variety of ways that anger can be handled so that it does not lead to violence. Reading Genesis is an act of moral education.

Chapter 13

Synthesis and Conclusion:
Hope in a World of Limitations

To understand both anger and ethics in Genesis, interpreters need to lay aside traditional Western assumptions. In the Hebrew Bible, irrationality is not a hallmark of emotion. Anger is not something best left to psychologists for interpretation. One does not need Freud to understand how this emotion works. Rather, anger is a common feature of the fractured world and imperfect humanity that Genesis envisions. It is a permanent mark of the exile from Eden. Anger cannot be avoided. It must be engaged, lest it ruin morality, community, and even life itself. Anger is thus not "merely a feeling." It is an ethical matter of the first degree.

To understand what Genesis teaches about the ethics of anger, one must lay aside modernist assumptions about not only emotions but also the ethical task. Genesis offers no set of principles for approaching this emotion, only stories of imperfect individuals who wrestle with anger's destructive power. Genesis never presents the highest good—only scenes in which good and evil are inextricably intertwined. Genesis does not uphold ideal images for simple emulation; instead, it presents fallible individuals who must struggle simply to prevent evil from destroying their lives.

Because of its realism about the human condition, the stories of Genesis are well suited to serve as "metaphors for life." The characters it portrays are not lofty, saintly types who remain forever separated from the rest of the human race. They are limited, fallible, and imperfect. Genesis is an anthology of moral difficulty. It is a collection of stories in which individuals face limitations of every type and must take extreme measures to prevent the eruption of violence in their midst. Genesis is not an ethical training manual for the morally elite but a survival guide for an imperfect humanity.

Genesis depicts archetypal features of the human condition, but at the same time, it is also aware of the diversity of human experience. Thus, it does not present a solitary rule or even a single narrative for guiding people about their anger. Instead, it offers readers approximately a dozen encounters with anger. Readers see this emotion among brothers, sisters, spouses, kinfolk, superiors, and groups of people. Although not comprehensive, this sampling of imaginative experiences provides readers with a lush pool from which they can make metaphorical transferences to their lives.

180

Among these stories, particular themes emerge and re-emerge. Readers who experience the world of Genesis find themselves on a stark landscape. Beyond paradise, they encounter a world of profound and pervasive limitations that frequently give rise to anger. Abundance and plenitude remained locked within the forbidden garden. Worshipers find a God who ignores sacrifices. Women find themselves unable to have children. Shepherds find land that will not support them. Children find parents who love other siblings more than themselves. Families find that separation is the only possible alternative to violence. Everyone finds morality in short supply.

Readers furthermore experience anger as one of the most devastating forces known to humanity. As soon as readers exit Eden, they see an angry individual kill his own brother, welcoming death into the world. Time and again, anger threatens to result in additional violence. The emotion imperils the house of Abraham and jeopardizes the heirs of divine promise. When it does not lead to bloodshed, anger tears apart the families of Genesis. This emotion presents a particular threat to the most vulnerable, regardless of how innocent they may be. God may intervene to help the innocent, but God will not overrule human freedom, even if it means that one of God's favorites dies in fratricide.

Genesis gives no simple solution to a force so complex and destructive. It never suggests that individuals can somehow become anger-immune, achieving an *apatheia* that sets them apart from worldly concerns. Rather, the book shows that every patriarch and even a number of the matriarchs must wrestle with this emotion simply to survive. All who share in the humanity depicted by Genesis need to engage this emotion, lest it lead to the loss of morality, community, and life.

By presenting anger as having the potential for such great harm, Genesis shapes the desires of its readers so they long for alternatives to this emotion's worst outcomes. When they witness it tearing families apart and resulting in bloodshed, they yearn to see anger engaged in ways that entail neither estrangement nor death. Readers of Genesis do not, however, have this desire fulfilled quickly or easily. Once anger's plots are set in motion in Genesis 4, readers must wait until the book's penultimate episode, just prior to the death of Joseph, before they finally see the worst effects of anger overcome. Only there do readers find brothers living together in unity, forgiven and reconciled after a lengthy history of anger and sin.

By setting forth so many cases of anger in which full forgiveness is not achieved, Genesis makes clear that the happy ending found by Joseph and his brothers is not always possible. Nevertheless, it suggests that at least violence can sometimes be avoided through a variety of means. The first is presented subtly in God's initial words to Cain: "Why are you angry? Why has your face fallen?" Cain refuses to respond to this invitation to express his anger directly to the one responsible for it. He turns down the opportunity to complain to the God who ignored his sacrifice. His anger festers until it issues in violence against Abel. Readers, however, are given alternatives. They can take a path different from the path that Cain took, directly confronting God for the injustices of life.

Another alternative to persistent anger is found with the book's final protagonist, who eventually entrusts vengeance to God. Initially, Joseph appears ready to repay evil for evil, harming his brothers just as they harmed him. However, when he learns of their changed character, Joseph changes as well. When his brothers fear that Joseph will punish them following their father's death, he asserts that such punishment is God's business, not his own. The person with power over the entire land of Egypt leaves vengeance to God.

Genesis also presents voluntary separation as a way of possibly preventing the worst effects of anger. Many characters in Genesis deem separation better than remaining together with the possibility that anger will erupt into violence. Abram and Lot, Isaac and the Philistines, and Laban and Jacob all face limited options. Amid their shortcomings, they do not overestimate their moral abilities or try to force good out of fractured relationships. They choose to separate to prevent bloodshed. The subsequent estrangement is far from ideal, but it avoids violence in a world of limited possibilities.

Readers also see that humility may prevent anger from leading to violence. Displays of humility are perhaps most prominent when Jacob encounters Esau in chap. 33 and when Joseph's brothers appear before Joseph in chaps. 42, 44, and 50. A humble spirit also appears in Abram's willingness to relinquish his rights as *paterfamilias* and give Lot his choice of land, as well as in Isaac's refusal to boast about his numbers and threaten the Philistines when they ask him to leave. Although these acts of humility do not in themselves heal all wrongdoing, they introduce dynamics that allow anger to dissipate. They signal alternative attitudes that allow for new ways forward.

Finally, readers learn that generosity can sometimes curb the worst effects of anger, particularly when paired with humility. Abram is obviously generous with Lot, offering him first choice of the land. His son Isaac displays something akin to generosity when he is willing to cede land rather than cause violence. Later, Isaac's son Jacob gives his brother 550 animals. Jacob's humility and generosity show Esau that his character has changed; they demonstrate his willingness to give back the blessing that was stolen by deceit. Jacob's sons similarly find in generosity a way beyond past wrongdoings. Joseph's brothers are willing to give gifts of choice food in the midst of a severe famine and to return silver they did not deserve. Judah makes a generous offer to be enslaved in the place of Benjamin. Through their generosity, Joseph learns that they are not the cruel individuals they were years earlier. Joseph, in return, showers his family with gifts and provisions. In Genesis, humility and generosity frequently combine to facilitate new beginnings.

However, Genesis is careful not to present acts of separation, humility, and generosity as simplistic solutions to anger. It makes clear that separation, particularly when forced on individuals with little power, such as Hagar, does not so much counteract violence as constitute it. The text also makes clear that humility does not immediately correct all wrongs. For Joseph's brothers, it takes many acts of humility and a variety of other factors before forgiveness is achieved. Finally, the narratives show that generosity sometimes diffuses anger, but readers also see Shechem's father, Hamor, making an extremely generous offer, only to have Dinah's brothers exploit it for bloodshed. Genesis presents no universal solutions for engaging anger. It speaks dialogically about this emotion, inviting readers to converse with the text and with themselves about the best ways to handle this destructive force.

Above (§12.2, fig. 2), I observed that God's word about anger to Cain in 4:7 chiastically corresponds to the beginning and end of Genesis. I note now, as a way of closing, that it also reverberates through many of the other stories in Genesis. The verse reads:

הֲלוֹא אִם־תֵּיטִיב שְׂאֵת וְאִם לֹא תֵיטִיב לַפֶּתַח חַטָּאת רֹבֵץ וְאֵלֶיךָ תְּשׁוּקָתוֹ וְאַתָּה תִּמְשָׁל־בּוֹ:

Is it not true that if you do good, then a lifting up? But if you do not do good, then at the entryway to sin is a creature crouching down. Its craving is for you, but you can rule over it.

In itself, this verse does not appear particularly life-changing. It essentially emphasizes doing good over the alternative. However, when the cumulative weight of the book of Genesis is brought to bear on this verse, it comes to life and sheds insights regarding one of humanity's most perplexing emotions. It makes clear that, even when individuals become angry through no fault of their own, they remain accountable for their actions. There is a dangerous attraction between anger and evil that can lead to grave outcomes.

But anger does not damn people to its worst consequences. For those who do what is good amid their limited resources and finite possibilities, there will be a lifting (נשא):

a lifting of eyes beholding a lush land like the Garden of Y$_{HWH}$ (נשא, 13:10)

a lifting of eyes that see an expansive land promised to countless descendants (נשא, 13:14)

a lifting of a slave boy, cast out into the wilderness and forsaken by all but God and his mother, nearly dead—but now near springs of life (נשא, 21:18)

a lifting of the face of a brother who once grabbed all he could but now wants to give back what he wrongfully took (נשׂא, 32:21[20])

a lifting of the crimes and sins of eleven brothers, who have nothing but themselves to offer the one they once enslaved (נשׂא, 50:17)

Amid the generations torn apart by the most destructive of emotions, Genesis offers realistic glimpses of hope. The good that it envisions is neither guaranteed nor easily achieved. But it is nevertheless present amid self-sacrifices, suffering, frailty, limitations, and evil. Genesis never hides the destructiveness of anger. Nor does it abandon hope, even for people who wander in the wilderness, homesick for Eden.

Appendix A:
The Statistics of
Biblical Language for Anger

The preceding discussion, especially chap. 5, presents several statistics about the likelihood of particular terms to appear with terms for anger. In this appendix, I explain how these numbers were obtained. I also present formulas for readers who wish to make similar calculations with different sets of words. In the discussion below, I use abbreviations not only for the sake of brevity but also for ease in expressing mathematical formulas.

One of the key pieces of evidence is the set of verses in the Hebrew Bible containing one or more words for anger. The number of verses in this set was obtained by conducting a graphical search on BibleWorks 8.0.017m.1 for verses that contain at least one of the following: אַף (nominal forms), אנף, זעם, זעף, חמה, חרה, חרון, חרי, כעס, כעש, עבר (Hithpael forms), עברה, קצף, רגז, and שטם. This number came to 640. Next, the specific results were examined with particular attention to "false positives," that is, instances in which a term that *can* refer to anger *does not* refer to anger (for example, Gen 2:7 where אַף means 'nostril', not 'anger'). One hundred twenty-one verses do not actually refer to anger, even though they contain a term that is often translated *anger* or something similar.[1] Thus, of the 640 verses returned on BibleWorks, only 519 verses refer to anger in both form and meaning. The number of verses containing one or more of the words for anger can be abbreviated $n(anger)$. Thus:

$$n(anger) = 519$$

---

1. For the purposes of these calculations, I considered the following to be false positives: Gen 2:7; 3:19; 7:22; 14:6; 19:1; 24:47; 36:20–22, 29–30; 40:6, 16; 42:6; 48:12; Exod 15:14; Num 11:20; 13:5; 22:31; Deut 2:12, 22, 25; 28:65; 32:24, 33; 33:10; 1 Sam 1:5–7, 16; 14:15; 20:41; 24:8; 25:23, 41; 28:14–15; 2 Sam 7:10; 14:4, 33; 15:28; 18:28; 19:1[18:33]; 19:19[18]; 24:20; 1 Kgs 1:23, 31; 20:43; 21:4; Isa 2:22; 3:21; 14:3, 9, 16; 23:11; 24:6, 23; 30:26; 32:10–11; 49:23; 64:1[2]; Jer 12:5; 22:15; 33:9; 50:34; Ezek 12:18; 16:12; 32:9; Hos 7:5; 10:7; Joel 2:1, 10; Amos 4:10; 8:8; Jonah 1:15; Mic 7:17; Hab 2:15; 3:2, 7, 16; Ps 6:8[7]; 10:14; 19:7[6]; 31:10[9]; 77:17[16]; 19[18]; 99:1; 112:10; 115:6; Job 3:17, 26; 6:2, 4; 9:6; 14:1; 17:7; 27:3; 30:28; 37:2; 39:24; 40:24, 26[41:2]; Prov 11:22; 30:21; Song 6:10; 7:5[4]; 9[8]; Qoh 1:18; 2:23; 7:3; Lam 4:20; Dan 1:10; Neh 3:20; 3:37[4:5]; 8:6; 1 Chr 1:39; 17:9; 21:21; 2 Chr 7:3; 20:18.

Determining these false positives is a matter of interpretation, and not everyone will agree with the decisions made here. For example, I consider 1 Sam 1:6, 7, 16 to be false positives. However, as observed on p. 58 n. 39 above, some scholars have contended that these verses do in fact refer to anger (see also §6.5, §15.1.3).

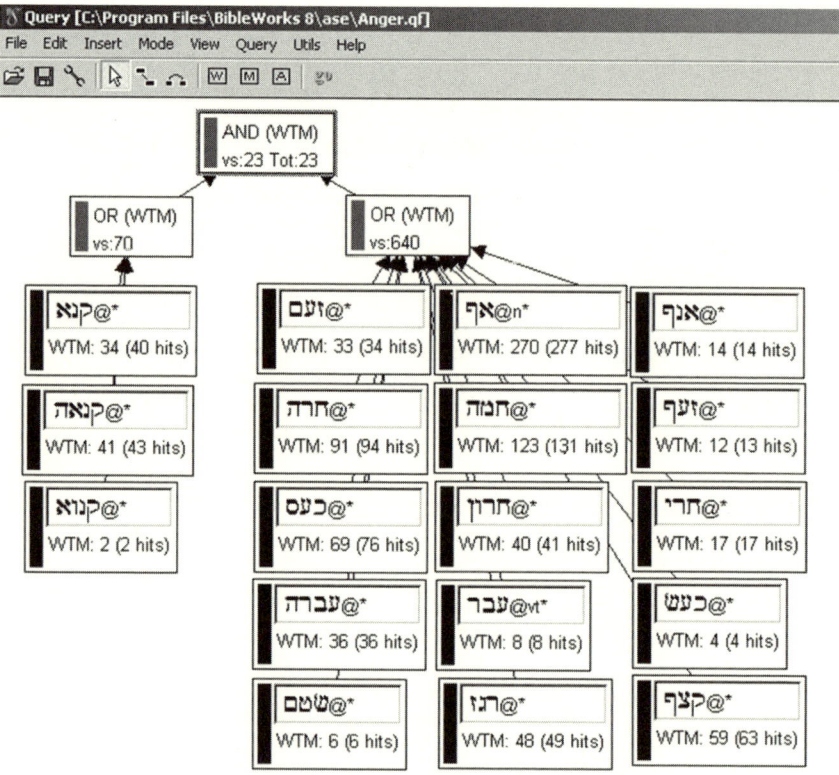

Figure 3. Example of Boolean Search.

The discussion above also focused on words that commonly appear alongside terms for anger. Again using the Graphical Search Engine on BibleWorks, I discovered the number of verses that contain one or more words from an interrelated set of search terms, something that I abbreviate here as *n*(*search*). For example, one can run an analysis of all verses that contain at least one appearance of קנא, קנאה, or קנוא (that is, words related to the concept of 'jealousy'). The number of verses in this particular set of search terms is 70.[2] Thus, if the search terms are defined as קנא, קנאה, and קנוא, then:

---

2. There are 34 verses containing קנא, 41 containing קנאה, and 2 containing קנוא. The sum total of these figures is 77. However, the number of verses containing one or more of these terms is 70 because there are 7 verses that contain more than one of these search terms (Num 5:14, 30; 25:11; Isa 11:13; Ezek 8:3; Zech 1:14; 8:2).

Note: Some search terms have homonyms that complicate matters. In these cases, an additional set of false positives needs to be created, and necessary adjustments need to be

$$n(search) = 70$$

Taking the analysis further, one can determine how frequently search terms appear among verses containing one or more terms for anger. Again, the Graphical Search Engine on BibleWorks is useful. An example of this sort of search (using the same words) is illustrated in fig. 3. This Boolean search reveals that 23 verses contained *both* one (or more) of the search terms *and* one (or more) of the anger terms. These 23 verses needed to be checked for accuracy using the list of false positives and decreasing the number if necessary. In this case, none of these 23 verses is part of the list of false positives, so the number does not need to decrease. Hence, when one defines the search terms as קנא, קנאה, and קנוא, then:[3]

$$n(search \cap anger) = 23$$

Building on the above data, one can determine what percentage of verses containing one or more of the search terms also contains at least one reference to anger. Or, to state things in terms of conditional probability, one can answer the following question: if a verse contains one or more of the search terms, then what is the probability that it will also contain one or more of the anger terms? Such a value can be abbreviated $P(anger \mid search)$.[4] One determines this value using the following formula:

$$P(anger \mid search) = \frac{n(search \cap anger)}{n(search)}$$

Thus, if the search terms are defined as קנא, קנאה, and קנוא, then:

$$P(anger \mid search) = \frac{23}{70} \approx 33\%$$

In other words, if someone selected a random verse from the 70 verses containing at least one appearance of קנא, קנאה, or קנוא, then there is approximately a 33% chance that the verse will also contain one of the words for anger.[5]

Making some adjustments, one can also determine what percentage of verses containing one or more terms for anger also contain one or more of

---

made. For example, ארך appears 143 times in the Hebrew Bible. In all but one of these appearances (Gen 10:10, where it is a proper locative noun), its primary meaning relates to 'length'. However, because of the one exception, the number 143 needs to be reduced to 142. With the 3 words related to jealousy, no reductions were necessary.

3. In conditional probability, the symbol $\cap$ means "and."

4. In conditional probability, $P(A \mid B)$ means "the probability of A, given B."

5. The symbol $\approx$ (meaning "is approximately equal to") and the term "approximately" are used above because 33% has been rounded to the nearest whole (percentage) number. The actual value of this fraction would be closer to 32.857143%. Similar approximations are used above in chap. 5 and below in this appendix.

the search terms. Again, the question can be stated in terms of conditional probability: if a verse contains one or more words for anger, then what is the probability that it will also contain one or more of the search terms? The value this time would be expressed as *P(search | anger)*. One determines this value using the following formula:

$$P(search \mid anger) = \frac{n(search \cap anger)}{n(anger)}$$

Thus, if the search terms are defined as קָנָא, קִנְאָה, and קַנּוֹא, then:

$$P(search \mid anger) = \frac{23}{519} \approx 4.4\%$$

So, approximately 4.4% of the set of verses containing a word for anger also mention at least one of these three words related to jealousy.

By itself, 4.4% may seem like a small and unimpressive number. To appreciate its full significance, however, one needs to compare this value with the probability that a verse containing one or more of the search terms would be randomly selected from the Hebrew Bible as a whole. Determining the probability that a verse would contain at least one appearance of קָנָא, קִנְאָה, or קַנּוֹא, given the set of verses in the entire Hebrew Bible, is relatively easy. It can be expressed as follows, where the abbreviation (*HB*) stands for all the verses in the Hebrew Bible, which number 22,946:[6]

$$P(search \mid HB) = \frac{n(search \cap HB)}{n(HB)} = \frac{70}{22,946} \approx 0.3\%$$

Thus, there is approximately a 0.3% chance that someone selecting a random verse from the Hebrew Bible as a whole will select a verse containing קָנָא, קִנְאָה, or קַנּוֹא. Obviously, this percentage is much lower than the 4.4% chance someone has of selecting a verse with one (or more) of these words from the set of verses mentioning anger. In fact, by dividing 4.4% by 0.3%, one finds that a verse containing anger is approximately 15 times more likely to mention jealousy than a random verse from the Hebrew Bible as a whole. This value can be called the *C*-value (for "collocation"), which I abbreviate *C*. It can be calculated as follows:

$$C = \frac{P(search \mid anger)}{P(search \mid HB)}$$

Alternate ways of calculating the value of *C* include:

---

6. This number excludes the 267 verses that contain only Biblical Aramaic. More is said about Aramaic (and the reasons for excluding it) at the end of this appendix.

$$C = \frac{n(search \cap anger)}{n(anger)} \bigg/ \frac{n(search)}{n(HB)}$$

$$C = \frac{n(search \cap anger)}{n(anger)} \times \frac{n(HB)}{n(search)}$$

$$C = \frac{n(search \cap anger)}{n(search)} \times \frac{n(HB)}{n(anger)}$$

$$C = P(anger \mid search) \times \frac{22{,}946}{519}$$

$$C = P(anger \mid search) \times 44.212$$

*Note that the value of 44.212 found on this last line is exclusive to this search for words involving terms for anger. Calculating a C-value for other sets of words would involve substituting a different number for the 519 found in the second-to-last line.

Consequently, when the search terms are defined as קנא, קנאה, and קנוא, then the value of C is approximately 15, as shown below:

$$C = \frac{P(search \mid anger)}{P(search \mid HB)} \approx \frac{4.4\%}{0.3\%} \approx 15$$

Alternatively:

$$C = P(anger \mid search) \times \frac{22{,}946}{519} \approx 33\% \times 44.212 \approx 15$$

This C-value of approximately 15 is highly significant, because it shows a high degree of attraction between terms for jealousy and terms for anger. Words that do not have a high affinity for appearing together have a C-value much closer to one (1).

Although the above examples defined the search terms as קנא, קנאה, and קנוא, one can substitute other sets of words to determine whether they are more likely to appear in conjunction with anger than in the Hebrew Bible as a whole (and if so, how much more likely).

Below is a summary of the abbreviations used here:

n(anger) = 519 = number of verses in the Hebrew Bible containing one or more words for anger
n(HB) = 22,946 = number of (Hebrew) verses in the Hebrew Bible

$n(search)$ = number of verses in the Hebrew Bible containing one or more of the search terms

$n(search \cap anger)$ = number of verses in the Hebrew Bible containing *both* one or more of the search terms *and* one or more of the words for anger

$P(anger \mid search) = \dfrac{n(search \cap anger)}{n(search)}$ = the probability that a verse will contain one or more words for anger, given the set of verses in the Hebrew Bible containing one or more of the search terms

$P(search \mid anger) = \dfrac{n(search \cap anger)}{n(anger)}$ = the probability that a verse will contain one or more of the search terms, given the set of verses in the Hebrew Bible containing one or more of the words for anger

$P(search \mid HB) = \dfrac{n(search)}{n(HB)}$ = the probability that a randomly selected verse from the Hebrew Bible will contain one or more of the search terms

$C = Collocation\text{-}value = \dfrac{P(search \mid anger)}{P(search \mid HB)}$ = the number of times more likely for one or more of the search terms to appear in a verse containing one or more words for anger than in a randomly selected verse from the entire Hebrew Bible

Table 3 presents values for various terms associated with anger. At times, search terms in the table have a superscript notation attached. These notations designate a limit on the search term, typically employed to prevent unwanted homonyms (that is, false positives among the search terms) from affecting the results. Thus, עוה[verb] means that the search was conducted for verbal forms of עוה. Because the search was limited to these verbal forms, the results focused on words having to do with 'iniquity', rather than the rare noun עֲוָה ('ruin') or the proper locative name עַוָּה ('Avva').

Earlier, I observed that the number of verses containing a word for anger needed to be adjusted for false positives from 640 to 519. At times, I needed to adjust the number of verses containing a search term as well. For example, searching for the consonants גדל not only revealed the verses containing the verb גדל ('be great'), the related adjective גָּדֵל ('great'), and the related noun גֹּדֶל ('greatness'). It also revealed the six verses that contain either the proper name גִּדֵּל ('Giddel', appearing 4 times) or the rare noun גְּדִל ('tassel', appearing 2 times). Consequently, the number returned by BibleWorks for a search of גדל needed to be reduced by 6 to account for these false positives. This reduction of 6 is noted with a superscript Arabic number in parentheses: גדל[(-6)].

A superscript Roman numeral refers to the homonym number found in *HALOT*. Thus, אֵשׁ[I] means all cases where this term refers to 'fire' and not the two instances where it means 'trifle'. Furthermore, the vowel pointing

Table 3. Detailed Statistics of Terms Associated with Anger

Search Terms	n(search)	n(search ∩ anger)	P(anger | search)	P(search | anger)	P(search | HB)	C
אָרֵן עוה[verb] עָוֹן	309	15	5%	2.9%	1.3%	2
ארך[(-1)]	142	16	11%	3.1%	0.6%	5
אָרֵךְ	15	13	87%	2.5%	0.1%	38
אֵשׁ[I]	347	36	10%	6.9%	1.5%	5
words related to 'fire' (listed in §5.4)	265	31	12%	6.0%	1.2%	5
all words in the previous two rows	551	54	10%	10.4%	2.4%	4
גָּדוֹל גְּדוּלָה גדל[(-6)]	632	26	4%	5.0%	2.8%	2
דִּין מָדוֹן[I]	55	5	9%	1.0%	0.2%	4
הרג הרגה	166	11	7%	2.1%	0.7%	3
חטא חטאה חטאת	493	24	5%	4.6%	2.1%	2
חרם[I]	65	5	8%	1.0%	0.3%	3
כלה	256	31	12%	6.0%	1.1%	5
למה ('why')	171	10	6%	1.9%	0.7%	3
מאד	278	23	8%	4.4%	1.2%	4
נטר	8	2	25%	0.4%	0.03%	11
נקם נקמה	59	7	12%	1.3%	0.3%	5
נתך	19	10	53%	1.9%	0.1%	23
עצב[II]	24	4	17%	0.8%	0.1%	7
פּשׁע	125	6	5%	1.2%	0.5%	2
קנא קנאה קנוא	70	23	33%	4.4%	0.3%	15
קצר	51	4	8%	0.8%	0.2%	3
קָצֵר[adj]	5	2	40%	0.4%	0.02%	18
יָרִיב[I] מְרִיבָה ריב	118	10	8%	1.9%	0.5%	4
רַע רֹעַ רָעָה[noun] רעע[I]	720	50	7%	9.6%	3.1%	3
שׁוב	956	59	6%	11.4%	4.2%	3
שׁמד[verb]	86	9	10%	1.7%	0.4%	5
שׁפך	112	23	21%	4.4%	0.5%	9

in אֵשׁ differentiates this word from אֵשׁ, which *HALOT* classifies as a term meaning 'there is/are'.

If a search term contains no vowels, then the various words with the relevant consonants are included in the results. Thus, the search for the consonants ארך includes the verbal forms of ארך, the adjective אָרֵךְ, the adjective אָרֹךְ, and the noun אֹרֶךְ. (It even includes the one appearance of the proper name אֶרֶךְ, which is then reduced from the total number of hits. Thus, one finds ⁽⁻¹⁾ארך in the table.) Meanwhile, the search for אָרֵךְ only presents the results for this one adjective. For this reason, the value of *n(search)* is 142 when the search term is ⁽⁻¹⁾ארך and 15 when the search term is אָרֵךְ.

Finally, the searches and statistics above include only Biblical Hebrew. Biblical Aramaic was excluded for a couple of reasons. First, although there are similarities with Biblical Hebrew (such as Dan 3:19, which mentions both 'anger' and words related to 'fire'), there are of course significant differences between the two languages. Many words overlap, but many words do not. Second, only 5 of the 269 verses containing Biblical Aramaic refer to anger (Ezra 5:12; 7:23; Dan 2:12; 3:13, 19). This set of verses in Biblical Aramaic is too small for adequate analysis. Thus, the footnotes in chap. 5 above and appendix B below mention Biblical Aramaic occasionally, but the statistics mentioned in this appendix derive solely from Biblical Hebrew.

Appendix B:
Hebrew Words for Anger

The discussion above touched in various ways on the Hebrew terminology for anger. However, a more technical discussion of this terminology was not possible at that point. Thus, this appendix provides a more in-depth look at the words for anger and their definitions. It is divided into three sections. In the first, I look at words designating more than one emotion (רגז, זעף, and כעס). In the second, I examine words related to a perceived physiological symptom (אף, חרה, and חמה). In the last, I analyze words referring to a specific type of anger (קצף, זעם, עבר, and שטם).

15.1 Words Designating More than One Emotion

15.1.1 רגז

Like its Semitic cognates, the word רגז means basically to 'shake'. It sometimes appears with its synonyms רעש ('quake'; 7x) and חרד ('tremble'; 2x), as well as its antonym נוח/נחת ('rest'; 5x). Of the 50 appearances of words from the root רגז, 18 do not refer to an emotion but to a literal shaking, typically of an impersonal object, such as the earth, mountains, or sky.[1] Almost all of the remaining cases refer to an emotional shaking—presumably, the feeling of being struck by a strong emotion and being unsettled. The majority of these (22x) refer to *fear* or *turmoil*.[2] The other 10 appearances of this word refer to *anger*, most commonly, human anger.[3]

---

1. The root רגז appears 7 times as the noun רֹגֶז, once as the noun רׇגְזׇה, 41 times as a verb (30 Qal, 7 Hiphil, 4 Hithpael), and once as the adjective רַגָּז, modifying לב ('heart', Deut 28:65). It is also found twice in Biblical Aramaic: once as the noun רְגַז (Dan 3:13) and once as a Haphel verb (Ezra 5:12).
   References to literal shaking include 1 Sam 14:15; 2 Sam 22:8; Isa 5:25; 13:13; 14:9, 16; Ezek 12:18; Joel 2:10; Amos 8:8; Hab 3:7; Ps 18:8[7]; 77:17[16], 19[18]; Prov 30:21; Job 9:6; 37:2; 39:24; 1 Chr 17:9. Most likely, one should include 1 Sam 28:15 as well. In this verse, Samuel, who is summoned from the grave, asks Saul why the king has *shaken* (הִרְגַּזְתַּנִי) him. While it may be that Samuel asks Saul why the king is *angering* him, anger is probably not the primary sense, given the extrabiblical evidence. A Phoenician inscription by the son of Šipiṭbaʿal from 500 B.C.E. found in Byblos/Gebal from the burial site of this king reads: 'You shall not open this resting place to *trouble* my bones' [אל תפתﬡ עﬥת המשכב] זן לרגז עצמי (KAI 9.A.5). A similar warning that also contains רגז is found in an inscription from Sidon from the end of the 6th century B.C.E. (KAI 13.4–7). The word רגז is thus repeatedly used in the context of the dead and refers primarily to disturbing their remains. However, there is also evidence that these disturbances may invoke cursing, which may imply secondarily the presence of anger (see KAI 191.B.2).
   2. Exod 15:14; Deut 2:25; 28:65; 2 Sam 7:10; 19:1[18:33]; Isa 14:3; 23:11; 32:10–11; 64:1[2]; Jer 33:9; 50:34; Ezek 12:18; Joel 2:1; Mic 7:17; Hab 3:2, 16 (2x); Ps 99:1; Job 3:17, 26; 14:1.
   3. Gen 45:24 (see also the LXX); 2 Kgs 19:27–28; Isa 28:21, 37:28–29; Ezek 16:43; Ps 4:5[4]; Job 12:6; Prov 29:9. Some of these references appear to refer to anger but have a

15.1.2 זַעַף

The word זַעַף appears in the Hebrew Bible only 13 times, mostly in later literature.[4] With so few appearances, lexicographers have had difficulty ascertaining its precise meaning. Most reference works (BDB, *HALOT*, *TDOT*, and *NIDOTTE*) consider it to mean primarily *rage*. However, there is then difficulty in determining what to do with the cases in which the word refers to *despondency* (Gen 40:6; 1 Kgs 20:43, 21:4) and *hunger* (Dan 1:10). Clearly, the subjects in these verses are not angry.[5] Some sources (*HALOT*, *NIDOTTE*) claim that the word in these verses is from a different root (same spelling) that is related to the Arabic word *ḍaʿīf*, meaning 'weak'. Although this possibility cannot be ruled out, the Arabic *ḍ* does not typically correspond to the Hebrew ז.[6] It seems preferable to understand זַעַף as instead meaning 'greatly disturbed' or 'in an uproar', a definition that works in all appearances of the word, including Jonah 1:15, where it describes the tumultuous sea.[7] Within this lexical rubric of *disturbed*, one can fit the various episodes of *despondency* (Gen 40:6; 1 Kgs 20:43, 21:4), the case of *hunger* in Dan 1:10, and the 8 cases in which the word refers to *anger*. In nearly every appearance, this word has close ties with authority. Whatever the type of disturbance, the subject is almost always an official of some type, except the two instances in which the subject is God and the case of Prov 19:3, "his heart is in an uproar (זַעַף) against YHWH."

15.1.3 כעס

Like רגז and זַעַף, the word כעס (spelled כעש in Job) can refer to not only 'anger' but also other forms of 'displeasure', such as 'sadness'. It makes 79 appearances, most commonly in Deuteronomistic works (8 times in Deuteronomy; 20 times in Kings; 11 in Jeremiah), and it carries the meaning of being 'troubled'.[8] Perhaps the most striking feature of this root is that

---

degree of ambiguity (such as Ps 4:5[4]). The two appearances of this word in Biblical Aramaic also refer to anger (Dan 3:13, Ezra 5:12).

4. It appears 7 times as the noun זַעַף, 4 times as a Qal verb, and twice as the adjective זָעֵף.

5. Koehler, Baumgartner, and Stamm assert that this word in 1 Kgs 20:43, 21:4 refers to being *furious* (*HALOT* [study ed.], "זָעֵף," 1.277). However, Ahab's responses of lying down, turning his face away, and refusing food have little in common with the typical responses to anger in the Hebrew Bible.

6. H. Ringgren, "זָעַף; זַעַף; זָעֵף," *TDOT* 4.111–12, esp. p. 111.

7. This definition of *disturbed* is not far removed from BDB's understanding of the word as meaning *vexed* (BDB, 277). It also is not far removed from the Aramaic זַעַף, which means *storm*, something we refer to as a *disturbance of nature*. While *anger* is sometimes expressed in English in terms of a tempest (for example, "He *stormed* off"), it is difficult to use expressions of this sort consistently to translate זַעַף.

The word appears in the Dead Sea Scrolls, referring both to *anger* (often on the part of those with authority; 1QpHab III 12; 4Q223–224 2 I 52; 4Q435 1 I 4 = 4Q436 1 II 2; 4Q511 35, 1) and to *disturbed* waters (1QHᵃ XIV 22; XV 4; 4Q429 4 II 1).

8. Many lexicons (BDB, *HALOT*) suggest that it means to be *vexed*, which is similar to the definition of being *troubled* proposed here. The translation *trouble* avoids the problems

its connotations differ depending on the social standing of the one who is troubled. When someone in a hierarchical position is troubled, the person tends to become *angry*. On the other hand, when someone in a marginalized or culturally inferior position is troubled, the person tends to experience *anguish* or *sadness*.[9] As with many terms for anger, issues of power determine how this emotion is experienced and expressed. Earlier (§5.2), I observed that the boundaries between anger and sadness are not as sharp in Biblical Hebrew as they are in American English. This observation is reinforced by the ways that רגז, כעס, and זעף can refer not only to anger but also to sadness or another emotion.

15.2 Words Related to a Perceived Physiological Symptom

15.2.1 אף

Although scholars are divided about the precise origins of אף and its root אנף, the substantive אף clearly carries double meaning in the Hebrew Bible.[10] In 234 cases, it refers to 'anger' (an additional 13 times, if one counts אנף, which is used exclusively of divine anger).[11] The other 42 appearances of this word refer to a 'nose' or 'nostril(s)'.[12] Lexicographers tend to assume

---

of the translation *offend*, which is associated with the degradation of honor, an association that is tangential to כעס/שׁ (N. Lohfink, "כַּעַס, כָּעַס," *TDOT* 7.282–88, esp. p. 285). Ellen van Wolde connects this word with the concept of jealousy (*Reframing Biblical Studies: When Language and Text Meet Culture, Cognition, and Context* [Winona Lake, IN: Eisenbrauns, 2009] 65). While there are clear associations between כעס and קנא, many other words for anger share this connection with jealousy, such as חמה and אף (see §5.1).

9. In the following texts mentioning כעס/שׁ, the person who is *troubled* is in a hierarchical position of power and is *angry*: Deut 4:25; 9:18; 31:29; 32:16, 19, 21a; Judg 2:12; 1 Kgs 14:9, 15; 15:30 (2x); 16:2, 7, 13, 26, 33; 21:22 (2x); 22:54[53]; 2 Kgs 17:11, 17; 21:6, 15; 22:17; 23:19, 26 (2x); Isa 65:3; Jer 7:18, 19; 8:19; 11:17; 25:6, 7; 32:29, 30, 32; 44:3, 8; Ezek 8:17; 16:26, 32; 20:8; 32:9; Hos 12:15[14]; Ps 78:58; 85:5[4]; 106:29; Job 10:17; Neh 3:33[4:1]; 2 Chr 16:10; 28:25; 33:6; 34:25. In the following texts that also mention כעס/שׁ, the person who is *troubled* is in an inferior position and experiences *anguish* or *sadness*: Deut 32:21b; 1 Sam 1:6 (2x), 7, 16; Ps 6:8[7]; 10:14; 31:10[9]; 112:10; Job 6:2; 17:7; Qoh 1:18; 2:23; Neh 3:37[4:5]. The following appearances of כעס/שׁ are marked by some level of ambiguity with respect to social standing: Deut 32:27; Job 5:2; Prov 12:16; 17:25; 21:19; 27:3; Qoh 7:3, 9 (2x); 11:10.

10. Bergman and Johnson, "אַף; אָנַף " *TDOT* 1.351.

11. When אנף is used in the Mesha Inscription, it also refers to divine anger—the anger of Chemosh (*KAI* 181.5). When it is used in Biblical Aramaic, it functions as a noun meaning 'face' (אֲנַף), which is used to describe the humility (Dan 2:46) and anger (Dan 3:19) of Nebuchadnezzar.

12. In many cases where אף can be translated 'nose', the meaning relates to some type of emotion. The term means 'nose' but refers to *humility* (esp. with the Hishtaphel form of חוה ['bow down']) in the following cases: Gen 19:1; 42:6; 48:12; Num 22:31; 1 Sam 20:41; 24:8; 25:23, 41; 28:14; 2 Sam 14:4, 33; 18:28; 24:20; 1 Kgs 1:23, 31; Isa 49:23; Neh 8:6; 1 Chr 21:21; 2 Chr 7:3; 20:18; see also Dan 2:46. In Ps 10:4, the term is associated with *haughtiness*. When a nose ring is mentioned, it frequently connotes *honor*: Gen 24:47; Isa 3:21; Ezek 16:12; Prov 11:22; see also Song 7:5[4]. Barbs, hooks, or ropes in the nose, on

that the two meanings are related, although they differ in how they parse this difference. On the basis of the expressions ארך אפים (lit., 'length of nostrils'; idiomatically 'slow to anger') and קצר אפים (lit., 'shortness of nostrils'; idiomatically 'quick to anger'), some scholars such as Dhorme see anger as marked by an increased rate of respiration, which is conveyed by referring to one's *nose* (אף).[13] Instances where רוח ('breath') appears in conjunction with references to anger substantiate this claim (Prov 14:29; see also Judg 8:3).[14] Others associate these references to the *nose* with a perception of *burning* or *heat* in the nose. There is a great deal of textual evidence for this connection. Fifty-seven times, אף is the subject of חרה, which is related to the idea of *burning*.[15] Thirty-nine times, the noun אף appears in a verse with חמה, which is related to ideas of *heat*, and typically the two words stand parallel to each other.[16] At least in terms of frequency, the *nose* appears to be connected with *anger* primarily on the basis of perceiving heat in one's face and secondarily on the basis of perceiving an increase in one's rate of respiration. In either case, the metaphorical connections appear to be dead in most biblical texts (see §6.4).

The word אף is the most common word for anger in the Hebrew Bible, and it has a relatively wide semantic range, referring to all types of anger. It is able to describe both the fairly minor anger of Jacob toward his wife (Gen 30:2) and the exceptionally violent anger mentioned in Ezek 23:25.[17] Of the 234 references אף makes to anger, 52 refer to human anger.[18] These

---

the other hand, refer to capturing someone or something, which can entail *humiliation* (2 Kgs 19:28; Job 40:24, 41:2; see also Prov 30:33).

13. E. Dhorme, *L'emploi métaphorique des noms de parties du corps en hébreu et en akkadien* (Paris: Librairie Orientaliste, 1963) 81–82. See also *TLOT*, which associates אף with "'snorting' (in anger)" (G. Sauer, "אַף *'ap* anger," *TLOT* 1.168).

14. There are also several cases in which the term means 'nose' and is connected with *breath* and *life*: Gen 2:7, 3:19, 7:22; Isa 2:22; Job 27:3; Lam 4:20; Song 7:9[8].

15. Gen 30:2; 39:19; 44:18; Exod 4:14; 22:23[24]; 32:10–11, 19, 22; Num 11:1, 10, 33; 12:9; 22:22, 27; 24:10; 25:3; 32:10, 13; Deut 6:15; 7:4; 11:17; 29:26[27]; 31:17; Josh 7:1; 23:16; Judg 2:14, 20; 3:8; 6:39; 9:30; 10:7; 14:19; 1 Sam 11:6; 17:28; 20:30; 2 Sam 6:7; 12:5; 24:1; 2 Kgs 13:3; 23:26 (2x); Isa 5:25; Hos 8:5; Zech 10:3; Ps 106:40; 124:3; Job 19:11; 32:2 (2x), 3, 5; 42:7; 1 Chr 13:10; 2 Chr 25:10 (2x), 15.

16. Deut 9:19; 29:22[23], 27[28]; Isa 42:25; 63:3, 6; 66:15; Jer 7:20; 21:5; 32:31, 37; 33:5; 36:7; 42:18; 44:6; Ezek 5:13, 15; 7:8; 13:13; 20:8, 21; 22:20; 23:25; 25:14; 38:18; Mic 5:14[15]; Nah 1:6; Ps 6:2[1]; 37:8; 78:38; 90:7; Prov 15:1, 18; 21:14; 22:24; 27:4; 29:22; Lam 4:11; Dan 9:16. In three of these cases (Isa 42:25, 66:15; Ezek 23:25), the two words form a construct relationship with one another.

17. Perhaps the most extensive treatment of the relationship between אף and anger is Mayer I. Gruber, *Aspects of Nonverbal Communication in the Ancient Near East* (Studia Pohl 12; 2 vols.; Rome: Pontifical Biblical Institute, 1980) 2.480–553.

18. The references to human anger are Gen 27:45; 30:2; 39:19; 44:18; 49:6, 7; Exod 11:8; 32:19, 22; Num 22:27; 24:10; Judg 9:30; 14:19; 1 Sam 11:6; 17:28; 20:30, 34; 2 Sam 12:5; Ps 37:8; 55:4[3]; 124:3; 138:7; Isa 7:4; 14:6; 37:29; Ezek 23:25; 35:11; Amos 1:11; Job 18:4; 32:2 (2x), 3, 5; 36:13; 40:11; Prov 14:17, 29; 15:1, 18; 16:32; 19:11; 21:14; 22:24; 25:15; 27:4; 29:8, 22; 30:33; Dan 11:20; 2 Chr 25:10.

references to human anger appear predominantly in Genesis (6 times), Job (7 times), and Proverbs (13 times).

15.2.2 חרה

Whereas אַף is the most common noun for anger in the Hebrew Bible, the word חרה is the most common verb, appearing 93 times.[19] As its various Semitic cognates suggest, this word is related to the meaning 'burn'. Aside from its rare appearances in the Tiphel and Hiphil stems, however, this verb refers to 'anger'.[20] In the 83 appearances of this word in the Qal stem, the text either says that someone's אַף '(nose) burned' (58 times), or it employs an impersonal subject (perhaps an implied אַף, see BDB) (25 times).[21] With the latter, a ־ל particle is typically employed to designate who is angry. Hence, an expression like וַיִּחַר לְקַיִן in Gen 4:5 is quite common, which literally could be rendered, 'It burned for Cain' but idiomatically means, 'Cain became angry'.[22] Never does one find the root חרה in the Hebrew Bible referring to fire in nonfigurative ways.[23] Like the term אַף, the word חרה is popular and describes many types of anger, ranging from Jonah's anger over a withered plant (Jonah 4:9) to Zebul's anger, which led to mass slaughter (Judg 9:30). Also like אַף, חרה functions as a common expression for anger that need not entail an actual description of the subject's physiological symptoms (see §6.4). The word חרה is one of the few terms used

---

19. The root חרה has two nominal forms that are used less frequently. The noun חָרוֹן is found 41 times and is used only of divine wrath, while חֳרִי is found 6 times and used of both humans (4x) and God (2x). When חרן is used in an 8th-century Aramaic stele from Sefire (*KAI* 223.B.12), it is connected with divine wrath, particularly a day of wrath (יום חרן), much like the Hebrew חרון (see Isa 13:13, Lam 1:12).

20. The Tiphel appears in Jer 12:5, 22:15. (See GKC §55h for more on the Tiphel stem.) The Hiphil appears only in Neh 3:20, which perhaps should be deleted on the grounds of dittography (see also the LXX). Job 19:11 should be repointed as a Qal verb.

21. This verb appears 83 times in the Qal (if one counts Job 19:11 [see n. 20 above] but not Isa 24:6 [see n. 23 below]), 3 times in the Niphal, and 4 times in the Hithpael. The meaning does not differ greatly between these three stems. The Hithpael appears in Ps 37:1, 7, 8; Prov 24:19, all of which employ a negative jussive, telling readers אַל־תִּתְחַר. In this stem, the word typically is translated *fret*. However, *fretting* tends to connote *worrying*, which does not seem to be in view here. Rather, these verses tend to be saying, *Do not anger yourself*, which works very well with how the Hithpael is frequently employed (reflexively) and with context (note the parallels between this word and קנא in Ps 37:1 and between this word, אַף, and חמה in Ps 37:8). Meanwhile, when the Niphal is used (Isa 41:11, 45:24; Song 1:6), the subject no longer needs to be אַף or impersonal (with ־ל). Finally, one should note the rare expression in Gen 31:35, 45:5: [(pro)noun] אַל־יַחַר בְּעֵינֵי. Literally, it would be rendered *Do not let it burn in* [*your/my lord's*] *eyes*. The expression is obviously referring to anger (see also Gen 18:30, 32).

22. Niko Besnier has an interesting discussion of how several languages convey emotion by having the one experiencing emotion not as the subject of the emotion-denoting verb but as its locative modifier, as is the case here ("Language and Affect," *Annual Review of Anthropology* 19 [1990] 419–51, esp. pp. 423, 425).

23. This assumes that חָרוּ in Isa 24:6 either derives from the root חרר (so BDB, 359) or another root also spelled חרה (appearing only here) that means 'diminish in number' (so *HALOT* [study ed.], 1.351).

more frequently to refer to human anger (46 times) than divine anger (41 times).[24] This word is most common in the books of Genesis and Numbers.[25]

15.2.3 חמה

The term חמה behaves similarly to אף and חרה in many respects. Its underlying meaning is 'heat'. Like many of its Semitic cognates, it can refer not only to 'heat' but also to 'anger'. In the Hebrew Bible, חֵמָה appears 125 times, 117 times in reference to 'anger' (spelled חֵמָא in Dan 11:44), 7 times in reference to 'venom' or 'poison', and once in reference to the 'heat' of wine.[26] It also appears an additional 6 times with the alternate pointing חַמָּה, referring to the 'sun' or its 'heat'.[27] The word חֵמָה tends to arise in later texts, and it is a favorite of Ezekiel, who mentions it 30 times, almost always with respect to divine anger. On 28 occasions, this word designates human anger, most commonly in Proverbs (9 times), while Esther is not far behind (6 times).[28] References to human חֵמָה tend to be quite serious and frequently involve at least the possibility of deadly violence.[29]

15.3 Words Referring to Specific Types of Anger

The words קצף, זעם, שטם, and עבר/עברה (Hithpael) refer to human anger only 14, 10, 4, and 11 times, respectively. Particular patterns emerge with each word, suggesting that each may designate a particular type of anger. However, with so few appearances, any conclusions are somewhat tentative.[30]

---

24. The references to human anger are: Gen 4:5–6; 30:2; 31:35–36; 34:7; 39:19; 44:18; 45:5; Exod 32:19, 22; Num 16:15; 22:27; 24:10; Judg 9:30; 14:19; 1 Sam 11:6; 15:11; 17:28; 18:8; 20:7, 30; 2 Sam 3:8; 6:8; 12:5; 13:21; 19:42; Isa 41:11; 45:24; Jonah 4:1, 4, 9; Ps 37:1, 7–8; 124:3; Job 32:2–3, 5; Prov 24:19; Song 1:6; Neh 3:33[4:1]; 4:1[7]; 5:6; 1 Chr 13:11; 2 Chr 25:10.

25. Genesis and Numbers both contain 11 appearances of this verb. It is unusually rare in the Latter Prophets.

26. Ezek 3:14 and 19:12 were counted in the number of references to *anger*. However, it is possible that they refer to *poison* and *heat*, respectively. Hos 7:5 speaks explicitly of the *heat* of wine (see also Deut 32:33, Isa 63:3, Jer 25:15, Esth 7:7). In Biblical Aramaic, one finds חֵמָא and חֵמָה referring to *anger* (Dan 3:13, 19).

27. Isa 24:23; 30:28 (2x); Ps 19:7[6]; Job 30:28; Song 6:10. While חַמָּה comes from the root חמם, חֵמָה appears to derive from the root יחם, which is an "alternate form of חמם" (*HALOT* [study ed.], 1.407; see also K.-D. Schunck, "חֵמָה," *TDOT* 4:462–65, esp. p. 462). A Meṣad Ḥashavyahu Inscription (1.10–11) also mentions the חם, *heat*, of the sun (F. W. Dobbs-Allsopp et al., *Hebrew Inscriptions: Texts from the Biblical Period of the Monarchy with Concordance* [New Haven, CT: Yale University Press, 2005] esp. pp. 359, 365).

28. References to human anger include Gen 27:44; 2 Sam 11:20; 2 Kgs 5:12; Isa 51:13 (2x); Ps 37:8; 76:11[10] (2x); Job 19:29; 36:18; Prov 6:34; 15:1, 18; 16:14; 19:19; 21:14; 22:24; 27:4; 29:22; Esth 1:12; 2:1; 3:5; 5:9; 7:7, 10; Dan 8:6; 11:44. See also Ezek 3:14. In Dan 3:13 (Biblical Aramaic) as well, חמה is used to refer to human anger.

29. Gen 27:44; Isa 51:13 [2x]; Job 19:29; Prov 6:34; 16:14; Esth 3:5; 5:9; 7:7, 10; Dan 8:6; 11:44.

30. Neither Dobbs-Allsopp et al., *Hebrew Inscriptions*, nor *KAI* mention these four words in their respective concordances. The only exception is עבר, but it carries meanings

15.3.1 קָצַף

The root קָצַף appears to refer to 'authoritative anger'.[31] This word conveys anger on the part of an official, king, leader, or someone with authority in arguably all of its appearances. Certainly, the 44 cases referring to divine anger can be seen as anger on the part of someone with great power. The word also designates anger on the part of several humans with authority:

- Pharaoh (פרעה, Gen 40:2, 41:10)
- Moses (angry with the people he leads; Exod 16:20, Lev 10:16, Num 31:14)
- The commanders of the Philistines (שׂר, 1 Sam 29:4)
- Naaman, the commander of the Aramean army (שׂר, 2 Kgs 5:11)
- Elisha, the man of God (איש האלהים, who exerts his authority in relation to the king of Israel; 2 Kgs 13:19)
- The officials who beat Jeremiah (שׂר, Jer 37:15)
- Various officials of King Ahasuerus (שׂר, Esth 1:18; סריס, Esth 2:21)
- King Ahasuerus himself (Esth 1:12)[32]

In Isa 8:21, the individuals who are angry are not officials or in a position of authority, but the verb in this case makes its sole appearance in the Hithpael stem. It is likely that the verb here is an *estimative-declarative reflexive*, whereby subjects can feign or pretend that they have particular qualities they do not have.[33] Thus, the subjects act as though they have stature and authority when they "become enraged (וְהִתְקַצַּף) and curse (וְקִלֵּל) their God and their king." In Qoh 5:16[17], קָצַף is not linked explicitly with authority, but even here the surrounding discussion focuses on wealthy individuals who have status higher than the עבד ('worker, slave') mentioned

---

there that have nothing to do with anger. For a more general account of the insufficiency of evidence in Biblical Hebrew, see Edward Ullendorff, *Is Biblical Hebrew a Language? Studies in Semitic Languages and Civilizations* (Wiesbaden: Harrassowitz, 1977) 16–17.

31. Its cognates tend to carry meanings of *anger*, although the Akkadian *kaṣāpu* and *keṣēpu* mean *think*. Of the 34 appearances it makes as a verb, 28 are Qal, 5 Hiphil, and 1 Hithpael. Van Wolde asserts that this word in its verbal and nominal forms "is almost exclusively used with reference to Yhwh" (*Reframing Biblical Studies*, 70). She overstates the case with the verb, which refers to divine anger 22 times and human anger 12 times. Of the 28 occurrences of קֶצֶף in the Hebrew Bible, 26 refer to divine anger and only 2 to human anger. (The number of references to divine anger assumes that 2 Kgs 3:27 is a reference to the perception of divine wrath on the part of the Moabite god Chemosh against Israel.) There is one other appearance of קֶצֶף (Hos 10:7), but it refers to a 'twig', not 'anger'. Biblical Aramaic contains two references to the root קצף, once as a Peal verb (Dan 2:12) and once as the noun קְצַף (Ezra 7:23). Both depict anger.

32. The two appearances of קְצַף in Biblical Aramaic also ascribe anger to individuals with authority, King Nebuchadnezzar in Dan 2:12 and God in Ezra 7:23.

33. As Waltke and O'Connor observe, "the *Hithpael* may denote esteeming or presenting oneself in a state, sometimes without regard to the question of truthfulness" as in 2 Sam 13:5, Prov 13:7, and perhaps Esth 8:17 (*IBHS*, esp. pp. 430–31, §26.2.f).

in 5:11[12] (see also vv. 9–14[10–15], 18–19[19–20]). Terms for *anger* tend to have connections with authority, and this is especially the case with קצף.

15.3.2 זעם

Most of the cognates of זעם refer to angry speech, which appears to be the case in the Hebrew as well.[34] The word זעם appears in conjunction with משל ('discourse'; Num 23:7), ארר ('curse'; Num 23:7), קבב ('curse'; Num 23:8, Prov 24:24), לעג ('mock'; Hos 7:16), לשון ('tongue, speech'; Isa 30:27, Hos 7:16, Prov 25:23), and שפה ('lip'; Isa 30:27). Lexicographers have suggested that, when the subject is human, זעם always refers to cursing.[35] Although it is not apparent that cursing is always in view (see Prov 25:23), the biblical and extrabiblical evidence make strong connections between this word and verbal communication.[36]

15.3.3 עבר, עברה *(Hithpael)*

Although the etymology of עבר is uncertain, a key pattern emerges in its usage in the Hebrew Bible.[37] In most of these cases, the word refers to 'unbridled' emotion, usually 'anger' although three cases refer to 'un-bridled pride' (Isa 16:6; Prov 14:16, 21:24; see also Jer 48:30).[38] The lack of restraint that characterizes the anger conveyed by these words is typically quite harsh, although it need not be marked by a total lack of control.[39] Isa 14:6 and Amos 1:11 illustrate the ferocity of this type of anger, the former speaking of "strik[ing] peoples in עֶבְרָה with unceasing blows," while the

---

34. These cognates include meanings such as 'attack verbally, scold' (Syr.), 'speak angrily' (Arab.), and 'quarrel' (Old South Arabic; B. Wiklander, "זָעַם, זַעַם," *TDOT* 4.106–11, esp. p. 107). The root זעם is found 34 times, 12 as a verb (11 Qal, 1 Niphal; 6 human, 6 divine) and 22 times as the noun זַעַם (4 human, 18 divine). The instances of human anger are Num 23:7–8; Jer 15:17; Hos 7:16; Mic 6:10(?); Prov 24:24; 25:23; Dan 8:19; 11:30, 36.

35. Wiklander, "זָעַם, זַעַם," 107. Even if this is the case, there appears to be anger implied in the cursing, something attested in other languages as well (Robert I. Levy, *Tahitians: Mind and Experience in the Society Islands* [Chicago: University of Chicago Press, 1973] 286–87; Besnier, "Language and Affect," esp. pp. 423–24).

36. C. A. Keller suggests translating זעם 'to snap at in anger, to scold strongly' ("קלל *qll* to be light," *TLOT* 3.1143). The word זעם appears with another term for anger in the following cases: Isa 10:5, 25; 30:27; Jer 10:10; Ezek 21:36[31]; 22:31; Nah 1:6; Hab 3:12; Zeph 3:8; Ps 69:25[24]; 78:49; 102:11[10]; Lam 2:6.

37. BDB, *HALOT*, and *NIDOTTE* all note the uncertain etymology. Schunck, "חֵמָה," 426, meanwhile, does the most to outline the various possibilities. The idea of a lack of restraint may be related to the idea of *crossing over* (עבר). The noun עֶבְרָה and the Hithpael forms of עבר appear 34 and 8 times, respectively. These words are used of human emotion in Gen 49:7; Isa 14:6; 16:6; Jer 48:30; Amos 1:11; Job 40:11; Ps 7:7[6]; Prov 14:16, 35; 20:2; 21:24; 22:8; 26:17.

38. Schunck, "חֵמָה," 10:426, uses the word "unbridled."

39. Thus, in Deut 3:26, Moses suffers the consequence of Yhwh's anger in that he will not cross the Jordan. While this result is harsh for the leader who has stood with the dis-obedient people so long, it is not as harsh as Yhwh's killing Moses would be. Likewise, Gen 49:7 refers to the anger of Levi and Simeon against the inhabitants of Shechem. While this anger is exceedingly harsh, it does not display a total lack of control, as shown in §3.3.

latter describes the destruction (שׁחת) of compassion, the constant tearing of anger (אַף), and the preservation of עברה. Not all appearances of this word give sufficient context to conclude that a lack of restraint is always in view (such as Prov 22:8), but the available evidence suggests that it typically is.[40]

15.3.4 שׁטם

The final word to consider is שׁטם, a rare verb appearing only 6 times, 3 of which are in Genesis.[41] All 6 of these instances involve the 'desire to cause harm', and most of them can be connected with 'buried anger' or 'harbored anger'—that is, 'bearing a grudge'. Whereas עברה suggests a lack of restraint, שׁטם suggests anger that is held in check, at least for a time. Thus, in Gen 27:41, Esau is the subject of the verb. He is clearly angry with Jacob and intends not only to harm his brother but to kill him. However, he restrains his anger, waiting until after his father's death before taking action. Gen 50:15 employs the same verb with a nearly identical situation: Joseph's brothers fear that Joseph has stored up anger against them for past wrongs, planning to harm them after their father dies. Among other things, שׁטם illustrates the tendency for biblical anger to result in violence that is not always immediate or uncontrolled.

---

40. To convey the lack of restraint, a number of sources (BDB, *TDOT*) recommend translating the noun 'outburst'. However, in English, the term *outburst* suggests a flash of anger that does not endure. As the above examples from Isa 14:6 and Amos 1:11 illustrate, this temporally bound connotation of *outburst* does not fit especially well.

41. Gen 27:41, 49:23, 50:15; Ps 55:4[3]; Job 16:9, 30:21. The verb always appears in the Qal stem, 4 times with a human subject and twice with a divine subject.

Bibliography

Abu-Lughod, Lila. *Veiled Sentiments: Honor and Poetry in a Bedouin Society.* Revised edition. Berkeley: University of California Press, 1999.

Ackroyd, Peter R. *Exile and Restoration: A Study of Hebrew Thought of the Sixth Century B.C.* Old Testament Library. Philadelphia: Westminster, 1968.

Adenzato, Mauro, and Francesca Garbarini. "The *As If* in Cognitive Science, Neuroscience and Anthropology: A Journey among Robots, Blacksmiths and Neurons." *Theory Psychology* 16 (2006) 747–59.

Albertz, Rainer. *A History of Israelite Religion in the Old Testament Period.* Translated by John Bowden. 2 volumes. Louisville: Westminster John Knox, 1994.

———. *Israel in Exile: The History and Literature of the Sixth Century B.C.E.* Translated by David Green. Society of Biblical Literature Studies in Biblical Literature 3. Atlanta: Society of Biblical Literature, 2003.

Alonso Schökel, Luis. *Dónde está tu hermano? Textos de fraternidad en el libro del Génesis.* Tesis y Monografías 19. Valencia: Institución San Jerónimo, 1985.

Alter, Robert. *The Art of Biblical Narrative.* New York: Basic Books, 1981.

Anderson, G. A. *A Time to Mourn, a Time to Dance: The Expression of Grief and Joy in Israelite Religion.* University Park, PA: Pennsylvania State University Press, 1991.

Anscombe, G. E. M. "Modern Moral Philosophy." *Philosophy* 33/124 (1958) 1–19.

Aristotle. *The Nicomachean Ethics.* Translated by H. Rackham. Edited by Jeffrey Henderson. Loeb Classical Library. Cambridge: Harvard University Press, 1934.

———. "Poetics." Pp. 1–141 in *Aristotle: Poetics; Longinus: On the Sublime; and Demetrius: On Style.* Loeb Classical Library. Cambridge: Harvard University Press, 1995.

The Assyrian Dictionary of the Oriental Institute of the University of Chicago. Chicago: Oriental Institute, 1956–2011.

Auerbach, Erich. *Mimesis: The Representation of Reality in Western Literature.* Translated by Willard R. Trask. Fiftieth-Anniversary edition. Princeton: Princeton University Press, 2003.

Aune, David E. "Review of: William Harris, *Restraining Rage: The Ideology of Anger Control in Classical Antiquity.*" *Journal of Religion* 83 (2003) 678–80.

Austin, J. L. *Philosophical Papers.* Edited by J. O. Urmson and G. J. Warnock. 2nd edition. Oxford: Clarendon, 1970.

Averill, James R. *Anger and Aggression: An Essay on Emotion.* New York: Springer, 1982.

Bakhtin, Mikhail. *The Dialogic Imagination.* Translated by C. Emerson and M. Holquist. Edited by M. Holquist. Austin: University of Texas Press, 1981.

———. *Problems of Dostoevsky's Poetics.* Edited by Caryl Emerson. Theory and History of Literature 8. Minneapolis: University of Minnesota Press, 1984.

———. *Toward a Philosophy of the Act.* Translated by Vadim Liapunov. Edited by Michael Holquist and Vadim Liapunov. University of Texas Press Slavic Series 10. Austin: University of Texas Press, 1993.

Balmary, Marie. *Abel ou la traversée de l'Éden.* Paris: Bernard Grasset, 1999.

Baloian, Bruce Edward. *Anger in the Old Testament.* American University Studies 7, Theology and Religion 99. New York: Peter Lang, 1992.

———. *The Aspect of Anger in the Old Testament.* Ph.D. thesis. Claremont Graduate School, 1989.

Barr, James. "Review of G. Johannes Botterweck and Helmer Ringgren, eds., *Theological Dictionary of the Old Testament*, Vol. 2." *Interpretation* 33 (1979) 90–91.

———. *The Semantics of Biblical Language*. London: SCM, 1961.

Barstad, Hans M. *The Myth of the Empty Land: A Study in the History and Archaeology of Judah During the "Exilic" Period*. Oslo: Scandinavian University Press, 1996.

Barton, John. *Ethics and the Old Testament*. 1st North American edition. Harrisburg, PA: Trinity Press International, 1998.

———. *Understanding Old Testament Ethics*. Louisville: Westminster John Knox, 2003.

Basset, Lytta. *Holy Anger: Jacob, Job, Jesus*. Grand Rapids, MI: Eerdmans, 2007.

Beardsley, Monroe. "Metaphor." Pp. 284–89 in vol. 5 of *The Encyclopedia of Philosophy*. Edited by Paul Edwards. New York: Macmillan & Free Press, 1967.

Bechtel, Lyn M. "Genesis 2.4b–3.24: A Myth about Human Maturation." *Journal for the Study of the Old Testament* 67 (1995) 3–26.

———. "Rethinking the Interpretation of Genesis 2.4b–3.24." Pp. 77–117 in *A Feminist Companion to Genesis*. Edited by Althalya Brenner. Princeton: Princeton University Press, 1993.

———. "What if Dinah Is Not Raped? (Genesis 34)." *Journal for the Study of the Old Testament* 62 (1994) 19–36.

Becker, A. L. "A Short Essay on Languaging." Pp. 226–33 in *Research and Reflexivity*. Edited by Frederick Steier. London: Sage, 1991.

Bellis, Alice Ogden. *Helpmates, Harlots, and Heroes: Women's Stories in the Hebrew Bible*. Louisville: Westminster John Knox, 1994.

Ben Yashar, Menahem. "Zu Gen 4:7." *Zeitschrift für die alttestamentliche Wissenschaft* 94 (1982) 635–37.

Berlin, Brent, and Paul Kay. *Basic Color Terms: Their Universality and Evolution*. Berkeley: University of California Press, 1969.

Berlyn, P. J. "His Brothers' Keeper." *Jewish Bible Quarterly* 26 (1998) 73–83.

Berman, Antoine. "Translation and the Trials of the Foreign." Pp. 284–97 in *The Translation Studies Reader*. Edited by Lawrence Venuti. London: New York, 2000.

Besnier, Niko. "Language and Affect." *Annual Review of Anthropology* 19 (1990) 419–51.

Birch, Bruce C. *Let Justice Roll Down: The Old Testament, Ethics, and Christian Life*. Louisville: Westminster John Knox, 1991.

Black, Edwin. "The Second Persona." *Quarterly Journal of Speech* 56 (1970) 111–19.

Black, Jeremy, Anthony Green, and Tessa Rickards. *Gods, Demons and Symbols of Ancient Mesopotamia: An Illustrated Dictionary*. Austin: University of Texas Press, 1992.

Black, Max. "Linguistic Relativity: The Views of Benjamin Lee Whorf." *The Philosophical Review* 68 (1959) 228–38.

———. *Models and Metaphors: Studies in Language and Philosophy*. Ithaca, NY: Cornell University Press, 1962.

Blenkinsopp, Joseph. "The Bible, Archaeology, and Politics; Or, the Empty Land Revisited." *Journal for the Study of the Old Testament* 27 (2002) 169–87.

———. "Ecclesiastes 3:1–15: Another Interpretation." *Journal for the Study of the Old Testament* 66 (1995) 55–64.

Booth, Wayne C. *The Company We Keep: An Ethics of Fiction*. Berkeley: University of California Press, 1988.

———. *The Rhetoric of Fiction*. Chicago: University of Chicago Press, 1961.

Boroditsky, Lera. "Does Language Shape Thought?: Mandarin and English Speakers' Conceptions of Time." *Cognitive Psychology* 43 (2001) 1–22.

Botterweck, G. Johannes, Helmer Ringgren, and Heinz-Josef Fabry, eds. *Theological Dictionary of the Old Testament*. 15 volumes. Grand Rapids, MI: Eerdmans, 1974–2003.

Brenner, Athalya. "Female Social Behaviour: Two Descriptive Patterns within the 'Birth of the Hero' Paradigm." *Vetus Testamentum* 36 (1986) 257–73.

Brett, Mark G. *Genesis: Procreation and the Politics of Identity*. Old Testament Readings. London: Routledge, 2000.

Briggs, Jean L. *Never in Anger: Portrait of an Eskimo Family*. Cambridge: Harvard University Press, 1970.

Briggs, Richard S. *The Virtuous Reader: Old Testament Narrative and Interpretive Virtue*. Studies in Theological Interpretation. Grand Rapids, MI: Baker Academic, 2010.

Brodie, Thomas L. *Genesis as Dialogue: A Literary, Historical, and Theological Commentary*. Oxford: Oxford University Press, 2001.

Brown, Francis, S. R. Driver, and Charles A. Briggs. *The Brown-Driver-Briggs Hebrew and English Lexicon, with an Appendix Containing the Biblical Aramaic*. Peabody, MA: Hendrickson, 2003.

Brown, William P. *Character in Crisis: A Fresh Approach to the Wisdom Literature of the Old Testament*. Grand Rapids, MI: Eerdmans, 1996.

———. *The Ethos of the Cosmos: The Genesis of Moral Imagination in the Bible*. Grand Rapids, MI: Eerdmans, 1999.

Brueggemann, Walter. *Genesis*. Interpretation: A Bible Commentary for Teaching and Preaching. Atlanta: John Knox, 1982.

———. *Theology of the Old Testament: Testimony, Dispute, Advocacy*. Minneapolis: Fortress, 1997.

Burke, Kenneth. *Attitudes toward History*. Berkeley: University of California Press, 1984.

———. *Counter-Statement*. Los Altos, CA: Hermes, 1953.

———. *Language as Symbolic Action: Essays on Life, Literature, and Method*. Berkeley: University of California Press, 1966.

———. "Literature as Equipment for Living." Pp. 253–62 in *The Philosophy of Literary Form*. New York: Vintage, 1957.

———. *Permanence and Change: An Anatomy of Purpose*. 3rd edition. Berkeley: University of California Press, 1984.

Butters, Ronald R. "Do 'Conceptual Metaphors' Really Exist?" *The SECOL Bulletin* 5 (1981) 108–17.

Cahill, Lisa Sowle. "Christian Character, Biblical Community, and Human Values." Pp. 3–17 in *Character & Scripture: Moral Formation, Community, and Biblical Interpretation*. Edited by William P. Brown. Grand Rapids, MI: Eerdmans, 2002.

Carr, David McLain. "Controversy and Convergence in Recent Studies of the Formation of the Pentateuch." *Religious Studies Review* 23 (1997) 22–31.

———. *Reading the Fractures of Genesis: Historical and Literary Approaches*. 1st edition. Louisville: Westminster John Knox, 1996.

Carroll, Robert P. "Exile! What Exile? Deportation and the Discourses of Diaspora." Pp. 62–79 in *Leading Captivity Captive: 'The Exile' as History and Ideology*. Edited by Lester L. Grabbe. Journal for the Study of the Old Testament Supplement 278. Sheffield: Sheffield Academic Press, 1998.

Cassirer, Ernst. *An Essay on Man: An Introduction to a Philosophy of Human Culture*. New Haven, CT: Yale University Press, 1944.

Castellino, Giorgio. "Genesis 4:7." *Vetus Testamentum* 10 (1960) 442–45.

Chapman, Stephen B. *The Law and the Prophets: A Study in Old Testament Canon Formation*. Tübingen: Mohr Siebeck, 2000.

————. "The Old Testament Canon and Its Authority for the Christian Church." *Ex Auditu* 19 (2003) 125–48.

Childs, Brevard S. *Biblical Theology in Crisis*. Philadelphia: Westminster, 1970.

————. *Biblical Theology of the Old and New Testaments: Theological Reflection on the Christian Bible*. Minneapolis: Fortress, 1992.

————. "Review of James Barr, *Semantics of Biblical Language*." *Journal of Biblical Literature* 80 (1961) 374–77.

Christensen, Duane L. "Anticipatory Paronomasia in Jonah 3:7–8 and Genesis 37:2." *Revue biblique* 90 (1983) 261–63.

Closen, Gustav Engelbert. "Der 'Dämon Sünde': Ein Deutungsversuch des massorethischen Textes von Gen. 4, 7." *Biblica* 16 (1935) 431–42.

Cohen, Norman J. *Self, Struggle and Change: Family Conflict Stories in Genesis and Their Healing Insights for Our Lives*. Woodstock, VT: Jewish Lights, 1995.

Collins, John J. "Historical Criticism and the State of Biblical Theology." *Christian Century* (July 28–Aug 4, 1993) 743–47.

Condit, Celeste M. "The Critic as Empath: Moving Away from Totalizing Theory." *Western Journal of Communication* 57 (1993) 178–90.

Cox, J. Robert. "The Die Is Cast: Topical and Ontological Dimensions of the Locus of the Irreparable." *Quarterly Journal of Speech* 68 (1982) 227–39.

Craig, Kenneth M. "Questions outside Eden (Genesis 4.1–16): Yahweh, Cain and Their Rhetorical Interchange." *Journal for the Study of the Old Testament* 86 (1999) 107–28.

Crenshaw, James L. "The Acquisition of Knowledge in Israelite Wisdom Literature." *Word and World* 7 (1987) 245–52.

————. *Defending God: Biblical Responses to the Problem of Evil*. New York: Oxford University Press, 2005.

————. *Old Testament Wisdom: An Introduction*. Revised edition. Louisville: Westminster John Knox, 1998.

————. "Prolegomena." Pp. 1–60 in *Studies in Ancient Israelite Wisdom*. Edited by James L. Crenshaw. New York: Ktav, 1976.

————. *Samson: A Secret Betrayed, a Vow Ignored*. Atlanta: John Knox, 1978.

————. "The Sojourner Has Come to Play the Judge: Theodicy on Trial." Pp. 83–92 in *God in the Fray: A Tribute to Walter Brueggemann*. Edited by Tod Linafelt and Timothy K. Beal. Minneapolis: Fortress, 1998.

Crenshaw, James L., and John T. Willis, eds. *Essays in Old Testament Ethics*. New York: Ktav, 1974.

Damasio, Antonio R. *Descartes' Error: Emotion, Reason, and the Human Brain*. New York: Putnam, 1994.

Davidson, Richard J., Klaus R. Scherer, and H. Hill Goldsmith, eds. *Handbook of Affective Sciences*. Series in Affective Science. Oxford: Oxford University Press, 2003.

Davies, Philip R. "Exile? What Exile? Whose Exile?" Pp. 128–38 in *Leading Captivity Captive: 'The Exile' as History and Ideology*. Edited by Lester L. Grabbe. Journal for the Study of the Old Testament Supplement 278. Sheffield: Sheffield Academic Press, 1998.

Davis, Ellen F. *Getting Involved with God: Rediscovering the Old Testament*. Cambridge: Cowley, 2001.

————. "The Poetics of Generosity." Pp. 626–45 in *The Word Leaps the Gap: Essays on Scripture and Theology in Honor of Richard B. Hays*. Edited by R. Wagner, K. Rowe, and A. K. Grieb. Grand Rapids, MI: Eerdmans, 2008.

————. "Preserving Virtues: Renewing the Tradition of the Sages." Pp. 183–201 in *Character and Scripture: Moral Formation, Community, and Biblical Interpretation*. Edited by William P. Brown. Grand Rapids, MI: Eerdmans, 2002.

Davis, Ellen F., and Richard B. Hays, eds. *The Art of Reading Scripture*. Grand Rapids, MI: Eerdmans, 2003.

D'Costa, Gavin. "Postmodernity and Religious Plurality: Is a Common Global Ethic Possible or Desirable?" Pp. 131–43 in *The Blackwell Companion to Postmodern Theology*. Edited by Graham Ward. Oxford: Blackwell, 2001.

De Groot, Christiana. "Genesis." Pp. 1–27 in *The IVP Women's Bible Commentary*. Edited by Catherine Clark Kroeger and Mary J. Evans. Downers Grove, IL: Inter-Varsity, 2002.

Derrida, Jacques. *"Des tours de Babel."* Pp. 209–48 in *Difference in Translation*. Edited by Joseph F. Graham. Ithaca, NY: Cornell University Press, 1985.

Deurloo, Karel Adriaan. "תשוקה 'Dependency': Gen 4,7." *Zeitschrift für die alttestamentliche Wissenschaft* 99 (1987) 405–6.

Dhorme, E. *L'emploi métaphorique des noms de parties du corps en hébreu et en akkadien*. Paris: Librairie Orientaliste, 1963.

Dirven, René, and Marjolijn Verspoor, eds. *Cognitive Exploration of Language and Linguistics*. Cognitive Linguistics in Practice. Amsterdam: John Benjamins, 1998.

Dobbs-Allsopp, F. W., J. J. M. Roberts, C. L. Seow, and R. E. Whitaker. *Hebrew Inscriptions: Texts from the Biblical Period of the Monarchy with Concordance*. New Haven, CT: Yale University Press, 2005.

Donner, H., and W. Röllig, eds. *Kanaanäische und aramäische Inschriften*. 3 volumes. Wiesbaden: Harrassowitz, 1962–1964.

Dube, Musa W. *Postcolonial Feminist Interpretation of the Bible*. St. Louis, MO: Chalice, 2000.

Duhm, Hans. *Die bösen Geister im Alten Testament*. Tübingen: Mohr, 1904.

Dupré, Louis. "Truth in Religion and Truth of Religion." Pp. 19–42 in *Phenomenology of the Truth Proper to Religion*. Edited by Daniel Guerrière. SUNY Series in Philosophy. Albany: State University of New York Press, 1990.

Ebeling, Erich, Bruno Meissner, Ernst Weidner, Wolfram von Soden, and Dietz Otto Edzard, eds. *Reallexikon der Assyriologie*. Berlin: de Gruyter, 1989.

Eichrodt, Walther. *Theology of the Old Testament*. 2 volumes. Philadelphia: Westminster, 1967.

Ellens, J. Harold, and Wayne G. Rollins, eds. *Psychology and the Bible: A New Way to Read the Scriptures*. 2 volumes. Praeger Perspectives: Psychology, Religion, and Spirituality. Westport, CT: Praeger, 2004.

Elliott, Matthew A. *Faithful Feelings: Rethinking Emotion in the New Testament*. Grand Rapids, MI: Kregel, 2006.

Enns, Peter. *Inspiration and Incarnation: Evangelicals and the Problem of the Old Testament*. Grand Rapids, MI: Baker Academic, 2005.

Exum, J. Cheryl. "The Accusing Look: The Abjection of Hagar in Art." *Religion and the Arts* 11 (2007) 143–71.

Fehr, B., and J. A. Russell. "Concept of Emotion Viewed from a Prototype Perspective." *Journal of Experimental Psychology: General* 113 (1984) 464–86.

Fewell, Danna Nolan, and David M. Gunn. "Tipping the Balance: Sternberg's Reader and the Rape of Dinah." *Journal of Biblical Literature* 110 (1991) 193–211.

Fish, Stanley. *The Trouble with Principle*. Cambridge: Harvard University Press, 1999.

Fishbane, Michael. *Text and Texture: Close Readings of Selected Biblical Texts*. New York: Schocken, 1979.

Fisher, Walter R. "Narration, Knowledge, and the Possibility of Wisdom." Pp. 169–92 in *Rethinking Knowledge: Reflections across the Disciplines*. Edited by Robert F. Goodman and Walter R. Fisher. Albany: State University of New York, 1995.

Fitness, Julie. "Anger in the Workplace: An Emotion Script Approach to Anger Episodes between Workers and Their Superiors, Co-workers and Subordinates." *Journal of Organizational Behavior* 21 (2000) 147–62.

Fokkelman, J. P. *Narrative Art in Genesis: Specimens of Stylistic and Structural Analysis.* 2nd edition. Studia Semitica Neerlandica 17. Sheffield: JSOT Press, 1991.

Foucault, Michel. *The History of Sexuality*, vol. 1: *An Introduction.* Translated by Robert Hurley. 3 volumes. New York: Vintage, 1990.

———. "Les mots qui saignent." *L'express* (29 Aug, 1964) 21–22.

Fox, Michael V. "Words for Wisdom." *Zeitschrift für Althebräistik* 6 (1993) 149–69.

Frege, G. *The Foundations of Arithmetic: A Logico-mathematical Enquiry into the Concept of Number.* Translated by J. L. Austin. New York: Philosophical Library, 1950.

Frei, Hans W. *The Eclipse of Biblical Narrative: A Study in Eighteenth and Nineteenth Century Hermeneutics.* New Haven, CT: Yale University Press, 1974.

Frei, Peter. "Persian Imperial Authorization: A Summary." Pp. 5–40 in *Persia and Torah: The Theory of Imperial Authorization of the Pentateuch.* Edited by James W. Watts. Society of Biblical Literature Symposium Series. Atlanta: Society of Biblical Literature, 2001.

Frei, Peter, and Klaus Koch. *Reichsidee und Reichsorganisation im Perserreich: Zweite, bearbeitete und stark erweiterte Auflage.* 2nd edition. Orbis biblicus et orientalis 55. Freiburg: Universitätsverlag / Göttingen: Vandenhoeck & Ruprecht, 1996.

Fretheim, Terence E. "Genesis." Pp. 321–674 in vol. 1 of *The New Interpreter's Bible: General Articles and Introduction, Commentary, and Reflections for Each Book of the Bible, Including the Apocryphal/Deuterocanonical Books.* Nashville: Abingdon, 1994.

Frymer-Kensky, Tikva Simone. "Patriarchal Family Relationships and Near Eastern Law." *Biblical Archaeologist* 44 (1981) 209–14.

Fuchs, Esther. "'For I Have the Way of Women': Deception, Gender, and Ideology in Biblical Narrative." *Semeia* 42 (1988) 68–83.

Fuller, Robert C. "Spirituality in the Flesh: The Role of Discrete Emotions in Religious Life." *Journal of the American Academy of Religion* 75 (2007) 25–51.

Furman, Nelly. "His Story versus Her Story: Male Genealogy and Female Strategy in the Jacob Cycle." *Semeia* 46 (1989) 141–49.

Galen. *On the Doctrines of Hippocrates and Plato*, vol. 1. Translated and edited by Phillip de Lacy. 3 volumes. Berlin: Akademie, 1978.

Garland, David E., and Diana R. Garland. *Flawed Families of the Bible: How God's Grace Works through Imperfect Relationships.* Grand Rapids, MI: Brazos, 2007.

Geeraerts, D., and S. Grondelaers. "Looking Back at Anger." Pp. 153–79 in *Language and the Cognitive Construal of the World.* Edited by J. R. Taylor and R. E. MacLaury. Berlin: de Gruyter, 1995.

Gibbs, Nancy. "The EQ Factor." *Time* (Oct. 2, 1995). http://www.time.com/time/classroom/psych/unit5 _article1.html (accessed April 13, 2010).

Gilbert, M., J. L'Hour, and J. Scharbert. *Morale et Ancien Testament.* Lex Spiritus Vitae. Louvain-la-Neuve: Université Catholique de Louvain, 1976.

Goldin, Judah. "The Youngest Son or Where Does Genesis 38 Belong?" *Journal of Biblical Literature* 96 (1977) 27–44.

Gossai, Hemchand. *Power and Marginality in the Abraham Narrative.* Lanham, MD: University Press of America, 1995.

Gowan, Donald E. *From Eden to Babel: A Commentary on the Book of Genesis 1–11.* Edited by Fredrick Carlson Holmgren and George A. F. Knight. International Theological Commentary. Grand Rapids: Eerdmans, 1988.

Gracián y Morales, Baltasar. *The Art of Worldly Wisdom.* Translated by Christopher Maurer. New York: Doubleday, 1991.

Green, Barbara. *Mikhail Bakhtin and Biblical Scholarship*. The Society of Biblical Literature Semeia Studies 38. Atlanta, GA: Society of Biblical Literature, 2000.

Greenspahn, Frederick E. *When Brothers Dwell Together: The Preeminence of Younger Siblings in the Hebrew Bible*. New York: Oxford University Press, 1994.

Griffiths, Paul E. *What Emotions Really Are: The Problem of Psychological Categories*. Chicago: University of Chicago Press, 1997.

Gruber, Mayer I. *Aspects of Nonverbal Communication in the Ancient Near East*. Studia Pohl 12. 2 volumes. Rome: Biblical Institute Press, 1980.

––––––. "The Tragedy of Cain and Abel: A Case of Depression." *Jewish Quarterly Review* 69 (1978) 89–97.

––––––. "Was Cain Angry or Depressed?" *Biblical Archaeology Review* 6/6 (1980) 34–36.

Gumperz, John J., and Stephen C. Levinson, eds. *Rethinking Linguistic Relativity*. Cambridge: Cambridge University Press, 1996.

Gunkel, Hermann. *Genesis: Translated and Interpreted*. Mercer Library of Biblical Studies. Macon, GA: Mercer University Press, 1997, 1901.

Gunn, D. M., and Danna Nolan Fewell. *Narrative in the Hebrew Bible*. Oxford Bible Series. Oxford: Oxford University Press, 1993.

Guyette, Fred. "Joseph's Emotional Development." *Jewish Bible Quarterly* 32 (2004) 181–88.

Hackett, Jo Ann. "Rehabilitating Hagar: Fragments of an Epic Pattern." Pp. 12–27 in *Gender and Difference in Ancient Israel*. Edited by Peggy L. Day. Minneapolis: Fortress, 1989.

Hallo, William W., ed. *The Context of Scripture*. 3 volumes. Leiden: Brill, 1997–2003.

Hamilton, Victor P. *The Book of Genesis: Chapters 1–17*. New International Commentary on the Old Testament. Grand Rapids, MI: Eerdmans, 1990.

––––––. *The Book of Genesis: Chapters 18–50*. New International Commentary on the Old Testament. Grand Rapids, MI: Eerdmans, 1994.

Hanson, Paul D. *Old Testament Apocalyptic*. Nashville: Abingdon, 1987.

––––––. *The People Called: The Growth of Community in the Bible*. Cambridge: Harper & Row, 1986.

Hardy, Barbara. "Towards a Poetics of Fiction: 3) An Approach through Narrative." *Novel: A Forum on Fiction* 2 (1968) 5–14.

Hardy, Daniel W. "Reason, Wisdom and the Interpretation of Scripture." Pp. 69–88 in *Reading Texts, Seeking Wisdom: Scripture and Theology*. Edited by David F. Ford and Graham Stanton. Grand Rapids, MI: Eerdmans, 2003.

Hauerwas, Stanley. "Character, Narrative, and Growth in the Christian Life." Pp. 441–84 in *Toward Moral and Religious Maturity: The First International Conference on Moral and Religious Development*. Morristown, NJ: Silver Burdett, 1980.

––––––. *The Peaceable Kingdom: A Primer in Christian Ethics*. Notre Dame, IN: University of Notre Dame Press, 1983.

Hauerwas, Stanley, and L. Gregory Jones, eds. *Why Narrative? Readings in Narrative Theology*. Eugene, OR: Wipf & Stock, 1997.

Hauser, Alan J. "Linguistic and Thematic Links between Genesis 4:1–16 and Genesis 2–3." *Journal of the Evangelical Theological Society* 23 (1980) 294–305.

Hays, Richard B. *Echoes of Scripture in the Letters of Paul*. New Haven, CT: Yale University Press, 1989.

––––––. *The Moral Vision of the New Testament: Community, Cross, New Creation; A Contemporary Introduction to New Testament Ethics*. San Francisco: HarperSanFrancisco, 1996.

Heard, R. Christopher. *Dynamics of Diselection: Ambiguity in Genesis 12–36 and Ethnic Boundaries in Post-Exilic Judah*. Atlanta, GA: Society of Biblical Literature, 2001.

Heffelfinger, Katie M. "From Bane to Blessing: The Significance of Food in Genesis 37–50." In *Rounded Stones: Literary Readings of Genesis Narratives.* Edited by Dennis Olson and Diane Sharon. Society of Biblical Literature Symposium Series. Atlanta: Society of Biblical Literature, Forthcoming.

Hempel, Johannes. *Das Ethos des Alten Testaments.* 2nd edition. Beihefte zur Zeitschrift für die alttestamentliche Wissenschaft 67. Berlin: Alfred Töpelmann, 1964.

———. "Ethics in the OT." Pp. 2:153–61 in *The Interpreter's Dictionary of the Bible: An Illustrated Encyclopedia Identifying and Explaining All Proper Names and Significant Terms and Subjects in the Holy Scriptures, Including the Apocrypha, with Attention to Archaeological Discoveries and Researches into the Life and Faith of Ancient Times.* New York: Abingdon, 1962.

Hendel, Ronald S. *Remembering Abraham: Culture, Memory, and History in the Hebrew Bible.* New York: Oxford University Press, 2005.

Heschel, Abraham J. *The Prophets.* 2 vols. Peabody, MA: Prince, 1962.

Hettema, Theo L. *Reading for Good: Narrative Theology and Ethics in the Joseph Story from the Perspective of Ricoeur's Hermeneutics.* Edited by H. J. Adriaanse and Vincent Brümmer. Studies in Philosophical Theology. Kampen: Kok Pharos, 1996.

Heyden, Katharina. "Die Sünde Kains: Exegetische Beobachtungen zu Gen 4,1–16." *Biblische Notizen* 118 (2003) 85–109.

Hill, Jane H., and Bruce Mannheim. "Language and World View." *Annual Review of Anthropology* 21 (1992) 381–406.

Hirschberg, Martin. "Er konnte es noch nicht wissen: Aggadasche und mystische Texte zu Kain und Abel." Pp. 123–55 in *Brudermord: Zum Mythos von Kain und Abel.* Edited by Joachim Illies. Munich: Kösen, 1975.

Hochschild, Arlie Russell. *The Managed Heart: Commercialization of Human Feeling.* Berkeley: University of California Press, 1983.

Hoffman, C., I. Lau, and D. R. Johnson. "The Linguistic Relativity of Person Cognition: An English-Chinese Comparison." *Journal of Personality and Social Psychology* 51 (1986) 1097–1105.

Hoffmeier, James K. "The Wives' Tales of Genesis 12, 20 and 26 and the Covenants at Beer-Sheba." *Tyndale Bulletin* 43 (1992) 81–99.

Hoglund, Kenneth G. *Achaemenid Imperial Administration in Syria–Palestine and the Missions of Ezra and Nehemiah.* Society of Biblical Literature Dissertation Series 125. Atlanta: Scholars Press, 1992.

Hughes, Richard A. "*Schicksalsanalyse* and Religious Studies." *Journal of Religion* 87 (2007) 59–78.

———. *Theology and the Cain Complex.* Washington, DC: University Press of America, 1982.

Humboldt, Wilhelm von. "From the Introduction to His Translation of *Agamemnon.*" Pp. 55–59 in *Theories of Translation: An Anthology of Essays from Dryden to Derrida.* Edited by Rainer Schulte and John Biguenet. Chicago: University of Chicago Press, 1992.

———. *On Language: On the Diversity of Human Language Construction and Its Influence on the Mental Development of the Human Species.* Translated by Peter Heath. Edited by Michael Losonsky. Cambridge: Cambridge University Press, 1999.

Hupka, Ralph B., Zbigniew Zaleski, Jürgen Otto, Lucy Reidl, and Nadia V. Tarabrina. "Anger, Envy, Fear, and Jealousy as Felt in the Body: A Five-Nation Study." *Cross-Cultural Research* 30 (1996) 243–64.

Huth, Werner. "Kain–Ein Hinführung zur schicksalsanalytischen Auffassung vom Bösen im Menschen." Pp. 37–56 in *Brudermord: Zum Mythos von Kain und Abel.* Edited by Joachim Illies. Munich: Kösen, 1975.

Illies, Joachim, ed. *Brudermord: Zum Mythos von Kain und Abel.* Munich: Kösen, 1975.

Jacob, Benno. *The First Book of the Bible: Genesis*. Translated by Ernest I. Jacob and Walter Jacob. Edited by Ernest I. Jacob and Walter Jacob. New York: Ktav, 1974.

Jacobs, Mignon R. "The Conceptual Dynamics of Good and Evil in the Joseph Story: An Exegetical and Hermeneutical Inquiry." *Journal for the Study of the Old Testament* 27 (2003) 309–38.

Janowski, Bernd. "Jenseits von Eden: Gen 4,1–16 und die nichtpriesterliche Urgeschichte." Pp. 267–84 in *Textarbeit: Studien zu Texten und ihrer Rezeption aus dem Alten Testament und der Umwelt Israels*. Edited by Klaus Kiesow and Thomas Meurer. Alter Orient und Altes Testament. Münster: Ugarit-Verlag, 2003.

Janzen, Waldemar. *Old Testament Ethics: A Paradigmatic Approach*. Louisville: Westminster John Knox, 1994.

———. "Review of Walter Kaiser, *Toward Old Testament Ethics*." *Interpretation* 39 (1985) 424–25.

Jastrow, Morris. *Aspects of Religious Belief and Practice in Babylonia and Assyria*. American Lectures on the History of Religions. New York: Putnam's, 1911.

Jeansonne, Sharon Pace. *The Women of Genesis: From Sarah to Potiphar's Wife*. Minneapolis: Fortress, 1990.

Jenni, Ernst, and Claus Westermann, eds. *Theological Lexicon of the Old Testament*. Translated by Mark E. Biddle. 3 volumes. Peabody, MA: Hendrickson, 1997.

Jerome, Saint. *To Pammachius: On the Best Method of Translating (St Jerome, Letter 57)*. Translated by Louis G. Kelly. Edited by B. Harris. Documents de Traductologie / Working Papers in Translatology. Ottawa: École de Traducteurs et d'Interprètes, Université d'Ottawa, 1976.

Johnson, A. R. *The Vitality of the Individual in the Thought of Ancient Israel*. Cardiff: University of Wales Press, 1949.

Johnson, William Stacy. "Reading the Scriptures Faithfully in a Postmodern Age." Pp. 109–24 in *The Art of Reading Scripture*. Edited by Ellen F. Davis and Richard B. Hays. Grand Rapids, MI: Eerdmans, 2003.

Kagan, Jerome. *What Is Emotion? History, Measures, and Meanings*. New Haven, CT: Yale University Press, 2007.

Kaiser, Walter C. *Toward Old Testament Ethics*. Grand Rapids, MI: Zondervan, 1983.

Kaminsky, Joel S. *Yet I Loved Jacob: Reclaiming the Biblical Concept of Election*. Nashville: Abingdon, 2007.

Kamionkowski, Tamar, and Wonil Kim, eds. *Bodies, Embodiment, and Theology of the Hebrew Bible*. Library of Hebrew Bible/Old Testament Studies. New York: T. & T. Clark, 2010.

Kamitsuka, Margaret D. "Toward a Feminist Postmodern and Postcolonial Interpretation of Sin." *Journal of Religion* 84 (2004) 179–211.

Kant, Immanuel. *Grounding for the Metaphysics of Morals; with, On a Supposed Right to Lie Because of Philanthropic Concerns*. Translated by James W. Ellington. 3rd edition. Indianapolis: Hackett, 1993, 1785.

Kassel, Maria. *Biblische Urbilder: Tiefenpsychologische Auslegung nach C. G. Jung*. Munich: Pfeiffer, 1980.

Kautzsch, E., ed. *Gesenius' Hebrew Grammar*. Translated by A. E. Cowley. 2nd edition. Oxford: Oxford University Press, 1910.

Kazen, Thomas. "Dirt and Disgust: Body and Morality in Biblical Purity Laws." Pp. 43–64 in *Perspectives on Purity and Purification in the Bible*. Edited by Baruch J. Schwartz, David P. Wright, Jeffrey Stackert and Naphtali S. Meshel. New York: T. & T. Clark, 2008.

———. "Emotions, Biblical Interpretation and the Ethics of Ethnicity." Paper presented at the Annual Meeting of the Society of Biblical Literature, San Diego, CA, November 18, 2007.

Keel, Othmar, and Christoph Uehlinger. *Gods, Goddesses, and Images of God in Ancient Israel*. Translated by Thomas H. Trapp. Minneapolis: Fortress, 1998.

Kille, D. Andrew. "Jacob—A Study in Individuation." Pp. 40–54 in *Jung and the Interpretation of the Bible*. Edited by David L. Miller. New York: Continuum, 1995.

Kirk-Duggan, Cheryl A. "Characterizations, Comedy, and Catastrophe: Divine/Human Relations, Emotions, and Rules of Law." Pp. 221–246 in *Genesis*. Edited by Athalya Brenner, Archie Chi Chung Lee, and Gale A. Yee. Texts@ contexts. Minneapolis: Fortress, 2010.

Klein, Joseph P. "How Job Fulfills God's Word to Cain." *Biblical Research* 9 (1993) 40–43.

Koch, Klaus. *The Prophets*. 2 volumes. Philadelphia: Fortress, 1983–84.

Koch, Susan. "Review of *Metaphors We Live By*." *Quarterly Journal of Speech* 67 (1981) 446–47.

Koehler, Ludwig, Walter Baumgartner, and Johann Jakob Stamm. *The Hebrew and Aramaic Lexicon of the Old Testament*. Translated by M. E. J. Richardson. Study edition. 2 volumes. Leiden: Brill, 2001.

Korte, Anne-Marie. "Significance Obscured: Rachel's Theft of the Teraphim: Divinity and Corporeality in Gen. 31." Pp. 147–82 in *Begin with the Body: Corporeality Religion and Gender*. Edited by Jonneke Bekkenkamp and Maaike de Haardt. Leuven: Peeters, 1998.

Koteskey, Ronald L. "Toward the Development of a Christian Psychology: Emotion." *Journal of Psychology and Theology* 8 (1980) 303–13.

Kotzé, Zacharias. "A Cognitive Linguistic Methodology for the Study of Metaphor in the Hebrew Bible." *Journal of Northwest Semitic Languages* 31 (2005) 107–17.

———. "Conceptual Metaphors for Anger in the Biblical Hebrew Story of the Flood." *Journal for Semitics = Tydskrif vir Semitistiek* 14 (2005) 149–64.

———. "Humoral Theory as Motivation for Anger Metaphors in the Hebrew Bible." *Southern African Linguistics and Applied Language Studies* 23 (2005) 205–9.

———. "In Response to van Wolde." *SBL Forum* (2007). http://www.sbl-site.org/Article.aspx?ArticleID=671 (accessed May 31, 2007).

———. "Metaphors and Metonymies for Anger in the Old Testament: A Cognitive Linguistic Approach." *Scriptura: International Journal of Bible, Religion and Theology in Southern Africa* 88 (2005) 118–25.

———. "Research on the Emotion of Anger in the Old Testament: Recent Trends." *Hervormde teologiese studies* 60 (2004) 843–63.

Kövecses, Zoltán. *Emotion Concepts*. New York: Springer, 1990.

———. "Introduction: Language and Emotion Concepts." Pp. 3–15 in *Everyday Conceptions of Emotion: An Introduction to the Psychology, Anthropology and Linguistics of Emotion*. Edited by James A. Russell, José-Miguel Fernández-Dols, Antony S. R. Manstead and J. C. Wellenkamp. Dordrecht: Kluwer Academic, 1995.

———. *Language, Mind, and Culture*. Oxford: Oxford University Press, 2006.

———. *Metaphor and Emotion: Language, Culture, and Body in Human Feeling*. Paris: Cambridge University Press and Editions de la Maison des Sciences de l'Homme, 2000.

Kramer, S. N. *Sumerian Mythology: A Study of Spiritual and Literary Achievement in the Third Millennium b.c.* Memoirs of the American Philosophical Society 21. Philadelphia: The American Philosophical Society, 1944.

Krüger, Paul A. "A Cognitive Interpretation of the Emotion of Anger in the Hebrew Bible." *Journal of Northwest Semitic Languages* 26 (2000) 181–93.

———. "A Cognitive Interpretation of the Emotion of Fear in the Hebrew Bible." *Journal of Northwest Semitic Languages* 27 (2001) 77–89.

———. "Depression in the Hebrew Bible: An Update." *Journal of Northwest Semitic Languages* 64 (2005) 187–92.

———. "'Nonverbal Communication' in the Hebrew Bible: A Few Comments." *Journal of Northwest Semitic Languages* 24 (1998) 141–64.

———. "The Obscure Combination of *mṣ'h kbd* in Isaiah 30:27: Another Description of Anger?" *Journal of Northwest Semitic Languages* 26 (2000) 155–62.

———. "On Emotions and the Expression of Emotions." *Biblische Zeitschrift* 48 (2004) 213–28.

Kuhn, Karl Allen. *The Heart of Biblical Narrative: Rediscovering Biblical Appeal to the Emotions.* Minneapolis: Fortress, 2009.

LaCocque, André. *Onslaught against Innocence: Cain, Abel, and the Yahwist.* Eugene, OR: Cascade, 2008.

LaFleur, William R. "Body." Pp. 36–54 in *Critical Terms for Religious Studies.* Edited by Mark C. Taylor. Chicago: University of Chicago Press, 1998.

Lakoff, George. *Moral Politics: How Liberals and Conservatives Think.* 2nd edition. Chicago: University of Chicago Press, 2002.

Lakoff, George, and Mark Johnson. *Metaphors We Live By.* Chicago: University of Chicago Press, 2003.

Lakoff, George, and Zoltán Kövecses. "The Cognitive Model of Anger Inherent in American English." Pp. 195–221 in *Cultural Models in Language and Thought.* Edited by Dorothy Holland and Naomi Quinn. Cambridge: Cambridge University Press, 1987.

Lambert, David. "Review of Michael Carasik, *Theologies of the Mind in Biblical Israel.*" *Review of Biblical Literature* (2007) 1–5.

Lambert, W. G. *Babylonian Wisdom Literature.* London: Oxford University Press, 1960. Reprinted Winona Lake, IN: Eisenbrauns, 1996.

Langacker, Ronald W. "Context, Cognition, and Semantics: A Unified Dynamic Approach." Pp. 179–230 in *Job 28: Cognition in Context.* Edited by Ellen van Wolde. Leiden: Brill, 2003.

———. *Foundations of Cognitive Grammar,* vol. 1: *Theoretical Prerequisites.* Stanford, CA: Stanford University Press, 1987.

Lapsley, Jacqueline E. "A Feeling for God: Emotions and Moral Formation in Ezekiel 24:15–27." Pp. 93–102 in *Character Ethics and the Old Testament: Moral Dimensions of Scripture.* Edited by M. Daniel Carroll R. and Jacqueline E. Lapsley. Louisville: Westminster John Knox, 2007.

———. *Whispering the Word: Hearing Women's Stories in the Old Testament.* Louisville: Westminster John Knox, 2005.

Lasine, Stuart. "Breaking the 'Spell of Identification': Ethics and the Evaluation of Biblical Characters." Paper presented at the Annual Meeting of the Society of Biblical Literature, San Diego, CA, November 18, 2007.

LeDoux, Joseph. *The Emotional Brain: The Mysterious Underpinnings of Emotional Life.* New York: Simon & Schuster, 1996.

Leeming, David. *Jealous Gods and Chosen People: The Mythology of the Middle East.* Oxford: Oxford University Press, 2004.

Léonard-Roques, Véronique. *Caïn et Abel: Rivalité et responsabilité.* Monaco: Rocher, 2007.

Lesser, Harry. "'It's Difficult to Understand': Dealing with Morally Difficult Passages in the Hebrew Bible." Pages 292–302 in *Jewish Ways of Reading the Bible.* Edited by George J. Brooke. Journal of Semitic Studies Supplement 11. Oxford: Oxford University Press, 2000.

Lester, Andrew D. *Anger: Discovering Your Spiritual Ally.* Louisville: Westminster John Knox, 2007.

Levinas, Emmanuel. *Humanism of the Other*. Translated by Nidra Poller. Urbana: University of Illinois Press, 2003, 1972.

LeVine, Robert Alan. "Levy's *Tahitians*: A Model for Ethnopsychology." *Ethos* 33 (2005) 475–79.

Levy, Robert I. *Tahitians: Mind and Experience in the Society Islands*. Chicago: University of Chicago Press, 1973.

Libolt, Clay. "Review of Walter Kaiser, *Toward Old Testament Ethics*." *Calvin Theological Journal* 20 (1985) 104–6.

Lichtheim, Miriam. *Ancient Egyptian Literature: A Book of Readings*. 3 volumes. Berkeley: University of California Press, 1973–80.

———. *Moral Values in Ancient Egypt*. Orbis Biblicus et Orientalis 155. Fribourg: University Press / Göttingen: Vandenhoeck & Ruprecht, 1997.

Lucy, John A. *Language Diversity and Thought: A Reformulation of the Linguistic Relativity Hypothesis*. Cambridge: Cambridge University Press, 1992.

Lundbom, Jack R. *Jeremiah 1–20: A New Translation with Introduction and Commentary*. Edited by William Foxwell Albright and David Noel Freedman. Anchor Bible 21 A. New York: Doubleday, 1999.

Luther, Martin. "*Sendbrief vom Dolmetschen*." Pp. 151–73 in *An den christlichen Adel deutscher Nation; Von der Freiheit eines Christenmenschen; Sendbrief vom Dolmetschen*. Edited by Ernst Kähler. Stuttgart: Reclam, 1970.

Lutz, Catherine A. *Unnatural Emotions: Everyday Sentiments on a Micronesian Atoll and Their Challenge to Western Theory*. Chicago: University of Chicago Press, 1998.

Lutz, Catherine A., and Geoffrey M. White. "The Anthropology of Emotions." *Annual Review of Anthropology* 15 (1986) 405–36.

Lyotard, Jean-François. *The Postmodern Condition: A Report on Knowledge*. Translated by Geoff Bennington and Brian Massumi. Theory and History of Literature 10. Minneapolis: University of Minnesota Press, 1984, 1979.

Mabee, Charles. "Jacob and Laban: The Structure of Judicial Proceedings (Genesis XXXI 25–42)." *Vetus Testamentum* 30 (1980) 192–207.

MacIntyre, Alasdair. *After Virtue: A Study in Moral Theory*. 2nd edition. Notre Dame, IN: University of Notre Dame Press, 1984, 1981.

———. *Three Rival Versions of Moral Enquiry: Encyclopaedia, Genealogy, and Tradition*. Notre Dame, IN: University of Notre Dame Press, 1990.

Mangan, Edward A. "A Discussion of Genesis 4:7." *Catholic Biblical Quarterly* 6 (1944) 91–93.

Matsuki, K. "Metaphors of Anger in Japanese." Pp. 137–51 in *Language and the Cognitive Construal of the World*. Edited by J. R. Taylor and R. E. MacLaury. Berlin: de Gruyter, 1995.

Matthews, Victor H. "The Wells of Gerar." *Biblical Archaeologist* 49 (1986) 118–26.

Matthews, Victor H., and Don C. Benjamin, eds. "Honor and Shame in the World of the Bible." *Semeia* 68 (1994) 1–161.

McEntire, Mark. *The Blood of Abel: The Violent Plot in the Hebrew Bible*. Macon, GA: Mercer University Press, 1999.

McGee, Michael Calvin. "The 'Ideograph': A Link Between Rhetoric and Ideology." *Quarterly Journal of Speech* 66 (1980) 1–16.

McKay, Heather A. "Confronting Redundancy as Middle Manager and Wife: The Feisty Woman of Genesis 39." *Semeia* 87 (1999) 215–31.

McKnight, S. "Cain." Pp. 107–10 in *Dictionary of the Old Testament: Pentateuch*. Edited by T. Desmond Alexander and David W. Baker. Downers Grove, IL: InterVarsity, 2003.

Meves, Christa. "Die Geschichte von Kain und Abel tiefenpsychologisch Gedeutet." Pp. 57–67 in *Brudermord: Zum Mythos von Kain und Abel*. Edited by Joachim Illies. Munich: Kösen, 1975.

Meyers, Carol. *Discovering Eve: Ancient Israelite Women in Context*. New York: Oxford University Press, 1988.

Miller, Cynthia L. "Response to Chapman." *Ex Auditu* 19 (2003) 149–52.

Miller, Patrick D. "Fire in the Mythology of Canaan and Israel." *Catholic Biblical Quarterly* 27 (1965) 256–61.

Mills, Mary E. *Biblical Morality: Moral Perspectives in Old Testament Narratives*. Aldershot: Ashgate, 2001.

Mitchell, Hinckley G. *The Ethics of the Old Testament*. Chicago: University of Chicago Press, 1912.

Moberly, R. W. L. "The Mark of Cain—Revealed at Last?" *Harvard Theological Review* 100 (2007) 11–28.

Moor, J. C. de. "The Sacrifice Which Is an Abomination to the Lord." Pp. 211–26 in *Loven en geloven: Opstellen van collega's en medewerkers aangeboden aan Prof. Dr. Nic. H. Ridderbos ter gelegenheid van zijn vijfentwintigjarig ambtsjubileum als hoogleraar aan de Vrije Universiteit te Amsterdam*. Amsterdam: Bolland, 1975.

Morson, Gary Saul, and Caryl Emerson. *Mikhail Bakhtin: Creation of a Prosaics*. Stanford, CA: Stanford University Press, 1990.

Mowinckel, Sigmund. *The Two Sources of the Predeuteronomic Primeval History (JE) in Gen. 1–11*. Oslo: Dybwad, 1937.

Muilenburg, James. "Form Criticism and Beyond." *Journal of Biblical Literature* 88 (1969) 1–18.

Murdoch, Iris. *An Accidental Man*. London: Chatto and Windus, 1971.

Murphy, Roland E. *The Tree of Life: An Exploration of Biblical Wisdom Literature*. 3rd edition. Grand Rapids, MI: Eerdmans, 2002.

Murray, John. *Principles of Conduct: Aspects of Biblical Ethics*. Grand Rapids, MI: Eerdmans, 1957.

Newsom, Carol A. "Bakhtin, the Bible, and Dialogic Truth." *Journal of Religion* 76 (1996) 290–306.

———. *The Book of Job: A Contest of Moral Imaginations*. Oxford: Oxford University Press, 2003.

———. "Spying out the Land: A Report from Genology." Pp. 437–50 in *Seeking Out the Wisdom of the Ancients: Essays Offered to Honor Michael V. Fox on the Occasion of His Sixty-Fifth Birthday*. Edited by Ronald L. Troxel, Kelvin G. Friebel, and Dennis R. Magary. Winona Lake, IN: Eisenbrauns, 2005.

Niebuhr, H. Richard. "The Story of Our Life." Pp. 21–44 in *Why Narrative? Readings in Narrative Theology*. Edited by Stanley Hauerwas and L. Gregory Jones. Eugene, OR: Wipf & Stock, 1997.

Niedenthal, Paula M., et al. "Embodiment in Attitudes, Social Perception, and Emotion." *Personality and Social Psychology Review* 9 (2005) 184–211.

Noordman, Leo. "Some Reflections on the Relation between Cognitive Linguistics and Exegesis." Pp. 331–36 in *Job 28: Cognition in Context*. Edited by Ellen van Wolde. Leiden: Brill, 2003.

Nussbaum, Martha C. *The Fragility of Goodness: Luck and Ethics in Greek Tragedy and Philosophy*. Rev. edition. Cambridge: Cambridge University Press, 2001.

———. *Love's Knowledge: Essays on Philosophy and Literature*. New York: Oxford University Press, 1990.

———. *Poetic Justice: The Literary Imagination and Public Life*. Boston: Beacon, 1995.

———. *Upheavals of Thought: The Intelligence of Emotions*. Cambridge: Cambridge University Press, 2001.

Oatley, Keith. "Do Emotional States Produce Irrational Thinking?" Pp. 121–31 in *Lines of Thinking: Reflections on the Psychology of Thought*, vol. 2. Edited by K. J. Gilhooly et al. Chichester: Wiley, 1990.

Olson, Dennis T. "Untying the Knot? Masculinity, Violence, and the Creation-Fall Story of Genesis 2–4." Pp. 73–86 in *Engaging the Bible in a Gendered World: An Introduction to Feminist Biblical Interpretation in Honor of Katharine Doob Sakenfeld*. Edited by Linda Day and Carolyn Pressler. Louisville: Westminster John Knox, 2006.

Osborn, Michael A., and Douglas Ehninger. "The Metaphor in Public Address." *Speech Monographs* 29 (1962) 223–34.

Otto, Eckart. "Of Aims and Methods in Hebrew Bible Ethics." *Semeia* 66 (1994) 161–72.

———. *Theologische Ethik des Alten Testaments*. Stuttgart: Kohlhammer, 1994.

Parker, Simon B. *Stories in Scripture and Inscriptions: Comparative Studies on Narratives in Northwest Semitic Inscriptions and the Hebrew Bible*. New York: Oxford University Press, 1997.

Parrot, André. *Assur*. Paris: Gallimard, 1961.

Parry, Robin Allinson. *Old Testament Story and Christian Ethics: The Rape of Dinah as a Case Study*. Paternoster Biblical Monographs. Milton Keynes: Paternoster, 2004.

Penchansky, David. "God the Monster: Fantasy in the Garden of Eden." Pp. 43–60 in *The Monstrous and Unspeakable: The Bible as Fantastic Literature*. Edited by G. Aichele and T. Pippin. Sheffield: Sheffield Academic Press, 1997.

Petersen, David L. "Genesis and Family Values." *Journal of Biblical Literature* 124 (2005) 5–23.

Plato. *Laws: Books 1–6*. Translated by R. G. Bury. Loeb Classical Library. Cambridge: Harvard University Press, 1926.

———. "Phaedrus." Pp. 405–580 in *Euthyphro, Apology, Crito, Phaedo, Phaedrus*. Edited by W. R. M. Lamb. Loeb Classical Library. Cambridge: Harvard University Press, 1914.

———. *The Republic: Books 1–5*. Translated by Paul Shorey. Loeb Classical Library. Cambridge: Harvard University Press, 1930.

Pleins, J. David. *The Social Visions of the Hebrew Bible: A Theological Introduction*. Louisville: Westminster John Knox, 2000.

Polliack, Meira. "Joseph's Journey: From Trauma to Resolution." Pp. 147–74 in *Genesis*. Edited by Athalya Brenner, Archie Chi Chung Lee, and Gale A. Yee. Texts@ contexts. Minneapolis: Fortress, 2010.

Pritchard, James B., ed. *The Ancient Near East: An Anthology of Texts and Pictures*. Princeton: Princeton University Press, 1958.

———, ed. *The Ancient Near East in Pictures Relating to the Old Testament*. 2nd edition. Princeton: Princeton University Press, 1969.

———, ed. *Ancient Near Eastern Texts Relating to the Old Testament*. 3rd edition. Princeton: Princeton University Press, 1969.

Purvis, James D., and Eric M. Meyers. "Exile and Return: From the Babylonian Destruction to the Reconstruction of the Jewish State." Pp. 201–29 in *Ancient Israel: From Abraham to the Roman Destruction of the Temple*. Edited by Hershel Shanks. Washington, DC: Biblical Archaeology Society, 1999.

Quinn, Naomi. "'Commitment' in American Marriage: A Cultural Analysis." *American Ethnologist* 9 (1982) 775–98.

———. "The Cultural Basis of Metaphor." Pp. 56–93 in *Beyond Metaphor: The Theory of Tropes in Anthropology*. Edited by J. W. Fernandez. Stanford: Stanford University Press, 1991.

Rad, Gerhard von. *Genesis*. Revised edition. Old Testament Library. Philadelphia: Westminster, 1972.

———. *Old Testament Theology*. 2 volumes. New York: Harper & Row, 1962.

Ramaroson, Léonard. "À propos de Gn 4:7." *Biblica* 49 (1968) 233–37.

Rawls, John. *Justice as Fairness: A Restatement*. Edited by Erin Kelly. Cambridge: Belknap of Harvard University Press, 2001.

———. *A Theory of Justice*. Cambridge: Belknap of Harvard University Press, 1971.

Richter, Wolfgang. *Recht und Ethos: Versuch einer Ortung des weisheitlichen Mahnspruches*. Munich: Kösel, 1966.

Ricoeur, Paul. *Figuring the Sacred: Religion, Narrative, and Imagination*. Translated by David Pellauer. Edited by Mark I. Wallace. Minneapolis: Fortress, 1995.

———. *Interpretation Theory: Discourse and the Surplus of Meaning*. Fort Worth, TX: Texas Christian University Press, 1976.

———. "Metaphor and the Main Problem of Hermeneutics." *New Literary History* 6 (1974) 95–110.

———. "The Narrative Function." *Semeia* 13 (1978) 177–202.

———. *Oneself as Another*. Translated by Kathleen Blamey. Chicago: University of Chicago Press, 1992.

———. *The Rule of Metaphor: Multi-disciplinary Studies of the Creation of Meaning in Language*. Translated by Robert Czerny, Kathleen McLaughlin, and John Costello. Toronto: University of Toronto Press, 1981, 1977.

———. *The Symbolism of Evil*. Translated by Emerson Buchanan. Religious Perspectives 17. New York: Harper & Row, 1967.

Roberts, Robert C. "Narrative Ethics." Pp. 473–80 in *A Companion to Philosophy of Religion*. Edited by Philip L. Quinn and Charles Taliaferro. Cambridge: Blackwell, 1997.

Roberts, Tyler T. "Theology and the Ascetic Imperative: Narrative and Renunciation in Taylor and Hauerwas." *Modern Theology* 9 (1993) 181–200.

Robinson, H. W. "Hebrew Psychology." Pp. 353–82 in *The People and the Book*. Edited by A. S. Peake. Oxford: Claredon, 1925.

Rodd, Cyril S. *Glimpses of a Strange Land: Studies in Old Testament Ethics*. Edinburgh: T. & T. Clark, 2001.

Rogerson, John. *Theory and Practice in Old Testament Ethics*. Edited by M. Daniel Carroll Rodas. Journal for the Study of the Old Testament Supplement 405. London: T. & T. Clark, 2004.

Rollins, Wayne G., and D. Andrew Kille, eds. *Psychological Insight into the Bible*. Grand Rapids, MI: Eerdmans, 2007.

Rorty, Richard. *Philosophy and the Mirror of Nature*. Oxford: Blackwell, 1980.

Rosaldo, Michelle Z. *Knowledge and Passion: Ilongot Notions of Self and Social Life*. Cambridge: Cambridge University Press, 1980.

Rosch, Eleanor. "Cognitive Representatives of Semantic Categories." *Journal of Experimental Psychology: General* 104 (1975) 192–233.

———. "Linguistic Relativity." Pp. 27–48 in *Human Communication: Theoretical Explorations*. Edited by A. Silverstein. New York: Halsted, 1974.

Roth, Martha T. *Law Collections from Mesopotamia and Asia Minor*. Edited by Piotr Michalowski. Society of Biblical Literature Writings from the Ancient World 6. Atlanta: Scholars Press, 1995.

Russell, James A. "A Circumplex Model of Affect." *Journal of Personality and Social Psychology* 39 (1980) 1161–78.

———. "Culture and the Categorization of Emotions." *Psychological Bulletin* 110 (1991) 426–50.

———. "In Defense of a Prototype Approach to Emotion Concepts." *Journal of Personality and Social Psychology* 60 (1991) 37–47.

Said, Edward W. *Orientalism*. 25th Anniversary edition. New York: Vintage, 2003.

Sapir, Edward. *Selected Writings of Edward Sapir in Language, Culture, and Personality*. Edited by David G. Mandelbaum. Berkeley: University of California Press, 1949.

Sartre, Jean-Paul. *Existentialism and Human Emotions*. New York: Philosophical Library, 1957.

Schleiermacher, Friedrich. "On the Different Methods of Translating." Pp. 36–54 in *Theories of Translation: An Anthology of Essays from Dryden to Derrida*. Edited by Rainer Schulte and John Biguenet. Chicago: University of Chicago Press, 1992.

Schlimm, Matthew R. "Biblical Studies and Rhetorical Criticism: Bridging the Divide between the Hebrew Bible and Communication." *Review of Communication* 7 (2007) 244–75.

———. "Different Perspectives on Divine Pathos: An Examination of Hermeneutics in Biblical Theology." *Catholic Biblical Quarterly* 69 (2007) 673–94.

———. "From Fratricide to Forgiveness: The Ethics of Anger in Genesis." Paper presented at the Annual Meeting of the Society of Biblical Literature, San Diego, CA, Nov. 18, 2007.

———. "The Necessity of Permanent Criticism: A Postcolonial Critique of Ridley Scott's *Kingdom of Heaven*." *Journal of Media and Religion* 9 (2010) 129–49.

———. "Teaching the Hebrew Bible amid the Current Human Rights Crisis: The Pedagogical Opportunities Presented by Amos 1:3–2:3." *SBL Forum* (2006). http://sbl-site.org/Article.aspx?ArticleId=478 (accessed July 31, 2008).

Schniedewind, William M. "Prolegomena for the Sociolinguistics of Classical Hebrew." *Journal of Hebrew Scriptures* 5 (2005). http://www.arts.ualberta.ca/JHS/Articles/article_36.pdf (accessed Aug. 16, 2007).

Scholz, Susanne. "Was It Really Rape in Genesis 34? Biblical Scholarship as a Reflection of Cultural Assumptions." Pp. 182–98 in *Escaping Eden: New Feminist Perspectives on the Bible*. Edited by Harold C. Washington, Susan Lochrie Graham, and Pamela Thimmes. Washington Square, NY: New York University Press, 1999.

Schroer, S., and T. Staubli. *Body Symbolism in the Bible*. Translated by Linda M. Maloney. Collegeville, MN: Liturgical Press, 1998.

Schultz, E. A. *Dialogue at the Margins: Whorf, Bakhtin, and Linguistic Relativity*. Madison: University of Wisconsin Press, 1990.

Schwartz, Regina M. *The Curse of Cain: The Violent Legacy of Monotheism*. Chicago: University of Chicago Press, 1997.

Schweitzer, Steven James. "Utopia and Utopian Literary Theory: Some Preliminary Observations." Pp. 13–26 in *Utopia and Dystopia in Prophetic Literature*. Edited by Ehud Ben Zvi. Publications of the Finnish Exegetical Society. Helsinki: Finnish Exegetical Society, 2006.

Scolnic, Benjamin Edidin. *Thy Brother's Blood: The Maccabees and Dynastic Morality in the Hellenistic World*. Studies in Judaism. Lanham, MD: University Press of America, 2008.

Scott, James C. *Domination and the Arts of Resistance: Hidden Transcripts*. New Haven, CT: Yale University Press, 1990.

———. *Weapons of the Weak: Everyday Forms of Peasant Resistance*. New Haven, CT: Yale University Press, 1985.

Segal, Naomi. "Review of Meir Sternberg, *The Poetics of Biblical Narrative: Ideological Literature and the Drama of Reading*." *Vetus Testamentum* 38 (1988) 243–49.

Seneca. "De Ira." Pp. 106–355 in *Seneca: Moral Essays*, vol. 1. Edited by John W. Basore. Loeb Classical Library. Cambridge: Harvard University Press, 1928.

Shaver, Phillip, Judith Schwartz, Donald Kirson, and Cary O'Connor. "Emotion Knowledge: Further Explorations of a Prototype Approach." *Journal of Personality and Social Psychology* 52 (1987) 1061–86.

Sherzer, Joel. "A Discourse-Centered Approach to Language and Culture." *American Anthropologist* 89 (1987) 295–309.

Shweder, R. A. *Thinking through Cultures: Expeditions in Cultural Psychology*. Cambridge: Harvard University Press, 1991.

Silva, Moisés. *Biblical Words and Their Meaning: An Introduction to Lexical Semantics*. Revised edition. Grand Rapids, MI: Zondervan, 1994.

Slobin, D. "The Development from Child Speaker to Native Speaker." Pp. 233–56 in *Cultural Psychology: Essays on Comparative Human Development*. Edited by J. W. Stigler, R. A. Shweder, and G. Herdt. Cambridge: Cambridge University Press, 1990.

Smith, Mark S. "The Heart and Innards in Israelite Emotional Expressions: Notes from Anthropology and Psychobiology." *Journal of Biblical Literature* 117 (1998) 427–36.

Smith, Michael K. "Metaphor and Mind." *American Speech* 57 (1982) 128–34.

Smith-Christopher, Daniel L. *A Biblical Theology of Exile*. Overtures to Biblical Theology. Minneapolis: Fortress, 2002.

Soden, Wolfram von, ed. *Akkadisches Handwörterbuch*. 3 volumes. Wiesbaden: Harrassowitz, 1965–81.

Solomon, Robert C. *Not Passion's Slave: Emotions and Choice*. Oxford: Oxford University Press, 2003.

————. *The Passions*. Garden City, NY: Anchor, 1976.

Sommer, Benjamin D. *A Prophet Reads Scripture: Allusion in Isaiah 40–66*. Edited by Daniel Boyarin and Chana Kronfeld. Contraversions: Jews and Their Differences. Stanford, CA: Stanford University Press, 1998.

Sorabji, Richard. *Emotion and Peace of Mind: From Stoic Agitation to Christian Temptation*. The Gifford Lectures. Oxford: Oxford University Press, 2000.

Soskice, Janet Martin. *Metaphor and Religious Language*. Oxford: Clarendon, 1985.

Speiser, E. A. *Genesis: Introduction, Translation, and Notes*. Edited by William Foxwell Albright and David Noel Freedman. Anchor Bible 1. Garden City, NY: Doubleday, 1964.

Spina, Frank A. "The 'Ground' for Cain's Rejection (Gen 4): *'adāmāh* in the Context of Gen 1–11." *Zeitschrift für die alttestamentliche Wissenschaft* 104 (1992) 319–32.

Stearns, Peter N. *American Cool: Constructing a Twentieth-Century Emotional Style*. New York: New York University Press, 1994.

Steen, Gerard J., and Raymond W. Gibbs Jr. "Introduction." Pp. 1–8 in *Metaphor in Cognitive Linguistics: Selected Papers from the Fifth International Cognitive Linguistics Conference, Amsterdam, July 1997*. Edited by Raymond W. Gibbs Jr. and Gerard J. Steen. Amsterdam: Benjamins, 1999.

Steinberg, Naomi A. *Kinship and Marriage in Genesis: A Household Economics Perspective*. Minneapolis: Fortress, 1993.

Steiner, George. *After Babel: Aspects of Language and Translation*. Oxford: Oxford University Press, 1975.

Steinmetz, David C. "The Superiority of Pre-critical Exegesis." *Theology Today* 37 (1980) 27–38.

Steinmetz, Devora. *From Father to Son: Kinship, Conflict, and Continuity in Genesis*. Literary Currents in Biblical Interpretation. Louisville: Westminster John Knox, 1991.

Stern, Ephraim. "The Babylonian Gap: The Archaeological Reality." *Journal for the Study of the Old Testament* 28 (2004) 273–77.

Sternberg, Meir. *The Poetics of Biblical Narrative: Ideological Literature and the Drama of Reading.* Indiana Studies in Biblical Literature. Bloomington: Indiana University Press, 1985.

Stone, Lawson. "Ethical and Apologetic Tendencies in the Redaction of the Book of Joshua." *Catholic Biblical Quarterly* 53 (1991) 25–35.

Strack, Hermann L., and Paul Billerbeck. *Kommentar zum Neuen Testament aus Talmud und Midrasch.* 6 volumes. Munich: Beck, 1922–61.

Strawn, Brent A. *What Is Stronger than a Lion? Leonine Image and Metaphor in the Hebrew Bible and Ancient Near East.* Orbis Biblicus et Orientalis 212. Fribourg: Academic / Göttingen: Vandenhoeck & Ruprecht, 2005.

Syrén, Roger. *The Forsaken First-born: A Study of a Recurrent Motif in the Patriarchal Narratives.* Journal for the Study of the Old Testament Supplement 133. Sheffield: JSOT Press, 1993.

Talmon, Shemaryahu. "The 'Comparative Method' in Biblical Interpretation: Principles and Problems." Pp. 320–55 in *Congress Volume: Göttingen, 1977.* Vetus Testamentum Supplement 29. Leiden: Brill, 1978.

Tavris, Carol. *Anger: The Misunderstood Emotion.* Revised edition. New York: Simon & Schuster, 1989, 1982.

Tigay, Jeffrey H. "The Image of God and the Flood: Some New Developments." Pp. 169–82 in *Studies in Jewish Education and Judaica in Honor of Louis Newman.* New York: Ktav, 1984.

Toorn, Karel van der, Bob Becking, and Pieter W. van der Horst. *Dictionary of Deities and Demons in the Bible.* 2nd edition. Leiden: Brill, 1999.

Trible, Phyllis. *Texts of Terror: Literary-Feminist Readings of Biblical Narratives.* Philadelphia: Fortress, 1984.

Ullendorff, Edward. *Is Biblical Hebrew a Language? Studies in Semitic Languages and Civilizations.* Wiesbaden: Harrassowitz, 1977.

Ulrich, Eugene, and Frank Moore Cross. *Qumran Cave 4.VII: Genesis to Numbers.* Discoveries in the Judaean Desert. Oxford: Clarendon, 1994.

Van Seters, John. *Prologue to History: The Yahwist as Historian in Genesis.* Louisville: Westminster John Knox, 1992.

———. "The Theology of the Yahwist: A Preliminary Sketch." Pp. 219–28 in *"Wer Ist wie Du, Herr, unter den Göttern?": Studien zur Theologie und Religionsgeschichte Israels für Otto Kaiser zum 70. Geburtstag.* Edited by Ingo Kottsieper et al. Göttingen: Vandenhoeck & Ruprecht, 1994.

VanGemeren, Willem A., ed. *New International Dictionary of Old Testament Theology and Exegesis.* 5 volumes. Grand Rapids, MI: Zondervan, 1997.

Vaux, Roland de. *Ancient Israel: Its Life and Institutions.* Translated by John McHugh. New York: McGraw-Hill, 1961.

Visotzky, Burton L. *The Genesis of Ethics.* New York: Crown, 1996.

Vogels, Walter. "Lot in His Honor Restored: A Structural Analysis of Gen 13:2–18." *Église et théologie* 10 (1979) 5–12.

Voloshinov, V. N. "'Language, Speech, and Utterance' and 'Verbal Interaction.'" Pp. 107–43 in *Bakhtinian Thought: An Introductory Reader.* Edited by Simon Dentith. London: Routledge, 1995.

Waltke, Bruce K. "Cain and His Offering." *Westminster Theological Journal* 48 (1986) 363–72.

———, and M. O'Connor. *An Introduction to Biblical Hebrew Syntax.* Winona Lake, IN: Eisenbrauns, 1990.

Waskow, Arthur I. "Brothers Reconciled." *Sojourners* 28 (1999) 42–46.

Watts, James W., ed. *Persia and Torah: The Theory of Imperial Authorization of the Pentateuch*. Society of Biblical Literature Symposium Series. Atlanta: Society of Biblical Literature, 2001.

Weber, Max. *Ancient Judaism*. Translated and edited by Hans H. Gerth and Don Martindale. Glencoe, IL: Free Press, 1952.

Webster, John. *Barth's Ethics of Reconciliation*. Cambridge: Cambridge University Press, 1995.

Wells, Samuel. *Improvisation: The Drama of Christian Ethics*. Grand Rapids, MI: Brazos, 2004.

Wenham, Gordon J. *Genesis*. Edited by David A. Hubbard and Glenn W. Barker. 2 volumes. Word Biblical Commentary. Nashville: Thomas Nelson, 1987.

———. *Story as Torah: Reading Old Testament Narrative Ethically*. Grand Rapids, MI: Baker Academic, 2000.

Wénin, André. "Adam *et* Éve: La jalousie de Caïn, 'semence' du serpent: Un aspect du récit mythique de Genèse 1–4." *Revue des sciences religieuses* 73 (1999) 3–16.

West, Gerald O. *The Academy of the Poor: Towards a Dialogical Reading of the Bible*. Interventions 2. Sheffield: Sheffield Academic Press, 1999.

———. *Genesis: The People's Bible Commentary*. Oxford: Bible Reading Fellowship, 2006.

———. "Review of R. S. Sugirtharajah, ed., *Voices from the Margin: Interpreting the Bible in the Third World*." *Review of Biblical Literature* (2007) 1–5. http://www.bookreviews.org/pdf/5534_5829.pdf (accessed June 13, 2008).

Westermann, Claus. *Genesis*. 3 volumes. Continental Commentary. Minneapolis: Fortress, 1984–2002.

———. "Kain und Abel: die biblische Erzählung." Pp. 13–28 in *Brudermord: Zum Mythos von Kain und Abel*. Edited by Joachim Illies. Munich: Kösen, 1975.

Westphal, Merold. "Phenomenologies and Religious Truth." Pp. 105–25 in *Phenomenology of the Truth Proper to Religion*. Edited by Daniel Guerrière. SUNY Series in Philosophy. Albany: State University of New York Press, 1990.

Whitelam, Keith W. "King and Kingship." Pp. 40–48 in vol. 4 of *Anchor Bible Dictionary*. Edited by David Noel Freedman et al. New York: Doubleday, 1992.

Whorf, Benjamin Lee. *Language, Thought, and Reality: Selected Writings of Benjamin Lee Whorf*. Edited by John B. Carroll. New York: Technology Press of MIT / John Wiley, 1956.

Whybray, R. N. "'Shall Not the Judge of All the Earth Do What Is Just?': God's Oppression of the Innocent in the Old Testament." Pp. 1–19 in *Shall Not the Judge of All the Earth Do What Is Right? Studies on the Nature of God in Tribute to James L. Crenshaw*. Edited by David Penchansky and Paul L. Redditt. Winona Lake, IN: Eisenbrauns, 2000.

Wierzbicka, Anna. "Everyday Conceptions of Emotion: A Semantic Perspective." Pp. 17–47 in *Everyday Conceptions of Emotion: An Introduction to the Psychology, Anthropology and Linguistics of Emotion*. Edited by James A. Russell et al. Dordrecht: Kluwer Academic, 1995.

Wiesel, Elie. *Messengers of God: Biblical Portraits and Legends*. Translated by Marion Wiesel. New York: Random House, 1976.

Wildavsky, Aaron. "Survival Must Not Be Gained through Sin: The Moral of the Joseph Stories Prefigured through Judah and Tamar." *Journal for the Study of the Old Testament* 62 (1994) 37–48.

Williams, Bernard. *Shame and Necessity*. Sather Classical Lectures 57. Berkeley: University of California Press, 1993.

Williams, James G. "Number Symbolism and Joseph as Symbol of Completion." *Journal of Biblical Literature* 98 (1979) 86–87.

Williams, Michael James. *Deception in Genesis: An Investigation into the Morality of a Unique Biblical Phenomenon.* Edited by Hemchand Gossai. Studies in Biblical Literature 32. New York: Peter Lang, 2001.

Wittgenstein, Ludwig. *Philosophical Investigations.* Translated by G. E. M. Anscombe. New York: Macmillan, 1953.

———. *Preliminary Studies for the "Philosophical Investigations": Generally Known as The Blue and Brown Books.* New York: Barnes & Noble, 1969.

Wolde, Ellen van. "Language of Sentiment." *SBL Forum* 5 (2007). http://sbl-site.org/Article.aspx?ArticleID=660 (accessed April 11, 2007).

———. *Reframing Biblical Studies: When Language and Text Meet Culture, Cognition, and Context.* Winona Lake, IN: Eisenbrauns, 2009.

———. "Sentiments as Culturally Constructed Emotions: *Anger* and *Love* in the Hebrew Bible." *Biblical Interpretation* 16 (2008) 1–24.

Wolff, Hans Walter. *Anthropologie des Alten Testaments.* Munich: Chr. Kaiser, 1973.

———. *Anthropology of the Old Testament.* Translated by Margaret Kohl. Philadelphia: Fortress, 1981.

Wright, Christopher J. H. *An Eye for an Eye: The Place of Old Testament Ethics Today.* Downers Grove, IL: InterVarsity, 1983.

———. *Old Testament Ethics for the People of God.* Leicester: Inter-Varsity, 2004.

Zornberg, Avivah Gottlieb. *Genesis: The Beginning of Desire.* Philadelphia: Jewish Publication Society, 1995.

Index of Authors

Index of Scripture

Hebrew Bible

228

Deuterocanonical Books

New Testament

Index of Key Hebrew Words

Note: Italicized page numbers refer to places where terms receive more extensive treatment.

237

Index of Subjects

green press INITIATIVE

Eisenbrauns is committed to preserving ancient forests and natural resources. We elected to print this title on 30% post consumer recycled paper, processed chlorine free. As a result, for this printing, we have saved:

3 Trees (40' tall and 6-8" diameter)
2 Million BTUs of Total Energy
310 Pounds of Greenhouse Gases
1,398 Gallons of Wastewater
88 Pounds of Solid Waste

Eisenbrauns made this paper choice because our printer, Thomson-Shore, Inc., is a member of Green Press Initiative, a nonprofit program dedicated to supporting authors, publishers, and suppliers in their efforts to reduce their use of fiber obtained from endangered forests.

For more information, visit www.greenpressinitiative.org

Environmental impact estimates were made using the Environmental Defense Paper Calculator. For more information visit: www.papercalculator.org.